THE 50 BEST*
COLLEGE FOOTBALL TEAMS
OF ALL TIME

(*THE MOST INTERESTING, INNOVATIVE, AND INFLUENTIAL, ANYWAY)

BILL CONNELLY

TABLE OF CONTENTS

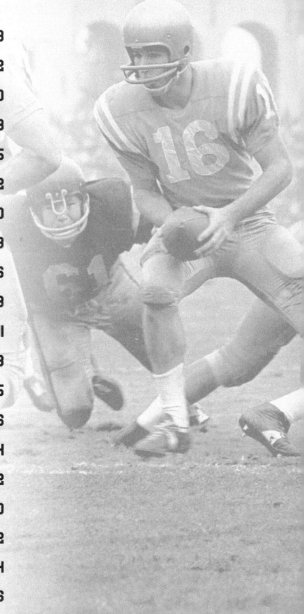

www.mascotbooks.com

The 50 Best* College Football Teams of All Time

For more information, please contact:
Mascot Books
560 Herndon Parkway #120
Herndon, VA 20170
info@mascotbooks.com

Library of Congress Control Number: 2016916339

CPSIA Code: PBANG1216A
ISBN-13: 978-1-68401-045-5

Printed in the United States

INTRODUCTION

Like a good counter play, the title of this book involves a little bit of misdirection. This is not a book about college football's best teams; it's a book about college football at its best. It's a book about championships and heartbreak, about rivalry and redemption, about innovation and adaptation. It is about all of college football, not just the handful of programs blessed enough to win more than others.

This book is also an attempt to tie pieces together. College football's history is uniquely, intensely regionalized. We remember our school's greatest players and greatest seasons, and we have a pretty good recollection of the successes of our rivals. My college football history is not your history; it is not that person's history over there. I felt there was an opportunity to tell 50 interesting stories while telling college football's at the same time.

In the following pages, you will read about incredible coaches (from John Heisman to Don James), offensive innovators (from Amos Alonzo Stagg to Chip Kelly), and defensive stalwarts (from

Bob Neyland to R.C. Slocum). You will read about burgeoning dynasties (from 1920s Notre Dame to 2000s USC) and spectacular mid-majors (from 1930 Utah to 2010 Boise State). You will read about greatness achieved (from 1931 USC to 2004 Texas) and greatness denied (from 1941 Northwestern to 2011 LSU). You will read about cultures that found themselves through football (1924 Notre Dame, 1925 Alabama). You will read about transcendent players (from Red Grange to Michael Vick), seasons full of transcendent moments (from 1965 UCLA to 2013 Auburn) ... and yes, you will read about some transcendent teams (hello, 1945 Army).

If you want to skip to your team's chapter, go for it. Each chapter should stand on its own. But if you start at the beginning and read straight through, you should also get a feel for the changes and challenges this sport faced from the beginning of the 20th century to the present. The sport has dealt with war and spectacular cultural shifts, and like the country in which it resides, it hasn't always handled change all that well.

Still, despite the contradictory, self-serving behavior of the sport's decision makers, and despite the frequently spastic whims of the 18- to 22-year old males who fill the uniforms, college football has, for more than a century, moved and entertained the fans who follow it, even while frustrating the hell out of them. If we could have quit on this game, we probably would have a long time ago. But we can't. And we might as well know our history.

When I pared the list of teams down to the ones I just *had* to write about, I ended up with 109 of them. Limiting this book to 50 creates holes in the plot lines and omits some key programs, but it also keeps the book under 1,000 pages. Guess I might just have to write a sequel one day. We'll call it *The REAL 50 Best* Teams*, just to make sure it sells.

1906 CHICAGO

Someone needed to become the Doc Brown of college football, the Christopher Lloyd in *Back to the Future*, the crazy experimenter who might prove that football could be watchable if 22 bodies weren't slamming together on every play.

Walter Camp wasn't going to be that guy.

Camp was 10 years old in 1869 when Rutgers and Princeton played in the first college football game, but the game didn't have a father figure until he took it in his hands. It was a disorganized mess, a chaotic, skull-cracking combination of rugby and soccer. Camp gave it a line of scrimmage (and actual lines) and a set of downs. He cut the number of required players from 15 to 11. He named All-American teams. He created about two-thirds of what we still see on Saturdays today.

Camp gave football an identity. But within that identity laid a dark side. At the turn of the 20th century, deaths on the playing field were rampant. Extracurricular violence within the field of play was common. This was a nasty sport, propped up by powerful people who enjoyed it

3

very much. President Teddy Roosevelt felt it had a place in American life. Princeton president and future Roosevelt successor Woodrow Wilson agreed. They saw it as an avenue for teaching young men about toughness and teamwork and all those generic, masculine values held dear in this country and most others.

In the current day, we hear plenty of sports personalities decrying a "war on football" because of an increased focus on head injuries and the long-term impact of the sport. There's a pushback from those who enjoy the sport just the way it is. We wouldn't want to weaken such a masculine sport by attempting to minimize certain types of contact, would we?

Just imagine if sports television or the Internet had existed in 1906, when the attacks on the sport were far more significant.

The fall of 1905 remains perhaps the most important in the history of college football. On one hand, the sport continued to thrive. In the first Game of the Century of the century, Chicago and Michigan played in front of 27,000 spectators on November 30; Amos Alonzo Stagg's Maroons took down Fielding Yost's Wolverines, 2-0, to end Michigan's 56-game unbeaten streak. But the outcry against the sport was growing in volume. The 1905 season featured 19 player deaths and 137 serious injuries. The popularity of the sport was clear, but there's a difference between physicality and brutality.

In October, Roosevelt met with college officials about potential solutions to the sport's ongoing issues. In November, Columbia University announced it was suspending its program because of the violence, and others announced they were considering doing the same. In December, not long after Chicago's epic win over Michigan, school representatives from around the East, South, and Midwest met to create a rules committee.

By March 1906, the Intercollegiate Athletic Association of the United States (IAAUS) had formed. Within five years, its name would change to the National Collegiate Athletic Association, with a much more aesthetically pleasing acronym: NCAA. The IAAUS' first task was to help open up the sport a bit.

If we think of every tactical pursuit as a way of trying to create situations in which there's one more offensive player in a given space than defensive players, and if we think of today's spread offenses as a way to create 2-on-1s or 3-on-2s, the pre-1906 sport was based around 11-on-11s. Push forward five or six feet at a time, then do it again. And that was the way Walter Camp liked it. He agreed to rules changes, but as the sport's original visionary, he wasn't interested in changing too much. This was his baby. (That his beloved Yale was really good at his version of the sport probably bolstered his stance.)

Still, change came. The first: A team had to gain 10 yards within three downs, not five. (A few years later, they would settle on four downs.) This meant that offenses couldn't persist by sending 11 bodies forward two yards at a time.

The second change: Rules would allow for a neutral zone on the line of scrimmage so that officials could maybe actually see some of the infractions that were taking place.

The biggest change: Teams could pass the ball. An offense was allowed to throw the ball beyond the line of scrimmage. You want to peel players off the line and open things up? This was a pretty good method.

Camp hated the idea of the forward pass. This was not his vision. He and others made sure that passing was still an immense gamble. You wanted to throw? Fine, but a pass had to cross the line of scrimmage at least five yards beyond where the passer received the ball from the center. Violating this rule meant a turnover. A pass could not cross the goal line. Violating this rule meant a turnover. The pass couldn't even hit the ground without resulting in a turnover.

As with any profession in need of change, you don't tend to get all that you need at once. These tweaks would not entirely alleviate the crisis facing the sport. By the end of the decade, after further on-field deaths, bigger shifts would take place, even with power brokers at Yale, Harvard, etc., dragging their feet.

But the 1906 rules changes gave people a glimpse of what the sport could become. And Amos Alonzo Stagg was the primary reason why.

Stagg was the Doc Brown, the tinkerer. He was a sportsman, not simply a football guy. Though mostly known as Chicago's head coach for 40 years, he spent 18 of those also coaching the Maroons' baseball team. He coached track and field, and he was good enough at it that he helped to lead the U.S. Olympic team in Paris in 1924. His friend James Naismith once consulted him regarding the early rules for a sport that would eventually become basketball. (Naturally, he also served as Chicago's basketball coach for one year.)

He enjoyed competition, creativity, and instruction above all else, and football was an outlet for all three.

Football offered him a blank canvas, and he was in no way married to the sport with a specific vision in mind. If anyone had more impact than Camp on how football is currently played, it was Stagg. The former Yale All-American is credited with inventing the huddle, the lateral, the linebacker, the tackling dummy, the onside kick, the quick kick, the end around, the QB keeper, the unbalanced line, motion, the Statue of Liberty play, and even padded goalposts.

Stagg had crafted a wonderful Chicago team with the old rules in 1905 (and in most of the decade preceding it), and with All-Americans like quarterback Walter Eckersall, halfback Walter Steffen, end Mysterious Walker, and tackle Ed Parry, he was guaranteed another good team that coming fall. But the rules changes piqued his imagination. He created new plays and patterns, and in the fall of 1906, it was time for him to unveil them … eventually.

The Western Conference (now the Big Ten) pared down its schedules to only five games in 1906, as much because of concerns of rampant commercialism as because of health risks. Because the game had already become so popular, fans were skeptical of the changes. As written in Chicago's 1907 yearbook, Cap and Gown, "There was much speculation as to what the new game would 'look like.' Some ventured to predict that it would be as interesting as ping-pong, only not so rough; others hoped that it might at least resemble the old game;

but few believed that any improvement would follow." We have forever rebelled against change.

In late October, Chicago's season opened with a pair of easy victories. Stagg's squad was superior to those of Purdue and Indiana under any rules, and the Maroons cruised to easy 39-0 and 33-8 victories, respectively. On November 10, however, Minnesota visited. Henry Williams' squad was the most powerful in the Western Conference. They had gone 65-4-5 over the past five seasons and were unbeaten when they visited the Windy City. The biggest game of the season would boast a raucous crowd of 20,000. It would have been a perfect canvas for Stagg to unveil his new tricks.

One problem: weather. A driving rainstorm produced a track so sloppy that the maroon tint of both teams' jerseys became a source of confusion. The conditions grounded whatever air attack Stagg would have preferred to unleash. Minnesota won an old-school, 4-2 slugfest, booting a muddy, four-point place-kick through the uprights and allowing only a safety. According to an account in the Minneapolis Journal, "Steffens [sic] could not navigate at all and floundered about like a hog on ice, a shouting spectacle to his admirers. Chicago's line, in fact, did much better work than the star backfield."

The next week, it was finally time to open things up a bit. Minnesota returned home and lost to Bemus Pierce's Carlisle Indians – the next year, Pop Warner would begin his second stint at Carlisle and unleash his own version of a dynamic passing attack – and Chicago welcomed Illinois to town. The team from Champaign was 0-2-1, having fallen 28-9 to Michigan and 16-6 to Wisconsin.

Long passes, short passes, wide runs, up-the-middle runs. Chicago's arsenal was unveiled a week later than intended, and Illinois was an unfortunate victim. Steffen scored on an 85-yard pass three minutes into the game, and the rout was on. The Maroons could have picked whatever score they wanted. They chose 63 and allowed Illinois nothing, and that was with the backups playing most of the second half.

The season ended with a non-conference matchup against Nebraska.

Amos Foster's squad put up a better fight, but only so much of one. The Maroons finished with a 38-5 win and capped year with a 4-1 record. Eckersall finished his career by booting five four-pointers; touchdowns came from Steffen and Harold Iddings, who would go on to coach football at Miami (Ohio) and basketball at Kentucky.

Chicago would go 4-1 again in 1907, beating Minnesota (with two touchdown passes, no less) but falling to Warner's Carlisle, 18-4, in the finale. This was significant. Stagg, Warner, and Saint Louis University's Eddie Cochems (a star at Wisconsin just a few years earlier) were the three coaches most directly tied to the early adoption of the pass. Cochems' 1906 squad completed the first known forward pass in college football history and scored 407 points in 11 games. And while it was mostly against non-major teams, SLU beat Kansas and Iowa by a combined 73-2 that year, then whooped Arkansas and Nebraska by a combined 76-6 the next.

Carlisle went 10-1 in 1907, handing both Chicago and Penn their only respective losses and falling only to a strong Princeton team in early November. Warner's Indians put the Chicago game away with a long touchdown pass, and the Chicago Tribune wrote that they "gave such an exhibition of [modern football's] possibilities as will not be forgotten by anyone."

Of course, Carlisle had one unfair advantage: The Indians had future Olympian Jim Thorpe in uniform.

Still, while Carlisle was a significant player in the sport until the school folded in 1918, Chicago was in the country's first powerhouse conference. That helped to make Stagg the face of the forward pass.

Stagg was, by most accounts, an almost unrealistically good person, one focused on clean, active living. He originally chose Yale because of its divinity school. He was offered a professional contract to play baseball but turned it down because he didn't think sport should lose its sense of amateurism. He frowned on drink or any disreputable activity. He valued sports because of the values and adversity they could create.

In the 1907 Cap and Gown, Ferdinand Schwill wrote, "Amos Alonzo

Stagg has never distinguished himself greatly in scholarship, nor does he shine, or aspire to shine, in the social arts of the drawing room, but he is admirable in the world which he has chosen, work which holds him up before a community of healthy undergraduates, engaged in out-of-door games, as a living example of grit, applied science, and fair play."

For his clean living, he was rewarded with a long life. Forced into retirement at Chicago when he hit 70 years of age, he ended up at the University of the Pacific in 1933 and, over the next 14 years, won five Northern California Athletic Conference titles. He retired at 83, officially ending his head coaching career with 314 wins — 10 at the YCMA School in Springfield, Mass. (1890-91), 244 at Chicago (1892-1932), and 60 at Pacific (1933-46).

That win total comes with an asterisk, though. From 1947-52, he joined his son Amos Jr.'s coaching staff at Susquehanna University in Pennsylvania. Amos Jr. was officially listed as the head coach, but the son later petitioned the NCAA to count the Crusaders' 21 wins from this period to his father's record. "We were co-equals," he said, "but he was in charge. Everybody knew that."

Stagg went on to coach special teams for Stockton College from 1953-58, then finally retired for good at age 96. President John F. Kennedy commemorated his 100th birthday in 1962, and he passed away on March 17, 1965, aged 102.

Chicago, meanwhile, quickly found that it couldn't win in a confer-ence of heavyweights without a coach of Stagg's caliber. (It especially couldn't do so with a university president as adamantly opposed to the sport as Robert Maynard Hutchins, who served in that role from 1929-45.) The slowdown began before Stagg left — after going 22-4-4 in his last of many golden ages (1921-24), the Maroons had managed just one winning record between 1925-32.

Former Minnesota fullback Clark Shaughnessy, a coach good enough to win the Rose Bowl at Stanford later in his career, went 11-11-2 from 1933-35, then went just 6-23-2 thereafter. In 1939, the university officially dropped football.

1917 GEORGIA TECH

Some people just have good timing. Joe Guyon boasted it on and off the field. Listed at 5'11 and around 190 pounds – the equivalent of, say, 6'2, 220, today – Guyon was a masterful rusher, blocker, passer, and even punter. He could run through or around you, he could pass and kick over you. He was a distinguished rusher and passer in 1917, and he earned All-American honors as mostly a blocking tackle in 1918.

Guyon's timing off the field was almost as good. An American Indian, he enrolled in Carlisle Indian Industrial School in 1912 and 1913. After three years at the Keewatin Academy in Chicago, he turned up at Georgia Tech in 1917 to complete his final two years of eligibility.

His coach at Carlisle: Pop Warner, namesake of awards and leagues and one of the co-fathers of the forward pass. His coach at Georgia Tech: John Heisman, author of the jump shift and the famed 222-0 victory over Cumberland and namesake of a pretty important trophy. Guyon's combined record at these two schools: 37-3-2. And wow, did he have some teammates. He played with Jim Thorpe at Carlisle, then joined what might have been the best backfield of all-time in Atlanta.

The 1910s were a time of relative upheaval in college football. Further rules changes had democratized the sport a bit, allowing for tactical experimentation; meanwhile, more of the country was discovering the sport. Whereas a list of the top programs of the 1900s would net you some combination of eastern (Yale, Harvard, Princeton, Penn) and Midwestern schools (Minnesota, Michigan, Chicago, Wisconsin), along with maybe a Southern school like Vanderbilt or Sewanee, the 1910s were wide open. Programs like Minnesota and Harvard were still good, sure, but so were teams like Nebraska and a small catholic school in South Bend, Ind., named Notre Dame.

Moreover, the South discovered both football and how much it liked football. Vanderbilt remained strong, but Auburn went on a 67-15-5 run under Mike Donahue from 1907-17. Georgia went 25-6-3 from 1910-13, then went 8-0-1 in 1920 after World War I. Texas lost either zero or one game seven times between 1912 and 1921.

Only Georgia Tech had Heisman, though. The Engineers (a.k.a. the Golden Tornado) hired Heisman away from Clemson in 1903 – the school literally hired him; he was the first football coach paid specifically to coach football – and found waves of success. They went 14-1-2 in 1904-05 before the rules changes, and after a decade of solid play, they caught fire in the mid-1910s.

Tech went 7-0-1 in 1915 and 8-0-1 in 1916, the year of the famous Cumberland win. The Golden Tornado would go 6-1 in 1918 as well. But everything clicked in 1917.

The New York Times called Heisman's 1917 squad "such a sensation" and "unquestionably the leading eleven of the last season." Tech was already loaded with future hall-of-fame halfback Everett Strupper (most notable for either being deaf or for scoring eight touchdowns against Cumberland in 1916), quarterback Buster Hill (the short-yardage guy), and fullback Judy Harlan. Guyon's arrival gave the team one more weapon than any opponent could account for, especially when deployed with Heisman's controversial jump shift.

College football offenses tend to be pretty straightforward in their labeling. Defenses can take you pretty far down the road of green dogs and quarter coverages and C-gaps, but offenses don't try to fool you. The spread offense is an offense that tries to spread you out. The wishbone is a backfield with backs arranged to look like a wishbone. And the jump shift was literally a method for offensive players to shift by jumping in unison.

That might sound a little bit primitive, but it worked to devastating effect for Heisman's offense. The quarterback, fullback, and halfbacks would line up in a straight line behind center – a dotted-I formation, if you will. In unison, the three backs who wouldn't be carrying the ball would shift in one direction or the other, creating an impromptu wall behind which the ball carrier-to-be could run. It was a primitive version of the single wing, and it helped to assure that the offense had more bodies at the point of attack than the defense.

As Heisman wrote in his Principles of Football, "The plan in such quick shifts is to throw against a particular section or point of the defense a preponderance of offensive strength, and do it so quickly that the defense will not have time to assemble its men to that location to stem the heavy onslaught before the ball shall have gone into play." The shifts would often include the linemen, too.

It's easy to envision how this would be effective, not only with its original intent, but with its potential counters. Backfield players shift in unison, then pause before the ball is snapped. The defense, thinking it now knows where the play is going, tries to attack that area of the field, only to get burned by misdirection.

This was a controversial formation because some thought it allowed the offensive players a running start. This was not a nationally televised sport, obviously, so word traveled via mouth and newspaper, and it didn't quite seem kosher. But in a letter written to the Washington Herald in 1918, Heisman emphasized that the pause before the snap made it legal, noting, "we have employed it in each of our games from 1910 in which some of the most famous officials in America have been involved – and not one has found fault with it." A fair point.

It looked like seamless movement because of disciplined, repetition-heavy orchestration. Heisman was a disciplinarian, a drill sergeant at heart (his punishment of those who fumbled the football was renowned and feared), and Tech's superior timing was a result of drills and drills and drills. He frequently created a superior product and had no problem telling others how strong his team was. To make matters even worse for opposing defenses, Heisman also had no problem working trickeration into his team's base offense. He was, after all, the inventor of the hidden ball trick.

The combination of incredible talent and unique, devastating tactics made Georgia Tech virtually unstoppable in 1917 – a preponderance of offensive strength indeed. Heisman himself said he considered the team his best ever.

Tech's early schedule presented a pair of unique challenges. First, Furman and Wake Forest both visited Atlanta for a doubleheader; the next week, eastern powerhouse Penn became the first Eastern team to head to the South for a big game.

To say the least, the Golden Tornado were ready for these tests. With mostly backups, they defeated Furman, 25-0 in a downpour. Buster Hill scored a couple of touchdowns in the easy rout. Against Wake Forest, Strupper and Guyon made their season debuts. Guyon's first Tech carry was a 75-yard touchdown run, and Strupper ran for 198 yards and three touchdowns. Tech 33, Wake 0.

Football was invented on the east coast, and at the time, Easterners had a justifiable belief in their historical superiority in the sport. But in the present tense, this was no longer the case. Penn was an excellent team, one that would have assuredly finished in the AP top five or top 10 had the poll existed at the time. Tech game aside, they would lose by only a 14-6 margin to a powerhouse Pitt team, winning nine other games by a margin of 239-16.

This confident Penn team had absolutely no answers for the jump shift, however. In front of what might have been the largest audience to watch a game in the South to date (estimates ranged from 10,000 to 25,000), Tech jumped ahead almost immediately. Strupper broke off a 68-yard score in the opening minutes, and at halftime, Tech had outgained its overwhelmed foe, 276-11. Strupper finished with 173 yards and two scores, Hill added 104 and three, respectively, and Tech cruised, 41-0.

For all intents and purposes, this game won Tech the mythical national title. To get attention in the 1910s, you had to beat an eastern team. Heisman's squad mauled an excellent one.

It perhaps makes sense that the team would suffer a little bit of a hangover the next week. Against a Davidson team that was better than its 6-4 record (among other teams, Davidson beat a strong Auburn squad later in the year), Tech actually trailed briefly by a 3-0 margin and led just 6-3 at halftime. Davidson was the only team to prevent a Tech back from crossing 100 rushing yards, and it took a late pick six by Harlan to ease Tech to a 32-10 win.

From that point forward, Tech would outscore its five remaining opponents by a margin of 360-7. And that was with games being called early.

On October 20, Washington & Lee visited Atlanta. The Generals had given the Engineers their only blemish the year before, holding them to a midseason 7-7 tie. Heisman was never one to resist proving a point – part of the reason the 222-0 rout of Cumberland occurred the year before was because Cumberland's baseball team had whipped Heisman's Tech baseball team that spring – and he certainly didn't here. W&L went a decent 4-3 that year, but this got out of hand almost immediately. Guyon knocked out the Generals' Turner Bethel early on, and in a 63-0 romp, Tech engineered 35 first downs to W&L's five. It got even worse the next week, when one-time Southern powerhouse Vanderbilt visited and got pasted, 83-0.

After a 48-0 win at Tulane in which Strupper, Guyon, Hill, and Harlan all rushed for 100-plus yards (Tech only hit 48 points because the game was called for darkness), the Golden Tornado returned to face a suddenly hapless Carlisle squad. The Carlisle Indian School was to close after this school year, and the once mighty Indians had nothing to offer. Even with Guyon getting pulled from the game in the second quarter, Tech would have hit 100 points if the game hadn't been called with 10 minutes left. Hill and Strupper scored five touchdowns each in a 98-0 romp.

That left Auburn. Heisman had watched the Tigers' scoreless draw with Ohio State the week before, but it probably didn't take too much scouting to develop an advantage here. Tech just had too much horsepower. Strupper had scoring bursts of 62 and 50 yards, but Guyon stole the show with four touchdowns and a spectacular defensive play: Auburn star Duke Ducote broke into the open field and seemed assured of a touchdown, but Guyon tracked him down from well behind to preserve the shutout.

After the game, legendary sportswriter Morgan Blake said, "I never saw Jim Thorpe. I never saw [Yale legend] Ted Coy. But I can't believe that America has ever produced a greater football player than Joe Guyon."

In nine games, Tech scored 471 and allowed 17. Take out the Davidson game, and the average score of the other eight games was Tech 57, Opponent 1.

The most incredible part: Almost the entire team was scheduled to return the next season – of the stars, only Hill was a senior – and Heisman was able to get Pitt on the 1918 schedule. It could have been as titanic a battle as any college football had seen. But real life intervened. Most of the team enlisted into the armed forces as the U.S. got more heavily involved in World War I. The 1918 Tech squad still featured Guyon but included only two other upperclassmen. Freshmen started in most positions.

Knowing that makes the 1918 team's accomplishments rather impressive in their own right. With Guyon playing mostly tackle, Tech outscored opponents by a 466-32 margin, topping 100 points three times (against Furman, the 11th Cavalry, and NC State) and whipping both Clemson and Auburn. But they were outmanned in the marquee matchup against Pitt and fell, 32-0.

Tech would remain mostly awesome in 1919, but that season was Heisman's last in Atlanta. He got divorced and agreed to live in a different city than his ex-wife to avoid any social awkwardness. He coached at alma mater Penn for three years, Washington & Jefferson for one year, and Rice for four years, retiring from coaching in 1927.

Heisman was named director of athletics at New York's Downtown Athletic Club, which would award the first Downtown Athletic Club trophy in 1935. He passed away due to pneumonia in 1936, however, and the club renamed the award in his honor.

1923 ILLINOIS

> *A streak of fire, a breath of flame*
> *Eluding all who reach and clutch;*
> *A gray ghost thrown into the game*
> *That rival hands may never touch;*
> *A rubber bounding, blasting soul*
> *Whose destination is the goal. – Red Grange of Illinois!*
>
> *-- Grantland Rice*

Around 1940, Northwestern head coach Pappy Waldorf discovered one of the greatest quarterbacks in football history, Otto Graham, on an intramural field. Not even two decades before that, Illinois' Bob Zuppke had discovered maybe the best college football player of all-time at a high school track meet.

Coaches should evidently keep their eyes open at all times. You never know when you might discover a player the famous Grantland Rice will write a poem about one day.

An artist, columnist, Kappa Sigma, and Milwaukee State alum, Zuppke was the most successful head coach in Illinois history. He was born when UI was still Illinois Industrial University, and he was almost literally the father of Illinois football. The school had fielded a team for 23 years before his arrival, sure, but he oversaw the building of Memorial Stadium on the west side of campus, and he was in charge when they took on the Fighting Illini moniker. He led them to shares of seven Western Conference titles and a claimed four national titles (1914, 1919, 1923, 1927). Attendance at Illinois games was below 5,000 per game when Zuppke arrived; soon, Illinois Field's capacity of 17,000 would become woefully insufficient.

Everything we know about the university's football team began with the Zuppke era. While consistency was an issue – Zuppke wasn't big on recruiting; in fact, he rarely actually did it – the program experienced quite a few highs under both him and his successor Ray Eliot. Though Zuppke's 1914 team and Eliot's 1951 unit might have a strong claim to being Illinois' best squad, those teams didn't have the Galloping Ghost.

Without Red Grange's presence on the 1922-24 squads, Zuppke's tenure would have still been a success. Indeed, the undefeated 1914 team was excellent, and the 6-1 squad of 1919 and the 7-0-1 team of 1927 each claim shares of the mythical national title. Zuppke would still have been known as an innovator and quarterback guru if Grange had simply played basketball and run track as he originally intended. He tinkered with an innovative 5-4-2 defense, and he did a lot to develop pocket passing and screen passes. He was successful and influential.

Zuppke took whoever showed up on campus and figured out how to maximize their athleticism. And while he may not have recruited off-campus, when he came across an athlete named Red Grange dominating foes on the high school track, he knew that guy needed to wear a football jersey.

Listed at 5'11, 175, Grange looked 40 years old when he was 20. He was a Wheaton, Ill., legend, the son of the chief of police who starred in football, basketball, track, and baseball. He earned money for his family (and developed strength) by toting ice. Indeed, Zuppke noticed him on the track and suggested to him that he might do pretty well on the football field in Champaign. Grange still wasn't convinced until his Zeta Psi fraternity brothers swayed him during his freshman year.

In 1924, as a junior, Grange became a college football legend in a game against Michigan. In seven other games that season, the Wolverines allowed only 15 points, but in front of 65,000 fans in Champaign, Illinois scored 39 thanks almost entirely to Grange. He returned the opening kickoff for a touchdown and scored three more times (on rushes of 67, 56, and 44 yards) in the first quarter. Gassed, he took a short break, then returned and rushed 56 yards for a fifth touchdown. Later on, he returned another kickoff for a score. He personally scored 36 of the 54 points Michigan would allow that year.

In 1925, just in case he wasn't already, Grange became a national name. On a muddy track, he rushed for 237 yards and three scores in a 24-2 win over Penn. Football was becoming more of a national sport, but football *writers* were still on the east coast. His exploits against Penn forced any lingering holdouts to acknowledge his legendary status. He even appeared on the cover of *Time* magazine.

Directly after the 1925 season ended, capping a career that featured more than 3,300 rushing yards, 250 receiving yards, 575 passing yards, and 31 touchdowns (nine of more than 50 yards) in just 20 games, Grange dropped out of school. He signed with the Chicago Bears and immediately became the face of the fledgling National Football League. He headlined a barnstorming tour that gave the league star power and sustainability.

In 1923, though, he was simply a stud sophomore on an Illinois team full of them.

Following a four-year run of excellent play – Illinois went 21-7-1 from 1917-20 – Zuppke's Illini had run into a difficult spell. They went just 5-9 in 1921-22, and in the latter season Zuppke's eye drifted more toward the junior varsity. His freshmen were dominant, led not only by Grange but also future stars like quarterback Moon Baker, halfback Paul Cook, and tackle Frank Wickhorst.

One problem: Those latter names all became stars elsewhere. Baker transferred to Northwestern, Cook to Michigan, and Wickhorst to Navy. Baker and Wickhorst would become All-Americans for their respective new schools.

Zuppke and Illinois, then, began 1923 facing uncertainty. Memorial Stadium was to open later in the fall, but it wasn't evident that the Illini would field a team worth watching. Cars were proliferating, and college football was becoming a sport worth driving to see. Illinois, therefore, had an incredible opportunity on its hands. Roads were improving in Illinois, and in *Red Grange and the Rise of Modern Football,* John M. Carroll notes that when the stadium opened, five million people would be within a five-hour drive of the stadium.

We hear all the time that college football can serve as the front door to a given university. That wasn't the case before cars, but it was certainly becoming that way. A packed Memorial Stadium would be an incredible advertisement for a state university now within a day's drive of both Chicago and St. Louis.

Illinois' sophomore class was not as loaded as it was supposed to be heading into 1923, but this was still a talented squad. Guard James McMillen would earn All-American honors and play a few years in the NFL. Enormous fullback Earl Britton (listed around 6'3, 215, a mammoth of a man in the 1920s) was invaluable as both a blocker and a place-kicker. Quarterback Harry Hall and end Frank Rokusek were strong contributors. End Ted Richards would play briefly for the Chicago Bears. Senior tackle Bunny Oakes had a football IQ so high that he would go on to become a coach at

Colorado and Wyoming.

Grange wasted no time turning a good team into a great one. In his October 6 debut against Nebraska, an emerging power in the Missouri Valley Conference, he scored three touchdowns. Held in check on the ground, he caught three passes for 45 yards and returned a punt for 66 yards. Nebraska would go on to hand Notre Dame its only loss of the year and fell to 8-1 Syracuse by only a 7-0 margin, but Illinois rolled, 24-7.

A week later, mid-major power Butler came to town. The Bulldogs had embarrassed the Illini with a 10-7 win in Champaign the year before, and it became quickly evident that Zuppke's plans to rest Grange would have to be abandoned. Playing primarily in the second half, Grange rushed for 142 yards and two scores, and Illinois needed every bit of that production in a 21-7 win.

Zuppke originally wanted to rest Grange against Butler because of what was on deck. Over the course of three Saturdays, Illinois would travel to Iowa, take on Northwestern at Cubs Park (which would become Wrigley Field in 1927), and play host to a Chicago team that was once again on a roll.

Iowa had won 20 games in a row when Illinois came to Iowa City. The Hawkeyes were 7-0 in both 1921 and 1922 and had outscored Oklahoma A&M, Knox, and Purdue by a combined 71-3 during a 3-0 start. Grange was knocked woozy on the opening kickoff and struggled for much of the game, rushing for just 58 yards. Britton bombed in a 50-yard field goal to put Illinois on the board, but Iowa took a 6-3 lead in the fourth quarter.

Illinois was forced to air the ball out a bit, but with Grange, that was a viable strategy. Hall connected with Grange three times and set the Illini up for a short Grange touchdown run and a 9-6 win. The Illini had survived their toughest test of the season. They would not allow a single point the rest of the way.

After disposing of Northwestern with ease in Chicago – in front of 32,000, Grange scored three touchdowns, including a 90-yard pick six, in a 29-0 win – Illinois returned home.

Homecoming against Amos Alonzo Stagg and Chicago would have been a big deal under any circumstances, but this was special. Memorial Stadium was opening in front of 60,000 spectators despite rainy conditions, and both teams were undefeated. Chicago had beaten Michigan State, Colorado State, Northwestern, and Purdue by a combined 77-6 and was in the middle of another golden age. The Maroons were 15-2-1 since the start of 1921 and would finish the season by outscoring Indiana, Ohio State, and Wisconsin by a combined 57-9.

With both offenses limited by the rain, the first half was taut and scoreless. Illinois made a goal line stand in the second quarter, Grange scored on a five-yard plunge in the third, and that was it. Grange added an interception, and Illinois survived, 7-0.

At that point, the drama was mostly over. Grange scored on a 26-yarder early against Wisconsin, Britton added a 33-yard field goal, and Illinois cruised to a 10-0 win, despite an injury that would keep Grange out of both the second half and the ensuing visit from Mississippi State. MSU had been outscored by strong Tennessee and Vanderbilt teams by only a combined 7-3 and would go on to tie a one-loss Florida team, but even without the Galloping Ghost, Illinois still had too much for a decent MSU team. The Illini rolled, 27-0.

That left a trip to Ohio State. The Buckeyes finished 3-4-1 but lost only to excellent teams (Illinois, Michigan, Iowa, Chicago). Ohio State sold out to stop Grange, who was once again healthy, and the game was scoreless through three quarters thanks to another big Illinois goal line stand. But Grange finally broke through late. He burst into the end zone from 31 yards out, and Britton added a 32-yard field goal to make the final margin 9-0.

Grange finished the season with 723 rushing yards, 178 receiving yards, and 12 touchdowns – at least one in every game he played. He earned All-American honors for the first of three years in a row. Illinois would earn a claim to the mythical national title, though the Illini had to split the Western Conference title with Michigan, which finished 4-0 in conference and 8-0 overall.

"I will never have another Grange," Bob Zuppke once said, "but neither will anyone else." (A quotable man, he also once said, "Alumni are loyal if a coach wins all his games." To put it lightly, that still rings true nearly a century later.)

But despite having Grange in uniform for two more years, he also never had another 1923. The schedules got tougher in 1924 and 1925, and Illinois wouldn't replicate the perfection of '23. The brilliant 39-14 win over Michigan in 1924 was followed a month later by a 21-21 tie with Chicago (the Maroons jumped out to a 21-7 lead in front of 33,000 before Grange dragged the Illini back) and a humbling 20-7 loss at Minnesota. Meanwhile, the 1925 season began with losses to Nebraska, Iowa, and Michigan and another tighter-than-it-should-have-been win over Butler before the Illini rallied.

The last four games of Grange's career briefly recaptured earlier brilliance. Grange's masterful performance in the 24-2 win over Pennsylvania kicked off a stretch that saw the Illini beat Chicago (13-6), Wabash (21-0), and Ohio State (14-9). Immediately after the win over Ohio State, Grange announced he was signing with the Chicago Bears. After changing what college football could become in the middle of Illinois, he did the same with pro football a few hours up the road.

1924 NOTRE DAME

Notre Dame had no business leading this game. Knute Rockne's plans had been foiled at every step by a physical, athletic Stanford team and its first-year head coach, Pop Warner. The Fighting Irish led 6-3 thanks to a shaky punt and short-field touchdown, but Stanford was driving, and the Indians' Ernie Nevers had been the best player on the field.

There was a lot on the line here. This was Notre Dame's first trip to the West Coast, and after a dominant season and cross-country publicity tour, all the attention was on the burgeoning Irish dynasty. They had Rockne, they had the Four Horsemen and the Seven Mules, and they had the attention of the entire country. They *especially* had the attention of the nation's Catholic population. But they had thus far proven inferior to Stanford's muscle.

Rockne always began games by softening opponents up with his second string, but Stanford had dominated them. The Four Horsemen entered and could barely move the ball. Stanford was about to take the lead, and while it was only midway through the second quarter, a Stanford lead could have meant disaster.

Luckily, Notre Dame had Elmer Layden. The Horseman had scored Notre Dame's first touchdown on a three-yard plunge, and with Stanford advancing, he stepped in front of a screen pass from Nevers and took it 78 yards for a score.

Notre Dame was used to being the superior team, but in Pasadena the Irish instead played with aplomb the role of opportunistic underdog. With Notre Dame still leading 13-3 midway through the third quarter, Stanford muffed a punt; Edward Hunsinger scooped it up and scored from 20 yards out. Hunsinger, a Mule, had nearly been sent home for breaking curfew in New Orleans during the lengthy pregame publicity tour. Instead, he was in place to put the game nearly out of reach.

It was 20-10 late when Layden again stepped in front of a short pass, taking this one 70 yards for another pick six. Outgained and outplayed for most of the game – Stanford had 316 yards to Notre Dame's 186, 17 first downs to the Irish's seven – Notre Dame still figured out a way to win handily.

According to Tex Noel's *Stars of an Earlier Autumn*, a 1943 *Esquire* magazine piece listed the 17 most memorable sports moments at any level; two were from college football: Red Grange's 1924 performance against Michigan and the 1925 Rose Bowl. And Notre Dame won it.

The Irish wouldn't return to Pasadena until a road game against UCLA in 2007. But they no longer needed the Rose Bowl. Notre Dame was *Notre Dame* now.

Take everything you know about this storied program and put it to the side. The fight song, "Play Like a Champion Today," Rockne, Lou Holtz, Ara Parseghian, all the Heismans, Touchdown Jesus, the NBC TV deal. Put it all aside.

Now think about Indiana in the 1920s. Steel, iron, and automobile manufacturing were thriving. So was the Ku Klux Klan, which had based itself in southern Indiana and, with help from a coded "law and order" message that has succeeded often in this country's history, infiltrated state government. As modernism and growth swept through

25

the country in the roaring 1920s, so, too, did a pushback, a desire to "save" the country from immigrants and technology and un-American influences. This is how a group like the KKK can thrive.

This was an exciting, angry time. A portion of Americans felt their country was being taken away from them. Some directed their hostility at the burgeoning Irish Catholic population. And, true to stereotype, plenty of Irish Catholics defended themselves.

Founded in 1842, the University of Notre Dame fought plenty of anti-Catholic rhetoric through the years – there's a reason, after all, that the team nickname is Fighting Irish. But it took on more notice when the football team began to act like it wanted to run the sport.

In 1913, former Wabash head coach and Amos Alonzo Stagg protégé Jesse Harper took over as Notre Dame's head coach. The school had beaten Michigan in 1909 and had an all-time record of 108-31-13 when Harper came to town, but everything went to a new level with him in charge.

Despite playing road-heavy schedules dictated by iffy facilities and what amounted to mid-major status, Notre Dame went 34-5-1 under Harper from 1913-17. Army and Texas were 15-0 in 1913 against teams not named Notre Dame, but both lost to the Fighting Irish at home by more than 20 points. The Irish did the deed again in 1915, and two days after beating Texas, they beat Rice in Houston, 55-2, for good measure. In 1916, they got revenge on a Nebraska team that had nipped them the year before. In 1917, they again handed Army its only loss. And in Harper's final game, they beat a strong Washington & Jefferson team, 3-0, in Pennsylvania. (W&J had lost by only a 13-10 margin to mighty, undefeated Pitt two weeks earlier.)

By the end of 1917, Harper felt he had done what he could for the university. American college enrollment was declining in general because of the approach of World War I, and the role of athletics within shrinking universities was uncertain. Plus, thanks in part to pushback from Notre Dame faculty, athletic facilities on campus were not where they needed to be. Harper had been tasked with making the program attractive to the prestigious Big Ten, but in that specific way, he had not been allowed to succeed.

Both Harper and the school had a pretty good successor in mind, though.

Knute Rockne turned only 30 years old in 1918, but the former Notre Dame end and Harper assistant had proven himself 10 times over. According to Murray Sperber in *Shake Down the Thunder: The Creation of Notre Dame Football*, "Harper also recognized Rockne's potential as a coach. The University of Chicago grad had installed the offensive 'shift' that he learned from his mentor, Amos Alonzo Stagg, and in 1913, Harper noticed that 'in the course of the development of the backfield shift,' captain Rockne 'worked out some very good ideas in regard to the ends shifting in the backfield.' Harper hired him as his assistant for the 1914 season, putting together a financial package for Rockne of about $1,000 a year from football, track (as N.D. head coach), and teaching chemistry part-time."

(This is not quite the version you may have seen in *Knute Rockne, All-American*. The version of Rockne played by Pat O'Brien in the 1940 film was torn between chemistry and football. The real Rockne almost certainly was not. He graduated magna cum laude in 1914 with a degree in pharmacy, sure, but he was always a sportsman at heart.)

Harper was so impressed with Rockne that, in earlier years, he wrote letters to other schools – Kansas, Wabash, Iowa State – to help him find a higher coaching position. Rockne ended up landing the perfect job simply by staying in town.

From 1918-23, Rockne's Fighting Irish were dominant. They went 48-4-3 – 4-0-1 against Army, 5-0 against Purdue, 4-0 against Indiana, 3-0 against Michigan State, 2-0 against Georgia Tech, 2-0 against Carnegie Tech. Two of their four losses in this span came at Nebraska, where Rockne was particularly frustrated by how obscenely his team was treated.

Granted, Rockne wasn't the purest of souls himself. Stagg, he was not. He grew up in the tough Logan Square neighborhood of Chicago, played semi-pro football on the side while attending Notre Dame, and, according to Sperber, was known to have bet on at least one Notre Dame game in 1916.

Still, he was the face of a movement, and he wanted his men treated with respect. Each trip back to Lincoln begat more nasty treatment than the one before it, and really, that made sense. Nebraska was farm country, and farmers were struggling in the 1920s – another product of modernization. Members of the population who are not doing as well are far more likely to fall back on resentment and/or anti-Semitism, and a group of Catholics from another region was an easy, almost conse-quence-free target. Regardless, Nebraska was coming to South Bend in the fall of 1924, and that was one of a few games Rockne had circled on the calendar.

That Rockne was still in South Bend in 1924 was a bit of a victory. He was frustrated by the pace at which some of his ongoing demands – a salary that befitted his status as one of football's best coaches, a new stadium to replace rickety Cartier Field – were being met, and despite his increasing influence, he supposedly gave serious thought to an offer from Iowa in the offseason following 1923.

Rockne and Notre Dame football played a role in an ongoing existential crisis for the school, one that just about every major foot-ball-playing university has gone through at some point. Sports success in general (and football success in particular) can do great things for a school – in the 1920s, for instance, enrollment at Notre Dame tripled. But you can go down a pretty bumpy road if you begin to cater to foot-ball at the perceived expense of other things. This was still a Catholic educational institution, and plenty of university higher-ups were uncomfortable with the increasing sway the football program held.

Rockne's relationship with university president Fr. Matthew Walsh was increasingly strained. Walsh did as much as Rockne to define Notre Dame in the 1920s, championing a major building and construction campaign. But he had also vetoed a proposed trip to the Rose Bowl in 1923, which created further animosity with Rockne and anxiety within the growing fan base.

Father John O'Hara, however, ended up becoming one of Rockne's best assets. O'Hara's father was the United State consul to Uruguay during the Teddy Roosevelt administration, and he spent time in Uruguay, Argentina, and Brazil while growing up. He graduated from Notre Dame in 1911, became ordained into the priesthood in 1916, and was serving as Prefect of Religion (basically the school's No. 3 in charge) for the university in the 1920s. He would eventually serve as university president, from 1934-39.

O'Hara's time in soccer-hungry South America taught him how imagery of sport and religion can intermingle, and in Notre Dame's gridiron success, he saw potential for both his university and his religion. He encouraged media to cover the team's traditional pregame communion, and he played a key role in securing the Rose Bowl bid following the 1924 season.

Whereas Notre Dame's football side and academic side could have (and did, for a while) produced conflicting stereotypes – angry Irish Catholic hooligans versus conservative, erudite conformists – O'Hara saw potential for a blending of the best of both worlds. He wanted to sell a vision of observant, wholesome Catholic gentlemen who would run you over on Saturdays, then help you up.

This was tough to pull off. The players were confronted frequently by anti-Semites, and, well, *you* try keeping a large group of high-testosterone 21-year olds all from engaging. In May 1924, a large group of Notre Dame students gathered in the South Bend train station and began to fight with members of the Ku Klux Klan coming to town to attend a rally.

O'Hara helped to secure the Rose Bowl berth, in part because he wore Walsh down; he also served as the driving force behind a massive, *three-week* publicity tour. The Irish would be hosted by alums and local Knights of Columbus groups in Chicago, Memphis, New Orleans, and other cities; they would go through more cities on the way back from Pasadena. The team would be displayed as gracious champions, good Catholics. They would represent the university and an entire people.

But first, they had to win some games.

Notre Dame's 1924 schedule was a feat. The Irish faced two eastern powers (Army, Princeton), hosted South heavyweight Georgia Tech, then took on three Midwestern 11s (Wisconsin, Nebraska, Northwestern) before finishing out east again against Carnegie Tech (now Carnegie Mellon) in Pittsburgh. If you want to become a national brand, that's a solid way of going about it.

The season began, however, with a pair of formalities. Notre Dame still struggled to schedule a full slate of solid home games, but part of this was likely by design: Rockne seemed to like starting with two cupcakes. The Irish began with Kalamazoo and Mount Union in 1919, Kalamazoo and Western Michigan in 1920, Kalamazoo and DePauw in 1921, Kalamazoo and St. Louis in 1922, and Kalamazoo and Lombard in 1923. Combined score of these 10 games: Notre Dame 428, Opponent 17.

In 1924, the designated victims were Lombard and Harper's former employer, Wabash. The fights didn't last long. Rockne would start games with his second-stringers, allowing the "shock troops" to absorb the opponent's early energy before unleashing hell with the starters. The starters didn't have to play in either of these games if they didn't want to. Ward Connell scored on a 60-yard run in the third quarter against Lombard, and Harry O'Boyle scored on two long runs of his own. After the 40-0 pasting of Lombard came an easy 34-0 win over Wabash. Then it was time to officially start the season.

If you wanted to find your place in 1920s football mythology, you had to play in front of Grantland Rice. The former Vanderbilt football and baseball player was in his heyday in the 1920s, writing a weekly Sportlight column for the *New York Tribune*. His writing was self-indulgent but poetic, verbose but quotable. He was college football's original tastemaker.

Rice made Red Grange a household name, and on October 18, 1924, he made Notre Dame's backfield immortal. In writing about the Fighting Irish's 13-7 win over Army at the Polo Grounds, Rice penned one of the sport's most famous passages:

> *"Outlined against a blue-gray October sky, the Four Horsemen rode again. In dramatic lore they are known as Famine, Pestilence, Destruction and Death. These are only aliases. Their real names are Stuhldreher, Miller, Crowley and Layden. They formed the crest of the South Bend cyclone before which another fighting Army football team was swept over the precipice at the Polo Grounds yesterday afternoon as 55,000 spectators peered down on the bewildering panorama spread on the green plain below.*
>
> *"A cyclone can't be snared. It may be surrounded, but somewhere it breaks through to keep on going. When the cyclone starts from South Bend, where the candle lights still gleam through the Indiana sycamores, those in the way must take to storm cellars at top speed.*
>
> *"Yesterday the cyclone struck again as Notre Dame beat the Army, 13 to 7, with a set of backfield stars that ripped and crashed through a strong Army defense with more speed and power than the warring cadets could meet."*

You would have thought Notre Dame won by 60. But six was enough. Layden scored in the second quarter, and James Crowley scored in the third; a late Army touchdown proved the Cadets' mettle, but the Irish controlled the game when it counted. They had cleared the first big hurdle of the season.

Having dispatched of one Eastern power, Notre Dame made quick work of another. On a visit to Princeton, Crowley rushed for 250 yards and two touchdowns, and the Irish never allowed the home team inside their 30-yard line. First downs: Notre Dame 23, Princeton 4. Now world-renowned as the Four Horsemen, the Notre Dame backfield controlled the ball, and only a Cowley fumble inside the Princeton 10 kept the game at 12-0.

The final scores didn't match the mythology to date. Notre Dame was clearly awesome, but the margins of these victories didn't scream "all-time great team." That began to change when the calendar flipped to November. The Irish returned home to face Georgia Tech; while this wasn't an amazing Tech squad, the Golden Tornado still finished 5-3-1 with wins over Penn State, LSU, and Auburn. They were competitive against an excellent Alabama team. They were not competitive in South Bend.

In front of a packed crowd of about 17,000 at Cartier Field, Tech kicked a field goal on its opening possession against Rockne's second-string shock troops. But as the second quarter began and the Notre Dame starters entered, the game turned. Quarterback Harry Stuhldreher was hurt against Princeton and missed the game, but thanks to the Seven Mules (the blockers up front) and the second-stringers, who played much of the second half, the lead kept growing. Final score: Notre Dame 34, Tech 3.

The dominance continued with a trip west. A shakier-than-normal Wisconsin hosted the Irish in Camp Randall Stadium, and it had no answer for Don Miller, who scored on a 19-yard run and a 28-yard reception, ripped off a 55-yard run to set up another score, and returned an interception inside UW's 20 to set up yet another. It was 3-3 when the shock troops left the game after 15 minutes; it was 38-3 45 minutes later.

Next up: revenge. With perhaps the most anti-Catholic squad and fan base on the schedule, Nebraska had indeed seen quite a bit of fortune against Notre Dame in recent years. The Irish were 17-2-1 in 1922-23 – 0-2 against NU and 17-0-1 against everybody else.

Rockne wanted this one badly, but he still began the game with the shock troops, and as was customary, this was a close game for a while. A fumbled punt snap set NU up inside the Notre Dame 5, and the Huskers took a 6-0 lead because of it. But the starters ended the game almost instantaneously. Stuhldreher found Miller for a 65-yard score, Crowley scored on a 70-yarder, and Rockne waited a little bit longer than normal to call off the dogs. The Irish won, 34-6, but the score didn't do justice to the dominance. First downs: N.D. 24, Nebraska 3. Total yards: N.D. 566, NU 76.

Strangely enough, this increasingly bitter rivalry set up another one. Nebraska beat Notre Dame again in Lincoln the next year, but hostilities were getting so bad that officials feared violence. Rockne canceled the series following the 1925 meeting, replacing it with one against USC. The Notre Dame-USC rivalry continues today.

As has so frequently happened in college football's history, a great performance was followed by a ragged one. Notre Dame had a couple of them. Against both Northwestern and Carnegie Tech, the game was even at halftime, but a combined 22-for-31 passing in the two games made the difference. Well, that and another Elmer Layden pick six. Layden provided the difference in a 13-6 win over Northwestern, and second-half scores created a 40-19 advantage in Pittsburgh against Carnegie.

That left Stanford and the long trip to Pasadena. Father O'Hara's plan came off perfectly: A massive PR success for both the Catholic religion and the University of Notre Dame got capped with a national title.

This was not the best Notre Dame team – hell, the Four Horsemen weren't even the best Notre Dame backfield of the era (that was probably the 1930 version that featured quarterback Frank Carideo and halfback Marchmont Schwartz) – but it was the most important. It created so much of what we now know about this university and its football program. Rockne's Fighting Irish would claim two more mythical national titles in 1929 and 1930, and he was finally able to get Cartier Field replaced. Notre Dame Stadium opened with a 20-14 win over SMU on October 4, 1930.

Rockne would only coach five games inside the stadium, though. On March 31, 1931, he was on a flight to Los Angeles to participate in a film called *The Spirit of Notre Dame*. One of the plane's wings separated, and TWA Flight 599 crashed in a field near Bazaar, Kansas, only about 100 miles from Jesse Harper's farm. Harper was called to identify the body.

Amos Alonzo Stagg was a head coach for 57 years. Pop Warner, Rockne's adversary in the 1925 Rose Bowl, made it 49 years. But Rockne made almost the same level of impact in just 13 seasons. He went 105-12-5, won shares of five national titles (not to mention the last 19 games he ever coached), created what we think of Notre Dame, and showed everyone, for better or worse, what a college football program can mean for not only a university, but for a large swath of American culture.

1925 ALABAMA

There was, for lack of a better term, a period of shame for Germany following World War II. In Adolf Hitler, the country had allowed a monster to take charge of its government and had paid the price. It was broken up into pieces and run by the people it had attempted to conquer. The country suffered from a malaise, a sense that it could not be allowed to experience pride or enjoyment.

Soccer helped to change that. In the 1954 FIFA World Cup in Switzerland, West Germany overcame an early blowout loss to Hungary, the best team in the world, to advance to the knockout round. They beat Yugoslavia, 2-0, then blew out Austria, 6-1, in the semis. Given another chance at Hungary in the title game, they pulled off the 'Miracle of Bern.' Down 2-0 after eight minutes, they scored twice in the first half and netted the game-winner six minutes from the end of regulation.

From guilt emerged bliss. Sport didn't actually change anything in anyone's day-to-day life, and there were plenty of negative forces the country had to deal with. But sport allowed Germans to feel good about themselves, if vicariously.

Now consider the American South. By the 1920s, the Progressive movement had found Southern states to some degree, but Jim Crow laws and segregation persisted. As a result, the South was in many ways separated from the rest of the country. But while the burgeoning National Football League had a team no further south than Kansas City, and the St. Louis Browns and Cardinals were the southernmost Major League Baseball team, college football was more democratic – anybody could try to form a team.

Of course, not just anybody could be considered great or allowed to prove their greatness.

By 1925, the Rose Bowl had become college football's showcase game. It was designed to pit an eastern team against a western team, in a gorgeous locale, in a de facto national title game. It conveyed status. It also hadn't yet invited a team from the South.

Georgia Tech might have gone in 1917 if not for the war enlistment that had stripped its roster down. But in every year in the first half of the 1920s, a Midwestern or northeastern team got the nod over a Southern team with an even or better record. The resulting pairings: Brown vs. Washington State, Penn vs. Oregon, Harvard vs. Oregon, Ohio State vs. California, Washington & Jefferson vs. California, Penn State vs. USC, Navy vs. Washington, Notre Dame vs. Stanford.

Technically, the Rose Bowl's streak of non-invitation should have continued in 1925. Undefeated Dartmouth was offered a bid, but school officials turned the invitation down in mid-November. The school was not prone to accepting such bids anyway, but in this case snowfall in New Hampshire was so significant that the school feared the team wouldn't get adequate practice time in to do the game justice.

Depending on who you believe, Colgate either turned down an invitation as well or got eliminated when it finished the season with a tie against a bad Brown team. Tulane, Princeton, Illinois, Michigan, and Yale were all supposedly approached as well.

Eventually, by either choice or the lack of any other options, the

Rose Bowl invited a dominant, unbeaten Alabama squad. And for the second straight year, the Rose Bowl and its result changed the trajectory of the sport's history, despite itself.

Alabama had been pretty good for a while, but the 1925 Crimson Tide were on another level. Wallace Wade took over two years earlier for Xen Scott, who had gone 29-9-3 in four seasons. With Scott, Bama was a bridesmaid – 8-1 in 1919 with a loss to powerful Vanderbilt, 10-1 in 1920 with a loss to unbeaten Georgia – before falling back a couple of steps and going just 11-7-3 the next two years.

Under Wade, however, the program appeared capable of taking a couple more steps forward. The Tide lost in their only chance to impress easterners, falling 23-0 to Syracuse in 1923, but they were otherwise 15-2-1 under Wade, and they secured their first Southern Conference title in '23.

With a backfield that featured halfback Johnny "Mack" Brown (a.k.a. the Dothan Antelope), quarterback Allison "Pooley" Hubert, and fullback Red "Lovely" Barnes, and a line that included All-American Hoyt "Wu" Winslett and three future pros (Bill Buckler, Bruce Jones, Claude Perry), the Tide rolled in 1925. The offense was strong, and, as with so many of the Alabama teams that would follow, the defense was ridiculous.

The season itself was a near-formality. While Georgia Tech began the season favored by most to win the conference, Alabama almost instantly proved itself the best team in the region.

After wins over Union (53-0) and Birmingham-Southern (50-7, a result noteworthy for the simple fact that Alabama allowed points) to begin the season, the Crimson Tide began Southern Conference play by outscoring LSU and Sewanee by a combined 69-0. But the score perhaps doesn't do justice to the magnitude of the wins: Both sets of Tigers would go on to finish .500 or better, but these two teams combined for just one first down.

For obvious reasons, Alabama was full of confidence when it traveled to Atlanta for the game of the year in the SoCon. Georgia

Tech had lost John Heisman to divorce and relocation after the 1919 season, but the Golden Tornado were still regarded as the South's best program. The home team was the favorite, coming off of a big win over Penn State in New York and an easy 23-7 win over Florida at home. Tech's *defense* was certainly strong enough to limit Alabama's offense. But not even the home of Heisman and the jump shift could produce an offense capable of moving the ball on this defense.

That the only touchdown of the game came from special teams was fitting. Brown returned a third-quarter punt 60 yards for a score, and Bill Buckler booted the PAT through the uprights. The 7-0 win made the Crimson Tide 3-0 in conference play and made them the overwhelming Southern favorites moving forward.

On the same day that Illinois' Red Grange torched Penn, Alabama put together a sloppy performance on a sloppy track, beating Mississippi State by only a 6-0 margin. But the offensive funk wouldn't last. On another wet field in Birmingham, Alabama handed Kentucky its first loss of the season in a 31-0 romp; the Tide then headed to Montgomery to manhandle Florida. Brown scored two touchdowns in each game, and a Pooley Hubert pick six put the Florida game away.

With one game remaining and another Southern Conference title all but official, Alabama trekked back to Birmingham on Thanksgiving to face a disappointing Georgia team. George Woodruff's squad had gone 7-3 in 1924, losing only to strong Yale, Alabama, and Centre teams, and the Bulldogs were regarded as a Southern dark horse heading into 1925. But another bad loss to Yale and tight losses to Virginia, Tennessee, and Georgia Tech meant they were just a .500 squad when they went to Birmingham. And they were no match for a Bama team on a mission. Final score: Alabama 27, Georgia 0. Combined score in seven Southern Conference games: Alabama 174, Opponent 0.

Regardless of who else had or hadn't been invited, by the first week of December Alabama had accepted an invitation to the Rose Bowl and was making plans to embark on the trip west the next week. The team from Washington would enter the game as the overwhelming favorite, but everyone in the South knew how important this game was to the region. Even Dr. Spright Dowell, president of rival Auburn, sent a good luck telegram Bama's way.

Washington was unbeaten at 10-0-1, having outscored opponents by a combined 461-39. But those numbers were rather inflated. Against six major opponents (Montana, Nebraska, Washington State, Stanford, California, and Oregon), the margin was only 94-30. The Huskies were clearly good – they had, after all, taken down Pop Warner and reigning Pacific Coast champion Stanford, 13-0. But to assume UW was the clear favorite was to assume terrible things about the quality of Alabama's opponents in the South.

Of course, those assumptions looked prescient early on the afternoon of January 1. In front of 45,000 at the Rose Bowl, with thousands listening via public news wire throughout Tuscaloosa, Washington went up 12-0. All-American George "Wildcat" Wilson picked off a pass to set up one touchdown, then threw a second score to Johnny Cole.

A hard hit late in the second quarter took Wilson out of the game for a while, but Alabama still found itself down 12 at halftime. The Crimson Tide had traveled 2,000 miles via train to lay an egg in their biggest ever game. They were pissed off, and Wade knew just how to push them over the edge.

Via Lewis Bowling's *Alabama Football Tales: More than a Century of Crimson Tide Glory*: "Wade knew his team, knew the pride it had in itself. He knew their faces, and what he saw pleased him to no end. … Wade, from looking at his boys, knew that his team, every single one of them, was now confronted with the choice of fighting or quitting, and he had absolutely no doubt they had chosen. To put them over the edge, he walked in and said in a rather low voice, 'They told me boys from the South would fight.' Then he left."

Wade won 171 games at Alabama and Duke, taking the two programs to five Rose Bowls. He was, by all accounts, a spectacular coach, but his best coaching job may have taken place in the locker room on this day. He made a couple of perfect tweaks to the game plan, and with one sentence he had his team primed to run through the locker room walls back out onto the field. On Alabama's first possession after half-time, Hubert ripped off a 26-yard run, then scored from one yard out to make the score 12-7. After a quick Washington punt, Grant Gillis went deep for Johnny Mack Brown. Fifty-nine yards later, Bama led.

The run continued. Washington lost a fumble, and on the ensuing snap, Hubert and Brown connected for a 30-yard score. After the perfect halftime speech, Alabama played seven perfect minutes and had a 20-12 lead to show for it.

With Wilson back in the game, Washington battled back. The Wildcat found John Cole for a 27-yard touchdown to make the score 20-19, but this brilliant Tide defense assured that there would not be another lead change. Gillis picked off a Wilson pass, Herschel Caldwell did the same, and the clock ran out.

According to Brown, whose good looks would lead to Wheaties box appearances and a movie career, a "bunch of farmers ... had won the Rose Bowl for the whole South." The entire South celebrated with Alabama. Tulane students cheered for the Crimson Tide when their train rolled through New Orleans. Local bands met them at other stops. The party continued with a parade in Tuscaloosa.

The championship of a sport created in the East, perfected in the Midwest, and showcased in the West, had gone to a school from rural Alabama. This changed everything. Southern teams would play in 13 of the next 20 Rose Bowls, winning five and tying one. The most dedicated teams from the massive, disorganized Southern Conference (which featured 22 teams in 1925, from Bama to Tulane to Washington & Lee) would split off and form the Southeastern Conference in 1933. Tennessee would get serious about the sport, as would LSU. Georgia and Georgia Tech already were.

The win was even immortalized in the Alabama fight song, "Yea Alabama."

"Fight on, fight on, fight on, men!
Remember the Rose Bowl we'll win then!

Go, roll to victory, Hit your stride,
You're Dixie's football pride, Crimson Tide!"

And to think, the Bama dynasty began at least partially because of a heavy snowstorm in New Hampshire…

1930 UTAH

Picked to defeat Nevada by only a touchdown in Reno, Utah drifts easily ahead with a 50-yard touchdown pass from Preston Summerhays to George Watkins. Despite an injury to a star, the Utes cruise in the closest game they will play all season. Utah 20, Nevada 7.

By 1930, every region of the United States had immersed itself in college football. The game had only become more popular after the rules changes of two decades earlier, and in the 1920s it had begun to produce truly bankable names.

Intercollegiate athletics – football, primarily – had grown so large that in 1929 the Carnegie Foundation put out a report mourning that "the athlete is the most available publicity material the college has. A great scientific discovery will make good press material for a few days, but nothing to compare to that of the performance of a first-class athlete. Thousands are interested in the athlete all the time, while the scientist is at best only a passing show."

While the popularity of the sport was increasing drastically, however, the power structure remained undefined. Some of the sport's earlier powers – Yale, Princeton, Penn, Michigan, Minnesota – carried heft. But Notre Dame had just emerged as a national power a few years earlier, the South was still getting its act together, and the West was, well, wild.

Forced to adapt its lineup due to injury, Utah somehow goes from good to untouchable. Frank Christensen, a fullback turned halfback, churns out seven-yard gain after seven-yard gain, and Utah is up 40-0 at halftime in the home opener against Wyoming. The reserves play most of the second half, but the margin gets so much worse. Utah 72, Wyoming 0.

Since 1915, California and Stanford had appeared in the Rose Bowl three times each, but USC was emerging under Howard Jones, and smaller schools were getting into the act.

In 1930, Saint Mary's, a small private school east of San Francisco, went 8-1 with wins over UCLA and Oregon and traveled to New York to take down emerging east power Fordham. The Gaels would begin 1931 by upsetting what turned out to be one of the best USC teams ever. Later in the decade, Santa Clara would finish twice in the AP top 10, winning two Sugar Bowls. Meanwhile, Montana and Idaho shared the Pacific Coast Conference with USC, Stanford, and the big boys. Nobody quite knew who was supposed to be good.

Between the coastal states and the Great Plains, there was quality football to be found as well, even if it involved teams just playing amongst themselves with minimal video evidence.

Ike Armstrong was only 35 years old when Utah's 1930 season began, but the Drake University alum had already built a scary Utes program. He was a Drake assistant when the Bulldogs pummeled Utah in Salt Lake City in 1924, and he liked the place and thought he could win there.

He was right. During his four years in charge, Armstrong was 28-5-3 with three unbeaten seasons and three Rocky Mountain Athletic Conference titles.

After a week off, Utah welcomes BYU to Salt Lake City on October 18. The rivalry game produces a tight 7-7 score at halftime. But a long pass from Ray Forsberg to Floyd Utter sets up a Christensen touchdown; Utter scores himself on the next bomb. After throwing three touchdown passes, Forsberg caps the scoring with a pick six. Utah 34, BYU 7.

Like the Southern Conference, the RMAC was a mishmash of regional programs, some serious about football, others not. In 1930, it consisted of Montana State, Wyoming, three schools from Utah (Utah, Utah State, BYU), and seven from Colorado (Colorado, Colorado State, Colorado College, Colorado School of Mines, Denver, Northern Colorado, and Western State). As with the Southern Conference, by the late-1930s, the more serious football schools in the group had split off and formed the Mountain States Athletic Conference.

This was football flyover country, and it would take Utah another 80 years before it found itself in a true power conference. Colorado, closer to the central portion of the country, caught on with what would become the Big 8 and Big 12 in the late-1940s.

Still, Utah was the clear BMOC of the RMAC at this time.

There was concern within the state, however, heading into 1930. The *Salt Lake Tribune*'s season preview announced that the "Approaching Title Race Appears Open," noting that, while Utah was the defending champion and returned 10 lettermen, the Utes had to replace serious talent, especially at fullback, where Earl "Powerhouse" Pomeroy had dominated the year before.

Caution reached an even higher ebb when presumptive new star halfback Preston Summerhays suffered a broken bone in his leg and ended up missing a good portion of the season.

Denver head coach Jeff Cravath had crafted the stingiest defense in the RMAC in 1929, allowing only 33 points in seven games. The Utes score nearly double that in 60 minutes. They score five times in the first half, then again pile on with the backups. The most memorable score comes when end Theron Davis carries a hapless tackler five yards into the end zone. Utah 59, Denver 0.

There was another reason for anxiety, however, and it had nothing to do with football. Utah was the wool capital of the United States in the 1920s, but as with so many other industries in the wake of the stock market crash and the impending depression, wool prices had tanked after hitting a peak of about a dollar per pound in May 1929. The price would fall as low as five cents per pound in the coming years.

In May 1929, stocks of American Wool were selling at 20 3/4. The price was down to 13 1/3 by the time of the market crash in October. And when Utah beat Utah State to cap a perfect 1930 season, it was at 6 1/4, less than a third of what it had been 18 months earlier.

This had an obvious effect on the local economy. Salt Lake City set up a relief committee in 1930, but funds for it had run dry by 1932. With wool prices back to pre-war levels and the labor force more than 50 percent more expensive than it had been at that time, jobs vanished. By 1933, Utah's unemployment rate was over 35 percent. Wage levels for the jobs that remained had declined by nearly 50. (The labor movement picked up in the state for equally obvious reasons.)

And that was before the massive mid-1930s drought.

Harry Hughes was successful enough to have a stadium named after him at Colorado State, and his Aggies beat Utah in Fort Collins in 1927. Three years later in the same venue, Utah wrecks Homecoming, scoring in every quarter. Four touchdowns come via pass, while Christensen continues to grind out six yards at a time. Utah 39, Colorado State 0.

Sports can serve as a distraction through hard times. And despite increasing economic woes, by the end of the magnificent 1930 season, Utah was drawing well over 10,000 people per game in an area that had only recently been bitten by the football bug.

As it turned out, Armstrong's biggest foe of 1930 was a spring bout with appendicitis. Leadership behind captain Ray Price was even stronger than that of the departed Bobbie Davis, and a big sophomore named Frank Christensen was not only a better fullback than Pomeroy; he was also a better halfback than Summerhays. Every potential obstacle for the RMAC crown fell by the wayside, usually more significantly than the one before it. Eight Utah players made the first-team all-RMAC list, and a ninth made the second team.

Armstrong would call this the best blocking team he had ever coached; it was also, to that point, one of the best passing teams in college football's brief history.

The biggest draw was Christensen, an eventual college football hall-of-famer. A three-time All-American (third-team in 1930 and 1931, first in 1932), Christensen still holds the career scoring mark with 235 points. He would go on to win an NFL championship with Detroit in 1935 and own the Christensen Diamond Products Company.

A Homecoming crowd of 12,000 is on hand to watch Utah host Colorado College. After another slow start, Utah scores four times in the third quarter -- two short runs (one by Christensen, one by Price), a 95-yard kick return by Davis, and a 43-yard touchdown from Forsberg to Utter -- to put the game away quickly. Utah 41, Colorado College 6.

Just as the Utes lost quite a few difference-makers from the 1929 team and improved, they barely got to see the lineup Armstrong envisioned in 1930 before Summerhays' broken leg forced some shuffling. Christensen moved from fullback to half and rushed for 100-plus yards for each of the final seven games of the season. Price, as a captain should, sacrificed yardage for more of a blocking-and-decoy role.

This arrangement, combined with a devastating, disciplined line, created an unstoppable Notre Dame- or Minnesota-style single wing. The base play: Christensen driving forward off tackle, with Davis and George Watkins driving out the defense's left tackle, Price and quarterback Ray Forsberg running the end away from the ball-carrier, guard Winfield Croft serving as a lead blocker/personal escort, and Utter blocking downfield. It got six to 10 yards anytime Utah needed it to. And when defenses were sufficiently distracted and/or worn down, Forsberg would throw to Utter or George Watkins over the top.

This was supposed to be a tough slate of Rocky Mountain teams, but it quickly became evident that Utah was too strong for the RMAC in 1930. The Utes needed intersectional competition to prove themselves, and this was the year to come up with something on the fly.

Unbeaten Colorado attempts a unique technique against Utah: Never mind Christensen and the ground game – focus on stopping the pass. Make Utah grind out scores on the ground. In theory, it almost makes sense, and Utah completes only three of 11 passes. Instead, the Utes … grind out scores on the ground. Lots of them. They gain 414 yards to CU's 60. Utah 34, Colorado 0.

Minor rumbles appeared after the win over Denver. First, the city of Denver wanted to host an exhibition between Utah and someone from another region, perhaps a minor opponent like North Dakota.

Then, as sentiment grew for a series of charity contests, with proceeds going to aid the unemployed, Utah seemed to find some options. They openly offered to play anyone in the country, and NYU volunteered to host a game at Yankee Stadium. Alabama, Colgate, and Utah were all mentioned as potential opponents. Staying in the west, the trio of Utah, USC, and St. Mary's basically all proposed games against each other. A game against SMC, USC, or NYU would provide the Utes with a wonderful chance to prove themselves.

USC seemed to be dragging its feet on an arrangement, however, especially as a game against undefeated Notre Dame on December 6 loomed. Utah didn't appear to want to face St. Mary's until it knew USC wasn't an option. Colgate, meanwhile, took the spot in Yankee Stadium.

Finally, as the calendar flipped to December, Armstrong called off the waiting game. A lot of his guys needed to focus on basketball if nothing was going to happen, and justifiably so – the Utes were awesome at that sport, too, going 21-6 that winter. So Utah finished an almost unknown 8-0. No one in the Rockies could come close to touching them, and no one else got the chance.

Armstrong coached at Utah until 1949. He won 141 games and shares of 13 conference titles. The team fell on hard times later in the decade at the same time the state did, then rebounded to go 16-2-2 in 1947-48. Still, while bigger names like Washington, USC, and Oregon State appeared on the schedule in later years, Armstrong's very best team, and the best the RMAC ever produced, didn't get to prove itself.

Cold and wind limit attendance for the season finale against Utah Agricultural (now Utah State). The Utes score four times in the second quarter, and in mostly familiar ways. Christensen scores on a plunge, then the Forsberg-to-Watkins combination hits pay dirt twice. Late in the quarter, Davis takes a punt return 64 yards to the house. Utah 41, Utah State 0.

There was another charity game arranged that year, by the way: On December 13 at Yankee Stadium, Army beat Navy, 6-0. The schools were casual rivals before then, playing in most but not every year. They haven't missed a date since.

1931 USC

Never mind Miami-Florida State. This was the original Wide Right, the original set of marquee rivalry games decided by faulty kicks. In 1926, USC lost to Notre Dame, 13-12. In 1927, it was 7-6. In 1929, 13-12. Three games in four years, all decided by one point, all involving a missed kick.

Even with a 27-14 win over the Irish in 1928, USC's status as a program was in some peripheral way being held back by the inability to make kicks against Notre Dame. The Trojans had earned a share of the mythical national title in 1928, going 9-0-1 with a scoreless draw against a good California team as the only blemish. They had romped over undefeated Pitt in the Rose Bowl to finish 1929. Their status was such that a two-loss season, as they suffered in both 1929 and 1930, was frustrating.

You can imagine the feeling, then, when Johnny Baker's PAT attempt was blocked early in the fourth quarter against Notre Dame in South Bend.

Los Angeles truly became what we know Los Angeles to be in the 1920s. The Hollywood sign, complete with four extra letters (L-A-N-D), went up. So did the Hollywood Bowl and showman Sid Grauman's flashy Egyptian Theatre, which hosted the first Hollywood movie premiere. In 1922, in a northern suburb named Pasadena, the Rose Bowl opened; the Los Angeles Coliseum went up a year later.

Pasadena had hosted the Tournament of Roses Parade since 1890 and for the 1902 celebration added a football game to the docket as a tourism booster. Unfortunately, the game was terrible – Michigan 49, Stanford 0 – so they held off on making it an annual event until more than a decade later.

From 1916-22, the game was played at Tournament Park, now owned and maintained by the California Institute of Technology. In 1923, with the event and the sport an obvious hit, a permanent home was erected.

It was clear Los Angeles had been bitten by the football bug. Rose Bowl attendance topped 60,000 in 1927 and 70,000 in 1929, when USC crushed Pitt. Meanwhile, the Trojans had played their home games at the chasmic Coliseum since it opened. UCLA would play there from 1933-81 before moving to the Rose Bowl. Professional sports had not yet found Los Angeles, but Los Angeles had found college football.

Winning didn't hurt. USC was a hit from the moment it attempted major college football; the Trojans went 10-1 in 1922, their first year, and would win three Rose Bowls and a Los Angeles Christmas Festival in their first decade.

USC and Notre Dame had filled Soldier Field, with over 100,000 in attendance, in both 1927 and 1929. In 1931, however, the rivalry made its Notre Dame Stadium debut. Knute Rockne had finally gotten the Irish's new home opened the year before, and considering the place only held 59,000, you can imagine how hot the ticket was in what had already become the sport's glamour rivalry.

Then there was the matter of the streak: Notre Dame hadn't lost since the 1928 defeat to USC. Hunk Anderson was chosen to succeed Rockne following the legend's tragic plane-crash death. He would only make it three years in the job, but he had, to date, kept the unbeaten streak going. Notre Dame was 6-0-1, with the only blemish a 0-0 tie against an awesome Northwestern team in Chicago. And early on November 21, the Irish gave no indication that the streak would be ending in 1931.

Defenses controlled the game early on, but Notre Dame seized the lead, as it was supposed to, late in the second quarter. A 35-yard pass from All-American Marchmont Schwartz to Charles Jaskwhich set up a short Stephan Banas touchdown and gave the Irish a 7-0 lead. And after USC began the third quarter with a punt, Banas raced 36 yards off of a lateral from Schwartz. Schwartz went off tackle from three yards out, and the Irish led, 14-0.

At halftime of USC's first game of the season, against powerful mid-major St. Mary's, Taps was played in honor of the fallen Rockne. St. Mary's head coach Slip Madigan had played on the line for Rockne in the late-1910s, and St. Mary's hired him to lead the football team barely a year after he graduated. Meanwhile, it was plainly obvious what the Notre Dame-USC rivalry had already meant for the growing USC program.

There was also the matter of USC trying to steal Rockne from South Bend. The Trojans bought out Gus Henderson's contract after the 1924 season – he had gone an incredible 25-5 over the last three seasons but was 0-3 against Cal (the school that was also accusing Henderson of paying players), which was a source of infuriation. He had fallen to St. Mary's as well in 1924.

The school was clearly ambitious and set its sights on nabbing

Rockne. But when Iowa came after him the year before after losing Howard Jones to Duke, he signed a 10-year contract extension. He was basically untouchable. So USC stole Jones from Duke instead.

Jones was a Yale alum, and his brother was the head coach in New Haven. He had bounced around, coaching Syracuse for one year and Yale for two, but made a name for himself at Iowa. He won 42 games in eight years, going 7-0 in both 1921 and 1922. He had just entered the first year of a five-year contract at Duke, but the draw of USC was too strong. One of the first things Jones did when he took the job out west was call Rockne to set up a series. It helped to shine a spotlight on the USC program, but the games themselves weren't working out incredibly well.

Following Notre Dame's second score in 1931, it looked like the game would finish a lot like the 1930 game, a 27-0 Irish win in L.A. But USC began to tilt the field in its favor. A drive deep into Irish territory stalled, but Notre Dame quickly gave the ball back to the Trojans, and early in the fourth quarter, USC great Gaius "Gus" Shaver scored to make the game 14-6. Baker's aforementioned PAT was blocked, however, and without a two-point conversion (it wouldn't come into effect until 1958), that meant it was still a two-score game. It would be too much to ask for any team to score three times in one quarter against Notre Dame, right?

Notre Dame went three-and-out following kickoff, giving USC the ball at the Trojans' 43. And on third-and-8, Notre Dame's tiring defense began to crack. A 32-yard pass interference penalty (it was a spot foul then) set up the Trojans at the Irish 24. Three plays later, Shaver went over right end for another score. 14-13.

Sensing his players were tiring, Hunk Anderson had subbed out quite a few starters by this point, and substitution rules meant they had to stay out for the rest of the half. Fatigue was common against USC. While Shaver was the most famous player on the team, the Trojans had maybe the most fearsome front in the sport. Johnny

Baker was not only a place-kicker — he was an All-American guard. Center Stan Williamson also earned All-American honors, and guard Aaron Rosenberg would the next year. Guard Byron Gentry and tackle Ernie Smith would both end up in the pros. Even though the offense wasn't picking up major ground in the first three quarters, physicality had its effect.

Anderson was protecting his defense with the subs, but it had an obvious effect on the Notre Dame offense. The Irish went three-and-out again, and Orville Mohler returned a punt inside Notre Dame's 40. Mohler lost a fumble, however; given a lifeline, Notre Dame earned just one first down, then punted again. USC's final attempt at a win would begin at its own 18.

USC had not completed a pass all game to this point, but it saved its two strikes for the most optimal time. On the second play of the drive, Mohler found Ray Sparling for 40 yards. One play later, Shaver hit recent sub Bob Hall for 23 more. With the clock ticking down, USC was suddenly in scoring position.

Notre Dame's gassed defense stiffened. Despite an offsides penalty, the Irish stuffed two run attempts for a loss of two. On third-and-7, Jones had a choice to make: Aim for the end zone and risk a turnover, or trust your kicking game despite plenty of reason to doubt it? Jones went with the latter. Convinced that Notre Dame's defense would be minding the pass and wouldn't effectively rush the kick, he asked Baker to attempt a spot kick from the Notre Dame 24. It split the uprights. 16-14.

Notre Dame got the ball back, but USC sacked Curtis Millheam, then picked off a Schwartz pass. Ballgame.

The day before Thanksgiving, on November 25, the USC team train arrived at Los Angeles' Arcade station at 8 a.m., welcomed by a mob of between 100,000 and 300,000 people. They were sent to city hall, where city authorities and another large crowd greeted them. They were given a parade through the Los Angeles business district.

The 1931 season had begun with a loss to small-but-mighty St. Mary's, a team that would go on to also beat 8-2 Cal, 6-2-2 Oregon, and 9-1 SMU. (The Gaels also lost to Olympic Club and a mediocre UCLA squad because college football sometimes refuses to make sense.) But since the buzzer sounded against the Gaels, the season was pure catharsis. The Trojans beat Cal, 6-0, then took down Stanford, 19-0.

And while a win like this can sometimes cause a hangover of sorts, it was a catalyst for the Trojans. Two weeks after Notre Dame, they hosted 5-2-1 Washington and rolled, 44-7. A week later, 8-1 Georgia came cross-country and was sent home with a devastating 60-0 defeat.

The Trojans hosted an awesome, unbeaten Tulane squad in the Rose Bowl; it was Bernie Bierman's final game as head of the Green Wave before he left to build a dynasty at Minnesota. The Green Wave were tenacious and unintimidated and had won shares of each of the last three Southern Conference titles. Play-for-play, they outgained USC (351 yards to 216), just as Stanford had against Notre Dame seven years earlier.

But like Stanford, the Green Wave were their own worst enemy. Finishing drives was as vital to the game of football then as it is now – USC did it, and Tulane didn't. The Trojans used the aggressiveness of Tulane's All-American end Jerry Dalrymple against him, doing damage with misdirection. Ray Sparling scored on a reverse to give USC a 7-0 lead at halftime, and Erny Pinckert scored twice on reverses of 30 and 28 yards to give the Trojans a 21-0 lead.

Tulane would win respect by continuing to plug away and eventually hitting pay dirt. They scored two touchdowns to make the final score 21-12, but USC wasn't going to be denied the national title.

In his *Stars of an Earlier Autumn*, Tex Noel named 1931 USC the best team of college football's first 68 years. Following this landmark season, the Trojans would not lose for nearly two more years. They stretched their winning streak to 20 by going 10-0 in 1932, handing Utah, Washington State, and Pittsburgh each their only respective losses of the season (each a blowout). They survived trips to Stanford and Washington, and they took down Notre Dame again, 13-0. Additionally, they would start 1933 with a 6-0-1 record before finally falling to Stanford, 13-7.

After a down spell – USC went just 17-19-6 from 1934-37 – Jones would rally the program to two more Rose Bowl titles in 1938 and 1939, garnering top-10 finishes both years. (The AP poll began in 1936.) Jones would coach through the 1940 season but passed away of a heart attack in the summer of 1941.

When it all clicks for USC, it's a beautiful thing. The stars get the celebrity treatment, and celebrities show up to watch the stars. Those that run the USC athletic department tend to think USC is such a special job that only someone with USC ties could understand how to succeed as football coach or athletic director. But the person who built USC into everything we think of as USC was a Yale guy who cut his teeth in Iowa. Again, this sport doesn't always choose to make sense.

1938 TCU

The quarterback lines up about six yards behind the center, with one receiver split wide right and four receivers bunched together on the left. The solo receiver curls inside, catches a short pass, and changes direction into an open swath of space on the right.

Two receivers are lined up wide left, with three receivers bunched together in a tight slot to the right. The quarterback finds a receiver on a left-to-right crossing route underneath a chaotic, confused secondary. As he swings to the right side of the field, he finds a trio of blockers clearing the way for a big gain.

The quarterback takes the shotgun snap and follows blockers off right tackle. At the last second, he lofts a jump pass, Tebow-style, to a receiver over the middle.

The QB rolls right behind a moving pocket, looking deep, then shovels the ball underhanded to a blocking back who scoots upfield for a short gain.

This is a pretty fun version of the spread offense, one with big-play goals and efficiency options. Someone's going deep on most plays, which stretches the defense and opens up safer, shorter passes. The offense's intent looks a lot like what we imagine from a West Coast offense, one that stretches a defense from sideline to sideline with the goal of eventually poking holes deep. (And really, there are only a couple of short steps from the West Coast offense to the modern spread.)

This selection of plays is on YouTube if you search for "Dutch Meyer TCU Spread." It is not from the 1970s or 1990s or 2010s – it's from the 1930s and 1940s. Everything old is new again.

So much of what made up football offenses on either side of World War II might seem primitive to a modern football fan. This was an era still defined by the single wing, the T formation, power football, and backfield misdirection. At least, it was outside of Texas.

Coaches were limited by the capabilities of the players at hand. With slingers like Sammy Baugh and Davey O'Brien at quarterback, TCU head coach Dutch Meyer was able to let his creative juices flow. After spending a few years under the tutelage of a legendary offensive tinkerer – Francis Schmidt, who went 47-5-5 in five years in Fort Worth before taking the Ohio State job – Meyer had plenty of ideas.

What he crafted shared a lot of characteristics with the double-wing formation (at times almost a *triple* wing) popularized by Pop Warner. And in 1938, TCU would still only average about 18 passes per game. But 18 in 1938 was like 50-plus today.

Of Meyer, Sammy Baugh would later say, "I didn't invent the modern passing game. Hell, I don't know who did. But I was ahead of people in the pro league because I had played under Dutch Meyer at TCU. … TCU's offense at the time was more sophisticated than anything they had in pro ball—and I just started putting those plays into the Washington offense."

Meyer changed what people thought about the forward pass, specifically its efficiency and risk. In 1938, he had an almost unfair advantage: O'Brien, the best player in college football. Meyer had a mantra regarding his passing game – "short, sure, and safe," the three S's – and that fall, just about anything was sure and safe in O'Brien's hands.

This wasn't supposed to be happening again so soon. In 1935-36, Meyer's Horned Frogs went 21-3-2 with Baugh behind center. In 1935, they claimed a share of the mythical national title with a 12-1 record. Baugh was a once-in-a-lifetime talent, eventually a two-time NFL player of the year, two-time NFL champion, and six-time first-team all-pro. In his junior and senior seasons, he won All-American honors by throwing for a combined 2,237 yards and 30 touchdowns. O'Brien, his replacement, was tiny (5'7, 150), one of the smallest QBs in college football. How was he supposed to replace a legend?

In 1937, the drop-off was obvious. TCU scored 20 points against Tulsa, 14 against Texas, and only 39 combined against eight other opponents. The Frogs went only 4-4-2, but they did finish strong, beating Texas, Rice, and SMU by a combined 24-2. The defense, led by a powerful line, was fantastic even if the offense was scuffling.

In 1938, however, Meyer had the experience he needed, and after a year of watching O'Brien, he was able to tweak the offense to allow his golden boy to thrive.

One such tweak appeared to be giving O'Brien better check-down options. If his deep man was not open, he didn't have to throw a jump ball – he instead looked for a halfback for a short gain. And with blockers more well-arranged nearby, those short passes often turned into long catch-and-run opportunities. Halfbacks Earl Clark, Pat Clifford, and Johnny Hall caught 42 of 66 passes for 870 yards and 12 touchdowns; passes targeting this trio were picked off only twice. More importantly, longer passes to ends Don Looney and Durwood Horner were picked off only once (they caught 30 of 64 passes for 418 yards and four scores). O'Brien's decision-making within this system was unmatched.

In 1938, TCU generated 39 first downs via pass, compared to 19 for opponents. Combined with O'Brien's running ability and that of big fullback Connie Sparks, TCU had an answer for whatever a defense wanted to attempt.

The state of Texas was ahead of everyone else when it came to the passing game, but TCU was leaps and bounds beyond anyone else in the state. The Southwest Conference was in transition in 1938 – Texas A&M was about to surge in 1939 but wasn't ready yet, Texas was two years away from its own surge under Dana Bible, SMU had struggled since reaching the Rose Bowl in 1935, Arkansas was replacing most of its contributors from a good 1937 squad, Baylor was solid but unspectacular, and Rice was rebuilding after a Cotton Bowl run in 1937. Plus, TCU's non-conference slate was almost suspiciously light; in 1937, Meyer had scheduled 6-2 Ohio State and 7-0-1 Fordham, but in 1938 they were replaced by 3-6-1 Temple and 1-7 Marquette.

With a soon-to-be-great quarterback, a creative playbook, and a huge, vicious line led by eventual hall-of-fame center Ki Aldrich, all-conference guard Forrest Kline, and all-conference tackle I.B. Hale, the team in purple had a golden opportunity. And it took full advantage.

As famed writer (and TCU alum) Dan Jenkins wrote in *Sports Illustrated* more than 40 years later, "[O'Brien's] long passes were beautiful spirals and they seemed to be guided by destiny into the arms of Don Looney, Earl Clark and Johnny Hall. In the meantime, Ki Aldrich and I.B. Hale blocked everybody and tackled everybody. The only suspense about 1938 was whether any of the Frogs or their rich and intimate fans would get drunk enough to fall off the stagecoaches they had hired to parade themselves around New York City when O'Brien went east to collect his awards."

The season opened with TCU hosting Centenary in front of 10,000 people. The Gentlemen from Shreveport had upset the Frogs, 10-9, in 1937, and threw a strange defense – a six-man line, only with a middle guard dropping back and attacking from different angles – at Meyer's charges in this one. It confused the mammoth TCU front, and the Frogs couldn't really get the running game going. But O'Brien hit Looney down the sideline for a 65-yard score in the first quarter, and a 47-yard catch-and-run for Hall set up a short Sparks plunge. That was all the scoring necessary in a 13-0 win.

More was required in Week 2. Thanks to a late touchdown, Arkansas became the only team all year to score more than once on TCU. But the game was notable mostly for the rushing output. Arkansas feared the pass and overcompensated, so the Horned Frogs rushed for 296 yards. TCU led 14-7 in the third quarter when, from midfield, O'Brien cut up-field for a gain of 20 yards, then lateraled to Sparks as he was getting tackled. The big sophomore rumbled another 30 yards for a score. The final score was 21-14; it was the closest any SWC team would come to an upset.

After a trip to Philadelphia to take on (and destroy) Pop Warner's Temple Owls by a 28-6 margin – in cold, rainy conditions, 25,000 showed up to watch what Warner himself would call the "greatest tosser I've looked at, and I've been looking a long time" after the game – the Frogs traveled to Kyle Field to face Texas A&M.

Timing means so much in sports. It doesn't only matter how good you are; it also often matters *when* you're good. In 1939, A&M head coach Homer Norton would unleash hell with junior fullback John Kimbrough. The "Haskell Hurricane" dominated, eventually finishing second in the 1940 Heisman voting, and the '39 Aggies surged to 11-0. But in 1938, Kimbrough was a sophomore, and Norton kept him behind senior Dick Todd in the backfield. Loyalty backfired, and the Aggies lost games by scores of 7-0, 10-7, and 7-6.

Kimbrough wouldn't have helped A&M much against TCU, though. In 90-degree heat in College Station, a crowd of 25,000 (the second-largest in A&M history at that time) showed up to watch Norton's "double shuffle" defense – it was known for lots of confusing pre-snap shifting – eventually get torched. The score was 13-6 heading into the fourth quarter, but O'Brien led two touchdown drives in the final stanza, and a pick six carried TCU to a huge 34-6 victory.

After throwing it into cruise control early in a trip to Marquette – O'Brien began the game 7-for-7 passing, TCU scored two quick touchdowns, and Meyer put in the backups quickly in a 21-0 win – it was time for a visit from Baylor. The Bears would finish a solid 7-2-1, but in front of another crowd of 25,000, BU had no answers. Sparks scored three touchdowns, O'Brien threw for three more, Earl Clark dominated at halfback, and TCU cruised, 39-7. An easy 21-0 win followed in windy Tulsa.

The formula and final scores were similar down the stretch. TCU faced Dana Bible's confusing 6-3-2 defense without four injured starters, but the Frogs still beat Texas easily, 28-6. They visited Rice and won, 29-7. Finishing up in Dallas against SMU, with wind whipping diagonally across the field, the TCU ground game powered a 20-7 win.

Meyer tended to take his foot off the gas as soon as possible and send in the second-stringers once TCU was up a couple of touchdowns. Even so, the Horned Frogs finished the regular season averaging 25.4 points per game while allowing 5.3. They finished the season No. 2 in the polls behind Notre Dame, but the Irish's loss to USC gave TCU an opportunity for a national title. Meyer accepted a bid to the Sugar Bowl, but with Oklahoma and Tennessee pairing up in the Orange Bowl and USC getting paired up with No. 3 Duke in Pasadena, that left No. 6 Carnegie Tech. The Tartans had handed then-No. 1 Pitt its only loss in early November and had lost only to Notre Dame by a 7-0 margin.

But first, a group of players and coaches had to head to New York because Davey O'Brien was to be awarded the Heisman Trophy. As far as research can tell, no one fell off of any stagecoaches.

The final game of O'Brien's career was the toughest of TCU's season. A long touchdown pass from Pete Moroz to George Muha gave Tech a 7-6 lead at halftime. It was the first time TCU had trailed all season.

You never know how a dominant team is going to respond to first-time adversity, but TCU did fine. On the first drive of the second half, O'Brien threw a dart to Horner for a 44-yard touchdown and a 12-7 lead. O'Brien strangely missed both extra points, but he made a short field goal to put the Frogs up 15-7 – a two-possession lead – with seven minutes left.

O'Brien finished 17-for-28 for 225 yards, and fittingly enough, he picked off a pass to shut down Tech's final scoring opportunity. Aldrich, meanwhile, made 19 tackles and picked off a pass of his own. Weeks earlier in the NFL Draft (which was then held in December), Aldrich had gone No. 1 to the Chicago Cardinals, O'Brien had gone No. 4 to the Philadelphia Eagles, and big I.B. Hale had gone eighth to the Washington Redskins.

After unearthing two of the most famous quarterbacks in college football history back-to-back, Meyer's luck ran out a bit. As the rest of the SWC began to develop and thrive, Meyer's success waned. He couldn't find another quarterback to do all he wanted to do. TCU did attend four more bowls under his watch and won two more conference titles in 1944 and 1951. But after the incredible success of the 1938 team, TCU wouldn't again finish in the AP top five until 2014.

Following the 1952 season, Meyer retired and wrote a book called *Spread Formation Football*. Again, everything old…

1938 TENNESSEE

To put it lightly, General Robert Neyland was a 'structure' kind of guy. An officer in World War I, a post-war aide for General Douglas MacArthur, and a brigadier general in World War II, he did pretty well within a rules-heavy environment. Turns out, he was good at creating rules, too.

Neyland was an assistant football coach at West Point in the early-1920s and took a shine to the profession. He became a military science professor at the University of Tennessee in Knoxville, and after just one year of serving as an assistant coach under then-coach Mark Banks, he took over the Volunteer program.

As head coach, Neyland created seven maxims of his own that perfectly outlined the way he believed a team won football games. He had his team recite them, believe in them, memorize them, take them to heart. Fans, too. If his team faithfully observed them, the Volunteers would probably win.

(He was rigid, but you can't say he was unreasonable – the original list had 38 maxims, but he cut it to seven. Things like and "1st rush equals 6 yds" and "Let none escape!" didn't make the final cut.)

The maxims were evidently pretty accurate: The Vols won a lot with Neyland in charge.

Results were immediate. In 1926, as a 34-year old first-time head coach, he led Tennessee to an 8-1 record with a loss only to powerful Vanderbilt. Progress was obvious: The Vols tied the Commodores the next year, then beat them in Nashville the year after that. Through seven years on the job, he only lost two games. His defenses earned him lasting notoriety – his team had allowed more than 14 points in a game just twice.

After a one-year Army assignment in 1935, he returned to Knoxville with some work to do.

In the mid-1920s, Alabama had introduced to the South what strong college football could look and feel like, and the rest of the South was becoming addicted. The late-1930s, then, were a time of transition for the SEC. Wallace Wade had left Alabama for the sanctity of a quieter (but no less successful) tenure at Duke, and successor Frank Thomas had done nothing but raise the Crimson Tide's profile since. Under Bernie Moore, LSU had surged.

Tulane hired Red Dawson in 1936 and continued its winning ways. Auburn was breaking loose of a couple of mediocre decades. Vanderbilt was still pounding out winning seasons. Harry Mehre was bringing a level of success to Ole Miss that hadn't existed before. Et cetera.

The Volunteers won six games in both 1936 and 1937 – they handed Duke its only loss in 1936 and throttled a good Georgia team in 1937 – but lost five times and fought to three draws. They were 0-3-1 against Alabama and Auburn and suffered scoreless ties with Duke and Ole Miss.

By 1938, the Vols were ready for a level of sustained defensive dominance college football hasn't seen since. Over the next 32 games, they would allow a grand total of 56 points. But either Neyland didn't know what he had at the beginning of the season, or he was keeping it under wraps. In the preseason, he predicted to a local paper that Alabama would win the SEC (Alabama and LSU were both considered national title contenders by the college football media) and that Tennessee would finish somewhere in the middle or lower half. "The boys have come along fairly well," he said, "but we're no further advanced than last year."

Maybe he really wasn't sure what he had that September. But he had his maxims, and he had a group of guys who personified them.

Maxim No. 1: The team that makes the fewest mistakes will win.

The season began with a ragged battle against struggling Sewanee. The University of the South was still a member of the SEC, but not for much longer. If all the teams listed above were winning, somebody had to be losing; the Tigers went 13-46 in seven seasons while in the SEC, went independent in 1940, and deemphasized athletics as a whole. It now has a Division III football program.

The Tigers were no match in this mistake-riddled affair. The Vols took control immediately with a 30-yard Bob Foxx touchdown, then blocked a kick in the end zone and scored again. Neyland was rattled by what he considered his team's poor play, but Tennessee certainly made fewer mistakes than Sewanee in a 26-3 win.

Maxim No. 2: Play for and make the breaks, and when one comes your way, SCORE.

Against Clemson in Week 2, the Vols ceded the early advantage to the Tigers, allowing a 64-yard scoring drive to fall behind, 7-0.

Forced to get a little bit creative, Tennessee went to the reverse: Sophomore Bob Andridge raced 59 yards for a touchdown on an end around. Later in the game, the Vols made a break and scored: Foxx reeled in a deflected Clemson pass and took it 23 yards for a touchdown. Final score: Tennessee 20, Clemson 7.

Maxim No. 3: If at first the game – or the breaks – go against you, don't let up. Put on more steam.

Tennessee's fourth-quarter prowess became both evident and necessary in a few specific moments. In Week 3, a visit from Auburn turned into a scoreless dogfight. The Tigers had yet to allow a point in 1938, and they were set to shut Tennessee out too. But Auburn's all-conference back, Spec Kelley, fumbled early in the fourth quarter. Bill McCarren recovered, and, with the break it needed, Tennessee's offense finally broke through. After three straight run plays, fullback Joe Wallen plunged into the end zone in an eventual 7-0 win.

Perseverance paid off in November as well. In a Week 8 trip to Nashville against 6-1 Vanderbilt, the Volunteers dominated – total yards: UT 255, VU 61; first downs: UT 15, VU 2 – but couldn't punch the ball into the end zone. Senior Walter Wood took the game over late, however, powering the Vols to two late scoring drives and a 14-0 win.

Maxim No. 4: Protect our kickers, our quarterback, our lead, and our ball game.

If there were any open spots on the bandwagon, they filled up after an October 15 trip to Birmingham. In front of 26,000 spectators, the Volunteers took an early lead, then protected it with abandon as Alabama put together scoring chance after scoring chance. George Cafego had a wonderful day on the ground (19 carries, 145 yards), but the game wasn't salted away until late.

The Associated Press began polling its members for a set of college football rankings in 1936. Tennessee's 13-0 win over Alabama vaulted the Vols to eighth in the country.

Maxim No. 5: Ball, oskie, cover, block, cut and slice, pursue and gang tackle. For this is the WINNING EDGE.

At the end of the 1938 season, a whopping *six* bowls were played on New Year's Day: the Rose, Sugar, Cotton, Orange, and Sun Bowls, plus the short-lived Poi Bowl in Honolulu. If Tennessee kept up its winning edge, the Vols were guaranteed to land their first ever bowl bid.

After such a huge win over Alabama, however, their focus wavered. Luckily, the schedule had let up. The Vols sleepwalked through the opening portions of a game against The Citadel in Knoxville. Frustrated with the first stringers, Neyland kept them in the game for a while until they got rolling. Eventually they did, in a 44-0 romp.

They found their edge against LSU, however. They also allowed points for the last time that season. In fact, they would go 15 games without allowing a score of any kind.

Neyland is known as one of the college football's greatest defensive coaches, but what exactly made his units so strong? He wasn't that experimental with his tactics — the Volunteers operated from a five-man front that was typical for its day — but he was innovative in his use of film study. (The innovation was that he used it at all.) His charges were incredibly well-prepared for their opponents, and it showed.

Neyland's longer list of 38 maxims hinted at what he preached every day in practice. He wanted brains ("Use your head. 75 percent of football is above the neck."). He demanded pursuit and pile-ups ("At least 3 men make every tackle, 'Gang Tacklers.'"). And as he showed in his substitution strategies, he was unafraid to use the second string to both give offenses new looks and wear opponents out ("Don't save yourself. Go to the limit. There are good men on the sidelines when you are exhausted.")

Neyland's 1938 team not only featured the veterans requisite for consistent, high-caliber football – senior Bowden Wyatt, one of the best ends of the decade; lightning-quick junior George Cafego, the No. 1 pick in the 1940 NFL draft (and a future lifer on the Tennessee coaching staff). It also included quite a few high-caliber sophomores that got major rotation time, including Bob Suffridge, whom Neyland called the "best lineman I ever saw." Sophomores in 1938 would go 31-2 in their collective playing career.

Maxim No. 6: Press the kicking game. Here is where the breaks are made.

In front of 36,000 in Knoxville – the Vols' schedule was home-friendly in 1938 – Tennessee's defense dominated against a team that had averaged nearly 17 points per game to date. LSU did score six points, but special teams carried the day for Tennessee. Neyland's troops were extraordinary kick blockers in 1938, never more than in this game. The Vols blocked *three* LSU punts, one of which led to a touchdown in a tough 14-6 win.

Cafego and Foxx were both injured against LSU and sat out the next game against Chattanooga. They were back for trips to Lexington and Memphis, however, and Tennessee beat Kentucky and Ole Miss, respectively, by a combined 93-0. (Against Ole Miss, they blocked yet another punt.)

By this point, Tennessee was still only fourth in the polls. Intersectional games were not widespread enough to assure strong non-conference slates. The result: No. 1 Notre Dame, No. 2 TCU, No. 3 Duke, and No. 5 Oklahoma had also survived the regular season unscathed. For that matter, No. 6 Carnegie Tech (now called

Carnegie Mellon) had lost only to Notre Dame (by a touchdown), and No. 7 Pitt had lost only to Carnegie Tech.

That's where bowls could come in handy. While there was already some handwringing from the TOO MANY BOWLS!!! chorus, TCU took on Carnegie Tech in the Sugar Bowl, Duke faced No. 8 USC in the Rose, and Tennessee challenged Oklahoma in the Orange. (USC had already knocked off Notre Dame on December 3.)

Maxim No. 7: Carry the fight to our opponent and keep it there for 60 minutes.

For a while, the Vols and Sooners would take Neyland's seventh maxim a little too literally, but the Vols' fight ended up being too much.

The Orange Bowl was the first bowl appearance for either of these eventually storied programs, and it showed. In the gorgeous new Orange Bowl stadium, both the Sooners and Volunteers were on edge, flagged for quite a few roughness penalties. Nevertheless, before the ebb of roughness reached its height in the third quarter, Tennessee had already secured a 10-0 lead. A short punt and a great Cafego return set up an early Foxx touchdown, and Bob Andridge recovered a fumble inside the OU 30, which set up a Wyatt field goal.

By the fourth quarter, the Sooners were toast. Fittingly, outgoing senior Walter Wood raced 19 yards to paydirt for the final score of the season, and the Vols won, 17-0.

Tennessee was simply too much, outgaining OU by a 260-94 margin and never allowing for a sliver of second-half hope.

Tennessee would finish second in the AP poll behind TCU but, via the College Football Researchers Association poll and others, would still claim a share of the mythical national title. It certainly doesn't take much affirmation for programs to claim titles from long-ago decades, but the Vols deserved a ring for the job they did. They maneuvered through a tricky schedule, handing Clemson, Alabama, and Oklahoma each their only respective losses of the season. With Cafego mastering his craft, they showed as much offensive upside as just about any Neyland squad would, and ... oh, that defense. It was always good, but in 1938, it began a run of true greatness.

By the time he retired, Neyland had manufactured elite play in Knoxville in four different decades: the 1920s, '30s, '40s, and '50s. His successors have experienced elite-level success here and there – Bowden Wyatt led the Vols to a No. 2 ranking in 1956, Doug Dickey did it in 1967, Johnny Majors reached the top five in 1985 and 1989, and Phil Fulmer scored an ever-elusive national title in 1998 – but Neyland's shadow over the Tennessee football program is as massive as the shadows that hang from Neyland Stadium over the Tennessee River as the sun sets.

1940 MINNESOTA

Each decade has its powerhouse coaches. In the late-1910s, it was John Heisman. In the 1920s and early-1930s, the big names were Knute Rockne, Howard Jones, Pop Warner, and Wallace Wade. In the postwar-1940s, Notre Dame's Frank Leahy, Army's Red Blaik, and Michigan's Fritz Crisler dominated. In the 1950s, Oklahoma's Bud Wilkinson ran the universe before Alabama's Bear Bryant took over.

The 1930s, however, are often overlooked. So much of the sport's power structure was up for grabs, with great teams emerging from every region of the country. The names you might remember are Alabama's Frank Thomas, Tennessee's Bob Neyland, or maybe Notre Dame's Elmer Layden, who replaced Hunk Anderson in 1934. But two names in particular sometimes get left out of the conversation. One is Pitt's Jock Sutherland, who succeeded Warner, went 56-6-6 from 1931-37, and won the 1937 national title. The other is Minnesota's Bernie Bierman.

There must have been an Elite Coaching major at Minnesota in the first half of the 20th century. Clark Shaughnessy, busy unleashing his version of the T formation on an unsuspecting college football

71

universe at Stanford in 1940, graduated in Minneapolis in 1914. Biggie Munn, who turned Michigan State into a sudden powerhouse in the early-1950s, graduated in 1932. Wilkinson followed in 1937.

Bierman was a 1916 grad. He wound his way around the country, leading the Montana, Mississippi State, and Tulane programs for 10 years before coming home. In his final three years at Tulane, he went 28-2 and shared two Southern Conference title.

Bierman needed only one year to get rolling in Minneapolis. After going 5-3 in 1932, Minnesota went 27-1-4 from 1933-36, winning the AP title in 1936. From November 19, 1932, to October 31, 1936 – nearly four full years – the Gophers did not lose. They did not play thrilling, light-up-the-scoreboard football (one of Bierman's most memorable quotes was, "A good running game behind good blocking is the smartest game. … Passing is a gambler's game."), but they proved impossible to conquer.

Relatively speaking, however, they had fallen on hard times. Minnesota went just 6-2 in 1937 and 1938 – granted, with mostly tight losses to elite teams (Notre Dame, for example) – and in 1939 finished 3-4-1. It was a deceiving record: The Gophers still outscored opponents by 72 points overall, and the four losses came by scores of 6-0, 23-20, 14-7, and 13-9. They lost to awesome Nebraska, Ohio State, and Iowa teams and beat an excellent Michigan team in Ann Arbor.

Still, in a loaded conference, expectations were low heading into 1940. Star Harold VanEvery was gone, and while Minnesota was sure to be solid, how could the Gophers expect to stand out?

The best coaches sometimes produce a second act that we didn't see coming.

Bierman was a public worrywart, an anti-showman. He never predicted big things before a given season (even the great ones), and with the Gophers sporting a mere 15-8-1 record over the past three seasons, nobody rolled their eyes at his preseason proclamation that "we'll have no championship team this year," and "with a little luck we may be able to improve on last season's record."

To be sure, Minnesota was going to be relying quite a bit on sopho-mores after losing 16 of 25 lettermen. And with excellent Washington and Nebraska teams on the non-conference slate before the typical run of brutal Big Ten games – at Ohio State, Iowa, at Northwestern, Michigan – the schedule was as tough as it had been in quite a while. In fact, only one of eight opponents (Purdue) would finish with a losing record, and the Boilermakers only finished 2-6 because of four tight losses.

Still, he had to know what he had. Halfback George Franck was the fastest player in the Big Ten, and junior Bruce Smith had emerged as a breakout star while Franck redshirted in 1939. With sophomore Bill Daley prepped to break out as well, Minnesota had three outstanding runners, the former two of which would go on to make the College Football Hall of Fame. (For that matter, so would tackle Dick Wildung, another one of those important sophomores.)

With a burly line and more halfbacks than a defense could stop, Minnesota had the ingredients to make a run at the Big Ten title. The passing game was as nonexistent as ever – Smith, the "leading" passer, completed seven of 30 for 161 yards, three touchdowns, and two interceptions – but this was, as always under Bierman, a rush-ing-and-defense team.

One more ingredient turned the Gophers into a national champion: good fortune. They had very little of it the year before, but maybe they were just saving up. And against this brutal schedule, even the best team would need some bounces.

In the opener against Washington, in front of 46,000 in Minnesota's Memorial Stadium, the Gopher line struggled against its Husky coun-terpart. But down 14-10 late in the second quarter, Franck returned a Washington kickoff 98 yards for a touchdown. Then good fortune came by way of bad snaps: One handed Minnesota a safety on an attempted Washington punt; another, recovered by team co-cap-tain Bill Johnson, doomed a late Husky drive that had gone inside Minnesota's 5. Washington would go on to lose only to Stanford; there were no apologies for needing a bounce or two to survive. *Minnesota 19, Washington 14.*

Next came a visit from Nebraska. With 41,000 in Memorial Stadium, Minnesota was itself almost doomed by special teams. The Gophers missed a field goal and had a punt blocked in the first quarter, had another field goal blocked in the second, then suffered what could have been a costly PAT miss in the fourth. But the Gopher defense was too stifling, and Daley had a well-timed "Hello, world" moment: His 47-yard run set him up for a two-yard score. A 42-yard strike from Smith to Johnson early in the fourth quarter put the Gophers ahead for good, and running by Franck and Daley helped Minnesota run out the clock on a long, late drive. *Minnesota 13, Nebraska 7.*

After a week off, Minnesota's first road trip of the season was to Columbus to face Francis Schmidt and his defending Big Ten champion Buckeyes. With more than 63,000 filling Ohio Stadium, Ohio State took an early 7-6 lead, but a long Smith run set up a short Smith touchdown to make it 13-7 Gophers.

Smith was the star of the day this time, rushing 16 times for 139 yards, but the Buckeye offense created more than enough chances to tie. The Gophers stuffed them at the 9 on one drive and at the 3 on another, and a bad snap from Ohio State center Claude White on a slippery field ended one last chance. There would be a new Big Ten champion in 1940. *Minnesota 13, Ohio State 7.*

The win in Columbus powered the Gophers to sixth in the AP poll. They would move to fourth after a Homecoming shellacking of Iowa. With 63,000 in attendance, Iowa scored first, then Franck scored four times – two via reception, two via rush. His 55-yard catch from Smith gave Minnesota a 14-6 lead, and power running took it from there. *Minnesota 34, Iowa 6.*

The challenges picked right back up again. Minnesota had already beaten the teams that would finish seventh (Nebraska) and 10th (Washington) in the final AP poll. Next up was the team that finished eighth. The Gophers hadn't beaten Northwestern in Evanston since 1929, when Bierman was still at Tulane. And after special teams turned on UM against Nebraska, special teams helped to take down Northwestern.

More than 48,000 were in attendance in Evanston, and while Minnesota was the far bigger team, Pappy Waldorf's Wildcats had enough speed to make up the difference. Minnesota fullback Bob Sweiger scored twice, but Joe Mernik, going 1-for-2 on extra point attempts, created the winning margin. The Gophers led 13-6 heading into the fourth quarter because Northwestern's own PAT had sailed just wide. After the Wildcats scored a touchdown on fourth-and-goal to begin the final stanza, NU's George Benson missed again. Minnesota picked off a pass on Northwestern's last-gasp possession and survived, once again, by the skin of its teeth. *Minnesota 13, Northwestern 12.*

Next up: the game of the year against Michigan. Minnesota came into the game now ranked second in the polls, the Wolverines third. Michigan boasted senior Tom Harmon, the national scoring leader and a two-time consensus All-American who would win the Heisman about a month later. He would finish his career 19-4-1 in three years in Ann Arbor. But three of the four losses came at the hands of the Gophers.

63,894 filled Memorial Stadium despite rainy November conditions, and this heavyweight battle was essentially decided on one play … and another missed extra point. Michigan had 15 first downs to Minnesota's five, but with four minutes left in the first half, down 6-0 because of a pretty Harmon-to-Forrest Evashevski lob (and a barely-missed Harmon PAT attempt), Bruce Smith took a handoff off left end, darted back toward the middle of the field, then raced down the left sideline for an out-of-nowhere, 80-yard score. It accounted for nearly half of Minnesota's 180 total yards, and Mernik's PAT gave the Gophers the lead.

The Gophers had already stuffed Harmon three times in a second-quarter goal line stand and, like a soccer team nursing a one-goal lead, they had to basically park the team bus in front of their end zone to hold onto the lead. They would only get inside Michigan's 30 on Smith's run and ended up playing defense nearly the entire second half. Michigan drove to the Gopher 4 to start the third quarter, but Evashevski fumbled and Urban Odson recovered. Minnesota thwarted every subsequent attack, holding Harmon to just 28 yards in 29 carries.

After the game, the *Detroit Free Press* proclaimed, "Michigan's luckless Wolverines pushed a giant Minnesota team all over the rain-soaked turf of Memorial Stadium this cheerless afternoon only to be subjected to one of the most bitter and truly undeserved defeats in Michigan's football history." Minnesota's presumable response: "Scoreboard." *Minnesota 7, Michigan 6.*

Michigan did the Gophers one more favor the next week: Thanks to the Wolverines' win over Northwestern, Minnesota could clinch the Big Ten title with a victory against Purdue. The game was over in approximately 10 seconds. Franck returned the opening kickoff 91 yards for a score, and the lead was instantly insurmountable. Minnesota rushed for 273 yards, while Purdue rushed for 10. This one was easy. *Minnesota 33, Purdue 6.*

The Big Ten wouldn't begin allowing its teams to play in bowl games until 1946, so Minnesota's unbeaten record and national title claim would require one final win over Wisconsin in front of 40,000 in Madison. The Badgers hadn't beaten anyone with better than a 3-5 record, but they came out on fire. A 72-yard touchdown pass gave them a 7-0 lead; two minutes later, Tommy Farris picked off a Smith pass and took it for a score. 13-0, Wisconsin.

Like a splash of cold water to the face, however, the pick six woke Minnesota up. Daley took a score in from 12 yards out, then picked off a Fred Gage pass and returned it to the 30. Eight plays later, Smith tied the game at 13-13.

Mernik knocked in a 25-yard field goal in the third quarter, then Minnesota received one last break: An iffy Mark Hoskins pass landed in Franck's arms, and he returned it 27 yards for the final touchdown of his career. *Minnesota 22, Wisconsin 13.*

Clark Shaugnessy's Stanford Indians finished the season unbeaten with a Rose Bowl win over Nebraska; they would move up from third to second in the AP poll after second-ranked Texas A&M struggled to get past No. 14 Fordham in the Cotton Bowl. However, the renown Minnesota had earned in surviving one of the toughest regular-season schedules imaginable was enough to keep the Gophers atop the poll. For the fourth time in seven seasons, they claimed a share of the mythical national title under Bierman.

They would earn a fifth ring in 1941, with Smith, Daley, and Dick Wildung leading the way. The slow slide of the late-1930s felt like a distant memory.

After serving in World War II like so many other coaches, Bierman would return to again lead the Gophers, but he managed only one more top-10 finish (No. 8 in 1949) and retired in 1950. Minnesota was one of the nation's powers in the first half of the 20th century. The 1940 and 1941 seasons were a last hurrah of sorts.

1941 NORTHWESTERN

Imagine being in the locker room. Imagine the feeling of disbelief, of downright grief in the visitors' locker room, deep in the bowels of Memorial Stadium in Minneapolis. With war on the horizon and an impossibly uncertain future, the present tense was supposed to belong to Northwestern. It did not.

Pappy Waldorf's Wildcats had waited their turn. In 1941, with Otto Graham emerging as one of the nation's most dynamic players and Bill DeCorrevont, the original blue chipper, coming into his own, Northwestern had the pieces it needed. But with the Big Ten title on the line, a bad snap and a penalty on a perfect pass had done the 'Cats in. Final score: Minnesota 8, Northwestern 7.

It was always something.

Waldorf had come to Evanston in 1935 after five consecutive strong seasons at Oklahoma State (then Oklahoma A&M) and Kansas State. His tenure was an unquestioned success, but it was racked by what-ifs.

In 1936, Northwestern moved to 7-0 and No. 1 in the country but got rocked by Notre Dame, 26-6, in the season finale.

In 1937, the Wildcats lost by a 7-0 margin to three different awesome teams (No. 12 Ohio State, No. 10 Minnesota, No. 12 Notre Dame).

In 1938, they upset No. 2 Minnesota, then got upset at home by Wisconsin.

1939 began in disappointing fashion, with bad losses to Oklahoma and Ohio State. But the Wildcats rallied and beat Minnesota again … and then, of course, got upset by Purdue.

In 1940, they lost by a missed PAT against Minnesota, potentially costing them a share of the conference title. And it appeared fortune wasn't planning on changing in 1941.

In recent years, Northwestern has attempted to brand itself as "Chicago's Big Ten Team," a label that derives a certain amount of mockery from rivals considering every school in the conference seems to have as many or more alumni in the area. But in the 1930s, it kind of *was* the city's team. Dyche Stadium held nearly 50,000, and big games filled the place. Only a few schools were a bigger draw. And the support was intense: After a 3-2 win over Michigan at Soldier Field in 1925, jubilant Wildcat fans returned to campus, set an abandoned fraternity house on fire, then allegedly created an impromptu bonfire in downtown Evanston.

Four years before the 1941 campaign, and barely 12 months after the Wildcats reached No. 1 in the country, Northwestern's future was impossibly bright. In fact, its future drew 120,000 at Soldier Field. The largest crowd to ever watch a football game in the United States had packed Chicago's famous stadium on November 28, 1937, to watch the Public League's Austin High School beat the Catholic League's Leo, 26-0, for the city championship. ("Packed" probably doesn't do it justice – Soldier Field only had about 76,000 seats at the time.)

DeCorrevont was the reason they were there. A five-star blue-chipper before the term even existed, he scored 35 touchdowns in 1937, and his real exploits were impossible to separate from the myths. He scored nine

79

touchdowns in 10 touches against McKinley High School, and he scored three touchdowns and passed for another against Leo and its own star, John Galvin. Galvin would go on to star for Purdue, but DeCorrevont, with an opportunity to play for any school he wanted, stayed close to home and his widowed mother. He elected to attend the school 18 miles north of Austin high. He brought four Austin teammates with him, including future Chicago Bear Alf Bauman.

DeCorrevont's career didn't start out incredibly well. In the first two games of 1939, his sophomore year, Northwestern was shut out – 23-0 against Oklahoma and 13-0 against Ohio State. But he found a rhythm in a Week 3 win over Wisconsin, and he ripped off a 61-yard, game-winning touchdown with four minutes left in a 14-7 win over Minnesota. He was thriving early in 1940 before a badly sprained ankle took him down. He had only one carry in the gut-wrenching 13-12 loss to Minnesota, but he rebounded to throw touchdown passes against both Michigan and Notre Dame. In 1941, he was healthy, and big things were expected.

Of course, DeCorrevont didn't even end up the biggest star on his own team. That was actually a basketball player. Otto Graham won first-team All-American honors on the hardwood as a senior and briefly played pro basketball for the Rochester Royals. He ended up at Northwestern because of a roundball scholarship, but when Waldorf discovered the music major throwing passes on an intramural field on campus, he talked the youngster into trying out for a spot on the gridiron. Needless to say, Graham made the squad, and he took the football world by storm as a sophomore in 1941.

The beginning of the season couldn't have gone better. Graham introduced himself against Kansas State with three touchdowns in a 51-3 win; one was a 93-yard punt return that still stands as the longest in NU history. The next week, Graham and DeCorrevont each scored twice in a 41-14 romp over Wisconsin.

Just two weeks into the season, Northwestern had already jumped to No. 5 in the AP poll. The Wildcats had a chance to make an even bigger statement when No. 6 Michigan came to town in Week 3. In front of 47,000, Michigan opened the game with a 78-yard scoring drive, but Northwestern tied things up with a fourth-and-goal lunge by Graham. Northwestern had the dagger in its hand for virtually the entire third quarter, but the Wildcats turned the ball over on downs at Michigan's 8 and 27 and lost fumbles at the 19 and 25. Given second (or third, or fourth) life, the Wolverines finally struck: Tommy Kuzma found Joe Rogers on a 47-yard pass to give Michigan a 14-7 lead.

Typical of this Wildcats team, Northwestern was just resilient enough to fall inches short. DeCorrevont and Bill Ohland connected on a 52-yard pass to get NU to the Michigan 12 in the final minute. But on the final play of the game, with Northwestern at the Michigan 4, the Wildcats were pushed backwards.

Conference title ambitions didn't end with the loss, however, and the Wildcats' rebound was impressive. Waldorf's squad traveled to Columbus to take on Paul Brown's Ohio State Buckeyes. Brown, the future Cleveland Browns head coach and Cincinnati Bengals owner, hadn't lost a game in four years; his prolific success at Massillon Washington High School, outside of Canton, earned him a shot at the state's largest institution. He would begin his Buckeye career 15-2-1, but his team couldn't do anything to stop Graham. In front of 71,896 at Ohio Stadium, Graham hit Bud Haase for a 43-yard score in the first quarter, then connected with Bob Motl for a third-quarter score. Northwestern won, 14-7, and Graham evidently made an impression on Brown, who would sign him to play for the Browns five years later.

Back to ninth in the polls, Northwestern still controlled its own destiny in the Big Ten thanks to Minnesota's 7-0 win over Michigan. If the Wildcats could pull an upset of the No. 1 Gophers in Minneapolis, they could take the title. They couldn't have come any closer.

It was Homecoming for the defending national champions, and a record Minnesota crowd of 64,464 showed up to watch Northwestern give the Gophers all they could handle. Minnesota's dominant line controlled the trenches for the most part, but with star halfback Bruce Smith injured – he got hurt against Michigan and touched the ball just once – the Gophers' offense was inconsistent. An early interception by Don Clawson ended a UM scoring opportunity, and Graham's passing kept Minnesota at bay, especially in the second quarter. Early in the quarter, Graham rolled right and fired a gorgeous strike to Motl for a 73-yard touchdown; only, the Wildcats were flagged for having an illegal man (lineman Leon Cook) downfield. The team protested, but the call stood.

Later in the quarter, a lucky break (Graham muffed a punt, but Ike Kepford recovered it and advanced it 20 yards upfield) led to a go-ahead score when Graham and Haase connected in the end zone.

The Wildcats could have used that Motl score, though. In the first quarter, a bad snap flew over DeCorrevont's head for a safety and a 2-0 Minnesota lead. In the third quarter, a short DeCorrevont punt set UM up in NU territory. On their second play of the series, the Gophers raced to the line of scrimmage and got set before the flat-footed Northwestern defense could do the same. Bud Higgins, the smallest man on the Minnesota roster, then raced 41 yards down the right sideline for a TD and an 8-7 lead. Northwestern never seriously challenged again, and the champs survived.

This was a gutting loss. Minnesota would go on to once again finish unbeaten and win the national title, and at best, Northwestern was now going to finish 6-2.

Make it 5-3. After Clawson scored twice from the fullback position to power Northwestern to a 20-14 win over Indiana, No. 8 Notre Dame came to town and handed the Wildcats one more gut-wrenching defeat. DeCorrevont was brilliant – he had rushes of 34 and 27 yards and picked off eventual Heisman winner Angelo Bertelli to end a scoring chance inside the Northwestern 10 – but as always, the Wildcats needed one more play. DeCorrevont's legs helped to set up a game-winning field goal attempt from the ND 17 as time expired, but it sailed wide. Notre Dame 7, Northwestern 6. One of the best, most star-powered teams in the country was 4-3.

At least the final act was a happy one. In the season finale against Illinois – in Illini head coach Bub Zuppke's final game – DeCorrevont had one of his finest afternoons. He scored three times: twice on five-yard runs (set up each time by DeCorrevont-to-Motl completions) and once on a 20-yard sweep. Northwestern cruised, 27-0, and the Wildcats could have made it worse if they'd wanted.

With today's scheduling and bowl slate, this Northwestern team would have finished about 9-3 with a bid in a strong January 1 bowl. But in the landscape of 1941, the season ended when the buzzer sounded on senior day at Dyche Stadium. Northwestern finished 5-3 and 11th in the country. Seniors like DeCorrevont joined the armed forces soon after – DeCorrevont enlisted into the Navy in March and spent some time on the Great Lakes Navy all-star squad of 1942 and the Bainbridge Navy squad of 1943. After the war, he played for four NFL teams in five years (including both the Chicago Bears and Chicago Cardinals), finishing with 10 interceptions and 233 rushing yards. He never had a chance to live up to the hype he received in high school, but he carved out a career for himself, and then mostly disappeared from public life, running a successful furniture-cleaning business in Chicago.

Graham, meanwhile, would go on to become the most famous Northwestern football alum of all-time. He finished his career with 2,072 career passing yards, which still ranks in the school's all-time top 15; his scoring average of 4.8 points per game remained top in the school record books into the 1990s. He served two years in the Navy Air Corps – he briefly played for the North Carolina Pre-Flight team (for which Bear Bryant was an assistant coach) in 1944 – then joined Paul Brown in Cleveland.

Graham led the Browns to four consecutive AAFC championships, and in the franchise's first year after moving to the NFL, he led the Browns to a league title there, too. They would also win in 1945 and 1955.

Waldorf, meanwhile, found success elsewhere, too. He coached Northwestern through the 1946 season, then landed in Berkeley, where he took the California Golden Bears to three consecutive Rose Bowls from 1948-50. He retired with 157 career wins in 1956; 49 of them came at Northwestern, where the Wildcats were close to so, so many more.

1943 IOWA PRE-FLIGHT

It is one of college football's ultimate butterfly effects.

1. Missouri head coach Don Faurot created his own version of the T formation to compensate for the loss of star quarterback Paul Christman.

In 1939-40, Pitchin' Paul finished in the top five of the Heisman voting twice and led Mizzou to the 1939 Big 6 title and the Tigers' first ever bowl bid, a trip to the 1940 Orange Bowl. They averaged nearly 24 points per game in 1940, with Christman leading the way, and the St. Louis native was selected by the Chicago Cardinals in the second round of the 1941 NFL Draft.

Christman's presence drove the Missouri offense, and in his absence, Faurot thought he might need to get creative to keep moving the ball. In his 1950 book, *Secrets of the "Split T" Formation*, he explained: "Christman fit nicely into our single wing and short punt formations. … There was no suitable replacement in sight among returning lettermen. However, our veteran backs had considerable speed, and the squad as a whole was versatile. The time seemed ripe for innovating the basic plays of the 'Split T.'"

Mizzou was in the process of upgrading its out-of-conference scheduling. To help pay for athletic department expenses, Faurot, with his athletic director hat on, took a series of payout games. Between 1940 and 1949, the Tigers would play at Ohio State an incredible eight times, at Minnesota three times, and at SMU twice; they would also visit to Pitt, Wisconsin, Fordham, Texas, and Navy. In *Secrets*, Faurot noted that the deception of the Split T he was tinkering with was attractive because it might allow his guys to compete with bigger, stronger teams. "We needed the deception of the 'Split T' together with its promise of more offensive punch to offset the superior man-power mustered by our opponents. If we couldn't beat them down to size, then we might bewilder them! It was worth a try."

Deception was long a part of football offenses, but *options* weren't. The premise of the Split T was to begin with your run-of-the-mill T formation and spread out the line further, giving them wider splits. Once the defense was spread out, you could find more gaps to exploit with speedy ball-carriers. But Faurot, once a basketball letterman at Mizzou, also saw a way to basically create miniature, 2-on-1 fast breaks. The QB could run the ball to the edge of the defense, and if a defender committed to tackling him, he could pitch the ball to a trailing halfback.

Faurot may have been the first college football coach to commit to option football. With film study still at a minimum, Missouri was able to constantly fluster unprepared opponents with it. He unveiled the offense in the second half of the 1941 opener against Ohio State, and while it was too late to help the Tigers against the Buckeyes in a 12-7 loss, the Tigers would proceed to go 16-4-1 over the next two seasons, 9-0-1 in Big 6 play. They reached the Sugar Bowl in 1941 and went 8-3-1 in 1942; their only losses were to a great Wisconsin team, Great Lakes Navy, and the Fordham team that had seen them the year before in the Sugar Bowl. They finished the 1942 season with one of the most impressive wins of the Faurot era: a 7-0 win over the Iowa Pre-Flight Seahawks in a Kansas City snowstorm.

2. With war efforts well underway, college-age males – including football players – were enlisting in the armed services.

Hostilities in Europe and Asia merged into one single World War in 1941, and after longstanding attempts to avoid combat, the United States officially joined the fray in December following Japanese attacks on Pearl Harbor. Millions of Americans enlisted in 1942, and to say the least, the effects were noticeable when it came to football rosters of able-bodied, athletic 18- to 22-year olds.

Football already had a grip on the country's consciousness, and many believed that it could be a useful tool within the armed forces – it helped to toughen men up, taught teamwork and discipline, etc. Beginning in 1942, teams from various Army camps and Navy bases began to play full schedules against not only each other, but also local college teams, many of which consisted of freshmen (who were previously ineligible to play) and/or players who were denied entry into the service for one reason or another.

These military teams frequently used recent college football players and sometimes even included a smattering of pros. Quite a few of these teams existed, and a few played schedules against mostly top-division schools. Here are the primary military teams from the years of 1942-44:

- 1942: Georgia Pre-Flight (7-1-1), North Carolina Pre-Flight (8-2-1), Jacksonville Naval Air Station (9-3), Great Lakes Navy (8-3-1), Iowa Pre-Flight (7-3), St. Mary's Pre-Flight (6-3-1).

- 1943: Iowa Pre-Flight (9-1), March Field (9-1), Great Lakes Navy (10-2), Del Monte Pre-Flight (7-1), Georgia Pre-Flight (5-1), Fort Riley (6-2-1), Coast Guard (6-3), Alameda Coast Guard (4-2-1), St. Mary's Pre-Flight (3-4-1), N.C. Pre-Flight (2-4-1), Camp Grant (2-6-2)

- 1944: Randolph Field (12-0), Norman Naval Air Station (6-0), Iowa Pre-Flight (10-1), Great Lakes Navy (9-2-1), March Field (7-2-2), Second Air Force (10-4-1), Alameda Coast Guard (4-2-2), Amarillo Field (5-3), Lubbock Field (5-4), Fort Warren (5-4-1), St. Mary's Pre-Flight (4-4)

3. The effect on college football was like scabs playing during an NFL strike.

College football typically employs heavy oligarchical tendencies – the sport's ruling class consists of teams that remain strong from generation to generation, and it is incredibly difficult to break into that ruling class.

The oligarchy is real, but as enlistment continued to grow and more of these military service teams began to field teams, up became down and left became right when it came to who ruled the sport. In 1943, for instance, teams like Nebraska, Pittsburgh, TCU, Yale, Wisconsin, and Georgia were all varying degrees of awful, while Iowa Pre-Flight, Great Lakes Navy, Del Monte Pre-Flight, March Field, and even Bainbridge Naval Training Station (which only played one top-division team: Maryland) finished ranked in the AP poll at the end of the season. Meanwhile, non-powers Tulsa, Dartmouth, Colorado College, and Amos Alonzo Stagg's Pacific also finished ranked.

It was the same story in 1944: Nebraska, Florida, and California were bad. Iowa, sharing its Iowa City facilities with the Iowa Pre-Flight squad (which, for obvious reasons, probably got some preferential treatment), was awful. But Randolph Field finished third, Bainbridge NTS finished fifth, and Iowa Pre-Flight finished sixth. El Toro Marines finished 16th, Second Air Force 20th. It might seem strange that an all-star team with some pros could be eligible for the national title, but special circumstances were special circumstances.

Meanwhile, it probably shouldn't be a surprise to learn that Army and Navy began to thrive at this time. In 1941, Red Blaik took over an Army team that had won just four games in two years but had the Cadets up to 11th in the AP poll in 1943 and first in 1944. Similarly, under a series of coaches, Navy went from 3-5-1 in 1939 to 7-1-1 and 10th in 1941 to 8-1 and fourth in 1943.

Another team benefited in its own way from wartime competitiveness adjustments. Notre Dame was struggling financially during the war, but the Navy made the school a training center for V-12 candidates and paid for usage of facilities. The Fighting Irish, then, were also able to maintain a stocked roster during this period. (This favor is why Notre Dame and Navy continue to play their long-running annual series and why they most likely always will.)

4. After beating Iowa Pre-Flight in 1942, Don Faurot took over Iowa Pre-Flight.

These service teams were coached by real, well-known college football coaches. Minnesota's Bernie Bierman, for instance, led the Iowa Pre-Flight team in 1942. When he was assigned elsewhere, another new enlistee took the reins in Iowa City: the 41-year old Faurot. Mizzou's head man spent a year with Iowa Pre-Flight, then took over Jacksonville N.A.S. in 1944.

You could legitimately say that Faurot's lone season with Iowa Pre-Flight changed college football. It's not because the Seahawks were good – though they certainly were – but because of the proliferation of the Split T. Among Faurot's assistants on the 1943 Seahawks: Bud Wilkinson and Jim Tatum.

Wilkinson was a guard on Bernie Bierman's Minnesota teams from 1934-36, when the Gophers went 23-1. After a short time as a Syracuse assistant, he landed back in Minneapolis, taking a job with Bierman and the Gophers.

Tatum, meanwhile, was a 6'3, 230-pound North Carolina graduate who, after a short time on staff at Cornell and UNC, was named head coach at his alma mater in 1942. He had just turned 29 when he led the Tar Heels to a 5-2-2 record that fall. (He also recruited Doc Blanchard, a relative of his who would end up winning the 1945 Heisman at Army.)

Faurot was not a secret keeper. He could have leaned on his single wing and "short punt" formations while at Iowa – goodness knows he had the talent on the roster to execute it well. Instead, he shared with his young assistants the ins and outs of his new baby, the Split T.

For football itself, this was great. This became a staple of many a college offense over the next couple of decades, and not necessarily because of Faurot. In 1946, after the war, Oklahoma hired Tatum as its new head coach, and Tatum brought Wilkinson along as an assistant. After one 8-3 campaign and Gator Bowl title, Tatum was pulled away by Maryland, and OU promoted Wilkinson. Tatum would win 73 games in 10 seasons at Maryland, finishing third or better in the AP poll three times and winning the 1953 national title. Wilkinson, meanwhile, coached for 17 years in Norman, won 145 games, finished in the AP top five 10 times in 11 years, and claimed shares of three national titles (1950, 1955, 1956).

Both Tatum and Wilkinson were better recruiters and perhaps better overall head coaches than Faurot; the tactical boost they got in Iowa City pushed both of their respective careers into the stratosphere, and they left their one-time mentor behind. Faurot would go on to reach two more bowls after the war, but he went an incredible 0-17 against Tatum and Wilkinson. The final loss of his career, in fact, was a 67-14 shellacking in Norman.

5. Iowa Pre-Flight damn near won the national title in 1943.

The Split T may have been originally designed with underdog tactics in mind, but Faurot's Seahawks had talent superior to most of their Midwestern foes in the fall of 1943. With another point or two in South Bend, there might be another, different colored national title banner hanging somewhere in or around Kinnick Stadium.

Pre-Flight's season began with a 32-18 cruise at Illinois in front of 8,500 fans. As was their custom, the Seahawks built an easy halftime lead (26-6 in this instance), then eased up. Dick Todd, a former Texas A&M Aggie and Washington Redskin, scored on a 51-yard run and threw a 30-yard touchdown pass to Clemson's Bob Timmons. Boston College grad and 1942 Chicago Bear rookie Frank Maznicki also scored.

The next exhibition was in Columbus. In front of 29,496 in the Horseshoe, Iowa took on an Ohio State team that a) won a share of the mythical national title in 1942 and b) returned virtually nothing from that team. A bunch of freshmen in the scarlet and gray had little to offer against the mighty Seahawks. Todd threw two more touchdowns to Timmons and rushed for a 37-yard score; it was 21-0 at halftime, 28-13 after 60 minutes. It was technically Ohio State's first season-opening loss since 1894 – and it was the only time Faurot would beat Ohio State during his decade of trips to Columbus – but that only sort of counted.

On October 2 in Ames against Iowa State, 10,000 fans watched the Seahawks ease out to only a 19-7 halftime lead. But Iowa scored to start the third quarter and cruised, 33-13. Maznicki scored another four touchdowns. Staying in state the next week, they took on Iowa in the teams' shared home stadium. Michigan State's Richard Kieppe scored twice, and Maznicki threw another touchdown pass. The Seahawks rolled to a 19-0 halftime lead and won, 25-0.

Next came the most awkward game on the schedule. A crowd of 12,000 in Kansas City watched Missouri give its head man a serious fight. Only a missed PAT separated the two teams – Iowa Pre-Flight 7, Mizzou 6 – heading into the fourth quarter, but eventually the Seahawks' depth was too much. Two late scores gave them a comfortable 21-6 win.

As the calendar began to flip from October to November, former Marquette star Art Guepe, scorer of the Hilltoppers' lone touchdown in a 1937 Cotton Bowl loss to Sammy Baugh and TCU, began to take over. He scored early in a 19-2 rout of Fort Riley, and against his alma mater on a muddy Sunday in Milwaukee, he rushed 14 times for 145 yards. He set up Iowa's first touchdown, raced 67 yards for the second, and burst around right end for a 19-yard score as well. It was 20-0 in the first quarter, and the only thing that kept it as close as 34-19 at halftime was a pair of kick return scores from Marquette's Paul Coupolus. Still, the outcome was obvious. Iowa scored a couple of times in the fourth quarter and rolled, 46-19. Total yardage: Seahawks 470, Hilltoppers 46.

Against Camp Grant on November 13, Illinois star Jimmy Smith scored on a lateral from Maznicki, then Todd threw a 31-yard touchdown pass to Timmons. An interception by linebacker and Chicago Cardinal Vince Banonis set up the third touchdown and gave the Seahawks a 21-0 halftime lead. However, on this one occasion, letting the foot off the gas almost backfired. Camp Grant scored twice in the second half, cutting the score to 21-13 midway through the fourth quarter. In the end, a 28-yard Guepe score put the game away, 28-13.

Iowa Pre-Flight's 1943 schedule featured plenty of schools that tended to field strong football teams – Ohio State, Iowa, Missouri, etc. Still, because of roster depletion, the Seahawks' schedule had not, to date, been nearly as strong as the 1942 slate that featured 7-3 Michigan, 7-2-2 Notre Dame, 9-1 Ohio State, and 8-3-1 Missouri.

It had a spectacular Notre Dame squad in the second-to-last game, though. The fortified Irish were 8-0 and boasted both the 1943 Heisman winner (Angelo Bertelli) and the eventual 1947 Heisman winner (Johnny Lujack, who would have his career interrupted by two years of Navy service) They had torn through an eight-win Georgia Tech team by 42, whipped Army by 26 in the Bronx, and handed Michigan and Navy their lone respective losses by a combined score of 68-18. This was a wrecking machine, and in front of 45,000 in South Bend, Faurot's Seahawks fought Notre Dame to a virtual draw.

A Guepe touchdown produced the only points of the first half; the second quarter ended with Notre Dame at the Seahawks' 4, unable to get off one last snap. The angry Irish opened the second half with a quick, easy, 64-yard drive, finishing it with a three-yard plunge by Bob Kelly. With the game tied at 7-7, Lujack lost a fumble late in the quarter, however, and Todd opened the fourth quarter by finding Dick Burk for a touchdown.

Unfortunately, the extra point drifted and pinged off the right upright. A 13-7 lead didn't feel nearly as safe as 14-7. Sure enough, Notre Dame quickly drove 55 yards for a score – Todd was knocked out of the game with a broken jaw on the drive – and a true PAT gave the Irish a one-point lead, 14-13.

Iowa wasn't quite done. Guepe connected with California's Perry Schwartz to advance to the Irish 11, but an eventual field goal attempt fell short. (Place-kicking was so much more of a crap shoot, and so much more of a potential advantage or disadvantage, decades ago.) Schwartz recovered a fumble in the final minutes, but a series of desperation passes couldn't find their mark. Notre Dame survived. The Irish would go on to win the national title, despite a loss the following week to 10-2 Great Lakes Navy.

The season ended with what seemed like it should be a heavyweight battle: Iowa Pre-Flight at Minnesota. But without Bierman and much of the roster, the Gophers were distinctly average. They went 5-4 in both 1942 and 1943 and went 5-3-1 in 1944. They were no match for what was now an angry Faurot squad. In front of 18,000, Minnesota put together a decent early drive but lost a fumble via bad snap deep in Iowa territory. The Seahawks drove straight down the field and scored on a five-yard Smith run. The score was only 6-0 at halftime, but Guepe ripped off a 53-yard touchdown run on the second play of the third quarter, then scored on a 66-yarder two minutes later. Iowa was forced to keep playing beyond halftime, unlike many of the games that season, but the result was eventually the same: The Seahawks' season ended with a 32-0 win.

By the end of 1943, the Axis powers were in retreat. The tide of World War II had slowly turned. But young men were continuing to train for combat, and service teams would hit the gridiron again in 1944. While Randolph Field would finish third in the polls that fall, that squad was beating mostly other service teams and depleted Rice, Texas, and SMU teams.

Iowa Pre-Flight, though, got a shot at Notre Dame in 1943 and nearly felled the champ. When the war was over and Faurot, Wilkinson, and Tatum returned to spread the gospel of the devastating Split T, Iowa Pre-Flight got yet another opportunity to make a lasting impact on the sport.

1945 ARMY

In 1951, the U.S. Army got dragged down by a cheating scandal. In the month before the football season began, 90 cadets were dismissed for what amounted to sharing answers on tests. A large number of those guilty were football players, enough that the dismissals took a team that was considered a national title contender and rendered it a lucky two-win squad.

The practice had been going on for four to five years. It came about like your normal frat or dorm cheating arrangement – two groups of students took the same exams at different times, and the second group would "get the poop" from the first group. This wasn't a practice isolated to the football team, but gridiron stars were a big part of it. The scandal furthered a divide that had grown for years within the academy. Football players were often resented for their preferential treatment.

Whatever divides existed before Red Blaik came to West Point, they had grown since. Blaik was a *football man*, and a good one. For seven years, he had fought with and antagonized professors at Dartmouth who thought that football was taking on too much emphasis. He rubbed plenty of Army men the wrong way as well, despite (or perhaps because of) his honorary colonel status.

But oh, did he win. He took advantage of increased enlistment and military stature during World War II to put together some of the most impressive collections of talent in the sport's history.

He also had an eye for coaching talent. He delegated and empowered smart young assistants, and 20 of his former assistants became head coaches.

Well, they didn't *just* become head coaches.

Frank Lauterbur (Army offensive line coach, 1957-61) won 23 straight games at Toledo and engineered a No. 12 finish for the Rockets in 1970. Eddie Crowder (backfield coach, 1955) inherited a listless Colorado program and took the Buffaloes to a No. 3 finish in 1971. Andy Gustafson (backfield coach, 1941-47) took on a nothing Miami program and finished No. 6 in 1956.

At Houston, Bill Yeoman (center, 1946-48) revolutionized college football offenses with his veer offense in the 1960s, pulled off four top-10 finishes between 1973-79, and influenced young, aggressive tinkerers like eventual Houston and Baylor head coach Art Briles.

Paul Dietzel (line coach, 1948, 1953-54) won a national title at LSU in 1958 and pulled off three top-five finishes in four years. Murray Warmath (line coach, 1949-51) won the 1960 national title at Minnesota, then finished in the top 10 in each of the next two years as well.

Sid Gillman (line coach, 1948) won an AFL title with the San Diego Chargers in 1963 and revolutionized passing in professional football.

And, of course, Vince Lombardi, Army assistant from 1948-53, is widely regarded as one of the greatest coaches in NFL history.

Football success is addictive. It boosts campus morale and brings positive PR. It can hook even a service academy. In the name of bringing more success, you find yourself willing to look the other way when it comes to shady activity or preferential treatment.

In fairness to Army, though, the Cadets hadn't simply experienced *success*. In 1945, they had experienced football perfection.

Many teams have a case for claiming the title of Best College Football Team of All-Time (no asterisk), especially considering there's really not any way to prove such a case wrong. But no one has the case that Blaik's '45 Cadets have: In nine games, Army took on five of the best teams in the country and beat them by an average score of 43-7.

Army had gone unbeaten in 1944, holding off another strong Ohio State team to claim the AP national title, and it was obvious the Cadets were going to be good again. Most of the previous year's major contributors were back, and Blaik had added some incredible new pieces. But the schedule stiffened up quite a bit, with a decent Wake Forest team replacing Brown and a strong Michigan squad replacing the Coast Guard. That was supposed to be an obstacle; it was not. Instead, the season that began six weeks after V-J Day and four weeks after the signing of the treaty that officially ended World War II, became a weeks-long victory lap, and for a few different reasons.

Most college football fans have heard of Doc Blanchard and Glenn Davis, and rightfully so. They are two all-time greats, and they won the Heisman in back-to-back years (Blanchard in 1945, Davis in 1946). Davis finished second in the voting in both 1944 and '45; in three years, he scored 51 touchdowns. Briefly dismissed from the academy late in 1943 after failing a math class, he was readmitted after completing remedial work, eligible just in time to put together one of the most storied careers ever.

In Red Blaik's *You Have to Pay the Price: The Red Blaik Story*, Davis' head coach said, "He was emphatically the greatest halfback I ever knew. He was not so much a dodger and sidestepper as a blazing runner who had a fourth, even fifth gear in reserve, could change direction at top speed, and fly away from tacklers as if jet-propelled." He averaged 11.5 yards per carry in 1944-45. Ridiculous. And for bonus points in the "I've mastered life" competition, he even dated Elizabeth Taylor for a bit in 1948.

That defenders had to pay so much heed to Blanchard gave Davis an almost unfair advantage. Blanchard was a 6'0, 205-pounder from Bay St. Louis, Mississippi, both a shot-putter and 100-yard dasher on the Army track team. In *You Have to Pay the Price*, Blaik called him "the best-built athlete I ever saw." Doc had "not a suspicion of fat on him, with slim waist, Atlas shoulders, colossal legs." He also knew what to do with the football in his hands. He didn't have Davis' speed, but no one did. He was speedy for his size, though, and he gained the tough yardage. His career stats were spectacular: 1,908 rushing yards and 38 touchdowns in three years. He passed on pro football to become an Air Force fighter pilot.

Writers like Grantland Rice and Damon Runyon poured all the panache they had – and they had quite a bit – into writing poetic passages about "Mr. Inside" (Blanchard) and "Mr. Outside" (Davis). But the stats and results back up the prose: Blanchard and Davis almost certainly made up the best duo of running backs the sport has seen.

What made this particular team so ridiculous, however, was depth. Because of loose wartime transfer rules, and because Blaik was relentless in milking every advantage he had, this Army team featured plenty of stars from other schools.

Halfback Shorty McWilliams was an All-American for Mississippi State in 1944 and returned to Starkville in 1946; in 1945, he was a backup good enough to finish eighth in the Heisman voting. Fullback Bobby Dobbs helped Tulsa to the Sun Bowl in 1942 and backed up Blanchard in 1945. Guard Joe Steffy played for Tennessee in 1944, when the Volunteers when unbeaten in the regular season again. End Barney Poole played for Ole Miss and would return to Oxford to lead the Rebels to the 1947 SEC title. End Hank Foldberg played for Texas A&M, halfback Dean Sensanbaugher played for Ohio State, fullback Bob Summerhays would thrive at Utah, etc. Plus, the show was run by quarterback Arnold Tucker, a steady enough hand to finish fifth *himself* in the Heisman voting (third on his own team) in 1946.

The skill positions were stocked three-deep with star power, and the line was extraordinary. It featured All-American captain John Green and future first-round pick DeWitt "Tex" Coulter, plus Herschel "Ug" Fuson, an athlete versatile enough to play both halfback and center and star at lacrosse. Coulter would later say that this team had better depth than the 1946 NFL East champion New York Giants team he would soon join.

September 29: Army 32, Louisville P.D.C. 0: The season began with a challenging tune-up against a team formed at Louisville's Air Force personnel distribution command. Louisville unleashed the most aggressive defense it could manage, and it slowed the Cadets down here and there. Army's depth advantages were obvious from the start, though. Davis opened the scoring with a weaving, brilliant 87-yard run in the first quarter, but with entirely different personnel coming in for the second quarter, Army scored twice. A 25-yard Bob Stuart punt return set up a two-yard McWilliams plunge. Then, Davis reentered the game and caught a 55-yard touchdown pass from Dick Walterhouse. Army led 19-0 at halftime and rolled.

October 6: Army 54, Wake Forest 0: Wake Forest barely fell to Tennessee in the first week of the season and lost by only seven to Duke the week after Army. The Demon Deacons would then finish the season 19th in the AP poll after going 5-0-1 down the stretch. But in rainy West Point (you'll notice Army didn't have to leave New York too much), Wake had no chance. Just two minutes into the game, Fuson burst around left end for a 51-yard score. Davis one-upped him with a 55-yarder, then McWilliams outdid them both with a 79-yarder in the second quarter. Army rushed for 443 yards to Wake Forest's 78 and scored twice in the first quarter, twice in the second, and three times in the third.

October 13: No. 1 Army 28, No. 9 Michigan 7: A crowd of 70,000 welcomed Army and Fritz Crisler's Wolverines to Yankee Stadium for what was supposed to be Army's first significant test. Michigan's line play frustrated Army, but while depth and size didn't produce as many advantages for the Cadets, star power carried the day. After a scoreless first quarter, McWilliams scored on a seven-yard run for Army's first touchdown, and Blanchard rumbled 68 yards just two minutes later. Michigan's misdirection offense caused Army some problems, but a particularly strong defensive day from Blanchard kept the Wolverines at bay. Up 21-7 in the fourth quarter, Army put the game away with a 70-yard sprint by Davis.

October 20: No. 1 Army 55, Melville PT Boats 13: To commemorate the closing of the Melville P.T. Base following the war, Army welcomed a team from the patrol torpedo base to West Point. The Cadets' second team, which started the game, even spotted the team 13 points. Shorty McWilliams lost a fumble, and Melville's John Welsh raced 30 yards for a score; later in the first quarter, Welsh ripped off a 60-yarder.

But that was enough fun. Army scored four times in the second quarter – Blanchard twice on short runs, Davis twice on long runs. Up 27-13 at half, Army scored twice more in the third quarter, then the backups piled on two more scores in an abbreviated fourth quarter.

October 27: No. 1 Army 48, No. 19 Duke 13: Duke would go undefeated against teams not named Army or Navy in 1945, but the Blue Devils suffered a program-worst 35-point defeat in front of 42,287 at New York's Polo Grounds. The deficit was only that small because of penalties: Army gained 524 yards and scored seven touchdowns but had a couple more called back.

McWilliams opened the scoring two minutes in with a 54-yard touchdown run, Bob Stuart and Blanchard scored twice each (once on a pass from Davis), and Davis added a tally. It was obvious to the 42,287 in attendance, almost from the moment the game kicked off, how the game was going to end up. It was 28-0 at halftime before Army reserves let Duke find a little bit of an offensive rhythm.

November 3: No. 1 Army 54, Villanova 0: Army and Villanova played for six consecutive years between 1943 and 1948. Final score of these six hours of football: Cadets 240, Wildcats 0. The only encouragement 'Nova could get from playing Army in 1945 was that the final score wasn't as bad as it had been the year before, when the Cadets laid a devastating 83-0 score on the board. The total yardage from this one was almost inhumane: Army 506, VU 25. Blanchard romped to two early scores, then scored two more later on. Villanova had one first down, even with the Army backups playing a considerable amount of the game.

November 10: No. 1 Army 48, No. 2 Notre Dame 0: Again, by comparison, this one wasn't as bad as it had been the year before. Reeling from a loss to Navy a year earlier, Notre Dame came to Yankee Stadium and got destroyed, 59-0. In 1945, having held Navy to a scoreless tie, the Fighting Irish came in more confident, and it made a difference … for a few minutes.

It was just 7-0 after one quarter before Army began to pour it on. The Cadets scored twice in the second quarter, then Barney Poole blocked a punt, setting up a 21-yard Davis score. For the day, Davis had three touchdowns, Blanchard two. Notre Dame gained 184 yards and threatened a couple of times. But against the second-best team in the country, Army gained a cool 441 yards and cruised. Again.

November 17: No. 1 Army 61, No. 9 Penn 0: Army would finish the season with two games in Philadelphia. The trip to Franklin Field didn't seem to bother the Cadets. Against a rock solid Penn team that had rolled over everybody but Navy, Army rolled up 61 points despite playing its third-stringers quite a bit. Army once again scored on its second play, rushed for 383 yards, and gained 139 yards on six pass completions.

These were legitimately good teams that Army was humiliating.

December 1: No. 1 Army 32, No. 2 Navy 13: Because of the war America had just won, the 1945 Army-Navy game might have been one of the most celebratory sporting events in the country's history. A crowd of 102,000, including President Henry Truman, packed Municipal Stadium in Philadelphia, which is now the site of a trio of professional ballparks in south Philly: the Wells Fargo Center, Citizens Bank Park, and Lincoln Financial Field, which continues to house Army-Navy games regularly.

What might have been the best ever Navy team battled this

incredible Army team to a draw for three quarters. The Midshipmen proved resilient and became the first team all year to score on Army's first team.

The problem: Those three even quarters were the last three. Army had already taken a 20-0 lead in the first 15 minutes. The Cadets took the opening kickoff and took seven plays to set up a Blanchard touchdown. Then Blanchard scored again. Then Davis went 51 yards. From that point forward, Navy outscored the Cadets 13-12. And that really was an achievement of sorts. They got to within 20-7 and 26-13, but they couldn't get any closer.

The buzzer sounded in Philadelphia, ending the run of maybe the best college football team in history. The 1946 Army team would be quite a bit weaker – a lot of the key additions to the 1944-45 squads had either run out of eligibility or headed back to their original schools of choice, leaving Blanchard, Davis, Arnold Tucker, and not nearly as many other stars. The offensive output fell from 46 points per game to 26, but Army kept winning. The Cadets' win streak reached 25 games until Notre Dame held them to a 0-0 tie midway through 1946, and the unbeaten streak stretched until 1947, when Columbia pulled off a 21-20 upset.

Red Blaik hired great coaches, attracted great talent, and won with it. Army went 2-7 in 1951, the year of the cheating scandal, then rebounded, eventually going 8-0-1 in 1958, his final season. The confluence of personnel rules, national sentiment, and the most dynamic backfield duo ever helped Blaik to create a perfect football team in 1945.

1947 NOTRE DAME

The 1947 college football season was defined on October 9, 1943. On that day, in front of a record 86,000 in what would become known as the Big House in Ann Arbor, Frank Leahy's Notre Dame Fighting Irish pasted Fritz Crisler's Michigan Wolverines, 35-12. In public, Crisler was beyond complimentary, saying that version of the Fighting Irish was "the greatest Notre Dame football team I've ever seen." However, according to a story in Jack Connor's *Leahy's Lads*, Crisler berated Leahy on the field after the game. "Leahy, this was the rotten-est, dirtiest football game I have ever seen and if I have anything to say about it, Michigan will never play Notre Dame again."

This story isn't well-corroborated, and other publications suggest Crisler had already made that decision well before the fall of 1943. Whatever the cause, his word held for more than 30 years: Michigan and Notre Dame wouldn't play again until 1978.

This is a shame because Notre Dame and Michigan were by far the two best teams of 1947. Their playing each other would have answered a lot of questions.

By the late-1940s, full-on Notre Dame resentment had set in. Thanks in part to assistance from the Navy, the Fighting Irish hadn't suffered the same type of roster drain other programs dealt with during the wartime years. With the war over and educational opportunities in the service academies getting phased out, that left the school in South Bend as football's only true national university. With Frank Leahy in charge of his alma mater, Notre Dame was both attracting bucket loads of talent and utilizing it properly.

It wasn't fun to play Notre Dame. Leahy's squad was 26-2-1 against teams not associated with the armed services (Army, Navy, Iowa Pre-Flight, Great Lakes Navy, etc.) in his four seasons in charge (1941-43, 1946). Seventeen of the wins had been by at least 19 points. A Leahy team was relentless and physical, and that's a scary combination when said team also has a clear talent advantage.

By this point, it also wasn't very much fun to interact with the Fighting Irish's fan base. In a story shared in Murray Sperber's *Onward to Victory: The Creation of Modern College Sports*, Gordon Graham, sports editor of the *Lafayette Journal & Courier*, said, "We never had a problem with Notre Dame officials, but after the war, some of their fans began driving us crazy. They began writing letters saying that other schools should imitate Notre Dame, not just in winning, but by winning absolutely cleanly and honestly. Sure, who doesn't want to do that? But no one could get players like Frank Leahy could. ... Also the fans said that Notre Dame sets an example that other schools *could* follow if those schools didn't like cheating so much." Sure.

Meanwhile, another kind of resentment was taking hold in the college football universe.

The world of college football has always been different from state to state and conference to conference, but in the 1940s, these differences were enormous. And with the NCAA carrying no enforcement power, you could say that states' rights ruled.

The arguments covered the same topics as they do today, but the viewpoints were even further apart. Schools in the Ivy League, Big Ten, and Pacific Coast Conference did not believe in paying players, but by "paying players," they meant, "giving them scholarships." You were supposed to play for the love of sport and school. In certain conferences, the kids were supposed to come to you – you didn't recruit off campus.

Teams from the SEC and Southern Conference felt that, with a less deep history with the sport (and an equal desire to dominate), they needed to do more to attract talent. They were insistent that they be allowed to recruit off campus and give scholarship assistance to the athletes they were recruiting; they had been doing so since 1935. NCAA President John Griffith disagreed, and those from the North had no problem using certain terms in reference to the South: At the NCAA convention in 1939, Ohio State athletic director Lynn St. John used an Abraham Lincoln quote, asserting that college athletics couldn't continue "half slave and half free." Never let it be said that pettiness in sports arguments is a new phenomenon.

Since the Carnegie Report of 1929 mourned the increasing commercialism involved in the sport, attempts at reform were constant. But war had interrupted those efforts. Now, in a period of special treatment for certain schools and unabashed transfer opportunities, the time had come.

In 1947-48, the NCAA debated and passed what was initially called the Purity Code; upon receiving mockery for the hypocrisy and haughtiness of that name, it was changed to the Sanity Code. It barred both athletic scholarships and off-campus recruiting; the latter ban would soon be lifted, but the scholarship ban remained until the mid-1950s. It gave NCAA schools the ability to kick rules violators out, too. And in the "history repeats" department, Southern schools seriously debated seceding from the NCAA.

Of course, this code didn't prevent coaches from setting up no-show jobs for kids. It didn't prevent under-the-table payments, and it really didn't stop cheating in any way. As one official put it, "This Sanity Code will make liars of us all." Said American Council on Education president George F. Zook at the time, "Many will vote for the code but are figuring out ways to beat it."

The supposed intent of the Sanity Code was to ensure a level playing field. More than anything, it simply helped the national brand that didn't have to cut too many corners to recruit. Surely there were payments and sketchy employment arrangements at Notre Dame, as in any other program, but Notre Dame was more well-equipped to compete in a "pure" environment than anyone.

At the same time, the Fighting Irish were finding it increasingly difficult to find opponents to play. Much of the Big Ten resented both the school's on-field superiority and off-field attitude. Additionally, they dropped vague hints (or blind items in newspapers) about Irish improprieties. In January 1947, in fact, Notre Dame president Father John Cavanaugh responded, calling both these hints and the supposed need for a Sanity Code, "the mere publishing of noble, high-sounding codes which are often hypocritically evaded in actual practice."

Father Cavanaugh also railed against reform attempts that amounted to reform in name only. "The type of reformers I refer to are those who play with the question for public consumption, who seem to say that an indefinable something has to be done in a way nobody knows how, at a time nobody knows when, in places nobody knows where, to accomplish nobody knows what. I wonder if there are not grounds to suspect that the reformers … protest too much, that their zeal may be an excuse for their own negligence in reforming themselves."

Schools like Iowa, Purdue, and Northwestern continued scheduling the Irish, in part because they liked the big crowds. But Michigan refused, Illinois and Wisconsin wouldn't play Notre Dame for 20 years, Ohio State didn't play the Irish for nearly 60 years, etc. Even Army got in on the act; the famed Army-Notre Dame series went black from 1948-57.

For the 1947 slate, Notre Dame lined up three Big Ten schools, the two service academies, one-time power Pitt, fading SEC program Tulane, USC (of course), and, for the first time since Knute Rockne swore off trips to Lincoln in 1925, Nebraska. Many of those teams had been good recently, but few were in 1947. In fact, only three of nine would finish with a winning record.

Notre Dame had perhaps the most talented team in its history and almost no one to play.

This was the Irish roster to which all others would be compared. A whopping 43 members of the 1946 and 1947 teams would go on to play professional football. Some, like Vince Scott, couldn't hardly see the field in South Bend. Scott, a defensive tackle, barely played at Notre Dame but went north of the border to Ontario and became a Canadian Football League hall of famer.

Fifty-two percent of Notre Dame's 1947 roster was made up of military veterans as well, taking advantage of extra eligibility and easy transfer opportunities. The first and second strings were nearly indistinguishable from a quality standpoint. They would basically alternate quarters. And the question wasn't whether a Notre Dame player would win the Heisman – it was which one. Eventually, the honor went to quarterback Johnny Lujack. Meanwhile, guard Bill Fischer and tackle George Connor were named consensus All-Americans, and halfback Terry Brennan, end Leon Hart, tackle Zygmont Czarobski, and center George Strohmeyer all earned All-American honors from at least one publication. Lujack, Connor, Fischer, Hart, Czarobski, and halfback Emil Sitko all ended up in the College Football Hall of Fame.

The season itself was the cakewalk it was supposed to be, though the Irish frequently took their time reaching their eventual destination. With full, hockey-style line changes after each quarter, finding a rhythm was difficult, but wearing down opponents in the second half was not.

The games were almost formulaic. Against Pitt, Notre Dame led just 13-6 at halftime but scored 20 points in the fourth quarter to run away with the game, 40-6. The next week at Purdue, it was 16-7 at half, but Lujack ran and passed for scores, and despite solid line play, Purdue couldn't threaten in a 22-7 Irish win. Against Nebraska in South Bend: same story. N.D. led 12-0 at halftime, then pulled away to a 31-0 win.

With help from three Notre Dame fumbles, Iowa put up a good showing on October 25 in South Bend. But on the day that Columbia ended Army's 32-game unbeaten streak, Notre Dame's own streak stretched to 13 with a 21-0 win.

In front of the largest Cleveland crowd to ever watch a sporting event at that point (84,070), Navy's line held up, but there was no stopping Notre Dame's pass. Lujack and Frank Tripucka combined to complete 18 of 27 passes for 263 yards and two touchdowns (one each). It was 13-0 after 30 minutes, 27-0 after 60.

No. 9 Army visited next. The Cadets' loss to Columbia had taken some of the shine off of the matchup, but it was the last battle in the rivalry for the foreseeable future. After the game, Leahy told the press, "There was no pep talk prior to the game. I just named the starting lineup, then told the boys: Army is waiting outside, now get going." It did the job: Terry Brennan returned the opening kickoff for 95 yards, and the game was essentially over. Notre Dame cruised, 27-7.

Notre Dame nearly fell victim to a post-rivalry game hangover. In front of 48,000 against Northwestern in Evanston, the Irish eased out to a customary halftime lead (in this case, 20-6). But muddy conditions led to turnovers (four each), and Northwestern scored to make it just 20-12 heading into the final 15 minutes. Lujack connected with Leon Hart for a late seven-yard touchdown to put the game away, but while the Irish outgained the Wildcats by a 410-132 margin, they only won 26-19.

At this point, it was a one-game season. Tulane visited on November 22, but Leahy was so unconcerned that he left to scout No. 3 USC instead of sticking around for the game. Assistant Moose Krause took over, and the game was over almost instantly. Brennan picked off a pass, which set up a Sitko touchdown. Tulane failed to field the ensuing pop-up kickoff, and Notre Dame's Ed Price recovered it. The next play: Lujack to Sitko for 21 yards. Notre Dame had scored two touchdowns in the game's first minute and cruised, 59-6.

So that left USC. A win would almost certainly give Notre Dame the AP title, and in front of a record 104,953 in the Los Angeles Coliseum, the Irish eased to only a 10-7 lead. But big plays put the game away in the third quarter. Sitko raced 76 yards for a score, and Bob Livingstone followed with a 92-yard run. Two more fourth-quarter scores made this tight game a laugher. Notre Dame 38, USC 7.

The postseason played out as planned: Lujack won the Heisman, Notre Dame won the mythical national title.

The irony: Unbeaten Michigan, which refused to play Notre Dame, was quite possibly the better team. Some computer ratings think so, and common results suggest the Wolverines were at least even. Notre Dame outscored Pitt, Northwestern, and USC by a combined 103-32; Michigan outscored the same three teams, 167-21. But the late Beano Cook's Heisman truism was never more broadly true than in 1947: To win any award, individual or team, you had to play for Notre Dame, or you had to beat Notre Dame.

1951 MICHIGAN STATE

Eventually Michigan State College simply gave the Big Ten no choice but to accept its application. Even when the timelines and demands change, even when the process is immensely frustrating, if you keep doing what is asked of you, you might eventually wear down the opposition. In movie parlance, State was the underling with big dreams that finally won over the big, powerful boss. (Choose your own specific movie reference for that: *Rudy. A League of Their Own. The Devil Wears Prada.*)

It sure did take a while, though.

In 1946, Chicago's membership in the Western Conference officially expired. The school had played its final football game in 1939, and the actual end of membership was a formality. But Michigan State had already applied to replace the school on the conference roster. John Hannah, school president since 1941, was wasting no time. The Spartans had only begun playing major college football full-time in 1925 (at which point Michigan had already completed nine undefeated seasons), but they were intent on making up for lost time.

When conference officials met at the end of May 1946, they were supposed to take up the issue of expansion. Michigan State and Pitt were both under serious consideration to fill Chicago's spot, but scheduling spats forced them to table the issue. Hannah presented State's case in May 1947, and it was tabled again. And then again in early 1948.

What was the problem? The Purity Code was basically the only thing members of the Big Ten could agree on. Schools were left to their own scheduling devices, and in an atmosphere in which gate receipts were the primary source of revenue (live television was only beginning to play a small role), the teams with big stadiums wanted to mostly play only the other teams with big stadiums. Indiana, for instance, had only been able to get Michigan on the schedule twice between 1929 and 1942. Purdue and Ohio State played twice between 1925 and 1939. Not only was this a point of contention, but the thought of adding a 10th team again to compete for these sparse opportunities didn't jazz the smaller schools up.

Michigan, meanwhile, was in no hurry to help its stepbrother out. When State was eventually accepted, Dean Lloyd C. Emmons, State's faculty representative during the Big Ten meetings, revealed that, through UM, State had been asked to complete a set of eligibility requirements. By some accounts, the goalposts were moved quite a few times in the process. "We knew from the beginning that there would be no friendly consideration of Michigan State's cause by the Big Ten if the University of Michigan had its way," Hannah would later say. "We anticipated that Ann Arbor would be unfriendly and critical and obstructive, and that is exactly what they were."

It would have been strange had Michigan *not* resisted State's ambition, though, at least for a while. In matters of conference expansion, the programs in the Southeastern Conference have for years been said to have in place a "gentlemen's agreement" that states the conference won't admit anyone from a state that already has a program. Why share flagship status, right? Why risk losing some of your dominance to a local rival?

Never underestimate sheer ambition, however. Knowing a long fight was coming, Hannah and his school doggedly kept meeting each checkpoint. He had a couple of allies, especially friend and Minnesota president Lewis Morrill. Morrill helped him through the process and pulled a few levers along the way. There was certainly a faction within the conference that didn't mind the thought of Michigan's power – from the perspective of both politics and football – getting tamped down a bit.

State did whatever the Big Ten asked, whenever. It grew its enrollment quickly, from 2,000 in the early-1920s, to 13,000 in 1946, to 16,000 in 1949. It doubled the size of its athletic facilities –- Macklin Stadium seated 26,000 in 1947, 51,000 in 1948.

When the issue of the Purity Code, very important to the Big Ten, was raised, State became its biggest champion. (This last part was key: Pitt was considered by many to be the leader for the 10th spot in the conference and had a champion in Ohio State athletic director L.W. St. John. But the conference didn't trust that it would commit to the Purity Code because of its history of compensating athletes during Jock Sutherland's successful run.) Basically, the only time State stepped into muddy waters was when it arranged to begin playing Notre Dame in 1948. That was not the best way into Michigan's heart.

Most importantly, however, the Spartans broke through on the gridiron. Funny how that always makes a difference. Following a disappointing 5-5 campaign in 1946, longtime Spartan coach Charley Bachmann resigned, and barely a week later, State hired Biggie Munn. The fact that he was a Minnesota grad – he played for Crisler there, then briefly served as an assistant for Bernie Bierman – and longtime Crisler assistant at Michigan probably didn't hurt his case too much.

But Munn was also a great coach. On November 27, 1948, Michigan State wrapped up a top-15 campaign. The Spartans had entered the AP poll for the first time in its 13-year existence. On December 13, not even a month later, the Spartans were voted into the Big Ten.

After the unanimous vote, Michigan athletic director Fritz Crisler, who had retired at the end of the undefeated 1947 campaign, quickly noted that, "It must be remembered that Michigan was on record prior to this meeting as definitely in favor of Michigan State's application."

That was a PR line, and everybody knew it, but it didn't matter.

The following May, it became official: State would become a member of the Big Ten. Eventually. While minor sports like cross country could begin competing soon, the Spartans wouldn't be able to join the conference in football until 1953 because conference schedules had already been drawn up through 1952. Apparently, nobody was in any mood to revisit that touchy subject.

The breakthroughs continued for Munn and his Spartans. In 1950, they beat No. 3 Michigan in Ann Arbor, breaking a 10-game losing streak to the Wolverines. They finished 8-1 and eighth in the AP poll, and they returned so many difference-makers that they began the 1951 second, behind only Tennessee.

State's only 1950 loss was in early October to Jim Tatum's Maryland squad. The Spartans would not lose again for more than three years. Munn's young squad was loaded with All-Americans present and future: tackle Don Coleman (MSU's first unanimous All-American *and* its first African-American player to earn All-American honors), quarterback Al Dorow, end Bob Carey, and safety Jim Ellis in 1951; guard Frank Kush (who would later win 176 games as Arizona State's head coach), linebacker Dick Tamburo, and halfback Don McAuliffe in 1952.

Ellis picked off six passes in 1951, but he nabbed half of those in the opening game against Oregon State. The Spartans needed each one, fending off an upset bid with a 6-0 win. But the season truly began the next week in Ann Arbor.

To keep Michigan on the schedule, the Spartans agreed to almost constant road games. To date, 33 of the 38 battles in the UM-MSU series had taken place in Ann Arbor, often before school had even begun at Michigan State. No matter. The Wolverines were beginning to fade under Crisler's successor, Bennie Oosterbaan. Michigan went just 9-9 in 1951-52, and the Wolverines were no match for Sparty on September 29. Up 12-0 at halftime, MSU calmly put the game out of reach with third-quarter scores by McAuliffe and Leroy Bolden. State outgained the

Wolverines, 307-6. This could have been much worse than 25-0.

The next game was an all-timer, the most memorable game of the season. State traveled to Columbus to take on first-year Ohio State coach Woody Hayes and 1950 Heisman winner Vic Janowicz in front of 82,640. The Buckeyes were seventh in the country, and while they would struggle on offense for much of the season, they gave Michigan State all it could handle.

Ranked No. 1 for the first time ever, the Spartans trailed the Buckeyes, 20-10, early in the fourth quarter. But after throwing a tough interception, Dorow settled in. He completed five passes on the ensuing drive, including a one-yard scoring strike to Paul Dekker on fourth-and-goal. Down just 20-17, the Spartans then caught the break they needed, recovering a fumble near midfield. A few plays later, they faced a fourth-and-5 from the OSU 28. Munn called for a trick.

Tom Yewcic, used primarily as a punter, entered the game and took a pitch from Dorow. He ran right, and appeared to get hemmed in with nowhere to run. That was the plan. Yewcic backed up and slung a perfect pass across the field to Dorow, running open down the left sideline. Dorow caught the pass, outran one defender, unleashed a devastating cutback to evade two more, and scored. Michigan State 24, Ohio State 20. The play became known as the "Transcontinental Pass" in East Lansing, and it kept the unbeaten season alive. (It was also a bit of foreshadowing: Yewcic would throw a few more pretty passes as MSU's starting quarterback in 1952.)

This wasn't the last comeback necessary in 1951. The next week, the Spartans trailed Marquette 14-6 heading into the fourth quarter before scoring two touchdowns and winning, 20-14. They trailed Penn State and Pitt in the proceeding weeks before surging and beating both teams easily – 32-21 over PSU, 53-26 over Pitt.

Thanks to a relatively weak schedule and a glut of undefeated teams (Tennessee, Illinois, Maryland, Princeton, USC, Stanford), the Spartans had fallen to fifth in the AP poll. But they surged to first after what they did to No. 11 Notre Dame on November 10.

Like Michigan, the Fighting Irish were faltering a bit; they had lost to SMU and would finish unranked for the second straight year. But nobody else did *this* to them. Fullback Dick Pannin burst up the middle for an 88-yard touchdown on State's first offensive play, State outgained Notre Dame 465-189, the Irish never once crossed the State 30, and the Spartans rolled, 35-0. It was the first time Notre Dame had been shut out since tying Army 0-0 in 1946.

Back to No. 1, the Spartans threatened to fall to Indiana in Bloomington. State burst out to a quick 14-0 lead but put the game into cruise control too early. The game was tied at halftime, but sophomore Billy Wells put State ahead for good with an 83-yard scoring run in the third quarter. The Spartans went up 30-14, but Indiana scored twice to make things interesting before the clock ran out on a 30-26 win.

State fell to No. 2 in the polls behind unbeaten Tennessee and would remain there despite a 45-7 win over a seven-win Colorado squad in the season finale. With the national champion now being decided before bowls, that was that: The Vols were champs. Of course, they then lost in the Sugar Bowl to No. 3 Maryland

The Spartans, meanwhile, had to turn down a bowl bid because of the Big Ten arrangement. Call it some last-minute hazing: They couldn't go to the Rose Bowl because they weren't Big Ten, but they couldn't go to a *different* bowl because they *were* Big Ten, and it was a single-bid league. (As they had an integrated roster, they would have been prevented from participating in the Orange Bowl regardless.)

Finishing second allowed the Spartans to shoot for another goal in 1952, and, in State fashion, they hit it. They went 9-0 again in 1952 with wins over No. 6 Notre Dame, No. 8 Purdue, No. 17 Penn State, and, once more, Michigan. And this time, the AP voted them No. 1.

The year after that, in their first try, they won the Big Ten and beat UCLA in the Rose Bowl.

Lots of schools have goals. Almost none achieve theirs as comprehensively as Michigan State did in the 1940s and 1950s.

1955 OKLAHOMA

*"It was once said—only half facetiously—that the three greatest organiza-
tions the world has ever known were the Imperial German Army, the Roman
Catholic Church and the Standard Oil Company. Inasmuch as the Imperial
German Army was demobilized in 1918, it is doubtless high time that a new
candidate be proposed to fill out the triumvirate, and one strong contender—most
sport fans would agree—is the University of Oklahoma football team."*

-- Tex Maule, *Sports Illustrated*, November 1957

In the 1950s, college football was in transition for a number of
reasons. First, it didn't really know what it wanted to be. The Sanity
Code, an attempt at some sort of common set of rules for player
compensation and recruiting, was mocked, ignored, and repealed by
1951. In the coming years, athletic scholarships would once again
become legal within NCAA rules, and in attempt to add nuance to
dealing with potential NCAA violations, a committee on infractions
had formed.

During this time, meanwhile, NCAA director Walter Byers cynically created the term "student-athlete" to avoid any direct or indirect insinuation that scholarship athletes were employees of a given university. As employees, after all, they would be eligible for workmen's compensation, and in a rather violent sport like football, that could be costly. Can't have that.

Meanwhile, substitution rules were changing frequently. Before World War II, if you were subbed out, you couldn't come back in until the end of the quarter. From 1941 to 1952, however, substitutions were unlimited, in part because wartime rosters featured less highly-skilled athletes. (Tennessee's Robert Neyland called football with substitutions "chickenshit football.") In 1954, the NCAA once again moved back to limited substitutions because it required fewer players and, with scholarships now rampant, it cost less money. In 1965, substitution limitations were again erased, this time for good.

Integration was ongoing but not comprehensive. Southern teams were not to play teams with integrated rosters, which made non-conference and bowl scheduling a tricky, limiting issue.

Ivy League schools, slowly deemphasizing athletics after the war, picked up that pace as scholarships proliferated.

On top of all of this change, un-change, and re-change, a generation of accomplished coaches was slowly fading away.

Alabama's Frank Thomas retired after 1946, Michigan's Fritz Crisler in 1947, Minnesota's Bernie Bierman in 1950, Neyland in 1952, Notre Dame's Frank Leahy and Michigan State's Biggie Munn in 1953, California's Pappy Waldorf and Missouri's Don Faurot in 1956, UCLA's Red Sanders in 1957, Army's Red Blaik in 1958. The generation that had defined the sport as it grew more and more popular was no more.

Amid such massive, multi-directional change, the sport's balance of power was altered. Alabama managed just one top-10 performance between 1948-58; it was the same story for programs like USC (one from 1948-61), Michigan (one from 1951-63), and Notre Dame (one from 1956-63). Hell, Nebraska had only one *winning record* between 1951-61. Meanwhile, Rice finished sixth in 1953, Miami finished sixth in 1956, and Maryland briefly became a national power.

This was a strange time.

Amid all this change, however, was one constant: Bud Wilkinson. His Sooners finished in the AP top five in 1948, 1949, 1950, 1952, 1953, 1954, 1955, 1956, 1957, and 1958.

Wilkinson was maybe the most organized coach of all-time. Every drill had a purpose, and there was no wasted motion. "It takes four hours of preparation by the coaches for one hour of practice," he once told *Sports Illustrated*. He believed that being the best required the best of everything – the best game plan, the strongest conditioning, the cleanest uniforms.

Originally a player for and protégé of Bierman at Minnesota, he got a tactical boost by learning Faurot's Split-T as an Iowa Pre-Flight assistant in 1943. He liked the Split-T for both its tactical prowess and, more importantly, his ability to teach it.

Everything Wilkinson did had a reason behind it. His system of grading players was demanding – you got a zero for doing things right and didn't get a positive score unless you went above and beyond. His team was smaller and faster than most because he felt running and balance were as or more important than size or brute strength. He hit small-town Oklahoma and West Texas hard in recruiting, both because they were under-recruited areas and because they contained the kind of churchgoers he preferred from a moral standpoint. He used the petroleum industry – the possibility of decent-paying rough-neck summer jobs and the availability of more high-up jobs after graduation – in his recruiting sales pitch. He compensated athletes as much as he was allowed … and in some cases, more so.

Wilkinson was pragmatic almost to a fault. He desperately sniffed out his own team's weaknesses and bad habits and was slow to make in-game adjustments for fear of moving to a less familiar, less rehearsed game plan. And while he was lauded for his integration of Oklahoma's roster to include African-Americans in the 1950s, some noted that his recruitment of Black athletes seemed to slow when it interfered with his ability to land important *white* athletes in West Texas.

Though he did run afoul of the NCAA at times – a Google search of "Bud Wilkinson" and "slush fund" does not come up empty – he spoke a big game about character and morals, and then he fielded a team that seemed to embody his words. After the Great Depression, a Minnesotan, fielding a team with an increasing number of Texans, made Oklahomans feel good about being Oklahomans again.

Wilkinson's 1955 team was supposed to take a step backwards. He even said so publicly; in *Sports Illustrated*, he predicted Colorado would win the Big 7 Conference. This was not uncommon – like many coaches, he was a public pessimist – but he had reason on his side. OU had to replace 14 lettermen from his unbeaten side of 1954, including three-quarters of a devastating offensive backfield.

These inexperienced Sooners averaged 36.5 points and 411 yards per game. After an early-season breaking-in period on defense (they allowed 35 combined points to Pitt and Colorado, the only two good opponents among the first six games), they allowed six points in five games after November 1. The depth he was able to cull – he would frequently put starter-caliber players on the second- or third-string just to even out the talent a bit – produced a team with solid talent and athleticism, even if it didn't have the requisite experience.

The Sooners featured future hall-of-famers at both guard (Bo Bolinger) and center (Jerry Tubbs) and two more at halfback (Tommy McDonald, Clendon Thomas). But the depth of talent spanned beyond those stars. Halfback Bob Burris – brother of former Sooner All-American Buddy and, like Bolinger, a product of Muskogee, Okla. – got his share of carries as well. And the Sooners also had Jimmy Harris running the show.

When Harris passed away of lung cancer in 2011, the *Daily Oklahoman*'s Berry Tramel put it beautifully in a tribute column: "Harris started 25 OU games at quarterback. He won them all. Basically ruined the position for everyone who ever followed." Harris was an ace punt returner, an eventual NFL cornerback, and a quarterback who moved as quickly and efficiently as Wilkinson demanded. He distributed the ball beautifully, and OU was unstoppable with him in charge.

Since starting 1953 with a loss to Notre Dame and a tie against Pitt, OU had won 19 straight games when it headed to Chapel Hill to start the 1955 season. After surviving an upset bid from North Carolina, they would not be challenged again.

The season almost couldn't have begun any worse, though. UNC recovered an OU fumble in the end zone for a touchdown and a 6-0 lead, and the Tar Heels stopped four drives inside their own 20 and two inside their five. But UNC eventually wilted. Burris capped a 74-yard scoring drive with an eight-yard touchdown to start the second half. And McDonald kicked off an All-American campaign by dominating a fourth-quarter drive, then scoring an insurance touchdown for a 13-6 lead.

At this point, it seemed Wilkinson's fears of a drop-off were prophetic. They wouldn't remain that way. No. 12 Pitt visited the next Saturday, and OU raced to a 19-0 halftime lead; after 60 minutes, despite a brief Pitt charge, they had rushed for 357 yards and outscored the Panthers, 26-14. In the golden-anniversary meeting with Texas in Dallas, Tubbs picked off three passes and the Sooners won easily, 20-0.

Conference play began as conference play *always* began for OU: with a win. The Sooners welcomed Kansas to town with a 47-game unbeaten streak within the Big 7. They spotted Kansas a 6-0 lead, then wrecked shop. The Jayhawks gained 71 yards on their first drive and only 120 thereafter, and six Sooners scored in a 44-6 romp.

Next up was the conference game of the year: a visit from No. 14 Colorado. Dallas Ward's Buffaloes had gone a solid 30-11-3 since the start of 1951 and would continue playing like the second-best team in the conference for the rest of the decade. And they put their best foot forward early, taking a 14-0 lead in the second quarter because of Sooner fumbles. But in front of a capacity crowd of 59,000 in Norman, the Sooners took over quickly. They scored three touchdowns in the final 10 minutes of the first half, took a 35-14 lead into the fourth quarter, then scored three more times with their backups. After some early glitches, Wilkinson's latest offensive wrinkle – a no-huddle attack he called "no recovery" wore the Buffaloes down quickly.

In Harold Keith's *47 Straight: The Wilkinson Era at Oklahoma*, Wilkinson credited McDonald for much of the genesis of the Sooners' extreme tempo:

"'McDonald is a funny kid,' Wilkinson said. 'He figures any play that doesn't go for a touchdown is a failure. When he carries the ball and doesn't score, he gets mad and wants to hurry up and take another crack at it. Tommy jumps up and tears back to the huddle, running almost as hard as if he had the ball. It's nothing we taught him. It's something God gave him, or his parents, or somebody. We didn't do it." A Texas reporter noted that at one point in the Texas game, he was surging so hard to get back to the huddle that he fell down.

After Colorado, the rest of the season was a predictable cakewalk. The Big 7 could barely be considered a major conference in the mid-1950s, and OU wrapped up conference play with wins over 4-6 Kansas State, 1-9 Missouri, 1-7-1 Iowa State, and 5-5 Nebraska by a combined 153-7. Two days after Thanksgiving, the Sooners beat in-state rival Oklahoma A&M (not yet a member of the conference, and not yet known as Oklahoma State), 53-0. The Cowboys had provided a surprising test the year before, falling by only a 14-0 margin; this time around, OU scored three touchdowns in the first half, poured it on in the second, and finished with 344 rushing yards.

From the moment Oklahoma left Colorado in the dust, it was clear the Sooners were going to finish unbeaten. And they knew well before the end of the regular season that they would be playing against Maryland in the Orange Bowl. Jim Tatum, one-time Wilkinson mentor, was about to leave for alma mater North Carolina, wrapping up a dominant stretch for the Terrapins. They had gone 73-15-4 in his time in College Park, finishing in the AP top 10 four times and winning the mythical national title in 1953. (That year, title in hand, they lost to Oklahoma in the Orange Bowl.)

In what Wilkinson would at the time call his most satisfying victory, OU's speed – both in feet and in tempo – wilted Tatum's Terps in front of 76,561 in Miami. Maryland led 6-0 at halftime, but a strong McDonald punt return set the Sooners up in Maryland territory, and they unleashed the hurry-up with great effect. McDonald scored to put the Sooners ahead, then backup quarterback Jay O'Neal sneaked in for another score on the next drive. With Maryland desperately playing catch-up late, Carl Dodd stepped in front of a Lynn Beightol pass and took it 82 yards for the final score in a 20-6 win.

Oklahoma had already won the AP title before the Orange Bowl, but the win over Maryland gave the Sooners total legitimacy.

Meanwhile, the win streak would continue. It was at 30 when 1955 ended and 40 a year later after a second straight national title. It would stretch to 47 before an upset loss to Notre Dame late in 1957.

The Sooners responded by winning 13 of their next 14.

1957 AUBURN

Legend says it was a panty raid. They were pretty popular in 1957. Male participation in college erupted after World War II, and female participation began trickling up in the early-1950s. As 18- to 22-year old males have never been bastions of good judgment, they began invading female dorms and stealing undergarments.

Auburn higher-ups, including head coach Ralph "Shug" Jordan, weren't impressed. Jordan enforced a moral code at what was still officially called the Alabama Polytechnic Institute, and "No panty raids" was beyond debate. To prove he was serious, when prospective starting quarterback Jimmy Cooke was caught in a female dorm at night – what he was doing was never confirmed, though the suspicion was obvious – he was booted from the team for a violation of team rules.

Jordan, a World War II Purple Heart and Bronze Star recipient, had been building toward 1957 for a while. He took over at his alma mater after four years as an assistant at Georgia. (In a bit of symmetry, he employed Vince Dooley for eight years, then Dooley became

Georgia's head coach.) After a couple of years of establishing himself, his Tigers took off in year 3. From 1953-56, Auburn went 30-11-2 with three Gator Bowl appearances and a top-10 finish (the school's first) in 1955.

The success had come with a cost: Thanks to the revelation that an assistant coach had paid two recruits, the NCAA, with its new sanctioning power, put Auburn on three years' probation. That included a postseason ban. Meanwhile, the Tigers got busted *again* and put on three *more* years' probation within a year.

There would be no bowl in 1957, and there was no starting quarterback. Jordan stuck backup halfback Lloyd Nix behind center and prepared his team to win games with defense. With the defense he had, that was a pretty good plan.

Granted, the offense ended up just fine. With Nix's ability to run the option (and not get caught in female dorms) and fullback Billy Atkins' ability to sniff out the end zone – he scored 11 touchdowns and, with place-kicking duties, placed third in the nation with 83 points – Auburn's scoring average rose from 17.4 points per game to 20.7. After a sluggish start, the Tigers averaged 25.2 over the final six contests.

Still, this team was built around an untouchable defense. Auburn allowed one touchdown each to Chattanooga (scored on the backups), Houston (scored by Houston's defense), Mississippi State, and Florida State (scored on the backups) ... and that's it. The first-string defense gave up seven points in 10 contests, and Auburn allowed just 133 yards per game.

The line was the best in the country, built around All-American Red Phillips, all-SEC Jerry Wilson and future Outland Trophy winner Zeke Smith. It allowed zero rushing touchdowns. Linebacker Jackie Burkett was a fantastic traffic director, and Atkins (whose son would play on Auburn's undefeated 1993 team) patrolled the secondary.

Atkins, by the way, also averaged 44.5 yards per punt. He did everything.

In 1957, college football's ongoing power vacuum picked up steam. There was no way of knowing that in the present tense, of course, but including 1956, the AP would vote for a different national champion for eight straight years. The eventual 1957, 1958, and 1959 seasons all produced first-time champions. In November, Oklahoma was upset at home by Notre Dame, bringing a literal end to a 47-game win streak and a figurative end to the Sooners' vice-grip on the sport.

For much of the season, it appeared that, if OU were to finally suffer a misstep, Bear Bryant's Texas A&M Aggies would be the team to take advantage it. But Bryant's and Auburn's respective fates would interact a couple of different times in the fall of '57.

Cooke's dismissal was certainly not the most auspicious way to start a title campaign, but the backfield would be missing another key face when the season began. Running back Tommy Hoppe, Auburn's second-leading rusher in 1956, was injured. Plus, the campus was dealing with an outbreak of the Asian flu. Bad signs, all.

Amid these issues, however, the Tigers opened the season with a brilliant performance. In front of 42,000 in Knoxville, they took down No. 8 Tennessee, 7-0. Early in the second quarter, Atkins scored on a short run (his specialty), and Auburn held Bowden Wyatt's Volunteers to just 84 total yards. A year earlier, Tennessee began an undefeated regular season with a 35-7 rout of Auburn; the Tigers had successfully turned the tables.

After a 40-7 home-opener win over Tennessee-Chattanooga – the first-stringers scored twice, then ceded the field to the backups – Auburn welcomed Kentucky to town. The game was scoreless into the third quarter, but Atkins broke up a lateral and covered it up at the UK 36. After a roughing penalty, Atkins once again scored the game's only touchdown in a 6-0 win.

Instead of scoring just one touchdown, Auburn raised the degree of difficulty against Bobby Dodd's Georgia Tech: The Tigers won with zero touchdowns. A year after losing to the Yellow Jackets, 28-7, they held Tech to 166 yards and won, 3-0. Tech failed on downs from the Auburn 4 in the second quarter, and Jimmy Phillips forced a fumble at the Auburn 5 in the fourth quarter.

Around this time, the polls started to move. Michigan State, which had just inched past Oklahoma for the No. 1 ranking, lost at home to unranked Purdue. No. 4 Minnesota, meanwhile, got rocked at Illinois. Suddenly, Auburn was fifth, and OU and A&M were back battling at the top.

AP Poll as of Oct. 21
1. Oklahoma (4-0)

2. Texas A&M (5-0)

3. Iowa (4-0)

4. Duke (5-0)

5. Auburn (4-0)

Auburn had reached the top five with almost no offense whatsoever. But at Houston on October 26, Jordan's plainsmen wasted no time taking their frustration out on the Cougars. On their first offensive snap, Nix hit Phillips for a 71-yard touchdown. It was 16-0 after the first quarter, and Auburn cruised, 40-7. The only Houston touchdown came on an 89-yard interception return – the Coogs could manage just 106 total yards.

With Iowa tying Michigan the next week, Auburn had a chance to move up further with a visit from No. 19 Florida. The Tigers held the Gators to just 83 total yards and needed only one score once again, but they got two: one from the normal Atkins plunge, and one from a 63-yard Nix-to-Phillips strike.

Then came a near-stumble. Against No. 17 Mississippi State in Birmingham, the Tigers' offensive momentum stopped, and MSU took a halftime lead with a 57-yard bomb from Tom Miller to Ned Brooks.

What was by all accounts a fiery halftime speech by Jordan seemed to turn things around. Auburn drove 76 yards for the tying score (by Atkins, of course) to start the second half, then took the lead with a blocked punt for a safety. Auburn put the game away when Mississippi State fumbled a lateral on a punt return. Auburn recovered at the MSU 10, and Atkins scored three plays later. Final score: 15-7.

For one final weekend, things appeared stable in the polls. And then all hell broke loose.

AP Poll as of Nov. 11

1. Texas A&M (8-0)

2. Oklahoma (7-0)

3. Auburn (7-0)

4. Michigan State (6-1)

5. Iowa (6-0-1)

Birmingham, Ala., Nov. 15 (UP): *A reliable source said today Texas A&M Coach Paul (Bear) Bryant will definitely succeed J.B. Whitworth as head football coach at the University of Alabama. … Bryant's Aggies Saturday meet Rice and would be a likely candidate to be host in the Cotton Bowl New Year's Day. Texas A&M is ranked first by the United Press Board of Coaches.*

Houston, Nov. 15 (UP): *Texas A&M football coach Paul (Bear) Bryant tonight issued a terse denial to reports he would move to the head coaching job at the University of Alabama. … "We're fighting for our lives here," Bryant said, "Both tomorrow and on Thanksgiving Day. I have recommended a coach for Alabama, and it isn't Paul Bryant."*

It had been known for a while that Jennings "Ears" Whitworth's contract would not be renewed at Alabama. The proud Crimson Tide had plummeted under Whitworth, who would finish his three-year tenure with a 4-24-2 record. The 44-year old Bryant had long been considered a logical candidate for the Bama job: He was a Bama grad and an SEC coaching veteran, having served as an assistant at both Alabama and Vanderbilt before the war and as head coach at Kentucky, battling Adolph Rupp's basketball team for attention, for eight years. To boot, his wife was from nearby Troy. After a dreadful first season as Texas A&M's head coach in 1954, he was at that point 24-2-2 since. His Aggies had overtaken OU for the top spot in the polls and needed only to beat No. 20 Rice and Texas to potentially secure the national title. He had kept his team focused even as Bear-to-Bama rumors began to swirl, but the day before the Rice game, the United Press noted that the move was all but official.

Texas A&M proceeded to lose to Rice, 7-6. Two weeks later, the Aggies lost to Texas, 9-7. For good measure, they finished with a third loss, 3-0 to Tennessee in the Gator Bowl.

On the same day in Norman, a Notre Dame team that had been blown out for two straight weeks – 20-6 at home to Navy, 34-6 at Michigan State – visited Norman and ended OU's winning streak.

Auburn darn near stumbled, too. Against a Georgia team that had recently lost to Whitworth's awful Alabama squad, the Plainsman offense went cold. Nix and Phillips connected for a touchdown late in the first half to give Auburn a 6-0 lead, but that was all the scoring. Georgia gained only 68 total yards, with just three first downs, but the Bulldogs still had two extraordinary chances to tie or win. Auburn lost a fumble at its 10 early in the third quarter, but the defense stuffed UGA on four plays. Auburn then lost *another* fumble, then stuffed Georgia *again*.

With a prime opportunity to move to No. 1 for the first time, Auburn barely got by Georgia. The result:

AP Poll as of Nov. 18

1. Michigan State (7-1)

2. Auburn (8-0)

3. Ohio State (7-1)

4. Texas A&M (8-1)

5. Ole Miss (8-1)

Michigan State's huge win over Notre Dame suddenly looked more impressive, and Duffy Daugherty's Spartans eked ahead of Auburn atop the rankings. Polls are not particularly rational entities, however, and the Spartans would fall behind Ohio State the next week because the Buckeyes had clinched the Big Ten title with a win over Michigan. (You only *thought* the "conference title bump" began when the College Football Playoff came into being.)

Sniffing a shot at a title, Auburn played maybe its two best games in the last two weeks. The Tigers visited Tallahassee and mauled Florida State, 29-7. FSU managed only 79 total yards, but did manage to score a fourth-quarter touchdown on Auburn's backups.

AP Poll as of Nov. 25

1. Auburn (9-0)

2. Ohio State (8-1)

3. Michigan State (8-1)

4. Texas A&M (8-1)

5. Oklahoma (8-1)

Fun fact about the AP poll in 1957 and before: Any eligible Associated Press subscriber was eligible to vote. As insane as that sounds, it worked pretty well until Auburn more or less gamed the system, and the AP went with the selected panel of voters it still uses now.

Auburn sports information director Bill Beckwith hit the phones, making sure that every small radio station and newspaper in the area knew it had a vote while pitching Auburn to these voters at the same time. The result: 135 additional votes were submitted in the final AP poll. Despite Ohio State's Woody Hayes doing some campaigning of his own, Auburn finished with a large poll lead. A lot of that was due to Beckwith's work, and Auburn's demolition of Alabama pushed the Tigers over the top.

"Demolition" might not be a strong enough word. This could have been as bad as Auburn wanted it to be. Playing in frigid temperatures in Birmingham, Alabama lost a fumble on the second play of the game to set up an easy score, Tommy Lorino and Jackie Burkett returned interceptions for touchdowns, and Auburn led 34-0 at halftime. Nix and Phillips connected for one last score, and with the backups playing almost the entire second half, Auburn rolled, 40-0.

Final 1957 AP Poll

1. Auburn (10-0, 210 first-place votes, 3,123 points)

2. Ohio State (9-1, 71 first-place votes, 2,646 points)

3. Michigan State (8-1, 30 first-place votes, 2,550 points)

4. Oklahoma (10-1, 22 first-place votes, 2,182 points)

5. Navy (9-1-1, 6 first-place votes, 1,915 points)

On Monday, December 2, Auburn officially became AP national champion, thanks in part to the late-season collapse of Bear

Bryant's Aggies. The same day, Bryant made official what everyone seemed to know was going to happen: He was indeed taking the head coaching job in Tuscaloosa. Auburn would beat Alabama the following November to finish up a 9-0-1 campaign.

The Crimson Tide would win nine of the next 10 Iron Bowl battles.

1959 OLE MISS AND SYRACUSE

Ole Miss averaged 48 yards per punt against LSU that evening. It was almost unfair that Jake Gibbs was good at this, considering how good he was at everything else, too. He was the Rebels' quarterback and would become the SEC's player of the year in 1960. A stud baseball player, he also led Ole Miss to its first SEC title in 1959 and ended up playing parts of 10 seasons as a catcher for the New York Yankees. He hit 25 career home runs and was named to the College Football Hall of Fame in 1995. Now *that's* well-rounded.

Good punting was also unfair, seeing how incredible Ole Miss' defense was. It was always strong under head coach Johnny Vaught, but it was particularly dominant in 1959. The Rebels allowed only three touchdowns all year, and all three were either because of special teams or a turnover deep in their territory. Opponents didn't sustain a scoring drive of double-digit yardage all year.

The defense was so good that Vaught often didn't even wait until fourth down to punt. Granted, quick kicks were still rather common in the late-1950s, but with Ole Miss it was almost a sign of arrogance. "Sure, our offense is pretty good, but we'll go ahead and give the ball back to you. You know you can't do anything with it."

For most of the season, Vaught was right. If Gibbs' kick with 10 minutes left in Baton Rouge had bounced out of bounds as intended, Ole Miss probably would have cruised to a 3-0 win in Baton Rouge in the biggest game of the season. With a win, the Rebels would have almost certainly become the SEC's third AP national champion in three years. It would have been the perfect culmination of what had become a 13-year building process for Vaught in Oxford.

Ole Miss had experienced scattered success before Vaught, but nothing like this. After going 17-3 in his first two years and winning both the SEC and the Delta Bowl in 1947, his Rebels had taken a brief step backwards, then surged forward again. Between 1952-63, Ole Miss would lose more than twice in just one season. The Rebs finished in the top 10 in 1952, 1954, 1955, and 1957, and finishing 9-2 and 11th in 1958 had been a source of disappointment.

From 1959-62, the Rebels would dominate college football in the South. But the 1959 squad was Vaught's best and one of the best in the sport's history. All the punt had to do was bounce out of bounds for Ole Miss to clinch immortality.

Unfortunately for the Rebels, it checked up. On a sloppy field on a muggy Halloween evening at Tiger Stadium, it bounced right up into Billy Cannon's hands.

They were born a month apart in 1909, one two hours northwest of Dallas, the other on the border of Ohio and West Virginia. They played on the line for home-state schools, entered the field of coaching, then served during World War II. They scored prime head coaching positions in their home region in the late-1940s and held those jobs until the early-1970s. A week apart in 1959, they each coached in the biggest game of their respective lives to date.

The parallels between Texas-born former Ole Miss head coach John Vaught and West Virginia-born Syracuse legend Ben Schwartzwalder are clear. The two combined for 168 career wins, and 13 top-10 finishes; 10 of those came from Vaught, but both men completely redefined what could be expected from their respective football programs.

For all intents and purposes, they could have been coaching in completely different countries. In more than two decades of coaching at their respective schools, they never coached against each other. For most of this period, they wouldn't have been allowed to.

Seven days after Ole Miss visited Baton Rouge and Gibbs punted to Cannon, Syracuse made the 240-mile trip south and west to Happy Valley to face Penn State for Eastern supremacy. It was the biggest moment yet for a team playing at its highest ever level. Schwartzwalder took over at Syracuse in 1949 after going 25-5 in three years at Muhlenberg College, now a Division III school in Allentown, Penn. Syracuse had made a wonderful hire when it brought Biggie Munn to town in 1946, but he left for Michigan State after just one year. Former Syracuse lineman Reaves Baysinger took over and went just 4-16 in two seasons.

It had taken Schwartzwalder a while to get rolling, but that was perhaps to be expected, considering the amount of turnover the program had dealt with before he arrived. He went 14-14 in his first three years, and after a top-15 finish and Orange Bowl appearance in 1952, the Orangemen went just 14-10-1 from 1953-55. However, with each progressive year, Syracuse's roster was slowly getting deeper and more interesting. Schwartzwalder was developing a reputation for recruiting and developing African-American players: Jim Brown was a first-round pick in 1957 after helping to lead the Orangemen to a top-10 finish and Cotton Bowl bid, and halfback

Ernie Davis – who chose Syracuse with encouragement from Brown – would become the first black player to win the Heisman in 1961. Heading into 1959, the Orangemen were coming off of another top-10 finish, and Davis was joining German-born captain Gerhard Schwedes in the backfield.

Syracuse's emergence was well-timed. In January 1959, an idea that had floated around for a few years began to look quite realistic: With the Pacific Coast Conference – which, until the end of the 1958 season, featured California, Idaho, Oregon, Oregon State, Stanford, UCLA, USC, Washington, and Washington State (Montana had left after 1949) – falling apart, the idea of an "Airplane Conference" was rapidly gaining momentum.

PCC mates Cal, Stanford, UCLA, USC, and Washington were to occupy the West division alongside Air Force; Army, Navy, Notre Dame, Penn State, and Syracuse would form an East division, joined by any number of candidates: Miami, Pitt, West Virginia, or maybe even Oklahoma.

A true, coast-to-coast super-conference? In 1959 or 1960? It was a distinct possibility. For most of 1959 and 1960, it seemed this was more of a "when," not an "if." At one point, when it appeared the ball was in Army's court, the Pentagon dragged its feet. And over time, Stanford appeared to want to include the other, non-Idaho members of the former PCC. By 1962, Washington State had joined what was now the Athletic Association of Western Universities with the other western schools; by 1964, Oregon and Oregon State had joined, and the idea of a super-conference was dead.

Still! If this power conference had taken shape, Syracuse would have almost certainly been a part of it. In 1950, that wouldn't have been the case.

The Orangemen were 6-0 and fourth in the country when they rolled into State College on November 7, 1959, having won their last five games by a combined 182-12. Rip Engle's Nittany Lions were peaking during his 10th year in charge. Their No. 7 ranking was their highest since 1948; after road wins over Missouri and Army (their first triumph over the Cadets since 1899) early in the season, they had most recently roughed up No. 13 Illinois in Cleveland and West Virginia in Morgantown.

The No. 1 and No. 2 teams in the country would both lose that day, meaning the 'Cuse-PSU winner would have a sudden claim to the top spot in the polls. The moment was not lost on the crowd of 32,800, the largest to fill Beaver Stadium to date; as many as 10,000 more ticket applications were turned down. (Penn State was in the process of expanding its stadium. It didn't expand it soon enough.)

A year earlier, college football adopted a two-point conversion option: After scoring a touchdown, you could choose to either attempt a one-point kick or line up with your offense and try to score a two-pointer from the 3. As Syracuse took a commanding 20-6 lead early in the fourth quarter, nobody was thinking about that rule change much. But they would soon enough.

Penn State's defense had its shaky moments, despite the Nittany Lions' unbeaten start. Colgate managed 20 points, and Boston University had scored 12. The PSU offense was rolling, scoring 58 against Colgate and at least 17 in every game to date, but against this Syracuse offense, it was clear PSU was going to have to score a few times to have a chance.

A large majority of the former Schwartzwalder players you can name are running backs – Brown, Davis, Larry Csonka, Floyd Little, Jim Nance, Schwedes. There's a reason for that. A Schwartzwalder team was built around running the ball and stopping the run. In 1959, Syracuse had too many weapons to account for. Art Baker, Schwedes, and Davis combined to rush 288 times for 1,760 yards, and eight other players rushed for at least 140 yards each. Quarterback Dave Sarette had his moments, completing 49 passes for 763 yards and 10 touchdowns, but this was a dominant, physical offense, one no defense had even come close to stopping. Davis averaged seven yards per carry, and Schwedes was one of the most well-rounded threats in the country, rushing for 567 yards and catching 15 passes for 231 yards. He threw two touchdown passes as well.

The only time Syracuse had been even slightly challenged to date was against Kansas in the season opener. Jack Mitchell's Jayhawks were building something solid – they would go 14-5-2 in 1960-61 – but just didn't have the depth to keep up. They took a 15-12 lead early in the second half, thanks in part to a kick return touchdown. But Bob Hart scored to give SU the lead, then Schwedes scored twice in the fourth quarter to put away a 35-21 win.

A decent Kansas team had capitalized on turnovers and special teams but couldn't stay within 14 points; in the process, the Orangemen had outgained the Jayhawks, 493-67. Penn State was deeper than Kansas, but on an unseasonably warm, wet November afternoon in State College, it looked like the Nittany Lions would wilt all the same.

PSU sophomore Roger Kochman gave them an early 6-0 lead thanks to a 17-yard run up the middle, and it could have been worse if not for a dropped potential touchdown pass a few minutes later. Nevertheless, Syracuse did what it did all year: lean on the opponent until it fell over. Schwedes scored on a six-yard run to give SU a 7-6 lead at halftime, and a four-yard pass from Sarette to Baker stretched the lead. When Davis plowed in on a two-yard score at the turn of the fourth quarter, SU's lead was 20-6. This was turning into a rout.

And then special teams reared its ugly head again.

It rained about a third of an inch on Halloween 1959 in Baton Rouge. High of 80, average humidity of 97 percent. It was a throwback to weeks earlier, a sticky late-summer day in mid-autumn. The soupy vibe permeated even the black and white footage of the game.

This might have been the most anticipated game in either program's history. Former Army offensive line coach Paul Dietzel had taken the LSU job in 1955 at the age of only 30; what his résumé lacked in quantity, it made up for in quality. He had played for Sid Gillman at Miami (Ohio) in 1946-47, spent two years as Bear Bryant's line coach at Kentucky, and spent three years under Red Blaik in West Point.

It took Dietzel only four seasons to pull off what Vaught hadn't yet accomplished: a No. 1 ranking. Utilizing a deep squad, he used a three-platoon system – the White team (first-stringers), the Gold team (second-stringers), and the Chinese Bandits (a third string made of LSU's most energetic, physical reserves) – to soften opponents up and roll to an 11-0 record. The Tigers beat Bear Bryant's first Alabama team by 10 in Mobile, shut out Ole Miss, and finished a perfect season with a 7-0 win over Clemson in the Sugar Bowl.

This didn't sit particularly well with Ole Miss or its fans. LSU had basically cut in line, and an already strong regional rivalry had grown nuclear. When Ole Miss came to town on Halloween, a packed house of 67,500 awaited. No. 1 vs. No. 3: This was the toughest ticket in college football. Legend has it that someone traded his car for seats. An even more creative legend tells that someone offered his wife. LSU hadn't lost for nearly two full years, and Ole Miss hadn't lost for nearly one. The winner would become the de facto national title favorite.

Because they reach both big cities and small towns and just about every state in the country, college sports at all times reflect the culture of the United States and each of its regions. With few exceptions, a pro team is a pro team, tied only to a certain area by its nickname. They rotate frequently. But Alabama is always going to be in Alabama, UCLA in L.A., Rutgers in New Jersey, etc. There is no escaping that the people of that area are going to make up a majority of your fans and, in some cases, your players.

The United States in 1959 was on the brink of massive change. Over the next decade or so, the country would pass major civil rights legislation, land on the moon, and kill both a sitting president and well-known civil rights leaders. Its best elements and its worst elements burst into view.

When the 1958 college football season ended, the singles charts were topped by "The Chipmunk Song" and Conway Twitty's "It's Only Make Believe." A decade later, it was The Beatles' "Hey Jude" and Marvin Gaye's "I Heard It Through the Grapevine." American culture invented itself in the 1960s. It also, so very slowly, began to acknowledge its baggage.

Let's look at 1959's preseason AP top 20, including one key piece of extra information for the non-service academies.

1959 Preseason AP football poll

1. LSU (not integrated)

2. Oklahoma (integrated)

3. Auburn (not integrated)

4. SMU (not integrated)

5. Army

6. Wisconsin (integrated)

7. Ohio State (integrated)

8. Ole Miss (not integrated)

9. Iowa (integrated)

10. Northwestern (integrated)

11. Purdue (integrated)

12. North Carolina (not integrated)

13. TCU (not integrated)

14. South Carolina (not integrated)

15. Air Force

16. Notre Dame (integrated)

17. Texas (not integrated)

18. Clemson (not integrated)

19. Michigan State (integrated)

20. Syracuse (integrated)

Over the next 10 to 12 years, the college football universe would finally become fully integrated. In 1959, however, it was still a foreign, unrealistic concept in certain areas. Among other things, it made Ole Miss' scheduling anything but novel. The Rebels played Memphis 23 times in non-conference play from 1949-74, Houston 17 times between 1952-70, and Arkansas 10 straight years from 1952-61. They played series against teams like North Texas, Chattanooga, Trinity (Texas), Hardin-Simmons, and Tampa throughout the 1950s and 1960s.

Predictably, then, the 1959 season started against Houston; a year later, the Cougars would start to become viable and interesting under former Blaik assistant and offensive mastermind Bill Yeoman. Under Hal Lahar, who was about to leave for his second stint at Colgate, the Coogs were just fine. But fine wasn't good enough against the Rebels.

A confusing new Houston offense had Ole Miss on its heels at the beginning of the game until the Rebels' Robert Khayat picked off a pass and took it 52 yards to set up a Jake Gibbs touchdown, and in front of 45,000 in Houston, Ole Miss cruised, 16-0.

The Rebel offense struggled a bit the next week in Lexington, too. But after a scoreless first half against Kentucky, Ole Miss drove 42 yards in six plays to take a 6-0 lead on a Cowboy Woodruff touchdown. Charlie Flowers, the fullback and indomitable captain, lost a fumble early in the fourth quarter, however, forcing the Mississippi defense to make a stop. No problem. As UK quarterback Lowell Hughes scrambled to find an open receiver, Ole Miss end Jerry Daniels yanked the ball away from him. A Khayat field goal put the game out of reach, and a late Doug Elmore touchdown gave Ole Miss a second-straight 16-0 win.

Ole Miss was all-defense so far. The offense would begin to play its part, at least until the trip to Baton Rouge.

Ole Miss and LSU had combined to allow just 13 points in 12 combined games. Defense that good doesn't only require down-to-down dominance; it also requires a little extra stiffening when the opponent gets a rare scoring opportunity.

Scoring chances were not particularly rare for Ole Miss in Baton Rouge, however, especially in a first half that took place mostly in LSU territory. Cannon fumbled at the LSU 21 early in the game, and Johnny Brewer recovered. After Flowers rumbled inside the 10 on third down, LSU stopped the Rebels on third-and-goal from the 3. A 22-yard Khayat field goal gave the Rebels a 3-0 lead.

When LSU lost two more fumbles (each recovered by Brewer), Ole Miss got more chances. Additionally, the Rebels saw drives end at the LSU 20, 22, and, in the dying seconds of the first half, 7.

At this point, Ole Miss had given up just seven points in 13 halves of football – there was reason to believe that a 3-0 lead would hold up over

30 more minutes. But after four brilliant offensive performances, these failures were particularly frustrating. Granted, LSU's defense was quite a bit better than Memphis' (Ole Miss won 43-0), Vanderbilt's (33-0), or Tulane's (53-7), but the Rebels had established a strong rhythm.

The offense may have unfortunately peaked a week too early. In a 28-0 romp over Frank Broyles' 10th-ranked Arkansas Razorbacks in Memphis, Ole Miss rushed for 201 yards and scored touchdowns on sustained drives of 80, 56, 49, and 20 yards. A little bit of that finishing power would have resulted in an easy win over LSU.

Syracuse had developed a pretty good formula, and everything was going according to plan in Happy Valley: Survive an early challenge, stuff the opponent's run, establish your own running game, wait for points. They didn't usually have to wait long. After a turnover-aided 29-0 win over Maryland, Syracuse took a tough early shot from Navy; the Midshipmen found some success in the passing game until a 96-yard pick six opened the game up. Syracuse grinded out touchdown drives of 59, 68, and 84 yards, passing effectively when Navy overcompensated for the run. It was 20-0 at halftime and 32-6 at the end of the game.

Navy would go on to rough up Army, tie 7-1-1 Penn, and lose by only three to Notre Dame, but the Midshipmen were not in Syracuse's weight class.

The easy wins continued. Holy Cross and Syracuse met in Norfolk, Va., with Holy Cross having pulled one-point upsets over the Orange in each of the last two years. An early pick six gave the Crusaders a 6-0 lead and may have caused a few flashbacks, but Syracuse scored three times in the second quarter, the highlight being a twisting 40-yard romp by Davis. Rushing yards: Syracuse 277, Holy Cross minus-28. Points: Syracuse 42, Holy Cross 6.

West Virginia actually managed 60 rushing yards, a pretty

impressive total against this defense. The problem: Syracuse had 455. Davis carried nine times for 141 yards and scored from 23 and 57 yards out; he also delivered a crushing block on a long Gerry Skonieczki run. It was 33-0 at halftime, and Syracuse used 42 players in a 44-0 blowout. The next week, it was more of the same: Syracuse gained 271 yards on the ground, while Pitt lost six. A 25-yard score by Davis made it 14-0 at half, and Pitt crumpled, 35-0.

While Syracuse was once again dominating the ground game coming and going against Penn State, the Nittany Lions used a different unit to crawl back into the game.

On the ensuing kickoff after Davis' touchdown gave the Orangemen a 20-6 lead, Roger Kochman fielded the ball near the right sideline, weaved toward the middle of the field to meet up with his blockers, cut back to the right at the 30, then outran everyone else to the end zone. PSU missed an attempted two-point conversion, but it was a game again, 20-12.

Moments later, PSU's Andy Stynchula burst through the Syracuse line and blocked Bob Yates' attempted punt. The Nittany Lions recovered at the 1, and Sam Sohczak scored with 4:15 left. Penn State suddenly needed only a two-point conversion to tie the game. PSU faked an option left, and quarterback Richie Lucas handed the ball to Kochman on a counter. He was stuffed on the 1. Syracuse got the ball back and completely took special teams out of the equation by rushing for enough first downs to kill the clock and escape with a 20-18 win.

Sometimes a play's importance, its magnitude, makes it seem greater than it really was. Take Alan Ameche's run in the NFL Championship nearly a year earlier. That it ended the first sudden death overtime playoff game in NFL history, and that it was nationally televised on NBC, made it great. The run itself was a relatively

141

simple, well-blocked run behind the right guard and tackle. Any long punt return, meanwhile, is going to be exciting and well-executed; it's probably going to feature at least one juke or broken tackle, too. We've seen a lot of them.

We haven't seen *this*, though. Billy Cannon's return really is every bit as spectacular as its reputation. It would have stood on its own as one of the sport's greatest returns. That it happened in a game of such importance made it something still discussed with reverence nearly 60 years later.

Again, the punt was supposed to go out of bounds. Instead, it checks up near the "0" in Tiger Stadium's 10-yard line marker. Cannon fields it at the 11 and gets to the 16 before he has to make his first move. He jukes inside then jukes back toward the sideline, evading one shoestring tackle. As he crosses the 20, he skates past a pile-up of bodies with three tacklers closing in, and if he can somehow get through those tacklers, there's open space ahead. But he is stopped dead to rights at the 27 as a tackler gets a full hold of his left leg. He bucks free of the tackler at the 30, however, and somehow regains his balance well enough to juke another tackler at the 35.

And now it's off to the races. That he squirted through the coverage team surprises even the cameraman, who loses track of him for a moment, then catches up to him as he is shaking off one last tackler at the 47. Only the official on the sideline can take him down now. He races the final 53 yards in peace in the middle of a stadium that is now shaking at its foundation. The house is packed, likely well past fire code restrictions, and everyone in attendance has just witnessed one of the greatest individual plays in a team sport's history.

Cannon himself was gassed – he later told media that he stuck to the right sideline instead of crossing the field because he was fried. And that was before the three killer jukes and at *least* three broken tackles. He had already picked off a pass and had spent most of the game running into Ole Miss' defensive front, fighting to gain two yards instead of one. He was almost walking by the time he hit the end zone.

Worse yet for Cannon: 10 minutes still remained. But suddenly all of Ole Miss' earlier missed opportunities were crystallized. If the Rebels had managed even another field goal earlier, they would have trailed by just a 7-6 margin. Instead, they would need a touchdown to win.

In response to this dagger of a return, Ole Miss mounted maybe its best sustained drive of the evening. LSU's Chinese Bandits were on the field for the start of the drive as Cannon and the starters caught their respective breath. But as the Rebels penetrated LSU's 30, it was time for the White team again. Still, Ole Miss charged forward. Now, with time running short, the Rebels earned a first-and-goal from the 6. After a dive play gained one yard, Ole Miss quarterback Doug Elmore rolled out and gained three. The play had worked as well as any other for the Rebels that day, and they would call on it one more time.

On third-and-goal from the LSU 2, Hoss Anderson was stuffed for no gain. Down four, the Rebels had no choice but to go for the touchdown. With just 18 seconds left, Elmore rolled to his left and appeared to have a lane toward the end zone. But a diving lineman got a hand on his shoe, and as he lunged toward the end zone, he was met first by all-SEC guard Ed McCreedy, then by, who else, Cannon.

Everybody involved called it the greatest game they had ever seen or played, and while such superlatives are frequently thrown about in the short-term, the sentiment remains among those still alive to talk about it. To media after the game, Vaught said simply, "The only thing wrong with that game was that they got the seven and we got the three."

That Ole Miss was able to respond well down the stretch after such a gutting loss is a credit to the coaching staff, but the schedule maker helped. The week after this titanic battle, as Syracuse was fending off Penn State, LSU was falling victim to the upset bug. The Tigers fell to No. 13 Tennessee in Knoxville, 14-13. The Rebels, meanwhile, got a recovery game against Chattanooga (a 58-0 win) to catch their breath, then blew out the Volunteers, 37-7, in Memphis.

Syracuse's win, combined with LSU's loss, vaulted the Orangemen to No. 1 in the country, and they responded with easy wins over Colgate (71-0) and Boston University (46-0). All that stood between Syracuse and a national title was an odd, end-of-year visit to No. 17 UCLA, a potential future Airplane Conference mate.

The bowl picture was beginning to take shape, and again, two different worlds were barely interacting. On November 14, the same day Syracuse destroyed Colgate, school officials accepted an invitation to play in the Cotton Bowl against the all-white champion of the Southwest Conference, be it Texas or Texas A&M. The Longhorns were No. 2 in the AP poll at the time of invitation, but any hopes of a No. 1 vs. No. 2 matchup died when Texas lost at home to No. 18 TCU. Still, they rebounded to dispose of A&M, 20-17, clinching a date with the Orangemen.

The Sugar Bowl, meanwhile, was staring at the possibility of pitting two SEC teams against each other, just as it had done in 1952 (Georgia Tech-Ole Miss) and just as it would do again in 1963 (Alabama-Ole Miss).

Slowly but surely, segregation was getting in the way of sports ambition.

According to Charles H. Martin's *Benching Jim Crow: The Rise and Fall of the Color Line in Southern College*, there were four stages in the relationship between college football and segregation. The first, which lasted into the 1930s, featured a gentlemen's agreement that teams with integrated rosters would not play their black players against a segregated Southern team. Being able to claim gridiron

superiority over strong Southern squads and avoid offending opponents outweighed sensitivity toward a team's own black players,
evidently. One prominent example: Bernie Bierman held out one
player (Dwight Reed) in a big early-1935 game against Tulane, then
held out two (Reed and Horace Bell) against Texas the next year,
citing non-existent injuries both times.

The second stage, which stretched through the 1940s, saw a
blurring of the agreement – some Southern schools were, at times,
willing to overlook the agreement if it meant scoring a big-time
matchup, while some integrated teams became more willing to question the agreement altogether. The country had just been through
a war, after all, and black Americans had fought in it just as white
Americans had.

The third stage, according to Martin, was when things began
to get awkward for Southern holdouts. Northern teams began to
freeze out teams with segregationist policies, and to some degree, it
worked. After the Supreme Court's *Brown v. Board of Education* decision overturned state-sponsored segregation, the pressure got even
stronger. Many Southern schools began to yield to pressure and at
least agree to play integrated teams, even if they themselves were
not yet integrated.

The fourth stage, then, was the integration of those teams.

The 1959 season took place well into the third stage. Almost no
school south of the Mason-Dixon line had yet integrated, but a lot
of them were willing to play integrated schools. In fact, Georgia,
which won the SEC when both LSU and Ole Miss fell, agreed to
play an integrated Missouri squad in the Orange Bowl that very
year, just as Texas agreed to play Syracuse in the Cotton.

Schools in the deepest of the deep South – Louisiana, Mississippi,
Alabama – were not there yet. In fact, state law still forbade them
from getting there. Seating at Tulane Stadium, home of the Sugar

Bowl at that time, was designated for whites only; it said so right on the ticket. Racism was in no way limited to the South, but it was certainly more ingrained in ordinances.

This made the sports teams at these schools sources of pride for those still clinging to the supposed glory of the Confederacy. They were unwitting fighters in the battle against change.

This *also* made finding Sugar Bowl pairings an increasingly difficult task. In some ways, in fact, the success of LSU and Ole Miss bailed the Sugar Bowl out. Without those schools to lean on, the bowl would have struggled even further. Aside from rare exceptions – Navy asserting pressure until the segregated seating was briefly lifted for the Navy-Ole Miss Sugar Bowl in 1955, for instance – the policy continued. From the 1956 season through 1963, eight Sugar Bowls featured 10 SEC appearances (five from Ole Miss, two each from LSU and Alabama), five SWC appearances (two from Arkansas), and one ACC bid (Clemson).

State pride or no state pride, frustration was building. Gibbs and Ole Miss won the 1959 SEC baseball title but had to refuse an NCAA tournament bid because of the possibility of playing an integrated team. Babe McCarthy's Mississippi State basketball team had to pass on tourney bids in 1959, 1961, and 1962 and watched Kentucky represent the league instead; in both 1959 and 1962, the Bulldogs were a tremendous 24-1, and in both 1961 and 1962, Kentucky went to the Elite Eight in MSU's place. While many players and fans probably shared their respective states' views on segregation, those who weren't completely committed to the idea grew irritated. They knew their sports legacies were being defined with an asterisk, and as Charlie Flowers said in a 2010 interview, "We just played who we were told to play."

Paul Dietzel's exhausted, banged up LSU Tigers weren't certain if they even wanted to play in a bowl to finish the 1959 season. They were weighing whether to pass altogether, accept a rematch with TCU in Houston's Bluebonnet Bowl (LSU had beaten the

Horned Frogs, 10-0, in September), or elect for a rematch with Ole Miss in New Orleans. They were waiting to see if Syracuse beat UCLA – if the Orangemen won, then LSU would have no possible claim to a mythical national title with a bowl win, and they could pass on a bid. If Syracuse lost, and the national title situation was still blurry, they would accept.

The Sugar Bowl needed to know as soon as possible, however, and forced a team vote on November 23, two days after LSU's shaky 14-6 win over 3-6-1 Tulane. The Tigers elected to play Ole Miss again. They shouldn't have.

On November 28, Ole Miss romped over Mississippi State, 42-0. Jake Gibbs threw two touchdown passes and rushed for two more; the Rebels outgained the Bulldogs, 422-115, and forced five turnovers.

On December 5, visiting Syracuse made a definitive statement, crushing UCLA, 36-8. In front of 46,636 in the Los Angeles Coliseum, the Orangemen began the game by driving 43 yards for one touchdown, and then went 71 for another. They led 21-8 at halftime, then scored twice more in the fourth quarter against the fading Bruins. UCLA had knocked off undefeated No. 4 USC in the Coliseum two weeks earlier. There would be no second upset.

LSU wasn't fully invested in playing on January 1 in New Orleans, and it showed. Dietzel was frustrated enough by how his team was pressured into playing that he passed on a Sugar Bowl bid in favor of the Orange Bowl two years later.

Ole Miss, on the other hand, had plenty to prove, and did so.

LSU's run defense was still intact; Flowers rushed 19 times for only 60 yards. But Rebel backup quarterback Bobby Franklin completed 10 of 14 passes for 148 yards, and Flowers caught four passes for 64. Ole Miss led 7-0 at halftime thanks to a 43-yard pass from Gibbs to Cowboy Woodruff, and the Rebels scored touchdowns in each quarter of the second half as well. Cannon carried six times for eight yards, and Ole Miss rolled, 21-0.

The Cotton Bowl was a little bit closer and a lot more intense. Texas players allegedly spit on Schwartzwalder's black players and called them predictable names. Accounts differ, and the circumstances likely weren't as egregious as what was depicted in *The Express*, the 2008 Ernie Davis biopic. Still, fights broke out on multiple occasions, and according to a *LIFE Magazine* account, one Syracuse player said after the game, "We've never met a bunch like that before."

Whether Texas players were expressing their feelings or attempting to bait superior Syracuse players into losing their cool, it had little effect. The Orangemen were too strong for a solid but outmanned Longhorn squad. Barely one minute into the game, Ger Schwedes found Davis, the Elmira Express, for a Cotton Bowl-record 87-yard touchdown pass. In the second quarter, Davis scored on a three-yard run, then caught a conversion pass from Schwedes. A three-yard score by Schwedes, accompanied by another Davis conversion, made the score 23-6 in the third quarter.

Syracuse won, 23-14. The majestic Orangemen had dominated virtually the entire season, aside from a few special teams blunders against Kansas and Penn State, and they capped the run with a thorough win over the No. 4 team in the country. That they couldn't play the No. 2 or No. 3 team in a bowl hardly seemed like it mattered at that point. They had made their case.

Davis had dominated for much of the second half of the season, and he would continue that form the next fall. In 1960 and 1961, he rushed 262 times for 1,700 yards and caught 27 passes for 298 yards. He won the Heisman Trophy in 1961. Before he could follow in Jim Brown's pro footsteps, however, he was diagnosed with acute monocytic leukemia in Summer 1962. He passed away the following May. He was posthumously elected into the College Football Hall of Fame, and the No. 44 jersey, worn by both Davis and Brown, was retired at Syracuse University.

In the fall of 1962, a black student named James Meredith enrolled at the University of Mississippi. As the federal government attempted to enforce his right to enroll in the face of state resistance, members of the football team, unbeaten and soon to claim a share of the mythical national title, were asked to help quell an Oxford riot.

In the spring of 1963, the Mississippi State basketball team, tired of passing on opportunities to prove itself and buoyed by a fan base with the same sentiment, sneaked out of Starkville on a plane to Nashville, then flew to East Lansing to face Loyola (Illinois) in the NCAA tournament.

In the fall of 1964, with segregated seating off the books, Tulane Stadium welcomed a Sugar Bowl battle between LSU and, as fate would have it, Syracuse. Thirteen days earlier, in the Bluebonnet Bowl in Houston, Tulsa beat Ole Miss, 14-7. Tulsa's Willie Townes, an African-American end from Hattiesburg, Miss., who would go on to play parts of six seasons in the NFL, was named the game's most outstanding lineman.

The world evolves more slowly than most would like. Sometimes, sports can help to, ever so slightly, speed the process along.

1960 IOWA

It was the biggest game of the season, and the quarterbacks had the stature to back it up. Wilburn Hollis, a bruising 6'2, 210-pounder who would lead the Big Ten in total touchdowns, had taken over the Iowa starting job and thrived. He churned through arm tackles, and his arm was one of college football's strongest – *too* strong, in fact. Despite decent accuracy, he completed only 35 percent of his passes in 1960 because receivers sometimes couldn't hold onto the bullets coming at them.

Minnesota junior Sandy Stephens, meanwhile, was an even sturdier 215 pounds. His passing numbers were similar to Hollis', and he didn't have to carry as much of the rushing load because of the work of fullback Roger Hagberg, who would go on to play five seasons with the AFL's Oakland Raiders.

Despite losing eight of 11 starters, head coach Forest Evashevski's Iowa offense was one of the nation's best in 1960; despite a brutal schedule, the Hawkeyes averaged 26 points per game, fifth in the

NCAA. Minnesota, meanwhile, averaged a healthy 22.8 per game.

The Big Ten was loaded in 1960, with eight teams spending part of the season ranked in the AP top 20. But Evy's Hawkeyes and Murray Warmath's Gophers stood out from the pack, and quarterback play was a major reason why. Both Stephens and Hollis would earn All-American honors.

That both teams had good quarterbacks wasn't particularly surprising. That both quarterbacks were black, however, was uncommon.

While the integrated portion of college football had already produced plenty of African-American stars by 1960, few got a shot at quarterback, and even fewer stuck there. Stereotypes both semi-positive (athleticism!) and ultra-negative conspired against them.

Stephens would get the best of Hollis when the two faced off on October 29. Despite a later Gopher loss, the win would eventually secure both the Big Ten title and pre-bowl national title for Minnesota. But you could perhaps forgive the Hawkeyes for a momentary glitch. They were playing their seventh ranked opponent in seven weeks, and there was an eighth on deck. Iowa played an almost impossible schedule in 1960 and nearly survived it unscathed.

Evashevski was, by all accounts, a real son of a bitch. A quarterback and key blocker for Michigan's 1938-40 teams, he somewhat literally paved the way for Tom Harmon's Heisman run. After the war, he served as an assistant under Biggie Munn at both Syracuse and Michigan State, then spent two years as Washington State's head coach in 1950-51. In 1952, he was summoned back to the Big Ten.

In the nearly three decades since Howard Jones had left for USC, Iowa had put together only about three or four good seasons. Powered by the heroics of Heisman winner Nile Kinnick, the Hawkeyes went 6-1-1 and finished ninth in 1939 in the AP poll. However, they had never again finished ranked, and they had still never been to a Rose Bowl. The Hawkeyes were second-class citizens in the conference of haves and have-lesses.

That would soon change. Upon both recommendation and warning from Fritz Crisler, Evy's former coach, athletic director Paul Brechler offered him the job. Crisler had endorsed Evashevski as a great coach but warned Brechler of the man's bull-headed streak. He would be proven right on both accounts.

After a 2-7 breaking-in season, Iowa went 5-3-1 and finished ninth in 1953, then reached and won its first Rose Bowl in 1956. The Hawkeyes claimed a share of the mythical national title by going 8-1-1 with another Rose Bowl win in 1958.

In less than a decade, Evashevski had definitively become Iowa's greatest coach. But his notorious stubborn streak was coming into view. He feuded publicly with Brechler in 1959 and, depending on the source, Brechler either left to take another job or got run out of town. Brechler had to know he wasn't going to win a public fight against a vastly successful football coach, even if he was the man who hired him.

Given a choice by Iowa's athletics board to either remain Iowa's head coach or take the now-vacant athletic director position, Evashevski chose the latter. The 1960 season, Evy's ninth in Iowa City, would be his last on the sidelines. (Perhaps predictably, his 10-year tenure as athletic director would prove turbulent, marred by feuds and accused vendettas.)

Evashevski was cranky and intimidating, but as a coach, he was also fair. He wanted to play the best players, regardless of class, background, or race. Longtime Iowa broadcaster Bob Brooks once shared an Evashevski quote with the *Minneapolis Star-Tribune*: "Nobody looks at what color [athletes are] when they cross the goal line." This created both competition and depth on the roster.

Little was expected of Iowa in 1960 – the 1959 squad had gone just 5-4 in a season defined by the Evashevski-Brechler feud, and beyond that, it had lost its most prominent contributors. Given a No. 15 preseason ranking mostly out of respect to Evy, the Hawkeyes proved themselves massively underrated.

Hollis was the catalyst. Saved from poverty and squalor in Possum Trot, Miss., in 1950 he came of age in Boys Town in Omaha. Boys Town was founded in 1917 by Father Edward J. Flanagan; it became a national shining example for juvenile care. It inspired both a Spencer Tracy movie and, indirectly, a song by The Hollies ("He ain't heavy, Father … he's m' brother!" was the caption of a famous Boys Town logo). It became Hollis' home at age 9; almost a decade later, Hollis moved to Iowa City.

As a sophomore, Hollis backed up chief passer Olen Treadway, rushing for 200 yards and throwing for 215. Treadway's departure was seen as a reason for 1960 pessimism, but Hollis quickly allayed concerns.

Hollis' bruising running opened up lanes on the outside for backs like Larry Ferguson, Joe Williams, Jerry Mauren, Sammie Harris, and Eugene Mosley. The depth came in handy against No. 10 Oregon State to start the season. Tommy Prothro's Beavers had begun the season a week early by knocking off No. 6 USC in Los Angeles, and they would prove resilient in Iowa City. Iowa led 9-0 at halftime and 16-12 after three quarters, but it took an 85-yard lightning-bolt run from Ferguson to finally put away a 22-12 win.

The Hawkeyes' first road trip of the year was to Evanston to face Ara Parseghian's sixth-ranked Northwestern Wildcats. NU had held Oklahoma to three points in a season-opening road win and would allow just 58 points in their final seven games of the season, but a vengeful set of Hawkeyes dominated. Mauren, the team captain, scored two touchdowns in about a minute in the first quarter, first on a 45-yard run, then on a 38-yard interception return. Hollis scored his first touchdown of the season in the second quarter, and as Northwestern mounted a drive in response, Ferguson picked off another pass and took it 70 yards for a score and a 28-0 halftime lead. Harris tacked on a 53-yard run late, and Iowa made a huge early-season statement with a 42-0 win.

In just two games, Evy's Hawkeyes had moved from 15th in the preseason poll to third. Things came close to falling apart in the third game of the year at No. 13 Michigan State. Iowa again raced to an early 14-0 lead, but two touchdowns by the Spartans' Carl Charon turned the tables and, with help from a two-point conversions, gave MSU a 15-14 lead midway through the fourth quarter. It got pretty dire when Iowa immediately lost a fumble, but fullback Joe Williams made a play that saved the season: He intercepted a lateral in the State backfield and rumbled 67 yards for a score. After an interception, Hollis put away a 27-15 win with a 23-yard touchdown up the middle.

The clutch play continued a week later. Hosting No. 12 Wisconsin, Iowa followed the formula: go up two touchdowns, then give it back. Wisconsin evened the score at 21-21 in the fourth quarter, but a long punt return gave the Hawkeyes one last chance to avoid a draw. In the game's dying seconds, Hollis threw a beautiful lob to Ferguson for a 34-yard touchdown, but Iowa was dinged by an offsides penalty.

No worries: On the next play, Hollis zinged a ball to a well-covered Harris in the end zone; defender Bill Hess got a hand on the ball, but Harris reeled in the tipped pass for an incredible, game-winning 39-yard touchdown.

Four wins over ranked opponents allowed Iowa to slip past unbeaten Ole Miss to rank first in the AP poll for the first time, and the Hawkeyes played like they enjoyed the top spot. Fresh off of a 24-21 win over No. 3 Ohio State, Purdue came to Iowa City for Homecoming ranked 10th in the country. But a Hollis touchdown gave Iowa a 7-0 second-quarter lead, and as Purdue was driving to score, a sack separated passer Bernie Allen from the ball; backup center Dayton Perry picked up the loose ball and sped 84 yards for the touchdown. Another Hollis touchdown made the score 21-0 in the third quarter, and while Purdue would tack on two late touchdowns with long drives, Iowa held on, 21-14. It was a similar story the next week against No. 19 Kansas: Touchdowns in each of the first three quarters (two by Hollis, one by Ferguson) gave Iowa a 21-0 lead before a Johnny Hadl touchdown made the final score 21-7. It could have been closer, but Kansas twice failed on fourth down in Iowa territory, then lost a fumble at the Hawkeye 5.

Iowa survived comfortably against Kansas, but there was a massive cost: Four guards and two tackles suffered injuries. Hollis, Ferguson, and Williams were all limping as well. The rugged schedule was beginning to take its toll, just in time for a visit to Minneapolis.

Despite residing in the same conference, Minnesota entered the game of the year much fresher. They had won at No. 12 Nebraska to start the season and upended Northwestern, 7-0, the week after the Wildcats were destroyed by the Hawkeyes. But in the three weeks prior to Iowa's visit, they had taken down Illinois, Michigan, and Kansas State by a combined 79-17. The Gophers were in contention for both their first conference title and first national title in 19 years.

While the Hawkeyes would take a 10-7 lead with a 20-yard Williams run to start the second half, they would soon fade. The Gopher front took over, and after a long touchdown drive gave Minnesota the lead again, a couple of Iowa fumbles finished the game off. In front of 65,610, Minnesota scored a 27-10 win, its first over Iowa since 1954.

The home stretch of the 1960 national title race was wild. Unbeaten Syracuse lost at home to unranked Pitt on October 29. Minnesota's win moved the Gophers to No. 1, but the Gophers responded by immediately losing at home to Purdue. New No. 1 Missouri fell to rival Kansas on November 19, only the Big 8 would later disqualify the Jayhawks for using an ineligible back (Bert Coan), so Missouri would finish "undefeated" but fall in the rankings nonetheless.

On the same day that Missouri "lost" to Kansas, Minnesota knocked off Wisconsin to win the Big Ten. The conference title bump was in effect: Minnesota leaped back ahead of Iowa in the AP poll and secured the top spot. The Gophers then proceeded to lose the Rose Bowl to Washington. They were a two-loss national champion.

Iowa's fate was already out of its own hands when Woody Hayes and new No. 3 Ohio State visited on November 12. (It probably goes without saying that Evashevski and the equally volatile Hayes didn't like each other very much.) On Dad's Day in Iowa City, Father Nichols Wenger of Boys Town served as Hollis' family on the sideline ceremony. The marching band spelled out "E-V-Y" before the game as a tribute to Evashevski in his final home game, and the Hawkeyes then pulled off a remarkable tribute of their own. Touchdowns from Hollis, backup quarterback Matt Szykowny, and Williams gave Iowa a dominant 28-12 lead at halftime. Iowa cruised to a 35-12 win, rushing for 361 yards on Hayes' defense.

Strangely enough, after a season full of ranked opponents, a visit to Notre Dame ended the streak. Joe Kuharich's second Fighting Irish team finished a miserable 2-8 and had nothing to offer against Iowa. They gained just 95 yards, and Iowa cruised, 28-0.

Iowa faced one of the most difficult schedules of all-time and finished with just one blemish. Quite possibly the best Hawkeye team of all-time sent Evashevski off as a winner and, through both its quality and its choice of quarterback, set a standard the rest of college football would struggle to match.

Stagg's Chicago Maroons (1906)

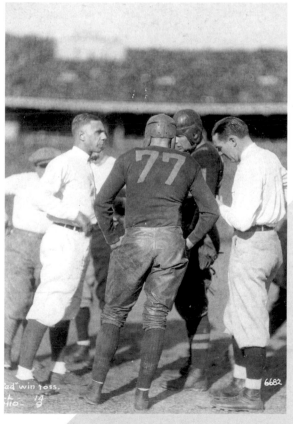

Red Grange (1923 Illinois)

John Heisman (1917 Georgia Tech)

Red Grange (1923 Illinois)

The Four Horsemen (1924 Notre Dame)

HERE IS THE PLAY THAT ROCKED THE STANDS. POOLEY, AFTER CARRYING THE BALL FIVE STRAIGHT TIMES, CRASHES THROUGH FOR A TOUCHDOWN. NOTE HOW ALABAMA'S LINE OPENED UP. THEN FOLLOWED THE CELEBRATED PASSES THAT MADE THE SOUTHERN CONFERENCE CHAMPIONS, VICTORS IN THE GREAT EAST-WEST CLASSIC.

Taking the Rose Bowl lead (1925 Alabama)

Ike Armstrong (1930 Utah)

A USC student stunt (1931)

Davey O'Brien (1938 TCU)

"Carry the fight" (1938 Tennessee)

Minnesota vs. Tom Harmon (1940)

Bill DeCorrevont (1941 Northwestern)

Don Faurot leads Iowa Pre-Flight (1943)

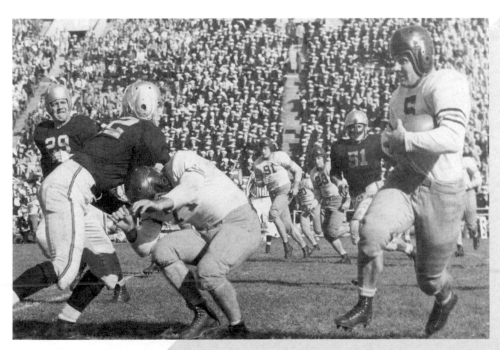

Iowa Pre-Flight and the troops (1943)

Glenn Davis & Doc Blanchard (1945 Army)

Johnny Lujack (1947 Notre Dame)

Biggie Munn (1951 Michigan State)

Bud Wilkinson (1955 Oklahoma)

Title Celebration (1957 Auburn)

John Vaught (1959 Ole Miss)

Ernie Davis (1959 Syracuse)

Iowa enters the field (1960)

Bob Devaney (1962 Nebraska)

Gary Beban (1965 UCLA)

Tommy Prothro (1965 UCLA)

Leroy Keyes (1968 Purdue)

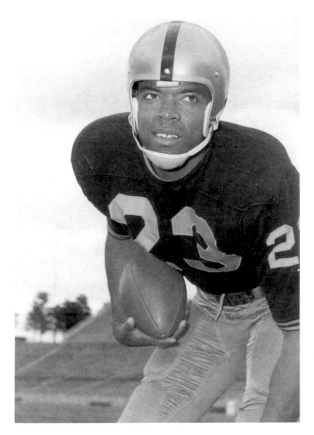

Leroy Keyes (1968 Purdue)

Darrell Royal & James Street (1968 Texas)

Bear Bryant (1970 Alabama)

1962 NEBRASKA

When Bob Devaney moved to Lincoln, Nebraska, fans almost certainly had high hopes. We all do when we get a fresh start. But the bar was probably pretty low.

According to Mark Fricke's *Nebraska Cornhusker Football*, Nebraska's first play of the 1962 season was an incomplete pass, but Husker fans stood and applauded all the same. Not only had the Huskers been terrible in recent years, but they had also been terribly boring. Nebraska's base offense was two runs up the middle and a punt on third down. Before worrying about wins, Husker fans just wanted to be entertained again.

In Bill Jennings' five years in charge, Nebraska had been held to seven or fewer points in 28 of 50 games. It wasn't just Jennings' aesthetics that clashed with Nebraska fan expectations; it was also his vision of reality. When he was dismissed after going 3-6-1 in 1961, he said, "There is an intense desire to do something good in this state, like elect a president or gain prominence in politics. But we can't feed the ego of the state of Nebraska with the football teams."

Outside of the political arena, it is possible that less true words have never been spoken.

Since finishing 8-2 and going to the Rose Bowl in 1940, Nebraska had spent two decades in football's wilderness. The Cornhuskers had only twice won more than five games in a season. Money and facilities were well behind the curve, and morale within the fan base was nonexistent.

New athletic director Tippy Dye was still finishing up his duties as Wichita State's outgoing AD when it came time to replace Jennings. He had his eye on three particular candidates, all from the Skyline Conference: Utah State's John Ralston, Utah's Ray Nagel (who would end up at Iowa and feud dramatically with new Iowa athletic director Forest Evashevski a few years later), and Wyoming's Devaney.

A 1939 graduate of tiny Alma college, Bob Devaney had bounced around in the Michigan high school coaching circuit until scoring his big break, a spot on the Michigan State coaching staff, in 1953. Wyoming asked him to lead its program three years later, and after going 4-3-3 in his first season, he would go 31-7-2 over the next four years, scoring a Sun Bowl win in 1958 and finishing 16th in the AP poll in 1959.

Dye had his eye on Devaney from the start. He had just signed a five-year contract extension at UW, and the school wasn't in a hurry to let him leave. A month after accepting the Nebraska job, he was finally released from his contract.

What Devaney found in Lincoln was insufficient. He was used to fielding a squad of more than 100 in spring practices at Wyoming, but his first NU squad had barely 90. His fall roster had 54 players, below the 60-plus he preferred.

Depth was lacking, but Devaney found some potential stars. Lineman Bob Brown was all-Big 8 in 1961 and All-American in

1962. Quarterback Dennis Claridge would become a two-time all-conference performer. Fullback Bill "Thunder" Thornton, NU's first black captain, was expected to have a huge year. The team had plenty of acumen as well: Junior tackle Monte Kiffin would go on to become one of football's most accomplished defensive assistants, and senior defensive back Warren Powers would win 46 games as Missouri's head coach in the late-1970s and early-1980s.

After that season-opening incompletion, Nebraska scored one touchdown in the first quarter against South Dakota, two in the second, three in the third, and another two near the end. The Huskers outgained their overmatched opponent 455-103 despite the fact that Thunder Thornton missed much of the game because of a separated shoulder. That 142 of their yards came through 11 completions surely got noticed by all 27,000 or so in attendance.

The season truly began the next weekend, however. From the moment he took the job, Devaney circled Nebraska's September 29 trip to Michigan as the time to make a statement. The Wolverines had hit a rough patch in the late-'50s, going just 11-15-1 as Bump Elliott took over for Bennie Oosterbaan. Elliott had engineered a 6-3 rebound in 1961, but he didn't have a very good team on his hands the following year.

Still, this was Michigan, and Nebraska was one of the losingest programs of the last 20 years. This was not supposed to be a contest.

Technically, it was not.

Thornton wasn't expected to play because of his shoulder injury, but he not only suited up, he scored two touchdowns and set up another with a 42-yard run. Nebraska took a 19-6 lead into the fourth quarter in front of a crowd of 70,287. Michigan scored to get to within 19-13, but Nebraska was playing for keeps. On the game-deciding drive, Claridge hit James Huge for exactly 16 yards on a third-and-16 pass, and on fourth-and-8 from the Michigan

24, he threaded a pass to Richard Callahan for exactly eight. Thornton's second touchdown iced a 25-13 win.

The *Lincoln Star* estimated that there were 3,500 Huskers fans gathered at the local airport that night to welcome the team back to town. This might not have been one of Michigan's best teams, but the symbolism was impossible to ignore. Devaney was looking to make a statement, and as the *Star* put it, the win "gave [fans] a chance to forget about studies, about their jobs, about Mississippi, Cuba, and everything else." Sports can provide an escape, a way to forget about real-world concerns. And as civil rights drama played out in the South and the Cuban Missile Crisis approached, Nebraska fans suddenly had a pretty nice outlet. With no professional team anywhere near, the Cornhuskers became a surrogate. They still are.

Against an Iowa State team that had narrowly lost to a great Oregon State team two weeks before, Nebraska rolled to a 36-22 win in front of 34,321. Thornton suffered a leg injury, but it didn't matter: Claridge rushed for three touchdowns and threw a 44-yard score to Huge, and NU led 28-7 at halftime. In front of an even larger crowd (36,867) the next week, Nebraska didn't experience the same happy start: The Huskers trailed NC State 6-0 at halftime and 14-7 heading into the fourth quarter, but two Dennis Steuwe touchdowns gave NU a 19-14 lead that stood up.

Easy wins over the worst teams in the conference – Kansas State (always bad) and Colorado (plummeting from 9-2 to 2-8) – gave Nebraska a stunning 6-0 start. To say the least, fans had noticed. On November 3, six days after the Cuban Missile Crisis ended, a sellout crowd of 36,501 welcomed the Huskers onto the field for Homecoming against Missouri.

A sellout crowd has greeted Nebraska every game since.

For a while, supply struggled to keep up with demand. NU expanded the stadium for four straight years between 1964-67; at the end of the projects, capacity had nearly doubled to 64,170. Five years later, it was expanded to 73,650. Today, it holds 85,000. And the sellout streak that began before Beatlemania continues.

Fan enthusiasm remained even as the 1962 team was exposed a bit. Missouri beat the Huskers, 16-7; the Huskers did score on the Tigers for the first time since 1957, but Dan Devine's defense still held them to 148 total yards and 3-for-14 passing with three interceptions. No. 10 Oklahoma did an even worse number on NU three weeks later, rolling up 373 yards, taking a 28-0 lead, and cruising, 34-6.

Still, there were a couple more highlights. On the road against a solid Kansas team that featured Gale Sayers and finished 6-3-1, Nebraska took a 32-0 halftime lead behind three Willie Ross touchdown runs. The Huskers rolled, 40-16, and that victory, along with a 14-0 win over Oklahoma State, got NU to the regular-season finish line at 8-2.

As remarkable as this turnaround was, it wasn't enough to score a major bowl bid ahead of the conference's two heavyweights at the time (8-2 Oklahoma and 7-1-2 Missouri). But thanks to a last-ditch effort by a terribly unorganized bowl committee, the Huskers found a postseason bid after all. On December 15, with the temperature hovering around 14 degrees and a paid attendance of only 6,166 at Yankee Stadium (*actual* attendance: far lower), Nebraska won a bowl game for the first time.

The game was called the Gotham Bowl. Created to raise funds for the March of Dimes, the game had good intentions and no organization whatsoever. In fact, it would never actually make enough money to give any to the charity.

In 1960, Oregon State accepted an invitation, but the bowl couldn't find an opponent. In 1961, Baylor and Utah State played in the cavernous Polo Grounds. And in 1962, Miami had agreed to play. While all other bowl invitations had gone out in November, Nebraska didn't get an invitation until December 4, 11 days before the game. Devaney wasn't particularly interested in accepting the bid, but the team was thrilled, and the game would go on.

Problem No. 1: The New York newspaper strike of December 1962 meant the game would get almost no publicity whatsoever.

Problem No. 2: When it was time for Nebraska to head east, the Huskers hadn't gotten their guaranteed expenditure money yet. The team sat in the Lincoln airport until a check cleared.

Problem No. 3: The weather was predictably New-York-in-December dreadful. Field conditions were hard, slick, and cold.

This was a doomed endeavor from the start, but ABC's *Wide World of Sports* cameras were there to take in the action, and against significant odds, there was incredible action. In what Devaney compared to a back-alley brawl (as in, nobody was watching it), Miami and Nebraska put on a show. Miami gained 502 yards to Nebraska's 296, but two early Miami fumbles set up a Nebraska touchdown, and two late picks cut off two Hurricane scoring drives.

Miami's All-American quarterback George Mira was the star of the show. He completed 24 passes for 321 yards and two early scores that gave Miami a 12-6 lead. But following the second score, Willie Ross returned the kickoff 92 yards for a touchdown. Miami scored on a short touchdown run, and Dennis Claridge (9-for-14 for 146 yards and, most importantly, no picks) found Mike Eger for a six-yard touchdown. It was 20-20 at halftime.

Miami struck first in the third quarter, but Thunder Thornton's one-yard score, followed by a Claridge conversion, gave NU a 28-27 lead. Then Claridge picked off Mira, setting up a short scoring drive. Ross' second score of the day, along with a Thornton conversion, made the score 36-27 early in the final period.

With Mira behind center, though, Miami kept charging. The Hurricanes scored to make it 36-34 with five minutes left, and after an NU drive stalled out in Miami territory, UM got one more chance. Perhaps fittingly, NU's All-American Bob Brown made the final play of the season. With Miami inside NU's 10 in the final minute, Brown dropped back into coverage and reeled in the Huskers' second interception of the afternoon. Ballgame.

To no one's surprise, the Gotham Bowl was not revived, but it had served its purpose in history: It put the punctuation mark on the first year of Nebraska football's second life.

Everything you know about Nebraska football began in 1962, from the wins, to the home sellouts, to the offensive prowess, to even the postseason battles with Miami: The teams would battle in the 1984, 1989, 1992, and 1995 Orange Bowls, along with the 2002 Rose Bowl, and the winner of four of those five games would become national champion.

The season also laid the groundwork for a four-decade coaching succession. Tom Osborne, a graduate assistant in 1962, would become offensive coordinator in 1969. The Nebraska attack was becoming stagnant; the Huskers had averaged just 14 points per game and gone 12-8 in 1967-68 when Osborne moved NU toward an I-formation, option attack. In 1970-71, NU would go 24-0-1 and claim shares of two national titles while averaging 37 points per game. Osborne would take over when Devaney retired in 1973.

Meanwhile, back in the gym in Lincoln, while the team was at the Gotham Bowl, a freshman named Frank Solich was lifting weights and trying to bulk up. The undersized fullback would captain the Huskers to a 10-1 record and top-five finish in 1965; 33 years later, he would succeed Osborne.

As it turned out, you could absolutely feed the ego of the state of Nebraska with the football team. That has been proven and re-proven every fall Saturday for more than five decades.

1965 UCLA

There comes a point, usually sometime in the third quarter, when the lighting in the Rose Bowl on January 1 is perfect. God's camera lens, aperture, shutter speed, filter, etc., are expertly calibrated, and the colors surrounding you are exactly as they were intended to be seen: the green of the grass, the blue of the sky, the golden tint of the sun.

Perhaps it was written in the cards, then, that a Michigan State team decked in green and a UCLA team with the colors of California blue sky and sunshine, would put on one of the Rose Bowl's most perfect spectacles.

UCLA would pull one of the great upsets of the 1960s, capping an incredible season of dramatic finishes and classic games by preventing Michigan State from winning the national title. But the Bruins would have to wait until Bob Stiles was conscious again to fully celebrate their first Rose Bowl title in six tries.

By the time UCLA began playing major college football, rival USC had already won a Rose Bowl and had already hired Howard Jones. When the Bruins pulled off their first winning season in 1932, Jones had already added three more Rose Bowl titles to the ledger. UCLA will always be the one that came on second in the rivalry.

Perhaps that makes the moments when the Bruins get the better of the Trojans twice as delicious. And it does happen from time to time. Red Sanders unleashed perhaps the school's most sustained run of success, going 34-5 and ripping off four straight top-6 finishes from 1952-55. Unfortunately, he died of a heart attack shortly before the 1958 season. George Dickerson was named interim head coach but was hospitalized twice – once for "nervous exhaustion" before the season, then for "physical exhaustion" three games in. He was replaced by Bill Barnes.

Barnes had some semblance of success – UCLA went 7-4 with a Rose Bowl bid in 1961 – but he resigned at the end of 1964 after going just 10-20 over his last three seasons. Not even a decade removed from major success, UCLA had sunk far back into underdog status.

Tommy Prothro was a perfect underdog coach. A masterful tactician and rousing motivator, he played for Wallace Wade at Duke and was a key piece of the Blue Devils' 9-1 Rose Bowl season and No. 2 AP finish in 1941. He joined up with Sanders as a Vanderbilt assistant and followed Sanders to UCLA before taking the Oregon State head coaching job in 1955. The Beavers had gone just 13-33 over the five seasons pre-Prothro but had only one losing record in 10 seasons with him leading the way. He took them to the Rose Bowl in 1956 and 1964, and quarterback Terry Baker won the Heisman under his guidance in 1962.

In search of another challenge, Prothro took over for Barnes in Westwood.

Prothro was fascinating. He carried a briefcase everywhere he went, and a la *Pulp Fiction*, nobody ever knew what, if anything, was in it. He maintained enough emotional distance from his players that he could properly use them as chess pieces instead of human beings, but he was still able to motivate these rooks and pawns into playing their best at key moments. He was as innovative in his practice techniques as in his tactics, and he taught many future head coaches how to coach. Pepper Rodgers spent two years under Prothro, then took over at Kansas and led the Jayhawks to an Orange Bowl berth in 1968. John Cooper was a Prothro assistant at both Oregon State and UCLA and would eventually win 194 games as head coach at Tulsa, Arizona State, and Ohio State. Terry Donahue, a defensive tackle on Prothro's 1965 and 1966 Bruin teams, would spend two decades as head coach of his alma mater.

Prothro inherited a team low on size but relatively high on speed. That was all he needed. Well, that, and a gifted sophomore quarterback. Barnes left one heck of a parting gift for Prothro in 6'0, 175-pound Gary Beban.

Beban was a graduate of Redwood City Sequoia High School near Palo Alto, but instead of attending Stanford or Cal, he chose to head a few hours south for college. He was a strong passer and a silky runner, and he would go on to win the 1967 Heisman, set the school's total yardage record, and win 24 games as UCLA's starting QB. In 1965, he was just a first-year varsity player who was, like the team he played for, trying to figure out a way to distinguish himself. The basketball team had just won back-to-back national titles under John Wooden and would soon open a sparkly new on-campus arena called Pauley Pavilion. The football team was just looking for eyeballs.

The start of the season was as inauspicious as possible. UCLA headed three time zones east to face Duffy Daugherty's Michigan State Spartans in East Lansing. MSU fullback Bob Apisa, who would rush for 715 yards and 10 touchdowns in 1965, scored on a 21-yard gallop up the middle, and the Spartans took a 10-0 lead into halftime.

Against what could become the best scoring defense in the country (State allowed barely six points per game), the Bruins were toast. They rushed for 200 yards but threw for only 69; they created scoring chances but managed only one field goal and fell, 13-3.

The Bruins had proven something by battling back and not getting blown out; two weeks later, on another trip east, they were rewarded for their efforts. Against Rip Engle's final Penn State team in Happy Valley, UCLA raced to an early lead. Beban scored the first two touchdowns of his career on runs of 16 and six yards. Then Mel Farr, a future All-American, NFL offensive rookie of the year, and two-time Pro Bowler, ripped off a 58-yard touchdown run. UCLA took a 24-7 lead into the fourth quarter, then held on for dear life as PSU scored twice in the fourth quarter. A late onside kick recovery sealed a 24-22 UCLA win.

The schedule continued to take UCLA throughout the country, and Prothro continued to figure out ways to generate fast starts. Against Syracuse back in L.A., the Bruins scored touchdowns on their first two plays from scrimmage – a 27-yard run by Beban following a fumble, and a 79-yard pass from Beban to Kurt Altenberg following a punt. The Orangemen scored two late touchdowns but still fell, 24-14. The next week, on the road against a Missouri team that would go on to finish 8-2-1 and win the Sugar Bowl, Beban and Byron Nelson connected for a 34-yard score to give UCLA a 7-0 halftime lead. They made it 14-0 early in the fourth quarter thanks to another Beban-to-Alternberg strike, but Mizzou scored on a kick return and a punt return to eke out a 14-14 tie.

After a 56-3 shellacking of California – Beban threw touchdown passes of 78 and 61 yards, and Farr scored on rushes of 21 and 45 – came another tricky road trip, this time to face Air Force in Colorado Springs. It was scoreless deep into the third quarter until Farr bolted off right guard for a 37-yard touchdown. The Bruins tacked on a field goal and won 10-0.

The going got rougher when the calendar flipped to November. Now ranked eighth in the country, UCLA hosted Washington and saw the tables turned. The Huskies quickly went up 14-0 on two long touchdown passes from Tod Hullin to All-American Dave Williams. A third connection between the two helped the Huskies to a 24-14 lead at halftime, but in the third quarter UCLA struck back. Beban raced 60 yards for a touchdown, then Prothro unleashed some all-time trickery: With UCLA lining up for a play at midfield, Dick Witcher stepped out of the huddle and walked toward the sideline like he was going off the field. He didn't. He stopped just short of the sideline and blended into the scenery, unnoticed by Washington defenders; Beban hit him with a short pass, and Witcher raced untouched for the game-winning score.

Washington head coach Jim Owens was still mad about the play – and the lack of a flag – years later. But for UCLA, the drama was only beginning.

A 30-13 win over Stanford set up the biggest UCLA-USC game in quite a while. The Bruins were up to seventh in the polls, and the Trojans were 6-1-1 and sixth. In front of 94,085 at the L.A. Coliseum, it was Beban and Farr against USC's soon-to-be Heisman winner Mike Garrett.

For 56 minutes, USC controlled the game. Garrett rushed 40 times for 210 yards, and after Farr started the game with a 49-yard touchdown run, the Trojans went on a 16-0 run to go up 10. It could have been worse, but turnovers and clock mismanagement led to a series of blown chances.

Only four minutes separated USC from only its second Rose Bowl in 11 years. But the Bruins were within shouting distance, and a pointy ball can bounce in funny ways sometimes. UCLA was given second life by a fumble recovery with about four minutes left, and a struggling Beban responded with just about his first strong pass of the night. He hit Witcher with a 34-yard touchdown strike, then found Nelson for a two-point conversion.

Suddenly, down only two and facing the prospect of Garrett generating first downs and running out the clock, Prothro called for an onside kick; it worked. Dallas Grider recovered, and UCLA quickly generated a first down. But a big loss quickly led to a third-and-24 from UCLA's 48. It was desperation time. Under pressure, Beban lobbed the ball high and far enough for a double-covered Altenberg to run under it. He took a hit and was laying on the ground when he heard the crowd react to Altenberg's catch.

Outgained by a 424-289 margin and playing from behind for much of the game, UCLA had pulled off a startling comeback and won, 20-16. UCLA fans tore down the goalposts. Garrett came to UCLA's locker room to congratulate Beban and others after a spectacular game. It was the Bruins' first win in four tries against USC, and it gave them the AAWU title and a Rose Bowl rematch against Michigan State. Pauley Pavilion was to open on December 3 with back to back games against Ohio State and UCLA, but not nearly as many people as usual were talking basketball.

Before Rose Bowl prep could begin, though, there came an oddly-timed, early-December trip to face No. 7 Tennessee in Memphis that made Prothro renounce the South.

No, seriously. "I'm embarrassed I'm a Southerner," the Memphis-born coach said after a series of controversial calls swayed a 37-34 shootout in Tennessee's favor. Laterals called incomplete passes, pass interference penalties, questionable clock stoppages when UT had the ball … Prothro was very clear that he didn't feel his Bruins got a fair shake. (On at least one of those stoppages, the ref blew the whistle because a UCLA player had kicked the ball away.)

Beban threw for 212 yards and two scores, but Tennessee backup Dewey Warren unexpectedly outdueled him, completing 19 of 27 passes for 274 yards. UCLA led this wacky shootout 34-29 with under four minutes left, but with the benefit of a couple of calls Prothro didn't like, UT worked the ball inside the UCLA 5 in the final minute. On fourth-and-goal from the 1, Warren rolled to his left, found no open receiver, and got walloped as he lunged toward the end zone. If he made it, it was by a few inches, but it was called a touchdown. Tennessee converted the two-point conversion and won, 37-34. *Sports Illustrated* diplomatically called it a "rowdy decision."

By the time January 1 came around, the UCLA team and its coach had regained their composure. Good thing, as they had a third straight classic to play, this time in the Rose Bowl. Top-ranked Michigan State and UCLA met in front of 100,087, with the perfectly green grass and the sky-blue sky.

UCLA's final game played out like so many of its other 1965 games, with the Bruins jumping out ahead and an opponent clawing back. In the first quarter, Bob Stiles picked off a Steve Juday pass near his goal line and returned it across midfield. The Bruins were forced to punt, but State's Don Japinga muffed the return; it was recovered by John Erquiaga at the Spartan 6. Two plays later, Beban plunged in from the 1.

One last bout of Prothro trickeration followed: UCLA pulled off a perfect surprise onside kick, and Grider was once again in place to recover it. Farr charged for 21 yards, Beban hit Altenberg for 27 yards, and Beban once again pushed in from a yard out. With 11:50 left in the first half, UCLA led the No. 1 team in the country, 14-0.

Just as the Bruins were good at letting opponents back into the game, however, State was good at coming back. The Spartans were undefeated despite suffering deficits in six games, but they blew chances to tie before halftime, first losing a fumble in Bruin territory, then missing a 23-yard field goal at the halftime buzzer.

The score was still 14-0 when State finally began to sustain drives. A bomb from Juday to Gene Washington got the Spartans inside the UCLA 40, and then State's other QB, Jim Raye, pulled off the prettiest option you'll ever see. Surging upfield for eight yards, he waited until Bruin tacklers converged, then pitched to a wide-open Bob Apisa on the sideline. Apisa raced the final 30 yards untouched. Since State missed the field goal in the first half, however, head coach Duffy Daugherty elected to take the kicking game out of the equation and go for two points; Juday's pass failed. 14-6, 6:13 left.

State quickly forced a punt, and All-American Bubba Smith partially blocked it. As the clock ticked under four minutes, the Spartans took over at midfield. They converted three punishing fourth downs, and with just 31 seconds left, Juday followed a line surge into the end zone.

The AP was now waiting to name its national champion until after the bowls. With No. 2 Arkansas losing to LSU in the Cotton Bowl and No. 3 Nebraska losing to No. 4 Alabama in the Orange Bowl, it was quite conceivable that a tie would have still secured a national title for Michigan State. But State needed to advance the ball three yards for two points and the draw.

It was option time once again: Raye glided right but found no space and had to pitch to Apisa earlier than he wanted. The 212-pound Hawaiian bulled past one tackler, but Jim Colletto charged down the goal line and jumped toward Apisa's shoulders as Stiles, 5'8 and 175 pounds, stood his ground around the 1. Stiles took on all of Apisa's weight and half of Colletto's. He was briefly knocked unconscious after the collision, but somehow he stood Apisa up short of the end zone. Final score: UCLA 14, Michigan State 12.

In 1965, UCLA played crazy games in three time zones, denied Michigan State the national title, won its first Rose Bowl, and finished fourth in the AP poll. The Bruins would go 9-1 in 1966, and Beban would win the Heisman in 1967, but nothing would top the ups, downs, and insane finishes of Prothro's first year in Los Angeles.

1968 PURDUE

The 1960s were what you might call the Big Ten's most democratic decade. In 1960, Iowa and Minnesota battled for both the conference title and national title. In 1962, Northwestern ascended to No. 1 in the country for a while, and Wisconsin finished No. 2. In 1963, led by Dick Butkus, Illinois went 8-1-1 and won the Rose Bowl. In 1965-66, Michigan State went 19-1-1 and finished No. 2 twice. And in 1967, Indiana, Purdue, and Minnesota all tied for the conference title, and John Pont's Hoosiers went to the Rose Bowl for the first (and, to date, only) time.

The conference's blue-blood programs were each suffering through ups and downs, allowing others a chance to shine. Ohio State still went 8-0-1 and finished second in the country in 1961, and Michigan still went 9-1 and finished fourth in 1964. But everybody got their turn.

1968 was to be Purdue's time. The Boilermakers had unleashed a sustained run of success under Jack Mollenkopf. A high school coach into his 40s, Mollenkopf landed on Stuart Holcomb's Purdue staff in 1947, then took over in 1956 when Holcomb became Northwestern's athletic director. After going 3-4-2 in his first year, he would never again finish below .500.

Purdue went 7-2-1 in 1965, and in 1966, because of the Big Ten's no repeats rule – nobody was allowed to go to the Rose Bowl two years in a row, so Michigan State was ineligible to make up for its gut-wrenching Rose Bowl loss to UCLA, despite a 9-0-1 record – the Boilermakers went to Pasadena for the first time and pulled off a thrilling 14-13 win over USC.

A frustrating loss to Indiana wrecked Purdue's chance at a solo conference title in 1967, but that was fine – 1967 was supposed to be the prelude anyway. In 1968, Purdue welcomed back quarterback Mike Phipps and running back Leroy Keyes from an offense that had averaged nearly 30 points per game.

Indiana-born Phipps was the second straight great Purdue QB, following in Bob Griese's footsteps. Like Griese in 1966, Phipps would finish second in the Heisman voting in 1969, merely 154 points behind Oklahoma's Steve Owens; he threw for 2,527 yards and 23 touchdowns that fall.

Keyes, meanwhile, was a product of Newport News, Va.; Southern schools were still primarily segregated when he was being recruited in 1964, and Mollenkopf was able to swoop in and score one of the nation's supreme talents. At 6-foot-3, 205 pounds, monstrous for 1968, he rushed for 1,989 yards, caught 78 passes for 1,186 yards, and scored a combined 34 touchdowns in 1967 and 1968. He also threw six touchdown passes. Oh, and he was PU's best cornerback for most of three seasons. He finished second to USC's O.J. Simpson in the 1968 Heisman voting.

From Phipps and Keyes, to fullback Perry Williams, to All-American linemen Gary Roberts (offensive guard) and Chuck

Kyle (defensive guard), the pieces were all in place for Purdue. The Boilermakers would begin the season as *Sports Illustrated* cover boys and the No. 1 team in the preseason AP poll. This was newfound territory for the program, but for his part, Mollenkopf welcomed the hype. As he told *SI*, "If you can't look at a season optimistically with our talent, you can't look at anything optimistically."

Against Virginia in the season opener, the team backed up the optimism. Kyle blocked a field goal attempt and Bill McKoy returned it 78 yards for a touchdown. While the offense started slowly, the Boilermakers scored 31 points in the second half of a 44-6 rout. Keyes suffered a bruised hip but still carried 11 times for 62 yards, caught eight passes for 94 yards, and completed two passes for 51.

What followed was the only No. 1 vs. No. 2 matchup in Purdue's history. The top-ranked Boilermakers visited South Bend for a meeting with Notre Dame, which had begun the season with a 45-21 thrashing of No. 5 Oklahoma. Irish quarterback Terry Hanratty was one of the college football's best, and the Irish would end up averaging nearly 38 points per game, fourth in the country.

In a shootout that featured 55 first downs and 933 total yards, Purdue was able to convert its chances, and Notre Dame wasn't. The Irish missed two early field goals; a 7-3 Irish lead should have been bigger. But Keyes swept left for a go-ahead touchdown, and the Boilermakers proceeded to score two more times within four minutes. Bob Yunaska intercepted a Hanratty pass, which led to a Keyes-to-Bob Dillingham touchdown; Bill Yancher then recovered a fumble, setting up another Keyes-to-Dillingham score. Purdue led 23-7.

Notre Dame scored a touchdown with three seconds left in the half, but another missed field goal in the third quarter wrecked an opportunity to get to within one possession. The Irish had punted only once but scored only twice. On the first play of the fourth quarter, Keyes scored from 18 yards out to ice the game. Purdue would go on to win, 37-22, probably its second-biggest win ever, behind 1967 Rose

Bowl; the Irish were done in by six turnovers – three that prevented Notre Dame scores, three that set up Purdue scores.

Following a 43-6 rout of Northwestern in Evanston – Keyes had 96 rushing yards, 46 receiving yards, and three scores – came a third road trip in three weeks.

A year earlier, Purdue had handed Ohio State one of its most humiliating losses of the Woody Hayes era, a 41-6 manhandling in Columbus. It was part of a 2-3 start for Ohio State that nearly got Hayes fired. The Buckeyes had begun to rebound, however. They won four straight to end 1967, and after two easy early-season wins over SMU (35-14) and Oregon (21-6), they had leaped to fourth in the country.

This was the second top-five team Purdue had faced on the road in three weeks, but the Boilermakers were still 13-point favorites. An Ohio Stadium record crowd of 84,834 awaited.

Hayes was never the most dynamic offensive tactician, but he hadn't for a while had the talent to win with his three-yards-and-a-cloud-of-dust attack. Recruiting had trailed off, and at one point in 1966-67, the Buckeyes lost four straight home games. The game had passed Hayes by, it seemed, and he was probably not going to make it much longer in Columbus. Ohio State hadn't averaged even 20 points per game since 1962, and during a 1966-67 span in which they lost eight of 13 games, they scored more than 14 points just three times.

That was the *previous* narrative, at least. Early in 1968, it appeared the Buckeyes were back. Stars like halfback Jim Otis combined with an incredible, program-changing 1967 recruiting class to suddenly make Ohio State, *Ohio State* again: Quarterback Rex Kern was an instant hit, backs Leo Hayden and Larry Zelina spelled Otis brilliantly, and tackle Jim Stillwagon (eventually a two-time All-American and 1970 Outland Trophy winner) and defensive backs Jack Tatum, Mike Sensibaugh, and Tim Anderson transformed the defense.

Tatum, a future first-round pick and three-time Pro Bowler, not only shadowed Keyes in Columbus, but was just about the only player to do it effectively. Keyes rushed for just 19 yards, and considering how many scoring chances Ohio State blew, Purdue was very lucky to get to halftime with a scoreless tie.

The Boilermakers' luck would run out. On the third play of the second half, Tatum jumped an out route and nearly intercepted a pass; minding Tatum on the next play, Phipps lost track of Ted Provost, who picked off his *next* pass and returned it 34 yards for a touchdown. Later in the quarter, Stillwagon picked off Pitts. With Kern injured, OSU backup Bill Long scrambled for a 14-yard touchdown and a 13-0 lead. Ohio State needed no more points.

This was the cruelest of reality checks. It was supposed to be Purdue's turn in the national spotlight, but as so many blue bloods have done through the years, Ohio State wrecked the Boilermakers' plans. The Buckeyes would finish unbeaten, wrapping up a national title with a 50-14 win over No. 4 Michigan and a 27-16 Rose Bowl win over No. 2 USC. The title that was supposed to be Purdue's would end up in Columbus with plenty of others.

Purdue nearly faltered again the very next week. Against an unlucky Wake Forest team that had lost three games by a combined 10 points, the Boilermakers were caught sleepwalking. Wake led 17-7 at halftime, and it could have been worse: Another Demon Deacon drive had stalled out at the PU 8.

Purdue still trailed 27-14 in the fourth quarter, but Keyes saved the day. Jim Kirkpatrick scored to make it 27-21, then Keyes, to wrap up a 25-carry, 214-yard day (which, granted, also featured four fumbles), scored from two yards out with 1:16 left. Purdue won 28-27, but Phipps injured his ankle holding for a PAT. It wouldn't matter the next week against Iowa – the Boilers attempted only three passes and rushed for 483 yards in a 44-14 win – but the season would continue to get more complicated.

On October 29, Mollenkopf was hospitalized with an infectious case of hepatitis. He would miss the rest of the season as assistant and former Purdue quarterback Bob DeMoss took over. On November 2, Purdue's offense slowed down with Phipps out again. Keyes rushed for only 81 yards, and the Boilermakers outgained Illinois by only 10 yards. An eight-yard Keyes touchdown and two punting miscues by the Fighting Illini – a blocked punt, followed by a bad snap – gave them a 28-3 lead and, eventually, a 35-17 win.

The seams were slowly popping for Purdue's 1968 squad, and on national television in Minneapolis, the fabric ripped entirely. Against a Minnesota team that was 3-4 and coming off of a home loss to the Iowa team Purdue had recently wrecked, the Boilermakers allowed three first-quarter touchdowns, all from Jim Carter. The 220-pound fullback had rushed for only 127 yards in seven games, but scored on a 49-yard run on the Golden Gophers' first possession. Keyes threw an interception, then backup quarterback Don Kiepert mishandled a snap; in both cases, Carter scored short touchdowns afterward. It was 21-0 after one quarter and 27-0 at halftime.

If there was a bright spot in Minnesota, it was Phipps' return. Kiepert had started the game as DeMoss attempted to establish the run, but with Phipps back in the lineup, Purdue scored 13 second-half points. It wasn't enough, but it hinted at a rebound. After a 9-0 win at Michigan State in snowy, windy East Lansing, Phipps was able to put together one last great performance before the season ended.

On November 23, Purdue and 6-3 Indiana, two teams disappointed in their seasons, played for both bragging rights and the 43-year old Old Oaken Bucket. Hoosier Bob Pernell ripped off a 64-yard touchdown run on Indiana's first possession, and Keyes responded with a 41-yard score. However, thanks to Harry Gonso's passing, IU seized control. He threw two touchdown passes to Jade Butcher and a third to Eric Stolberg, and midway through the third quarter, the Hoosiers, 17-point underdogs, were up 28-10.

Indiana had dominated field position, playing with a gusty wind in both the first and third quarters. In the fourth quarter, however, the field tilted in the other direction. Down 35-24, Phipps scrambled away from pressure, planted his feet, and threw a bomb 60 yards in the air. Keyes had drifted behind the defense and was waiting for it in the end zone. 35-31.

With just 96 seconds left, Keyes scored to give Purdue its first lead of the day. The Boilermakers held on, 38-35.

College football's present-day structure is more forgiving: If you suffer a couple of devastating losses or battle some key injuries, some of your goals end up off the table but you get a soft landing. In 2015, this Purdue team would have finished about 10-2 with a berth in the Capital One Bowl.

But in 1968, it was Rose Bowl or bust. Purdue's goals were off the table by mid-October. Still, the Boilermakers showed fortitude in battling disappointment and injury to finish 8-2. Keyes finished as the leading rusher in Purdue history and one of the leading receivers. Mollenkopf would return in 1969 – his last before retiring – and Phipps would lead the Boilers to another 8-2 campaign.

Unfortunately for Purdue, the Boilermakers' timing was off. After waiting patiently for their turn at the top, they had to settle for simply being very good. Ohio State's resurgence was well underway, and Michigan would hire Bo Schembechler at the end of 1968. The Big Ten's experiment with democracy would soon come to an end.

1968 TEXAS

Ohio State's Woody Hayes wasn't the only coach rebuilding his career in 1968. About 1,250 miles southwest, in Texas' capital city, Darrell K Royal had hit his own dry spell of sorts. His Texas Longhorns had gone 40-3-1 from 1961-64, with four consecutive top-five finishes and the 1963 national title. But, as was the case for Hayes, recruiting had trailed off. Ranked second in the 1965 preseason, Texas went 6-4. They lost four games in each of the next two years, too.

Still only 43 at the end of the 1967 season, Royal had already lived a full coaching life. A quarterback and defensive back for Bud Wilkinson at Oklahoma in the late-1940s, he became the head coach of the CFL's Edmonton Eskimos at age 29, spent two years leading Mississippi State and one at Washington and, having bounced around long enough, landed the gig at his alma mater's rival by the age of 32.

Royal was folksy and strange – his middle name was K; that wasn't an initial – and lived the same "Three things can happen when you pass, and two of them are bad" ethos attributed to the run-heavy Hayes.

Another similarity: Both Hayes and Royal signed phenomenal recruiting classes in 1967. For Texas, that meant blue-chip running back Steve Worster and receiver Cotton Speyrer headlining a group that would also feature four of 1968's nine leading tacklers.

Still, an accumulation of exciting sophomores alone wasn't going to get Texas back into college football's ruling class. To move the Longhorns back up the mountain, they were going to need some tactical assistance.

The season begins much earlier now than it used to, but even on September 22, there is potential for some truly miserable central Texas weather. That was certainly the case in 1968, when Houston (second game of the year) and Texas (first) kicked off. High in Austin: 90 degrees. Humidity at one point reached 94 percent. After three quarters of chasing each other around, both the Cougars and Longhorns became mistake-prone near the end.

Houston had been waiting for this opportunity for a while. Bill Yeoman's Cougars had gone 15-5 over the previous two seasons, at one point reaching No. 2 in the AP poll in 1967. They had led the nation in total offense each year, averaging about 33 points in the process. But they were not yet a SWC member – that would not come until 1976 – and getting opportunities against perceived heavyweights was tough. They played zero ranked teams in 1966, falling 27-6 to the only big name on the schedule (Ole Miss). In 1967, they took advantage of two huge opportunities, beating No. 3 Michigan State by 30 points and beating Georgia, 15-14, in November. But they squandered these gains by losing to NC State, Ole Miss, and Tulsa.

The Cougars visited Austin in 1968, having already beaten Tulane, 54-7. They were ranked 11th, and the perpetually respected

'Horns were ranked fourth. A sweaty crowd of 66,397 witnessed two different glimpses of the future.

Yeoman had basically invented and mastered the veer offense; it featured a running back on either side of the quarterback, each behind a guard. The linemen lined up with large splits, and Houston's triple option would send a talented back on a dive in between those gaps, then send another back wide, ready to take a pitch from the QB depending on the signal caller's read.

This triple option was devastating, especially with the speedy personnel Yeoman was able to recruit to UH. It was hitting its peak in 1968, too – the Cougars would score 71 points on Cincinnati, 77 on Idaho, and a patently absurd 100 on Tulsa in a *94-point victory* on November 23.

It wore Texas' defense out, too. But the Longhorns' defense managed to come up with a few key stops in the final quarter. And, for a while at least, Houston had equal trouble with the strange formation Texas was deploying.

A Texas grad and longtime Texas high school coach with three state titles to his name, Emory Bellard landed on Royal's staff in 1967. He was originally hired as linebackers coach, but Royal named him offensive coordinator heading into 1968. Despite plenty of talent, Texas had averaged only 18 points per game in 1966-67 and had scored 13 or fewer points in seven of eight losses in those years. Good teams were figuring out how to stop Royal's predictable attack.

Texas had a wealth of backfield talent, and Bellard's task was to figure out how to most effectively take advantage of it.

The first step was instituting the triple option, which was in use not only by Yeoman, but also by Texas A&M under head coach Gene Stallings. That made multiple backs *and* the quarterback a run threat at all times. The second step was adding another back to the backfield.

Bellard essentially started with an old-fashioned Split-T formation, with two halfbacks and a fullback behind the QB. He asked the fullback to line up ahead of the other backs so that, in the triple option, the fullback could either fulfill the dive role or get into his blocking responsibilities as quickly as possible.

The formation itself was not brand new. Clark Shaughnessy, transient coach who made his biggest impact at Stanford in 1940-41, had long ago adopted the T-formation but stuck the fullback slightly ahead of the halfbacks, forming a bit of a V. Meanwhile, Spud Cason, a junior high coach from Fort Worth, had utilized it to great effect nearly two decades earlier. But Cason wasn't using it as a muse for the triple option. With someone as talented as Worster at fullback, the potential was endless. The formation quickly got a name. Houston sportswriter Mickey Herskowitz is credited with saying that it looked like a "pulley bone," which was changed to something slightly more aesthetically pleasing: the wishbone.

In this battle of triple-option power vs. triple-option newbie, the big plays came fast and furious. Houston went 59 yards in 11 plays on the first possession of the game, and Paul Gipson scored from a yard to give the Cougars a 7-0 lead. Texas needed only three plays to respond, with Chris Gilbert ripping off a 57-yard score to make it 7-7. Despite scoring threats, the score remained the same at halftime.

Early in the third quarter, a 40-yard Ted Roy burst set up an eight-yard Gilbert score and gave UT the lead. Then it was Houston's turn to respond immediately: On the second play after kickoff, Gipson exploded for 66 yards. Royce Berry picked off a Bill Bradley pass, and after a short drive, Gipson scored his third touchdown to give UH a 20-14 lead. The PAT sailed wide, however.

Houston was on the verge of taking the game over, especially with how much Bradley was struggling. (For the game, he completed just one of seven passes for five yards and three interceptions.) After UT's Bill Atessis recovered a Ken Bailey fumble, backup

James Street entered the game. After a couple of shaky plays, he hit Speyrer on a 14-yard slant on third-and-15. Gilbert squirted through a couple of tacklers for three yards on fourth-and-1, and Koy capped the game-tying drive with a four-yard score in the first minute of the final quarter.

This PAT *also* sailed wide. 20-20.

Houston dominated the rest of the fourth quarter but could not figure out how to put the winning points on the board. The Cougars sliced through the tiring Longhorns' defense to set up a goal-to-go situation, but Ronnie Ehrig and Glen Halsell stuffed Jim Strong on third down from the Texas 2, forcing a field goal. Jerry Leiweke, fresh off the missed PAT, pushed this one wide, too.

Houston quickly got the ball back and came charging again. But on fourth-and-1 from the UT 2, Yeoman decided to forego a field goal and go for it: James Strong stuffed Gipson. Houston picked off another pass, but the Longhorns' Fred Steinmark nabbed one right back.

The game ended in a 20-20 tie. Through three quarters, the Longhorns had outgained the vaunted veer by a 301-267 margin before the Cougars controlled the fourth quarter. (Final tally: 408-314, Houston.) They lost control late but continued to make the plays they needed to make.

Bradley's struggles throwing the ball were the primary impediment early on, which caused some consternation. A former high school all-American and blue-chip recruit, Bradley could throw with either hand and punt with either foot and came to Austin with the nickname of "Super Bill." He had already been drafted by baseball's Detroit Tigers, but he turned down baseball and set his sights on becoming a Texas great.

It wasn't really working out. In two seasons behind center, the senior had thrown for 1,716 yards and rushed for 778, but his 22 interceptions and 47 percent completion rate were crippling, even by 1960s standards. He had thrown three more picks in his first seven passes of 1968. Street had shown a little something in coming up with the big pass to Speyrer, but replacing a blue-chipper is always a dicey proposition. Bradley was adapting well in practice, but it didn't translate against UH.

Bradley remained in the starting lineup when Texas traveled to Lubbock the next week to face Texas Tech. With the wishbone still in beta stage, J.T. King's Red Raiders jumped out to a 21-0 halftime lead, and with Bradley 1-for-4 with an interception, Royal again sent Street into the game. Texas scored three times in the third quarter to get to within 28-22 before Tech added a field goal to ice the game. Street ended up 8-for-17 for 108 yards. He ran the option better than Bradley, too.

Texas was winless after two games, but Royal and Bellard were beginning to figure things out. After the game, Royal told the media, "We have eight games left. You can't throw in the sponge when you're getting started. A lot of things can happen."

Two specific things happened in the coming days: First, Bellard made a formation tweak, moving Worster slightly further back so he wasn't running into the quarterback or hitting the line before it established its blocks. (What a problem to have – a fullback who was too fast.) Second, Royal made Street the quarterback.

Texas wouldn't lose again for 27 months.

Street completed a 60-yard pass to Speyrer in the first quarter against Oklahoma State the next week, and Texas cruised, 31-3. The next week against Oklahoma in Dallas, UT trailed 14-6 at halftime and 20-19 with 2:37 left. But Street completed passes of 18, 21, and 13 yards to Deryl Comer before handing to Worster for gains of 13 and seven. Worster carried two tacklers into the end zone for the game-winning points with 39 seconds left. Texas won, 26-20, and wouldn't score fewer than 35 points in any game from that point forward.

No. 9 Arkansas was the first victim of the fully weaponized wishbone. Gilbert and Worster rushed for 190 yards, and Texas burst out to a 39-15 lead before a couple of late Razorback touchdowns. Rice managed to keep the score an even 7-7 at halftime in Houston the next week, but the floodgates opened in the second half. Texas rushed for 440 yards and won, 38-14.

No. 13 SMU had no answers in Austin. Street rushed for two short touchdowns in the first quarter, and then completed a 59-yard pass to Comer to put a 38-7 win out of reach. Baylor led 13-12 at halftime in Waco, then gave up five second-half touchdowns in a 47-26 Texas win; Gilbert and Worster combined for 349 yards and six scores.

Texas moved to 7-1-1 with a 47-21 romp over TCU. Then, against triple-option rival Texas A&M, the Longhorns unleashed their masterpiece, bolting to a 35-0 halftime lead, then throwing it into cruise control in a 35-14 win.

Royal's 'Horns were pitted against Doug Dickey's 8-1-1 Tennessee Volunteers in the Cotton Bowl, and even with a month to prepare, the Vols had no solutions. Worster scored on a 14-yard run to give Texas a lead, and two minutes later, a 78-yard Street-to-Speyrer pass virtually put the game away. It was 28-0 at half, and another bomb to Speyrer sealed a 36-13 romp. Street finished 7-for-13 for 200 yards, and the trio of Worster, Gilbert, and Koy rushed for 212 yards.

The beating was sound enough to make a lasting impact on Tennessee assistant Ken Hatfield. Hatfield brought the triple option to head coaching stops at Air Force (1979-83) and Arkansas (1984-89). "When you get beat like that," he said, "you remember."

A creative formation and two tweaks had turned a 0-1-1 team into an 8-1-1 juggernaut, and the Texas Tech loss was the last one Street was associated with. He would never lose a start, leading the Longhorns to an 11-0 record and national title in 1969. Texas would go 10-1 in 1970 and 1972, and the wishbone would proliferate quickly. One UT rival, A&M, would hire Bellard to replace Stallings in 1972; another, Oklahoma, would master the wishbone with Barry Switzer in charge. Alabama's Bear Bryant would adopt it, as well, when his program needed a shot in the arm.

The smallest tweaks can make the biggest difference.

1970 ALABAMA

There is far more romance in myth than in reality. There is also far more simplicity. Race is already a complicated enough subject as is, so when we get a chance to simplify, we do so.

Alabama head coach Bear Bryant scheduled USC in Birmingham to start the 1970 season with the idea that the Crimson Tide would lose, and that Alabama fans would realize they had to recruit black players to compete at the highest level.

After USC whooped Bama in Birmingham, powered by Sam Cunningham's 12 carries, 135 yards, and two touchdowns, Bryant brought Cunningham into the Alabama locker room and announced that this, Cunningham, was what a football player really looked like.

As former Bryant assistant Jerry Claiborne is credited saying, Cunningham did more for Alabama race relations in 60 minutes than Martin Luther King Jr. did in 20 years. Because of this game, Bryant was free to recruit black players, and voila, the national titles flowed in a tide for Bama in the 1970s.

This is the legend. A simple, convenient legend. It has been passed along from writer to writer, from father to son, and from football fan to football fan. Almost none of it is actually true, mind you, but truth rarely matters in storytelling.

As is everything on Earth, the truth is more complex than we want to make it. So let's talk about what we know with some degree of certainty about the 1970 Alabama football team, a fragile squad about to transition toward something great.

1. Alabama had already lost to plenty of integrated teams.

It's not like USC was the first. Back in 1959, in only his second year in charge in Tuscaloosa, Bryant made waves by agreeing to pit his team against Penn State's integrated squad in the Liberty Bowl. He did so despite warnings from racist groups like the Citizens Council of West Alabama within the state. The Crimson Tide lost that game, 7-0. Heading into 1970, it was the last time they had been shut out.

An integrated Missouri team thumped Bama in the 1968 Gator Bowl, 35-10. The following October, in front of a record crowd at Legion Field in Birmingham, a Tennessee team with three black players destroyed Alabama, 41-14. Linebacker Jackie Walker and receiver Lester McLain were two of UT's biggest stars, and Tennessee beat the Tide so badly that a third black player, reserve Andy Bennett, saw the field as well.

2. Alabama had already recruited black players before Cunningham ran all over Legion Field.

In 1966, No. 1 Notre Dame and No. 2 Michigan State famously tied in South Bend, 10-10. Despite No. 3 Alabama being unbeaten and untied, these two teams remained in the top two spots in the rankings, and 9-0-1 Notre Dame ended up winning the AP national title.

For going on 50 years, many have believed that Alabama was, to some degree, punished for the segregationist values still strongly held throughout much of the state (and for the segregated team it was still putting on the field). Maybe. But the fact that the Texas' all-white 1969 team won the national title over a segregated Penn State squad throws at least a little bit of water on that.

Regardless, Bryant had been attempting to work African-American players into the roster for quite a while. He had supposedly begun scouting black athletes as early as 1966, but he didn't appear to pursue them with any urgency until a few years later. Plus, for obvious reasons, black players weren't necessarily in a hurry to join a non-integrated team in a state dominated by segregationist governor George Wallace.

Five walk-ons were allowed to try out for the squad in 1967, but none made it. Meanwhile, other local stars ended up choosing schools with other black players already on the roster. Bryant lost Huntsville's Bo Matthews, a future All-American, to Colorado and warned future Tennessee starting quarterback Condredge Holloway, also from Huntsville, that the state certainly wasn't yet ready for a black *quarterback*.

One-time Birmingham native Clarence Davis, meanwhile, played for USC. He would reside on the visitors' sideline in 1970's season opener.

Whether Bryant pursued integration with enough urgency, or whether he could have used the political clout he had built up with his run of early-1960s success – five top-five finishes and three AP national titles between 1961-66 – will always be a matter of debate. But after the 1969 season, Bryant indeed signed his first African-American player: Wilbur Jackson. As the school's athletic director, he oversaw the integration of the basketball team in the winter of 1970 with the signing of Birmingham's Wendell Hudson.

Jackson was an electric athlete who was eventually picked in the first round of the 1974 NFL Draft. He carried 212 times for 1,529 yards in his career, an average of 7.2 yards per carry that still ranks atop the Alabama all-time list. Jackson wasn't available in 1970, however, as freshmen were still not allowed to play varsity football. When he debuted in 1971, six of 10 SEC schools had already been integrated. Everybody else would by 1972.

3. Alabama definitely needed a shot in the arm.

Be it because of Alabama's segregated roster, Bryant's brief, late-1960s flirtation with the NFL, or any other reason, the Crimson Tide's roster did not feature as much relative talent as it used to as the new decade dawned. After going 60-5-1 from 1961-66, Bama fell to 8-2-1 in 1967, 8-3 in 1968, and 6-5 in 1969. In that downward slide, Bama went just 3-6 against ranked opponents; the Tide had gone 9-2 against such teams over the previous six years. The "game has passed him by" murmur had begun among fans and media in Tuscaloosa.

In 1964, Alabama boasted four All-Americans. The 1966 and 1967 teams had three each. But there had been only one in 1969 (lineman Alvin Samples), and there would be only one in 1970 (running back Johnny Musso). And the '70 squad was about to suffer from the same uneven, uncertain play as previous Tide iterations.

4. Cunningham most certainly ran all over Alabama.

So did a lot of his teammates.

Beginning in 1970, the NCAA began allowing teams to schedule an 11th regular season game. It was a revenue boost, though most schools used it to schedule easy wins against smaller schools. Bryant and USC head coach John McKay, however, had other ideas. Longtime friends, they met in Los Angeles and agreed on a home-and-home series for 1970-71. The first game would be in Birmingham, the second in Los Angeles.

Like Bryant, McKay had quickly established a level of dominance when hired. After getting his feet wet for two years – USC went 8-11-1 in 1960-61 – his Trojans surged to 11-0, winning the Rose Bowl and the 1962 national title. Heading into 1970, they were the preseason No. 3 team in the country, having attended four straight Rose Bowls and gone 29-2-2 over the previous three seasons.

It was quickly clear which team had the more athletic lineup. In front of 72,175 fans at Legion Field, USC outgained the Crimson Tide, 559-264. While Cunningham's two first-quarter touchdowns, including a powerful 22-yarder, stole most of the headlines, what might have been even more noteworthy was that every USC touchdown was scored by a black player. Cunningham put the Trojans up 12-0, and a seven-yard score by Charlie Evans made it 22-7 at halftime. Quarterback Jim Jones (USC even had a black quarterback) hit Davis for a 23-yard touchdown to make it 29-7, then Bill Holland, in what was by now a mostly empty stadium, caught a six-yard pass to make it 42-13.

5. Bryant did speak with Cunningham after the game.

Cunningham finished with 135 rushing yards, and Jones added 76 in the 42-21 romp. Bryant never brought Cunningham to the Alabama locker room, but Cunningham has since told media that the coach did congratulate the young USC back after the game. And according to the late Craig Fertig, a USC assistant at the time, he saw Bryant approach McKay and say, "John, I can't thank you enough." Whatever the motivation for scheduling the game, Bryant appeared to get what he thought he needed out of it.

6. There was symbolism to this occurring in Birmingham.

According to Charles H. Martin's *Benching Jim Crow*, to accommodate the USC team, the Alabama band offered not to play "Dixie" until the second half of the game. (A whole half! That probably seemed like more of a sacrifice to them than it would to outsiders.) And the game wasn't officially approved at all until the schools got assurance from Birmingham's civic leaders that there would be no discrimination of any sort for the Trojans' visit – no problems with lodging, restaurants, etc. You could probably understand the concern.

For a long time, the facade on the upper deck of Legion Field featured a sign that proclaimed, in a cursive, italic font, that it was the "Football Capital of the South!" Indeed, it was, for reasons good and bad.

Before Alabama went to Pasadena to win the Rose Bowl in 1930 and 1934, the Crimson Tide closed out unbeaten regular seasons with easy wins at Legion Field. When Tennessee handed Alabama its only loss of 1938 on the way to a share of the national title, it happened there. Alabama handing Georgia its only loss of 1941 ... Alabama handing Tennessee its only loss of 1942 and 1945 ... Alabama handing Georgia Tech its only loss of 1947 ... those moments all happened on that field. When Auburn and Alabama resumed their bitter rivalry in 1948, they chose the Football Capital of the South! as the location for the annual battle, and they wouldn't start playing home-and-homes for more than 40 years.

Alabama played two or three games per year there. Auburn played one or two a year and up to three a few times in the 1960s. If something famous happened in the SEC, it seemed there was about a 50-50 chance it happened at Legion Field.

And with its segregated seating policy remaining into the 1960s, the stadium also served as a symbol of the stubborn South in the city at the heart of so much civil rights strife.

U.S. history books and sports history books don't tend to cross-pollinate, and it is jarring to begin to think of these two worlds existing in unison in the 1960s.

When black students were admitted into Central High School in Little Rock in 1957, Fred Shuttlesworth, pastor of Birmingham's Bethel Baptist Church, attempted to enroll two daughters into J.H. Phillips High School and was beaten and hospitalized. Just under three months later, Auburn blew out Alabama at Legion Field, about three miles from Phillips, to secure the national title.

In 1961, a bus full of civil rights activists, known as Freedom Riders, was firebombed in nearby Anniston in May. A few months later, Alabama beat Tennessee, Georgia Tech, and Auburn with ease at Legion Field on the way to the national title.

In September 1963, segregationists and Ku Klux Klansmen bombed the 16th Street Baptist Church in Birmingham, killing four children. Two months later, Auburn upset Alabama, 10-8, barely two miles away.

Over time, we have separated these events into their historical categories, but at the time, they were far more intertwined.

The USC-Alabama game of 1970 wasn't a turning point so much as a consummation. It was not that the Trojans beat the Tide with an integrated roster; it's that they did it with a *fully* integrated roster that featured well over 20 black athletes. The magnitude of both the roster and the result was perhaps what mattered above all else. As Birmingham was indeed the symbolic capital of the South, it gave this blowout even deeper meaning.

Bryant didn't decide to *start* recruiting black athletes at the conclusion of this game, but the result gave him free rein to do what he needed in order to restore the level of talent on the Alabama roster. By the end of the evening of September 12, 1970, any lingering white pride had taken a backseat to Tide pride. And while other Southern programs would continue to struggle recruiting black athletes, even well past when official integration began, Bryant did not. Once black players were brought in, they were treated as family.

7. The rest of the season revealed a young, unstable team that was close to putting the pieces together.

It wasn't like Alabama had a half-black roster beginning in 1971. Bryant's recruiting efforts would slowly bear fruit, but the Tide turnaround would begin the very next fall. First, a young 1970 squad needed to take some lumps and learn from mistakes.

When things clicked for Alabama in 1970, they clicked fully. Back in Birmingham the next week for a game against Virginia Tech, the Crimson Tide dominated, outgaining Jerry Claiborne's Hokies, 582-362. It was 30-6 after 30 minutes and 51-18 after 60. Against No. 13 Florida in Tuscaloosa the next week, the story was similar. Yards: Alabama 486, Florida 279. Points: Alabama 46, Florida 15.

Against lesser teams, the success continued. Alabama outgained Vanderbilt by 190 yards in a 35-11 win on October 10 and outgained Mississippi State by 229 yards in a 35-6 conquest on Halloween. In a late-season trip to the Orange Bowl to face Miami, the Tide eased to a 14-0 halftime lead and cruised, 32-8.

However, against the more talented teams on the docket, fragility showed. Alabama committed four turnovers in Jackson against No. 7 Ole Miss the week after the big Florida win. Rebel quarterback Archie Manning threw three touchdown passes and rushed for two more, and after allowing a 26-3 lead to fritter away to 26-17, Ole Miss cruised, 48-23.

Against No. 14 Tennessee in Knoxville on the third Saturday in October, Alabama quarterbacks completed 26 passes for 271 yards but threw an incredible eight interceptions in the process. Alabama outgained the Volunteers, 358-213, but fell 24-0. It was their first shutout loss since the Liberty Bowl loss to Penn State 11 seasons earlier.

The turnovers god smiled on Bama in a trip to face No. 15 Houston in the newly-built Astrodome. Houston committed five of them while gaining 409 yards, and with Alabama having taken a

23-21 lead late in the game, Alabama's Steve Higginbotham picked off a pass and took it 80 yards for the game-clinching touchdown. But the balance shifted back on November 7 in Birmingham. No. 11 LSU forced four Bama turnovers and knocked off the Tide, 14-9. Once again, Alabama had outgained its opponent rather significantly (in this instance, 328-245) in a loss.

The regular season ended with a particularly wild Iron Bowl affair. Alabama raced to a 17-0 lead thanks to a 14-yard Johnny Musso run and a touchdown pass from Scott Hunter to David Bailey. (Russo finished the season with 1,137 rushing yards and 30 receptions, while Bailey finished with 55 catches for 790 yards, a massive total in 1970.)

Once again, however, turnovers got in the way. Six Bama give-aways and solid play from future Heisman winner Pat Sullivan paved the way for a massive comeback. Auburn took a 27-20 lead in the fourth quarter on a 17-yard pass from Sullivan to Robby Robinett, but Bama responded with a 54-yard strike from Hunter to George Ranager. Uninterested in a tie, Alabama went for two and got it on a two-point conversion pass to Bailey. With 5:18 left, it was 28-27.

It took Sullivan and the Tigers barely a minute to respond. A couple of big Sullivan passes set up a three-yard run by Wallace Clark, giving Auburn its second straight Iron Bowl win, 33-28.

8. There is more symbolism in the season ending against Oklahoma.

Despite a mediocre 6-5 record, Alabama was still a marquee draw for bowl organizers. There were just 11 bowls in 1969, but the Crimson Tide accepted an invitation to play No. 20 Oklahoma in Houston's Bluebonnet Bowl.

Unbeknownst to anyone outside of his inner circle, Bear Bryant was considering a significant offensive change. When Alabama took the field at the L.A. Coliseum to begin the 1971 season, Bryant unveiled a wishbone attack that he had installed under cloak and dagger after spring practice. That same fall, OU offensive coordinator Barry Switzer would introduce his version of the increasingly popular offense. From 1971-80, Oklahoma would go 105-11-2 under first Chuck Fairbanks, then Switzer, finishing in the AP top five nine times; Alabama would go 107-13 with seven such finishes. In a decade dominated by bluebloods, these two schools stood out.

In 1970, however, they were disappointing young teams battling program stagnation. In front of 53,822 in the Astrodome, they fought to a draw. OU took a 21-7 lead on two long touchdown runs by Greg Pruitt, but Alabama broke ahead in the fourth quarter when Musso took a handoff from Hunter, then threw back to Hunter for a 25-yard score.

Oklahoma tied the game on a 42-yard Bruce Derr field goal, but Fairbanks ordered an onside kick in attempt to avoid a draw, and Alabama recovered. Musso gained 21 yards on a draw play to get inside the OU 20, but OU's John Shelley blocked a 34-yard field goal at the buzzer. An unstable season ended with a frustrating result and a 6-5-1 record.

9. In 1971, Bear Bryant's second life as Alabama head coach began.

Following the 1970 season, Bryant signed three more African-American athletes: Tuscaloosa's Sylvester Croom and Montgomery's Ralph Stokes and Mike Washington. He also inked junior college defensive end John Mitchell, who would officially become the first black Alabama football player to see the field. Alabama had nine black starters by 1973, including Wilbur Jackson, who earned all-conference honors.

Between improved recruiting and the surprising shift to the wishbone, Alabama quickly found the shot-in-the-arm that it was looking for. The Crimson Tide shocked USC in the 1971 opener on the way to an 11-0 start, then claimed shares of the mythical national titles in 1973, 1978, and 1979.

Few coaches get a second act of dominance, but during a time of drastic cultural evolution in the country, Bryant figured out a way to evolve as well.

1970 DARTMOUTH

In late-1985, after back-to-back two-win seasons, Dartmouth fired head coach Joe Yukica. Well, it tried to, anyway. With a year left on his contract, he sued to keep his job, saying the school was legally bound to continue employing him.

It was a Hail Mary of a claim, and he won via formality – the court ruled that athletic director Ted Leland basically hadn't followed proper procedure. Yukica got his job back and won three games in 1986. His contract was not renewed.

The case drew national attention, in part because of who testified on behalf of Yukica and his competence. According to *Sports Illustrated*, with Penn State head coach Joe Paterno on the stand, Dartmouth lawyer Tommy Rath, a former team manager, asked him the most pressing of questions: "Coach Paterno, before we get down to the business at hand, and as long as I have you under oath, I'd like to ask you one question: Did you really think you could beat that 1970 Dartmouth team?"

Penn State had won the Lambert Trophy, awarded to the East's best team, each year from 1967-69 and would do so again 14 times between 1971-90. But in 1970, that crown went to Dartmouth, the last great Ivy League team, and maybe the *greatest*.

By the end of the 1960s, it had long grown clear that the Ivy League didn't have much of a role to play in top-division college football. Though programs like Harvard and (especially) Yale had helped to literally define the sport in the late-1800s, and though the best Ivy teams continued to play at a high level into the 1930s – 1933 Princeton, 1935 Princeton, and 1939 Cornell all claimed shares of the mythical national title with undefeated seasons – college football's post-war organization of rules, talent, and scholarships had left the league behind.

Heading into 1970, only one Ivy League team had finished a season ranked by the AP in the last 17 seasons: Yale's undefeated 1960 squad. This shift had come rather quickly – from 1936-40, the Ivy produced nine top-15 teams, and in the postwar years, teams like 1945 Penn, 1947 Penn, and 1950-51 Princeton still produced top-level teams. But then it pretty much ended. The league still produced high-level talent – Yale receiver Calvin Hill was a first-round NFL pick in 1969, and Cornell running back Ed Marinaro would finish second to Auburn's Pat Sullivan in the 1971 Heisman Trophy voting – but not nearly as much of it.

Bob Blackman's Dartmouth program had been the shining light of the 1960s Ivies. Then called the Indians, they finished either first or second in the conference 10 times between 1957 and 1970. Their 9-0 squad won the 1965 Lambert Trophy over a weak crop – Syracuse went 7-3, Colgate 6-3-1, Boston College 6-4, Penn State 5-5.

After a down year in 1968, Dartmouth surged the following fall. The Indians destroyed Boston College, 42-6, in a preseason scrimmage, then started the season 8-0, winning every game by at least 14 points. But they stumbled over the final hurdle, suffering a

35-7 shellacking at the hands of Princeton. That created a potent combination of talent, experience, and residual bitterness.

A captain of the USC freshman team in 1937, Blackman's football career ended early when he contracted polio. Originally given no chance of walking again, he recovered enough to don the pads as a sophomore in 1938, but he was clearly limited, and head coach Howard Jones instead made him an assistant coach on the freshman team.

After the war, he got his first head coaching job at Pasadena City College in 1949 and led the Lancers to JUCO national titles in 1951 and 1952. He moved on to the University of Denver, a member of the Skyline Conference, in 1953, and by 1954 he was dominating. The Pioneers went 9-1 with a prolific offense and road wins over Utah, BYU, and Utah State.

Blackman's reputation was quickly growing. Following the 1954 season, he was considered for the head coaching jobs at Oregon State, Dartmouth, and the NFL's Los Angeles Rams. The Rams hired eventual legend Sid Gillman, Oregon State went with Tommy Prothro, and Dartmouth selected Blackman upon a key recommendation: Paul Brown, by then nine years into his legendary tenure with the Cleveland Browns, was asked to take a look at DC's potential candidates, in part because his son Mike was a Dartmouth quarterback at the time. Brown recommended Blackman over the other primary candidate, Navy assistant Ben Martin. (Martin would eventually hold the Virginia job for two years before coaching Air Force through most of the 1960s and 1970s.)

Blackman was thorough and innovative. He was an early adopter of Clark Shaughnessy's V-formation, a wishbone predecessor in which the fullback lined up a little bit ahead of the halfbacks in the typical T-formation. He was organized and ambitious in his recruiting practices, opening up the Dartmouth umbrella to include most of the country and creating a national network as a talent base. He was miles ahead of the game from a scouting perspective, using computers to spot play tendencies long before most realized this was even an option.

Put it all together, and Dartmouth was bigger, stronger, more talented, and more well-prepared than any other team in the Ivy League.

In 1970, quarterback Jim Chasey was capable of posting big numbers with his arm and did enough to win the Asa Bushnell Cup (awarded to the Ivy League's most outstanding player), but he only got so many chances because most games were over after two or three quarters. Halfback John Short was steady and reliable, and the Dartmouth defense was untouchable. Rover back Murry Bowden, safety Willie Bogan, and defensive lineman Barry Brink all landed on 1970's All-East team, and sophomore end Fred Radke quickly came into his own.

To top things off, the Indians were great in special teams: Tim Copper was the best punt returner in the country this side of Nebraska's Johnny Rodgers, and Wayne Pirmann was one of the country's more reliable place-kickers.

The Indians had an almost unfair advantage over most opponents, but with Chasey missing the season opener against UMass with an ankle injury, it took a while for the domination to begin. The Minutemen not only held Dartmouth scoreless in the first half; the Big Green gained only 46 total yards. But thanks to special teams, DC eventually worked out the kinks. John Macko blocked a punt to set up a short field, and Short scored the first touchdown of the season from 12 yards out. Copper followed up with a 73-yard punt return score, and Dartmouth tacked on two more scores in the final period to win, 27-0.

Blackman's squad officially found its rhythm the next week. On the road against a Holy Cross team that was rebuilding after a hepatitis outbreak – 90 of 97 players were ill the year before, forcing the school to cancel the season after two games – Chasey made his season debut. HC knocked the Dartmouth offense for an 11-yard loss on the first play of the game. From that point forward, the Indians outgained the Crusaders, 430-127. Holy Cross had one first-half first down, and three short touchdowns (two from Stu Simms, one from backup quarterback Bill Pollock) made it 24-0 at halftime. Dartmouth cruised, 50-14, then got spectacular revenge on Princeton the next week. In front of 20,306 at home in Hanover, the Indians outgained the Tigers, 306-100. Chasey, Simms, Short, and Mike Roberts scored on short runs, and Copper took another punt to the house. Final score: DC 38, Princeton 0.

On October 17, Dartmouth used three return touchdowns (fumble, short kick, interception) to race to a quick 28-0 lead over Brown and cruised, 42-14. Then, in front of 35,000 in Cambridge, Short scored three touchdowns and threw for a fourth (a 49-yarder to Bob Brown) to go up 31-0 on Harvard; the Indians cruised, 37-14.

Late in the game, Harvard's Eric Crone hit Ted DeMars for a 75-yard touchdown. It had no impact on the game, but was noteworthy for one reason: It was the last time an opponent would score on Dartmouth, even on the backups. It was only October 24.

On Halloween, it was off to New Haven for the biggest Ivy League game in years. Powered by Dick Jauron and Don Martin (who would combine for 1,515 rushing yards, 343 receiving yards, and 15 touchdowns), Yale was off to a spectacular start itself. The Eli were 28-3-1 since the beginning of the 1967 season and were unbeaten thus far in the fall of 1970. Both teams were ranked in the UPI top 20, and the winner would almost assuredly crack the AP rankings as well.

A crowd of 50,000 was expected at the Yale Bowl; 60,820 showed up, the largest Yale crowd since a 1954 game against Army, and they saw what you might call one of the most dominant 10-point victories in the sport's history. Dartmouth outgained Yale, 489-190, completely shutting down the Yale running attack. Chasey threw for 237 yards, as well, but in the first half, Dartmouth was its own biggest enemy. The Indians threw three interceptions (two in the end zone), lost a fumble, failed on a key fourth down, and suffered three key penalties in the first half.

With Yale holding no hope of scoring, the game remained scoreless until John O'Neill, Dartmouth's leading rusher on the day, broke through with a three-yard touchdown run. A 30-yard field goal from Pirmann in the third quarter put the game virtually out of reach; a late Dartmouth interception officially sealed the deal. The final score was 10-0. It could have been 45-0.

The run continued after the big game. Columbia visited Hanover and went home with a 55-0 shellacking. Chasey ripped off a 75-yard run in the second quarter, and Copper returned yet another punt for a score. Columbia would get its revenge the next year, ending a 15-game Dartmouth winning streak with a 31-29 win in New York City, but the Lions had no answers in 1970.

In Ithaca the next week, Dartmouth outgained Cornell 429-193 and completely shut down the explosive Marinaro. But thanks to two goal line stops by Cornell, the score was only 3-0 in DC's favor heading into the fourth quarter. A three-yard score by Short, a 41-yard scoring strike from Chasey to Brown, and a one-yard plunge by O'Neill made the final a more indicative 24-0.

Now 16th in the AP poll, Dartmouth finished the season against 4-4 Penn in Philadelphia. The Quakers' Pancho Micir entered the game as the Ivy League's leading passer; Dartmouth's absurd defense sacked him nine times and picked off four passes. Short ran for 154 yards, and a 34-yard pass from Chasey to Short made the score 21-0 at halftime. One last Short touchdown meant the season ended with a 28-0 thrashing.

The final AP poll of 1970 is a fascinating contrast. The top five is predictable enough: Nebraska, Notre Dame, Texas, Tennessee,

Ohio State. But Ole Miss and Oklahoma tied for 20th, Penn State was 18th, USC 15th … and tiny Dartmouth, the no-scholarships program from New Hampshire, 14th. Because the Big Green weren't allowed to play in the postseason, and because they were Division I in name only, playing only select, small eastern schools in non-conference play, they didn't get much of a chance to prove themselves against the powers of the sport.

Still, they averaged 34.6 points per game, sixth in the country. They allowed just 4.7 points per game, first. Their preseason thrashings of Boston College in 1968 and 1969 had proven they could compete athletically with bigger Division I programs, and their devastation of every Ivy League club proved that, weak strength of schedule or not, this was a phenomenal club.

Dartmouth was awarded the Lambert Trophy, to Joe Paterno's slight chagrin. He grumbled to the press that Dartmouth and 7-3 Penn State should play in a postseason game to determine the East's truly best team.

Blackman disagreed. "If we were allowed to play a postseason contest, I would prefer to play a team that had a better record."

1972 TAMPA

On one sideline, you had three future coaching greats and one of the best linebackers of all-time. On the other, you had Mr. Wonderful, Sloth, and a future NFL receiver playing quarterback. The 1972 Tangerine Bowl was one of the more noteworthy, star-heavy minor bowls ever played, even if nobody had any idea at the time.

By the early-1970s, the high school talent within the state of Florida was growing, and the end of segregated rosters was creating huge new recruiting battles. College football's oligarchy, its ruling class, doesn't add members very frequently, but by the mid-1980s, both Miami and Florida State were turning into national powers. Florida was close as well. In the 1990s, Central Florida and South Florida would make the move to Division I-A; USF would spend parts of two seasons (2007 and 2008) in the AP top 10, and in 2013 UCF would win the Fiesta Bowl.

The University of Tampa got a significant head start on either UCF or USF, and when the Spartans were peaking in 1972, Miami was stagnant. If FSU was ahead of Tampa, it wasn't by much.

Within three years, however, UT had dropped football altogether.

For most of its existence from the 1930s to the mid-1970s, Tampa existed as a typical mid-major with upside. The Spartans beat Florida State in 1952, Mississippi State in 1968, Miami in 1970 and 1972, and Vanderbilt in 1972. In the 1960s, as they were moving toward Division I status, they were in the rotation as SEC fodder against programs like Tennessee, Alabama, and Ole Miss.

They were creative in the scheduling department, playing everyone from FSU to Delta State, and they even played Cuban and Mexican teams from the 1930s (Athletico de Cuba) to 1963 (Mexico Poly). They won the 1951 Beach Bowl (against Brandeis), the 1952 Cigar Bowl (against Lenoir-Rhyne), and the 1954 Cigar Bowl (against Charleston).

This was a decent program, and it was drawing attendance in the 10,000-20,000 range. But it didn't have any particular rivals, any sense of regional belonging. In the 1970s, there were attempts at kindling a rivalry with Miami and Florida A&M, and maybe that could have gone somewhere. But in the three decades after World War II, the Spartans didn't play anyone more than 13 times. There was passion, sure: Fans once mobbed a referee after a controversial loss to Birmingham Southern in 1934. But there was never a major connection, something that brought 40,000 or 50,000 to Phillips Field or, later, big Tampa Stadium. And there was never total support from school administration.

In 1970, under head coach Fran Curci, Tampa pummeled Miami, 31-14. It was such a momentous win, evidently, that it helped to convince Miami to hire away Curci, who had gone 25-6 in three years. The Spartans replaced him with Florida offensive line coach Bill Fulcher; Fulcher went 6-5 and was hired away by Georgia Tech.

That brought Earle Bruce to town. UT chose him over Kansas offensive coordinator Charlie McCullers and Michigan offensive line coach Chuck Stobart. An Ohio State grad who had spent the previous six seasons under Woody Hayes at his alma mater, Bruce would only spend a year in Tampa himself before Iowa State hired him away as well. (He would end up succeeding Hayes in Columbus a few years later.) But he didn't have to wait long to make a statement.

In the first game of 1972, the Spartans hosted Toledo, purveyors of a 35-game winning streak, the longest in college football. The Rockets hadn't lost since the last game of 1968. Head coach Frank Lauterbur left for Iowa after going 23-0 in 1969-70; Jack Murphy took over and went 12-0 in 1971.

Toledo had won three straight Tangerine Bowls and finished in the AP top 15 for two straight years, but the win streak was over when the Rockets left Tampa. In front of 23,803 at Tampa Stadium, running back Alan Pittman rushed 13 times for 90 yards and caught a touchdown pass, and Dave Bankston came away with both an interception and fumble recovery in a runaway 21-0 win.

Bankston spent a lot of time in the Toledo backfield, and he usually met a teammate back there: star end John Matuszak.

The Tooz had lived a transient existence before he reached Tampa. He spent his first year at Fort Dodge junior college in Iowa, then signed with Dan Devine's Missouri Tigers in 1970. Devine kicked the backup tight end off the team, however, after he got into a fight at a post-game party, and he ended up in Florida.

At 6'7, 275 pounds, Matuszak was beginning to harness his immense tools while staying out of trouble just enough to stay on the field. As his mid-1980s autobiography, *Cruisin' with the Tooz*, would suggest, he wasn't staying out of trouble altogether. But he did well enough. He would end 1972 with All-American honors, and the following spring, he would become the first pick in the NFL draft.

Tooz ended up playing a role in two Super Bowl champions in Oakland before retiring in 1981, but he is perhaps most well-known for what happened after his playing days. He appeared in the December 1982 issue of *Playgirl* magazine and ended up in Hollywood, starring in episodes of everything from *M*A*S*H* and *The A-Team* to *Silver Spoons* and *Perfect Strangers*. He most notably played Baby Ruth-loving Sloth in *The Goonies* and Stain in *One Crazy Summer*. (His Bacon Number is 2, by the way: He was with Josh Brolin in *The Goonies*, and Brolin was in *Hollow Man* with Kevin Bacon.) Eventually, his wild ways caught up to him; he passed away in 1989 at the age of 38, due to heart failure following an opioid overdose.

Hollywood was not yet part of the equation in 1972, however. The dominance of Matuszak and Bankston against Toledo meant Bruce's tenure started out with a huge win. Not only did UT steal headlines for ending the Rockets' streak; the Spartans also gave Bruce some bragging rights over his Ohio brethren.

Tampa then traveled to Marquette, Michigan, of all places, to face the Northern Michigan Wildcats. (Again, scheduling regionally appeared to be an issue.) Tampa quarterback Buddy Carter ripped off a 56-yard touchdown run in the first quarter, but it wasn't until Alex Edlin reeled in a 34-yard pass from Carter to make it 28-21 in the third quarter that Tampa could begin to feel safe in an eventual 34-21 win. It got easier against another directional Michigan school the next week. EMU visited Tampa, and after a slow Spartan start – something of a trend this season – UT pulled away, scoring two touchdowns in each of the final three quarters and winning, 42-0.

Edlin caught two more touchdown passes against EMU, but the star of the day was fullback Paul Orndorff.

The Brandon Bull scored 21 touchdowns in his career and would eventually get selected in the 12th round of the 1973 NFL Draft. But within a couple of years, Orndorff found his true calling: professional wrestling. Carved out of granite and capable of playing a good heel, he feuded with the likes of Jerry Lawler on the southern wrestling circuit before landing in the WWF in 1983. As Mr. Wonderful, he was part of the WrestleMania I main event, teaming with Rowdy Roddy Piper against Hulk Hogan and Mr. T.

Tampa piledrove EMU, but struggled through another awkward road trip. At Kansas State on September 30, the Spartans outgained the host Wildcats by a 371-313 margin but committed six turnovers in a 31-7 loss. Back home against Louisville, Tampa's Morris LaGrand fumbled the opening kickoff, which set up a short Howard Stevens touchdown run; Stevens later returned a punt for a touchdown as well, and Louisville survived, 17-14.

At this point, the season could have gone south pretty quickly. Two error-prone losses had killed hopes of a national ranking, and any thought about a bowl bid would die with any further missteps. But the team rallied, and the schedule helped. Tampa outscored Southern Illinois and Drake by a combined 68-7. Ernie Dubose rushed for 146 yards against SIU, then Alan Pittman hammered out 105 against DU.

When November rolled around, it was time for a pair of burgeoning rivalries. Against Florida A&M in front of 31,350, Wilbur Grooms recovered a bombed punt snap in the end zone for an early touchdown, and Tampa scored 10 fourth-quarter points to put away a 26-9 win. The next week, Curci returned to Tampa as Miami's head coach and left with a 7-0 loss. Miami lost two fumbles inside the Tampa 10, and an 18-yard LaGrand touchdown run in the first quarter held up.

The star of the Miami win, with 114 yards on 29 carries: Freddie Solomon. The junior platooned at quarterback with Buddy Carter and offered the Spartans a speedy option for moving the chains and winning the field position battle.

A product of Sumter, S.C., Solomon played in segregated Lincoln High School before it merged with all-white Edmunds High his senior year. He wasn't much of a passer, but he offered one hell of a change of pace. He would move to receiver and enjoy a long NFL career with the San Francisco 49ers. Just as he helped to beat Miami in 1972, he would help to beat the Miami Dolphins in Super Bowl XIX 12 years later. He retired from the NFL in 1985, having caught 371 career passes, and he created a ministry to help at-risk children in the Tampa area. He passed away of colon and liver cancer in 2012.

By mid-November, it was down to Tampa and East Carolina in the running for a bid in the Tangerine Bowl opposite the MAC champion. Dubose scored three touchdowns in a 29-22 win over Bowling Green, and in the regular season finale against Vanderbilt in the rain, Tampa just got out of the way and let the Commodores stumble to the ground. Eddie Caldwell picked off a pass and re-turned it 55 yards for a score, and the Spartans cruised, 30-7, thanks to seven Vandy turnovers. That sealed the deal: On December 29 in Tampa Stadium, the Spartans would host Kent State in the Tangerine Bowl, their first top-division postseason bid.

Kent State was led by head coach Don James and featured a safety named Nick Saban, a tight end named Gary Pinkel, and a linebacker named Jack Lambert. James would go on to win 212 games and the 1991 national title at Washington; Saban would win multiple national titles at LSU and Alabama; Pinkel would lead Missouri back from a destitute period in the 2000s; Lambert would become a nine-time Pro Bowler and NFL Hall of Famer with the Pittsburgh Steelers.

Lambert would lay a huge hit on Buddy Carter at one point, and Pinkel would catch five passes for 97 yards. But Kent State had Orndorff, Solomon, and surer hands. After a muffed punt gave UT the ball at Kent's 15, Orndorff caught a 15 yard pass from Carter for a touchdown. After Tommy Thomas picked off Kent's Greg Kokal, Orndorff flared out and rumbled for a 35-yard score. Solomon scored to make it 21-0 at halftime, but Kent charged back. The Golden Flashes scored three second-half touchdowns but missed two PATs and a two-point conversion. Tampa held on, 21-18. Solomon finished with 103 rushing yards and was named the game's co-MVP with Lambert.

Despite the midseason blip, this was Tampa's greatest season. Matuszak would go first in the 1973 draft, and both McQuay and tackle Ron Mikolajczyk were picked in the fifth round. Two years later, tackle Darryl Carlton was picked in the first round, Solomon in the second. Guard Noah Jackson, a junior in 1972, would spend 10 years in the pros.

Administrative support still lagged, though. In 1975, school president B.D. Owens announced that the school's endowment fund was getting used to support football debt, and the school's board of trustees voted to drop football. There was outcry, but the decision stood. In 1989, the school conducted a feasibility study for bringing the sport back, but another school president, Bruce Samson, killed the idea.

Any lingering bitterness over this decision would continue to fester as so many other schools began to find their footing in top-division college football. And when nearby USF was able to establish itself, any future thought to bringing UT Football back was quashed.

There will always be the 1972 team, however: an all-time mix of athleticism and personality.

1973 MICHIGAN

"You can see over there on that eastern sideline right now. The two Ohio State captains – the elected captains are Hare, the second-string quarterback, and Middleton, one of those fine linebackers making up the trio: Middleton, Koegel, and Gradishar.

"HERE they come … Hare, Middleton, and the Buckeyes … boy, look at Hicks, he's an active captain today … and they're TEARING DOWN MICHIGAN'S COVETED M-CLUB BANNER! THEY WILL MEET A DASTARDLY FATE HERE FOR THAT. THERE ISN'T A MICHIGAN MAN IN THIS STADIUM WHO WOULDN'T LIKE TO GO OUT AND SCALP THOSE BUCKEYES RIGHT NOW.

"THEY HAD THE AUDACITY … THE UNMITIGATED GALL … TO TEAR DOWN THE COVETED 'M' THAT MICHIGAN WAS GOING TO RUN OUT FROM UNDER. BUT THE MEN – THE 'M' MEN WILL PREVAIL BECAUSE THEY'RE GETTING THE BANNER BACK UP AGAIN – AND HERE THEY COME!! THE MAIZE AND BLUE! TAKE IT AWAY, 105,000 FANS!"

That's Michigan radio announcer Bob Ufer, describing one of the crazier pregame scenes in college football history. Woody Hayes' Ohio State Buckeyes charged and tore down the "Go Blue: M Club Supports You" banner under which the Michigan team always runs before home games. This was as delightfully petty as college rivalry can get. But the 1973 game, perhaps the biggest in the history of the rivalry, would only get more bitter from there.

Cecil Coleman, Illinois' athletic director, voted for Ohio State. He heard about the injury to Michigan quarterback Dennis Franklin and got spooked, deciding the Buckeyes would be the better team to represent the conference. Michigan head coach Bo Schembechler raged at Big Ten commissioner Wayne Duke for sharing information about Franklin's injury before the vote.

Bump Elliott of Iowa voted for his alma mater, Michigan. He said he knew Franklin's injury was an issue for some, but he went with the Wolverines.

Wisconsin's Elroy Hirsch, a former Michigan end, voted for Ohio State. Schembechler assumed it had something to do with hurt feelings after Schembechler said negative things about Hirsch in a recent Joe Falls book called *Bo Schembechler, Man in Motion*. Hirsch swore it was because of Franklin.

Indiana A.D. Bill Orwig, *also* a former Michigan end, voted for the Wolverines. Two athletic directors who actually had no Michigan connections – Purdue's George King and Minnesota's Paul Giel – split their votes, King going Buckeyes, Giel going UM.

Northwestern's Tippy Dye, former Ohio State quarterback, voted for the alma mater Buckeyes. He and Michigan A.D. Don Canham hadn't seen eye to eye in recent years, and allegedly some resentment had festered. He, too, referenced Franklin's injury.

Considering Canham's predictable Michigan vote and an equally predictable Ohio State vote from Buckeyes A.D. Ed Weaver, this gave OSU five votes against Michigan's four.

These athletic directors were voting to select the conference's Rose Bowl participant because Ohio State and Michigan had tied, 10-10, in Ann Arbor the previous day. That meant both teams finished 7-0-1 in conference play, and per the conference's list of tiebreakers, the conference would decide who would attend the only bowl Big Ten teams were allowed to attend. As Ohio State had gone to Pasadena the previous year, a tie vote would give the bid to Michigan. Michigan State's vote would make the difference, one way or the other.

There is a balance between tradition and progress, one that college football has toed since the 1890s. Historical significance about a given game, a given season, or a given result adds gravitas to this sport. Still, there is a difference between celebrating the past and living in it. At quite a few times in its history, the Big Ten's greatest export has been The Way Things Used to Be.

In 1973, there were 11 bowls. Of the 22 bowl bids, 17 went to teams in the AP top 20 and five went to unranked teams. The three ranked teams that would be postseason-free were unbeaten Oklahoma (on NCAA probation) and the losers of Ohio State-Michigan and UCLA-USC. The Big Ten and Pac-8 were each holdouts to a previous era, holding onto the "Rose Bowl or nothing" mantra long after other conferences had begun allowing non-champions to bowl.

All-or-nothing circumstances can certainly create an extra layer of drama. Both Michigan and Ohio State were well aware of that. In 1969, in Schembechler's first year, Michigan upset the top-ranked Buckeyes, denying Woody Hayes' Buckeyes both a national title and a Rose Bowl. In 1970, unbeaten Ohio State beat unbeaten Michigan. In both 1972 and 1974, one-loss Ohio State beat undefeated Michigan.

After spending so much of the 1960s in flux, the Big Ten had turned into a two-team league. The Wolverines and Buckeyes finished first and second in some order in all but one year between 1969 and 1977. (That one exception: In 1971, Ohio State finished 5-3 in conference play, a half-game behind second-place Northwestern.)

Hayes and Schembechler were in so many ways mirror images of each other; they were both great motivators, they were both old-school conservatives in a time when colleges had become more liberal, and they both viewed the game of football as an extension of war. Their similarities made sense, considering Schembechler played for Hayes at Miami (Ohio) in 1949-50 and spent six years as a Hayes assistant at Ohio State.

Schembechler treated rivals as enemies and never relinquished some of the anger he felt against the athletic directors who voted against him and his team in 1973. Beating Ohio State and making the Rose Bowl was the be-all and end-all for Schembechler's program, to such a degree that, then the Wolverines *did* make the Rose Bowl, they usually suffered letdowns and lost – it took him six tries to actually win one. (Well, five: He was hospitalized during the 1970 Rose Bowl after suffering a heart attack.) As he put it in *Bo*, his autobiography, "Jonah had his whale. Captain Hook had his crocodile. And I have January 1. Let's be honest here: my bowl record stinks."

Despite those lapses, however, the level of concentration required to pull off what Michigan was doing in the early-1970s was staggering. The Wolverines lost to Michigan State in October 1969 and Purdue in November 1976; in between, they only lost games that were either in Pasadena or against Ohio State.

Ohio State sophomore running back Archie Griffin, who would go on to win the Heisman in 1974 and 1975, rushed 30 times for 163 yards against Michigan. He burst ahead for 38 yards on the first play of the second quarter to key a 10-play, 66-yard field goal drive. Blair Conway's 31-yard boot gave Ohio State a 3-0 lead. After an exchange of punts, Griffin plowed out chunks of yardage and set up freshman fullback Pete Johnson, who dragged tacklers into the end zone for a five-yard score. At halftime, in front of 105,223 at Michigan's Big House, Ohio State led 10-0.

Michigan opened the season at Iowa, led 17-7 at halftime, and cruised, 31-7. The next week, Stanford and Michigan faced off for the first time since Stanford's 13-12 Rose Bowl win over the Wolverines, a result that prevented UM from finishing unbeaten. Schembechler clearly had revenge on his mind: Michigan scored three times in the first quarter and led 34-0 at halftime before Schembechler called off the dogs in a 47-10 win.

Two things were noteworthy from this win: The ruthless team efficiency and the powerful leg on Mike Lantry. The lefty was the last of a dying breed – he was a "toe kicker," approaching the ball from straight on and booting with his toe – and bombed in a 50-yard field goal in the second quarter. A Vietnam vet, the junior was already 25 years old, and he would eventually earn All-American honors.

Michigan's next two performances were their least impressive. The Wolverines beat a weak Navy team, 14-0, thanks mostly to four turnovers by the Midshipmen. The next week against visiting Oregon, the Wolverines forced four more turnovers and won 24-0, despite gaining only 278 yards.

With conference play resuming, however, Michigan went into fifth gear. In a steady downpour in East Lansing, the Wolverines led Michigan State 17-0 at halftime thanks to a 53-yard Chapman run, and the Spartans continuously self-destructed, fumbling a slippery ball nine times and losing six of them. Final score: 31-0.

Rinse, repeat. The Wolverines led Wisconsin 21-0 at halftime and cruised, 35-6. Then they went to Minnesota and took a 24-0 halftime lead over the Golden Gophers before rolling, 34-7. Indiana threw a kink into the script by actually scoring in the first half against UM, but that was okay – the Wolverines had already scored six times, held a 42-7 halftime lead, and won 49-13.

Michigan was 8-0 when Illinois came to town and handed the Wolverines their first deficit of the year. The Fighting Illini scored twice on field goals, but Walt Williamson recovered a fumble at the Illinois 36, and Ed Shuttlesworth gave Michigan a 7-6 halftime lead. Chapman scored on the first drive of the second half, and UM cruised, 21-6. After another sluggish first half at Purdue – Michigan led only 6-3 at halftime – Franklin scored twice in the third quarter and Bob Thornbladh scored twice in the fourth. Michigan won, 34-9.

Then came the big game. And the big vote.

Michigan simply could not sustain any offensive momentum. But near the end of the third quarter, the Wolverines stuffed Buckeye quarterback Cornelius Greene for just one yard on fourth-and-2 from the UM 34. Shuttlesworth finally started finding some holes. Michigan advanced to the Ohio State 12 before Chapman was stuffed on third down. Mike Lantry booted a 30-yard field goal early in the fourth quarter. Ohio State 10, Michigan 3.

Shuttlesworth's rhythm continued after an Ohio State punt, and Dennis Franklin hit Paul Seal for a 27-yard gain to get inside the Ohio State 20. After three Shuttlesworth rushes gained nine yards, everyone in the stadium assumed a fourth run from Easy Ed was coming. Ohio State lined up all 11 defenders in the box. Instead, Michigan ran an option to the left, and Franklin glided untouched for a 10-yard touchdown. Lantry's extra point made it 10-10.

After another Buckeye punt, Michigan took over and began moving the ball once more. But on a pass to Shuttlesworth near midfield, Franklin was hit hard by end Van DeCree and, upon landing on the unforgiving Michigan Stadium turf, fractured his collarbone. Larry Cipa came in, Michigan ran for three yards, and Lantry trotted out for a massive 58-yard field goal attempt with a minute left. Damned if it didn't look good when it left his foot. Eventually, it drifted just wide.

With a minute left, Hayes, also struggling to stomach the thought of a tie, sent in his passing quarterback, Greg Hare, to attempt the Buckeyes' first pass of the day. Michigan's Tommy Drake, however, picked it off and returned it inside the OSU 35. Schembechler didn't trust Cipa to throw the ball, so after one Chapman run and a Cipa spike, out came Lantry again with just under 30 seconds left. Despite the shorter distance, he missed badly. Three desperate Hare incompletions later, the game was over. 10-10. Michigan had controlled much of the game and dominated down the stretch, but the Wolverines had to settle for a tie.

"The Big Ten will live to regret this decision." That's how Schembechler responded to news of the vote. Michigan State's Burt Smith, with the full decision in his hands, chose Ohio State to make it 6-4 in favor of the Buckeyes. Of course he did. He could have been swayed by Franklin's injury, too, but if he held a grudge, few would have blamed him. Michigan was the team that passive-aggressively fought against Michigan State's addition to the Big 10. Michigan was the program battling them over local television rights. Michigan was the big brother.

Of course, Michigan was *also* Smith's alma mater.

The next year, with all the same stakes, Lantry trotted onto the field in the final seconds to attempt another game-winner, this time from 33 yards away. If he missed it at all, it was by an eyelash. The refs in Columbus said it was no good, Ohio State won 13-12, and the Buckeyes went back to the Rose Bowl again. The Buckeyes did it *again* in 1975, but by then the Big Ten had finally loosened up its bowl restrictions. A flawed Michigan team accepted an Orange Bowl bid that year, two seasons too late.

1974 MIAMI (OHIO)

The word "idyllic" was created to describe Oxford, Ohio, the town of about 21,000 that houses the redbrick college known as Miami University, or Miami of Ohio. It is not part of the industrial vision we have of northern Ohio – with a few steps west or south, it could have just as easily been part of Indiana or Kentucky. It's almost like Oxford holds its fall colors all year long. It is a nurturing environment, especially if you want to become a successful football coach one day.

Weeb Ewbank graduated from Miami and went on to win 130 games and a Super Bowl as head coach of Baltimore and the New York Jets. Paul Brown succeeded Ewbank as Miami's starting quarterback in the 1920s and later led the Cleveland Browns to four AAFC titles and three NFL titles.

Red Blaik played for three seasons at Miami, spent two years as an assistant there, and ended up winning 121 games and shares of three national titles at Army. Paul Dietzel played for Miami after the war, spent three years as a Blaik assistant, and won a national title at LSU.

Sid Gillman spent two years as a Miami assistant and four years as Miami's head coach; he would become one of football's most influential offensive coaches and is a member of both the pro and college football halls of fame. Woody Hayes succeeded Gillman in Oxford, then spent 28 seasons with Ohio State, winning shares of five national titles in the process.

The list goes on. Ara Parseghian played for Miami for two years after the war, spent five years leading the program after Hayes left, then moved on to lead Northwestern to 36 wins (and a brief No. 1 ranking) and Notre Dame to 95 and two national titles. Bill Arnsparger graduated from Miami, spent a year on Hayes' Miami staff, then became one of the most influential defensive coaches in football in 12 seasons with another Miami (the Dolphins).

John Pont played for Hayes and Parseghian at Miami, took over for Parseghian in 1956, and later led Indiana to its only Rose Bowl bid. Carmen Cozza was in Pont's class and spent seven years as a Miami assistant before winning 179 games in three decades as Yale's head coach.

Bo Schembechler played for Gillman and Hayes at Miami, roomed with Pont, then succeeded Pont as head coach in 1963. After six seasons at UM, he would win 13 Big Ten titles in 21 years as Michigan's head coach.

And on and on. Bill Mallory played for Pont, succeeded Schembechler, and won 168 games at Miami, Colorado, NIU, and Indiana. Dick Crum was an assistant under Mallory, succeeded Mallory, and won 113 games leading Miami, North Carolina, and Kent State. Jim Tressel spent two years as Miami's quarterbacks and receivers coach before winning 135 games and four Division 1-AA titles at Youngstown State and 94 games and 1-A title at Ohio State.

John Harbaugh attended Miami and led the Baltimore Ravens to a Super Bowl title. Et cetera.

For decades, it seemed the best way to make it as a coach was to be touched by the school in Oxford. Play there and/or serve as an assistant there, and you'll win ring after ring later in life. That's how you get away with calling yourself the Cradle of Coaches with a straight face.

The best team in Miami history, however, may not have been one coached by Brown or Hayes or Parseghian or Schembechler. The most influential coach involved with the team was a starting running back at the time.

Dick Crum graduated from Mount Union, the future Division III football powerhouse, in the late-1950s, and after six seasons coaching in the Ohio high school ranks, he landed a spot on Mallory's staff when Schembechler left for Michigan. When Mallory was hired away by Colorado following an 11-0 breakthrough in 1973, Crum was anointed the successor. Good choice.

Despite entering the season with a 12-game winning streak, having finished 15th in the AP poll the year before, the Redskins (as they were then called) began 1974 unranked. It would take about a month for the voters to right their wrongs.

After an easy 39-0 win over Eastern Michigan, controlled by Randy Walker's rushing and Steve Sanna's passing, Miami took a trip to West Lafayette. Purdue hadn't kept up its cruising altitude of the late-1960s, but while the Boilermakers were iffy enough to fade and finish 4-6-1 in 1974, their upside was obvious early in the season: The week after playing Miami, they went to South Bend and thumped No. 2 Notre Dame, 31-20.

Sanna completed 23 of 36 passes for 227 yards against Purdue, but he was picked off twice, and Miami lost two fumbles. With Miami down 7-0, Sanna lobbed a fluttery, 35-yard touchdown pass to tight end Ricky Taylor to tie the game. With just seconds left, Purdue's Bill Stinchcomb missed a 42-yard field goal, but Miami was called offside. From 37 yards, Stinchcomb missed again.

Miami was called offside again! Stinchcomb missed again from 32. The game finished tied, 7-7. Somehow.

A 42-0 romp at Marshall set up the next proving-ground game, the Redskins' third straight on the road. In Lexington, the Tribe faced a Kentucky team that would go on to finish 6-5. Former Tampa and Miami coach Fran Curci was in his second year in charge of the Wildcats; he would briefly gain traction, going 18-5 in 1976-77, and against a Miami team that was once again starting to receive votes in the AP poll, UK surged out of the gates. On the second play of the game, quarterback Mike Fanuzzi burst up the middle for a 64-yard score, and Kentucky led 10-0 after seven minutes.

With backup quarterback Sherman Smith entering the game in the second quarter, however, the tide began to turn. Smith and Walker formed a nice 1-2 punch in the backfield, and early in the third quarter, Smith hit Taylor for a six-yard touchdown. Four minutes later, Miami's Brad Cousino blocked a UK punt in the end zone. Brad Miller recovered it for a touchdown and a 14-10 lead.

Midway through the fourth quarter, Fanuzzi again raced up the middle for a 40-yard gain, but was tracked down from behind by a hustling Cousino. Miami's defense stiffened, stuffing the Wildcats at the three on fourth down and eventually running out the clock. The reward for the 14-10 win: enough votes to jump back into the AP top 20.

A fourth straight road trip resulted in a 31-3 win over Ohio, and Bowling Green left Oxford with a 34-10 pasting a week later. Next came a huge road battle against a Toledo team that was 3-0 in conference play. While Toledo's Gene Swick completed 25 of 38 passes for 341 yards, he threw two interceptions, and Miami's running game eventually took over. Toledo led 14-7 in the second quarter when the Redskins ripped off a 31-0 run. A 49-yard Carpenter score gave Miami a 24-14 lead early in the fourth quarter, and a two-yard Carpenter score capped a 38-22 win.

After clinching at least a tie of the conference title with a 31-0 win over Western Michigan – it could have been a lot worse: Miami gained 585 yards to WMU's 231 – it was time to seal the deal outright. Maybe.

Now unbeaten in 20 straight games and up to 13th in the country, Miami hosted Kent State. And when Kent's Larry Poole leaped over the goal line to give the Golden Flashes a 17-16 lead with 58 seconds left, it looked like the streak was about to end.

This moment gave Crum a chance to show his fearless side. On the first play from scrimmage after the kickoff, Smith pitched to Walker, who threw back to Smith for a 26-yard gain to get near midfield. Sanna entered the game because he was a better passer, and he hit Schulte for gains of 12 and 18 yards on the sideline. With just six seconds left, kicker Dave Draudt, Sanna's roommate, came in to win the game. He had made only four of 14 kicks all year, a major slump that hadn't mattered because Miami was so dominant. But he nailed the only truly vital kick he would attempt all year – his 39-yarder sailed perfectly through the uprights, and his teammates mobbed him as the buzzer sounded on a 19-17 win.

Following a dominant 27-7 road win over rival Cincinnati, it was time for the annual trip to Orlando. The Tangerine Bowl was attracting pretty decent opponents each year to take on the MAC champion. In 1973, Miami handled Florida, 16-7, to finish 11-0. In 1975, the Redskins finished an 11-1 campaign with a 20-7 thumping of South Carolina. In 1974, Vince Dooley's Georgia Bulldogs met Crum's 15th-ranked Redskins.

Dooley and UGA would gain traction in a few years, but they were scuffling a bit since finishing 11-1 in 1971. Despite an impressive win over No. 6 Florida in Jacksonville, they were just 6-5, having followed up the Florida win with three losses in four games. They had an awesome duo of running backs in Glynn Harrison and Horace King, but they were prone to shootouts – they would finish 14th in the country in scoring offense and just 94th in scoring defense.

Miami linebacker John Roudabush recovered a fumble on the first play of the game, and six rushes later, Carpenter plunged in to give Miami a 7-0 lead. Georgia passed its way to a field goal response, but it was 14-3 Miami after one quarter and 21-3 after two. The Tribe got sloppy with the ball in the second half, but the defense was awesome, holding UGA to 74 rushing yards and riding Carpenter (30 carries, 114 yards) and Smith (22 for 90) to a 21-10 win.

For the season, Carpenter finished with 656 rushing yards, 125 receiving yards, and a scene-stealing 13 touchdowns. Walker had done most of the pre-touchdown dirty work, rushing 214 times for 873 yards. And while Sanna finished with 724 passing yards, Smith mixed 711 rushing yards with 218 passing. The trio returned the next season, with Smith passing the 1,000-yard rushing mark and throwing for 729, Walker contributing 604, and Carpenter erupting for 1,142.

Elsewhere during bowl season, No. 10 Maryland, No. 11 Texas, No. 12 Baylor, and No. 13 NC State all lost. Though Miami had fallen to 15th before the bowls, the win over a team with Georgia's stature bumped the Redskins to 10th in the final AP poll. They would nearly match this the next year, going 11-1, losing only to Michigan State (14-13 in East Lansing), winning a third straight Tangerine trophy, and finishing 12th. And after a 3-8 misstep in 1976, they surged right back to 10-1 in 1977.

The Cradle of Coaches sprouted a few more branches in the mid-1970s. With three 10-win seasons under his belt, Crum was hired away by North Carolina, where he inherited star pass rusher Lawrence Taylor and went 21-3 in 1980-81. Miami was relatively mediocre through the 1980s, then brought a familiar face to revive the program: Walker. The former star halfback led the renamed RedHawks for nine seasons. He went 10-1 in 1998, then took the Northwestern head coaching job. And in Evanston, he and offensive coordinator Kevin Wilson (a Crum recruit at UNC who landed on Walker's Miami staff in 1990 – small world) were able to craft one of the country's first dominant, up-tempo, run-first spread offenses.

Walker passed away of a heart attack in 2006, aged just 52.

Smith, meanwhile, was a little bit ahead of his time as a quarterback. Selected in the second round of the 1976 NFL Draft, he was the first offensive player chosen by the expansion Seattle franchise. As a running back, he ended up rushing for 3,429 yards, catching 210 passes for 2,445 yards, and scoring 38 combined touchdowns with the Seahawks. He predictably ended up a coach, spending two seasons as the Washington Redskins' offensive coordinator in the late-2000s.

One more future coach dressed out in Miami's red and white jerseys in 1974. Junior defensive back Ron Zook, a former walk-on, would become a starter and co-captain in 1975; by the age of 27, he was a college defensive coordinator. Then, in the early-1990s, he became Steve Spurrier's first defensive coordinator at Florida. A decade after that, he succeeded Spurrier in Gainesville. In 2007, he led Illinois to its first Rose Bowl bid in nearly 25 years.

There's something about the water in Oxford, apparently.

1978 MISSOURI

Missouri announcer Steve Bassett: "Missouri's got plenty of time showing on the clock. They've also got two timeouts left." Color commentator Bob Rowe: "Let's just hammer the ball down the field, pick up three or four, give it to our horses — Ellis, Wilder — let 'em pick up three or four at a time, get Kellen down across the middle, then score!"

By college football's standards, the 1970s were rather orderly — few usurpers, few surprises. Nine programs — Alabama, Michigan, Nebraska, Notre Dame, Ohio State, Oklahoma, Penn State, Texas, and USC — accounted for 41 of the 50 year-end top-five spots between 1970 and 1979. The national title race was so frequently dependent on which of these powers played each other and when.

Sometimes, it was also dependent on who did and did not play Missouri.

At the end of the 1970 season, Mizzou head coach Dan Devine left Columbia to take the reins of the Green Bay Packers, ending a tremendous 13-year run that featured 92 wins, two conference titles, and four top-10 finishes. Longtime Devine assistant Al Onofrio would take over when Devine left.

After a 1-10 reset in his first season in charge, Uncle Al, as he was called, unleashed five of the most mystifying seasons imaginable.

In 1972, the Tigers beat No. 8 Notre Dame and No. 12 Iowa State. In 1973, they beat No. 2 Nebraska and No. 19 SMU. In 1974, No. 5 Nebraska and No. 7 Arizona State were the victims. In 1975, Mizzou handed Alabama its only loss of the season in a 20-7 nationally televised pasting in Birmingham. In 1976, the Tigers pummeled USC in Los Angeles in week one (the Trojans' only loss of the year), won at No. 2 Ohio State two weeks later, and beat No. 3 Nebraska and No. 14 Colorado.

Despite these incredible wins, Mizzou never finished better than 8-4 in any of these seasons because, while the Tigers took on all comers in non-conference play, they almost always ran out of gas before November. And they almost always lost to rival Kansas.

When Onofrio had a more customary season in 1977 – 2-5 against teams with winning records, losses by double digits to USC and Nebraska, and of course another season-ending loss to Kansas – that was the end. Onofrio was done, replaced by Washington State head coach and former Nebraska defensive back Warren Powers. The 37-year old had spent eight years as NU's defensive backs coach under both Bob Devaney and Tom Osborne before heading to Washington at the start of 1977.

Rowe: "Watch this, watch Wilder. We've said it once, we've said it a thousand times: This guy is just tremendous. He's one of the greatest backs in the Big 8. How he was overlooked for second-team or honorable mention, I'll never know."

Powers inherited a team without the depth of an Oklahoma or Nebraska, but the Tigers had star power. Future Seattle Mariners outfielder Phil Bradley would throw for 1,780 yards and rush for

301 at quarterback, future second-round pick James Wilder and future fifth-round pick Earl Gant would combine for 1,662 rushing yards, future Minnesota Vikings return man Leo Lewis would catch 28 passes for 376 yards, and future NFL Hall-of-Fame tight end Kellen Winslow would lead the team with 479 receiving yards and six touchdowns. Powers would deploy this skill position talent with his own preferred offense, the veer.

Mizzou began its campaign with a trip to South Bend to face its former coach, Devine, and the defending national champions. Joe Montana had emerged three games into the 1977 season and turned the Irish into the best team in the country. They were early favorites to repeat in 1978. Montana was back, and Notre Dame was a 17-point favorite.

Hoping to inspire his defense, Powers told his offense that he only needed a field goal from them because they were going to shut the Fighting Irish out. Somehow, they did just that. Notre Dame would create nine solid scoring opportunities, but they were always left needing one more play.

The game was scoreless at halftime, but an iffy punt gave Notre Dame the ball near midfield early in the third quarter. The Irish quickly advanced to the Mizzou 11 and elected to go for it on fourth-and-1; Mizzou stuffed a Montana sneak. The Tigers immediately lost a fumble but, three plays later, stuffed Notre Dame on fourth-and-short once more. Notre Dame forced a three-and-out, and Montana, just 4-for-17 on the day, completed a pass to the Mizzou 3. But receiver Kris Gaines, fed up with trash-talking Mizzou cornerback Russ Calabrese, slapped Calabrese on the helmet after his big gain and drew a personal foul penalty. Sent back to the 18, Notre Dame went three-and-out and attempted a field goal … only to bobble the snap.

Late in the third quarter, the frustrated Irish defense finally cracked. A couple of screen passes to Gant and a third-down completion to David Newman put Mizzou in field goal range, and Jeff Brockhaus split the uprights on a 33-yarder. Powers had his field goal. After one more defensive stand, Notre Dame muffed a punt and Missouri recovered and ran out the clock. Final score: Missouri 3, Notre Dame 0. Fans back in Columbia sneaked into Memorial Stadium and tore down the goalposts.

The celebration was short-lived, however, because a week after playing No. 5 Notre Dame, it was time to welcome Bear Bryant and No. 1 Alabama to town.

In front of a record crowd of 73,655 at Faurot Field, Bama charged to a 17-0 lead, then watched it disappear. Gant scored to make it 17-7, and after an Alabama punt, Bradley hit the right sideline on an option keeper and raced for a 69-yard touchdown. Two plays later, Calabrese stepped in front of a Jeff Rutledge out route and weaved into the end zone for a pick six. The Tigers would add a field goal and zip into the locker room with an out-of-nowhere 20-17 halftime lead. There was another upset in the works.

Unfortunately, for Missouri, whatever fire Bryant was able to light under his team in the locker room burned pretty hot. E.J. Junior blocked a Monte Montgomery punt, and Ricky Gilliland returned it 35 yards for a touchdown. Mizzou fumbled, and Alabama scored. Mizzou fumbled again, and Alabama scored again. The Tigers faded to a 38-20 loss.

The first test of Missouri's resilience went well. Against visiting Ole Miss, Missouri rushed for 327 yards, passed for 207 (Bradley was 14-for-19), and sacked Rebel quarterbacks 10 times. It took four Missouri fumbles to keep this 45-14 game within 31 points. Next up: a trip to Norman to face the third top-five team (and second No. 1) of the month.

With Alabama losing to USC, Oklahoma was the new top team in the country, and the Sooners weren't taking any chances against the giant-killing (or at least giant-*threatening*) Tigers. Billy Sims and the Sooner offense began the game with three straight touchdown drives of 80-plus yards and raced to a 21-0 lead on the way to a 45-23 win. Mizzou scared countless giants in the 1970s but could never get a read on Barry Switzer's Sooners.

After returning home and destroying a bad Illinois team, 45-3, Missouri hosted an Iowa State team that was peaking under Earle Bruce. A few months later, Bruce would accept the Ohio State job, replacing the departing Woody Hayes. But he had the Cyclones ranked 20th when they visited Columbia. The Tigers raced to a 19-7 halftime lead but went conservative on offense, and after cutting the lead to 19-13, Iowa State was driving with under 10 minutes left. But Mizzou end Wendell Ray, father of future Tiger All-American Shane Ray, sniffed out a trick play pass from halfback Dexter Green and picked it off. A Gant touchdown finally put the game out of reach, 26-13. A 56-14 romp at Kansas State followed.

Missouri returned home and again took its foot off the gas. In front of 71,096 in Columbia, the Tigers took a 27-7 lead on Bill Mallory's 5-2 Colorado Buffaloes late in the third quarter. The Tigers had a 6-2 record and a top-10 ranking in their sights, but Colorado scored twice to make it 27-21, and after a Mizzou three-and-out, Colorado scored once more to take a one-point lead. Mizzou responded by driving into CU territory, but after Gant dropped a sure touchdown pass, a shaky field goal snap meant a 42-yard field goal attempt by Brockhaus fell well short. After fighting so hard against so many ranked teams, the Tigers had once again tripped up against an unranked foe. To make matters worse, an increasingly banged up Mizzou squad then went to Stillwater and lost to 2-6 Oklahoma State, 35-20.

After they held hopes for a major bowl bid in mid-October, it looked like the 5-4 Tigers wouldn't go bowling at all. And even after the Tigers destroyed the hated Kansas Jayhawks, 48-0, back in Columbia – Gant and Wilder combined for 294 yards and six touchdowns – Mizzou would still probably have to pull a huge upset of No. 2 Nebraska in Lincoln to return to the postseason for the first time in a half-decade.

Bassett: "Bradley's gonna pass. HE'S GOT WINSLOW OVER THE MIDDLE. COMPLETE! AT THE 20 … 15 … 14 … FIRST DOWN." Rowe: "ALRIGHT, KELLEN. Here we go again! The famous pass – Phil Bradley to Kellen Winslow! We just sent Kellen down the seam … guy's sittin' right there, behind the linebackers, in front of the defensive backs. A guy that high, you've gotta give him room." Bassett: "Oh, I can't stand it. What a football game we've got today."

Sometimes games become classics simply because the stakes are so high. Sometimes it's because they're just so intensely well-played. For Missouri's 35-31 win over Nebraska, it was both. Tom Osborne's Cornhuskers were one win from a shot at the national title after years of taking a backseat to Oklahoma. And on the first play of the game, NU's Rick Berns raced 82 yards for a touchdown. This was going to be the year that Osborne escaped Bob Devaney's shadow.

Mizzou responded with an easy touchdown drive, capped by a nine-yard Wilder score. Led again by Berns, NU struck right back. Bradley found a tiptoeing Winslow in the corner of the end zone, and at halftime, Mizzou trailed by just three.

The Nebraska lead had expanded to 10 when Bradley, on fourth-and-goal from the 1, bobbled the snap; he recovered just enough to stick the ball in Wilder's belly, however; the Sikeston Train dove in to cut the lead to 24-21. Mizzou linebacker Chris Garlich then picked off a pass in NU territory, and a gorgeous, spinning, 27-yard run by Bradley set up another Wilder touchdown. Mizzou led for the first time. Naturally, NU immediately responded, milking seven points out of a 16-play drive.

A bad exchange between Bradley and Gant wasted a scoring opportunity, and as NU chipped away at a tired Tiger defense four yards at a time, it looked like this upset bid would come up short. But on fourth-and-5 for the Huskers from the Mizzou 27, the Tigers snuffed out a swing pass and stopped it two yards short. With the game on the line, the offense unleashed a perfect drive.

Wilder and fullback Gerry Ellis pounded away, Winslow caught a monstrous 33-yard pass up the seam, and Wilder fought to the Nebraska 6. Then, in one of the meanest plays in the sport's history, Wilder ran into a tackler at the NU 2, shoved him aside, and plunged into the end zone.

Bassett: "WILDER!" Rowe: "WILDER!" Bassett: "JIM WILDER!" Rowe and Bassett: unintelligible loud noises. Rowe: "DID YOU SEE THAT?? DID YOU SEE HIM?? DID YOU SEE HIM TAKE THAT MAN AND THROW HIM DOWN?? Bassett: "You will not believe what Wilder did." Rowe: "He had a guy wrapped around his waist, he just grabbed hold of him and threw him into the ground like he was a piece of turf!" Bassett: "Unbelievable!"

Nebraska had time to respond and did so. But on fourth-and-11 from the MU 33, with barely a minute to go, the Tiger pass rush forced an early pass from Tom Sorley, and his desperation heave fell incomplete. Mizzou had wrecked Nebraska's national title plans and sealed a Liberty Bowl date with LSU.

In Memphis, Mizzou threatened to let another one get out of its control. The Tigers from the north took a 20-3 halftime lead thanks to touchdowns by Gant and Winslow. But LSU scored twice to make it 20-15 in the closing minutes. Mizzou recovered the penultimate onside kick, however, and took the trophy.

Between 1972 and 1978, Missouri beat six top-five teams and 16 top-15 teams, and never finished better than 8-4. Despite the exhilaration at the beginning and end of the '78 season, this year still produced only an 8-4 record.

Still, the late win over NU made it seem like big things were on the horizon for Powers and the Tigers. Instead, it set a standard

Powers struggled to meet. He would go either 7-5 or 8-4 in four of the next five seasons and got dumped after his first losing year, a 3-7-1 campaign in 1984.

As so frequently happens when a program gets tired of merely being decent and makes a rash move, Mizzou fell into the wilderness, winning just 36 games over the next 12 seasons.

1980 GEORGIA

On April 7, 1980, Georgia secured the signature of a running back from Wrightsville, a town of about 2,000 in east central Georgia. The Dawgs have won plenty of recruiting battles in the state's small towns by simply showing up, but this recruitment lasted a little bit longer than most. Head coach Vince Dooley had to fend off a majority of the nation's powers – Alabama, USC, Ohio State – along with other local schools like Clemson and Georgia Tech. This back was named the nation's best; he was a 6'2, 216-pound behemoth who had, the previous fall, rushed for 3,167 yards and 45 touchdowns while leading Johnson County High School to the Georgia Class A state title.

You could say that Georgia won the 1980 national title the day Herschel Walker signed.

Even blue-chip freshmen usually take a while to become acclimated, to grow into a large role within the game of college football. Hell, until recent years, freshmen weren't even allowed to play;

234

they had to wait until their sophomore seasons to make an impact. Though the rules changed, most coaches still lived with the belief that freshmen had to be eased in, that you wouldn't be able to count on them to make a difference that early in their respective careers.

Usually, this approach was acceptable, and for one simple reason: Most recruits weren't Walker.

A former Auburn quarterback and Auburn assistant, Dooley took over for Johnny Griffith in 1964, when UGA was at a low ebb. The Dawgs had finished ranked only once since 1949, but by his third year, Dooley had the Bulldogs back in the top five. Georgia won the SEC in 1966 and 1968, but results had grown more sporadic in the 1970s, as integration changed life for many SEC programs. The Dawgs went 19-5 in 1975-76, then fell to 5-6 in 1977. They went 9-2-1 in 1978, then fell to 6-5. They were ranked 16th in the preseason AP poll heading into 1980, and honestly, they may have indeed been the 16th-best team in the country. But throughout one of the wildest, most unlikely runs in the sport's history, Walker carried a heavier load than anyone thought imaginable, and the Dawgs consistently found a way to make the one play they needed to make.

Absolutely, positively necessary play No. 1: Pat McShea recovers a Glen Ford fumble.

The first game of the season took place in front of the largest crowd to ever watch a football game in the South. A crowd of 95,288 filled Knoxville's Neyland Stadium to watch Tennessee host Dooley's Dawgs, and the home crowd was happy for a while. Georgia quarterback Buck Belue fumbled the ball in the end zone in the second quarter for a safety, and Tennessee led 9-0 at halftime. The Vols quickly expanded the lead to 15-0, but after Georgia got a safety of its own when UT fumbled out of the end zone, Walker took over.

His first career touchdown was perhaps his most memorable; Walker ran through an ankle tackle at the line of scrimmage and, at the 5, ran over Tennessee safety Bill Bates like he was driving a corn harvester. Bates, by the way, would go on to become an all-pro safety for the Dallas Cowboys. Walker flattened him like Bates was an overwhelmed 15-year old playing against Johnson County High.

Legendary Georgia announcer Larry Munson yelped, "My God Almighty … he drove right over orange shirts just driving and running with those big thighs! My God, a freshman!" Walker would score again on a nine-yard sweep to give Georgia a 16-15 lead and would finish with 84 yards. He had begun the game on the third string; he would never be anything less than a first-stringer again.

Georgia still had work to do, though. As the minutes wound down, Tennessee moved the ball inside the Georgia red zone and all the way to the 1. But Ford fumbled, and McShea recovered. Georgia had only gained 240 total yards to UT's 310, but four Vol fumbles made as much of a difference as Walker did.

Walker made his home debut in front of 60,000 at Sanford Stadium the next weekend, and against a weak Texas A&M team, the Dawgs left nothing to doubt. Walker rushed for 145 yards and three touchdowns and shook off tackler after tackler on a 76-yard burst late in the third quarter.

Absolutely, positively necessary play No. 2: Frank Ros tips a Clemson pass into the air, and Jeff Hipp picks it off.

Now 10th in the country, Georgia played host to rival Clemson. The Dawgs and Tigers were in the middle of a crazy series of tight non-conference battles, and this one was no different. Early on, Georgia's Scott Woerner nearly won the game by himself. He returned a punt 67 yards for a touchdown, then made a leaping interception in the Georgia end zone and raced 98 yards to set up a short Belue touchdown.

Georgia led 14-0 in the first quarter, but despite Walker ending up with 121 rushing yards, the Dawg offense was stagnant. Clemson was able to cut the lead to 20-16 by the fourth quarter and was driving to possibly take the lead. However, Ros tipped a ball at the line of scrimmage and Hipp won a fight for the ball at the UGA 1. A 20-yard Walker run allowed UGA to run out the clock on a second narrow victory.

Another home game, this time against a weak TCU squad, offered a little bit of a respite. Belue threw two touchdown passes and, nursing a sprained ankle, Walker carried just nine times for 69 yards in a 34-3 win. But while the Dawgs were now sixth in the country, the challenges would continue.

Absolutely, positively necessary play No. 3: Carnie Norris rips off a 20-yard run against Ole Miss.

"It never seems to come easy," Dooley told media after Georgia's 28-21 win over Ole Miss. The Rebels were not doing very well under third-year head coach Steve Sloan and had already lost at home to the Texas A&M team that couldn't hang with Georgia. They trailed by just three heading into the fourth quarter.

Amp Arnold caught a 34-yard pass from Belue, and the Dawgs led 17-0 in the closing seconds of the first half. But James Otis picked off a Belue pass and returned it 32 yards for a score with just nine seconds left in the second quarter, and Rebel quarterback John Fourcade scored on a one-yard sneak midway through the third. A 25-yard Walker run set up a 43-yard Rex Robinson field goal to stretch UGA's lead back to 20-14, but the game wasn't out of reach until third-string running back Carnie Norris' 20-yard run set up a one-yard Belue touchdown with six minutes left. A late Ole Miss touchdown made the final score 28-21.

Norris finished with 15 carries for 150 yards, picking up the slack beautifully for Walker.

The extra rest for Walker paid off. Over the next two weeks, he would rush for 418 yards and four touchdowns as the Dawgs beat

Vanderbilt 41-0 and Kentucky 27-0. That set up the biggest game of the season to date.

Absolutely, positively necessary play No. 4: Tim Parks recovers a George Rogers fumble at the Georgia 16.

South Carolina came to Athens on a roll. Behind eventual Heisman winner (and Georgia native) George Rogers, the Gamecocks were 6-1. Rogers had rushed for 142 yards in a 17-14 upset of Michigan in Ann Arbor, and their No. 14 ranking was their highest since 1959.

Against Georgia, Rogers was good, rushing 35 times for 168 yards. But the game was mainly remembered for two plays. On the third play of the third quarter, with Georgia leading by just a 3-0 margin, Walker exploded down the right sideline. Three different Gamecock defenders looked like they had an angle to catch him, and none did. The 76-yard score made it 10-0. It showcased Walker's speed in the same way that his harvesting of Bates showed his power.

Walker finished with 219 yards on 43 carries, but Georgia's lead shrank to 13-10, and South Carolina was driving with five minutes left. Once again, the resourceful Georgia defense, the Junkyard Dawgs, saved the day. Rogers powered what could have been a game-winning drive, but he was shaken up on a run inside the 20. On his final carry of the day, the ball was stripped and flew into the air. Tim Parks fell on it, and after a roughing the punter penalty gave Georgia one last break, Walker plowed away at the rest of the clock.

Rogers would go on to win the Heisman, in part because Heisman voters just couldn't fathom giving it to a freshman.

Absolutely, positively necessary play No. 5: Lindsay Scott runs and runs.

Walker did everything he could against Florida the next week in

Jacksonville. Georgia still needed more. His 37 carries and 238 yards gave him the school's single-season rushing record – In the ninth game of the season! Despite battling injury for a couple of weeks! – and his 72-yard run opened the scoring in the first quarter. But Georgia still found itself trailing Charley Pell's 20th ranked Gators, 21-20, in the closing minutes. Rival Georgia Tech tied No. 1 Notre Dame, so the Dawgs could ascend to No. 1 for the first time since 1942 with a win. But a Florida punt bounced out of bounds at the UGA 8 with 1:35 left.

On first down, Belue scrambled but found no one open and got pushed out of bounds at the 7. On second down, he threw incomplete to the sideline. At this point, he was 6-for-15 for 52 yards, a touchdown, and two interceptions.

Again rolling to his right, however, Belue then threw the most famous pass of his life. Take it away, Larry Munson: "Buck back, third down on the eight. In trouble! Got a block behind him. Gonna throw on the run ... complete on the 25 ... to the 30 ... Lindsay Scott 35, 40 ... Lindsay Scott 45, 50, 45, 40. Run, Lindsay! 25, 20, 15, 10, 5, Lindsay Scott! Lindsay Scott! Lindsay Scott!"

It went down in history as "Run, Lindsay, Run!", maybe the most celebrated play in school history. Belue rolled to his right, then threw back toward the middle of the field to Scott, who was running the opposite direction of most of the defenders. He turned the corner and raced up the left flank for the game-winning touchdown – a member of UGA's 400-meter relay team, he was not going to get caught. He was immediately mobbed by fans in the end zone.

UGA followed one huge rivalry game with another, visiting Auburn on November 15 as the No. 1 team in the country. Auburn did a pretty good job of playing spoiler, trailing just 10-7 near the end of the second quarter. The Dawgs had made it to the Auburn 1 with nine seconds left in the half, but Belue fumbled the snap in what was supposed to be the last play before attempting a field goal. Georgia didn't have any timeouts, but the refs had to stop the clock to clear up the pile, and that gave Belue time to get his team lined up as soon as the ball was placed. With one second left, Belue took the snap and threw to Norris Brown for a touchdown and a 17-7 lead.

Auburn attempted a surprise onside kick to start the second half, but Georgia recovered it and drove 34 yards for the score. Walker rushed for just 77 yards, but he wasn't needed: Georgia went up 24 points before a couple of late Auburn touchdowns made the final score 31-21.

The Georgia Tech game was the Walker Show. UGA wrapped up an undefeated regular season by racing to a 17-0 halftime lead and winning 38-20. Walker rushed 35 times for 205 yards, and his 65-yard, fourth-quarter touchdown both iced the game and set the NCAA's single-season freshman rushing record at 1,610 yards.

Absolutely, positively necessary play No. 6: Trainers pop Herschel Walker's shoulder back into place.

On Georgia's second play from scrimmage in the Sugar Bowl against No. 7 Notre Dame, the greatest freshman running back ever separated his shoulder. With so many close wins and only two victories over ranked teams, the Bulldogs were seen as a relatively soft No. 1. It wasn't hard to find someone predicting the 9-1-1 Irish to take down the Dawgs, and that was with a full-strength Walker.

The record-setter barely missed any time. His shoulder was popped back in on the sideline, and he carried the ball 36 punishing times for 153 yards. Ridiculous.

Late in the first quarter, Rex Robinson nailed a 46-yard field goal to tie the game at 3-3, and the Irish fumbled the ensuing kickoff. UGA recovered at the 1 and took a 10-3 lead on a diving Walker touchdown. Frank Ros soon forced a fumble, and Chris Welton recovered. Walker scored to make it 17-3, and the game took on the typical Georgia script: UGA takes an early lead, the opponent begins to come back, and Georgia's defense makes repeated stops near the end. Up 17-10 in the final period, Georgia came up with a big third-down sack to force a field goal that missed, and on ND's final surge, Scott Woerner, the All-American and hero of the Clemson game, picked off a fourth-down pass. For the first time in 38 years, Georgia was national champion.

This wasn't the best Vince Dooley squad. Hell, it probably wasn't even the best *Herschel Walker* squad – you could make the case that either the 10-2 team of 1981 or the 11-1 team of 1982 was better. But this team simply refused to lose. It had the best player in the country (Heisman voting be damned), and just about every player on the team made a key play at a key time. While everybody else in the country slipped up at an inopportune time, Georgia simply won every game on the schedule and made both Walker and Dooley immortal in the process.

1981 FLORIDA STATE

It probably isn't a coincidence that three of the more recent additions to college football's ruling class – Florida, Florida State, Miami – all hail from one of the most talent-rich states in the country. Segregation kept the in-state schools from taking full advantage of the talent in their backyard; both Midwestern schools and Historically Black Colleges and Universities were able to raid the state and build long-term connections that FSU and company could not immediately overcome.

However, with charismatic coaches like Miami's Howard Schnellenberger and Florida's Charley Pell (both hired in 1979) and, of course, FSU's Bobby Bowden, the recruiting tide began to turn. In the history of the AP poll, these three schools had combined for two top-10 finishes before 1979, a span of more than four decades. But in the 35 seasons between 1979 and 2013, they would combine for 11 national titles and 50 top-five finishes.

Each of these three schools took their own approach to dominance.

Florida's path took a little bit longer thanks to an extended bout with NCAA sanctions in the 1980s. But for Florida State, the turnaround began pretty quickly after Bowden came to town.

The Seminoles had fallen into a spectacular funk. Larry Jones was dismissed after going 0-11 in 1973, and in two years, Darrell Mudra – engineer of turnarounds at Adams State, North Dakota State, Arizona, and Western Illinois – had gone just 4-18. Athletic administrators announced that they did not intend to fire him, but a group of boosters, led by Tallahassee lawyer James Smith, raised nearly $100,000 to pay off the rest of Mudra's $30,000/year contract. Money talked.

FSU indeed dismissed Mudra, and after getting turned down by Pittsburgh's Johnny Majors and Indiana's Lee Corso (an FSU alum and future ESPN *College GameDay* stalwart), the school interviewed four men: former FSU coach Bill Peterson (winner of 62 games in 11 seasons before taking the Rice job in 1971), Tallahassee Leon High School coach Gene Cox, ECU head coach Pat Dye, and Bowden, a former FSU receivers coach who had spent the last six years at West Virginia. Bowden had found himself in the hot seat following a 4-7 campaign in 1974, but bounced back to go 9-3 the next year.

On January 12, Bowden took the job, saying to the media about the school's impatient, desperate-to-win fan base, "There's only one answer and that's to win. You can go around and be nice, but a coach is judged by winning. The people around here want to win. I'm going to lose some and these people are going to get on me." He was right, eventually. But it wasn't until the mid-2000s when he started to lose a little bit too much.

Bowden undertook a major youth movement out of the gates and went just 5-6 in 1976, but his first batch of stars quickly began to thrive, going 10-2 in 1977, 11-1 in 1979, and 10-2 in 1980. The Seminoles lost to Barry Switzer's Oklahoma Sooners in the Orange Bowl in both 1979 and 1980 but finished in the top 10 both years.

In 1981, Bowden faced two incredible challenges: rebuilding and taking on the most difficult schedule imaginable. FSU had produced six All-Americans in 1980: offensive lineman Ken Lanier, defensive tackle Ron Simmons, linebacker Reggie Herring, defensive back Bobby Butler, kicker Bill Capece, and punter Rohn Stark. In 1981, only Stark remained. A defense that had allowed just 8.6 points per game in 1980 would replace eight starters in all; the Noles would allow 26 points per game in 1981.

FSU's attitude was to schedule like a power team, and the Noles became even more aggressive with Bowden in charge. In 1978, they thumped Oklahoma State, Miami, and Florida, but lost to Houston, Mississippi State, and No. 15 Pitt. In 1979, they whooped Arizona State, Miami, Mississippi State, and South Carolina and beat LSU and Florida on the road. In 1980, they won at No. 3 Nebraska and LSU and beat No. 4 Pitt and Florida at home.

As he rebuilt his two-deep in the winter of 1981, Bowden faced down a truly ridiculous slate. That coming fall, the Seminoles would play Nebraska, Ohio State, Notre Dame, Pitt, and LSU on the road. Consecutively. "It's going to be an interesting year," he told media following the 1981 Orange Bowl loss. "That's why I've got a five-year contract."

The season's warm up went well enough, as FSU allowed only five combined points in wins over Louisville and Memphis. The offense was taking its time figuring things out, however. The Noles beat UL 17-0 and UM 10-5, averaging only 316 yards per game in the process.

The reality check came soon after. In the first game of the amazing five-game road trip, FSU's offense faltered repeatedly. No. 17 Nebraska led just 10-7 at halftime but returned a punt and a fumble for touchdowns in the third quarter, then sealed a 34-14 win with a 94-yard run by future San Francisco 49er Roger Craig.

FSU got a bye week following the trip to Lincoln, and the regrouping time paid off: The Noles were ready for Octoberfest. Bowden's squad next flew to Columbus to face No. 7 Ohio State and did things to the Buckeye run game that a team hadn't done in decades. OSU rushed 31 times for just 38 yards, rendered completely reliant on quarterback Art Schlichter's arm. Meanwhile, Bowden elected to attack the edges of Ohio State's defense, attempting to take advantage of quarterback Rick Stockstill's arm – the future Middle Tennessee head coach would end up an honorable mention All-American – and an inexperienced Ohio State secondary, coached by a young assistant (and future Alabama dynasty creator) named Nick Saban.

Schlichter finished 31-for-52 for 458 yards, and Stockstill was 15-for-41 for 299. Both teams finished with 496 yards. The difference ended up coming down to special teams and a goal line stand.

FSU's Ron Hester blocked and returned a punt for a touchdown in the first quarter, and holder Kelly Lowrey took a fake field goal five yards for another score in the second. The Noles led 30-21 when a Schlichter bomb got OSU to the FSU 2. However, FSU made a dramatic goal line stand (three run stuffs, followed by a dropped pass on fourth down) and put the game away with a 99-yard touchdown drive.

FSU won, 36-27. It was the Seminoles' first ever game against a Big Ten team, and it was a landmark victory. They wouldn't have to wait very long for another one.

The first meeting with Notre Dame went just as well. Following Dan Devine's retirement, the Fighting Irish were in Year 1 of a fascinating trial: Able to select just about any coach in the country to replace Devine, the school chose Gerry Faust, head coach of Moeller High School in Cincinnati, a football dynasty that had won four national prep titles and five state titles in six years. It was called "The Bold Experiment." It would end up a disaster. Ranked first in the country by the second week of the season, the Irish fell on the road to Michigan and Purdue and would go on to finish 5-6 in 1981 and just 30-26-1 in five years under Faust.

When FSU came to South Bend, though, it still felt like a grand opportunity. Driven by backs Ricky Williams and Michael Whiting, who combined for 206 yards on 30 carries, FSU outgained Notre Dame by more than 100 yards. Three Stockstill interceptions and a missed field goal kept the game tied at 13-13 midway through the fourth quarter. Then, James Harris picked off Notre Dame's Blair Kiel, and Stockstill hit Whiting with a five-yard touchdown pass with 7:41 left. Final score: FSU 19, Notre Dame 13.

Bowden called it the biggest win of his career. He admitted that he figured his team would be 2-3 at that point; instead, the Noles were 4-1 and drawing national title buzz.

The hype wouldn't last long, however, because the tests weren't over. The next trip was to No. 3 Pitt, a team looking for revenge. In 1980, the Seminoles had handed the Panthers their only loss of the season, denying them a second national title in five years. Scores on two returns (interception, punt) gave Pitt a 21-0 second-quarter lead, and two third-quarter touchdown passes by Pitt's Dan Marino turned this into a 42-14 rout.

FSU still finished with a winning record on its brutal road trip, though. The fifth of the consecutive road games sent the Noles to Baton Rouge, where Jerry Stovall's struggling Tigers awaited. Forced to again prove their resilience, the Noles did so, and quickly. Stockstill threw touchdown passes to Dennis McKinnon and Phil Williams, and freshman Greg Allen scored on a 15-yard run to put FSU up 24-7 at half.

Allen was the story of the 38-14 win – he carried 31 times for 202 yards, and the next week he rushed 32 times for 322 against Western Carolina. He had to carry that many times because the defense had fallen apart and Stockstill was struggling, but he did what was needed in a 56-31 win.

Unfortunately, though Allen would earn All-American status in the future and finish his FSU career with 3,769 yards and 43 touchdowns, he wasn't much help the rest of the year. Neither was anyone else. The team completely ran out of gas down the home stretch. Of course it did. This was a young team, thin on experience, and it had just run through an incredible gauntlet. The defense gave way against Western Carolina, and the offense began to do the same the next week against No. 13 Miami in Tallahassee. Schnellenberger's Hurricanes blocked three kicks (two field goals and a PAT), and that, plus a failed FSU two-point conversion, made the difference in a 27-19 Miami win. It was Bowden's second straight loss to Schnelly.

And then things got worse. Southern Miss, 8-0-1 with a tie at No. 7 Alabama, came to town with a point to prove. The Golden Eagles were ranked 14th and would rise to ninth after putting together maybe the program's most impressive performance ever. They led FSU 51-0 midway through the third quarter – *In Tallahassee! On ABC!* – before Seminole backup Blair Williams threw a couple of garbage time touchdowns. USM won, 58-14, and took the Tangerine Bowl bid that looked intended for FSU.

With nothing to play for and nothing in the tank, FSU limped to Gainesville and took its first loss in five tries to rival Florida. Stockstill completed five passes to his team and three to Florida in a 35-3 Gator romp.

In 34 seasons as Florida State's head coach, Bobby Bowden won fewer than seven games just twice: in his first season and in 1981. This was an endurance test more than it was a football season, and looking at November results, the Seminoles didn't necessarily pass. But though they lacked staying power, they earned respect and a "road warriors" reputation. The wins over Ohio State and Notre Dame were their most symbolic yet under Bowden.

The scheduling would never be *this* ridiculous again, but the challenges continued. FSU went back to Ohio State and won again in 1982. They went back to LSU the next two years and split. They went back to Nebraska in 1985 and 1986, then went to Michigan as well in 1986. The schedules kept the win totals tamped down – they were a decent-not-great 39-18-3 from 1982-86 – but recruits saw them fighting blue blood after blue blood, and more and more of them signed with FSU. And when the Noles broke back through with an 11-1 campaign in 1987, they remained in the top five every year thereafter until 2001. It was perhaps the most sustained run of greatness ever.

Florida State agreed to play anybody, anytime, anywhere, to prove they were worthy. Eventually, they were.

1982 PITTSBURGH

Fourth-and-5 from the Georgia 33, 42 seconds remaining. Pitt has dictated the entire Sugar Bowl, outgaining Vince Dooley's second-ranked Bulldogs by more than 200 yards. The Panthers have held junior Herschel Walker well under 4 yards per carry, and star quarterback Dan Marino is a decent 25-for-40 for 228 yards against a good UGA defense. But five turnovers have hurt the cause, to say the least, and Pitt trails, 20-17.

Marino takes the snap, and his blockers pick up an all-out blitz. Instead of checking down for first-down yardage to one of his backs crossing near the line of scrimmage, he looks deep and fires a perfect ball to receiver-turned-tight-end John Brown in the end zone. Touchdown. Ballgame. In that moment, Pitt becomes the preseason No. 1 team for 1982.

Heading into 1982, the Panthers returned 18 starters from a 1981 team that began the season 10-0 and spent a month ranked No. 1. The program was a proven entity, with five top-10 finishes in the last six years. Marino had the strongest arm anyone had ever seen, and he was a likely top pick in the 1983 NFL Draft.

The talent in the trenches was ridiculous. An incredible defensive line was headlined by future pros Bill Maas, Chris Doleman, and Dave Puzzouli and future All-American J.C. Pelusi. The offensive line featured tackles Jimbo Covert (the sixth pick in the 1983 draft) and Bill Fralic (the second pick in the 1985 draft). Six of Marino's top seven receiving targets were back, too, including running back Bryan Thomas (1,132 rushing yards and 451 receiving yards in 1981), split end Julius Dawkins (767 receiving yards) and Brown (530 receiving yards).

Just about the only thing Pitt wouldn't return in 1982 was its head coach. After allegedly getting turned down by Michigan's Bo Schembechler, Texas A&M opened its checkbook and made Jackie Sherrill the most well-paid coach in college football. Pitt had increased its spending and commitment over the past decade, but it wasn't ready to take that step. Instead, Sherrill's celebrated defensive coordinator, Foge Fazio, took the reins. On paper, it made perfect sense. On paper, *everything* about this team made sense.

The 1982 season would represent the last go-round for Marino, Covert, Thomas, Puzzuoli, cornerback Tim Lewis, and a class of Panthers that had come oh, so close, losing exactly once in each of the last three seasons. Their loss in 1979 was in Week 2 at North Carolina, before Marino had fully staked out the starting job. The 1980 loss at Florida State featured four lost fumbles. And in 1981, they lost only at the end of the season, blinking in the face of expectations in the biggest Pitt-Penn State game ever. But as bad as the Penn State loss was – and 48-14, at home, as the top-ranked team in the country is awfully bad – the Sugar Bowl win had repaired most of the damage.

An experienced team like this often circles the wagons and lives up to hype. But a sport that features a pointy ball and 22 players on the field – almost all of whom are 18- to 22-year old males, some of the least stable, least predictable people on the planet – doesn't always follow a predictable story line.

The pressure was immense heading into the fall. Thanks to the 1970s success of not only the Panthers, but also the NFL's Steelers and MLB's Pirates, Pittsburgh natives were accustomed to championships and fulfilled expectations. And unlike football heavyweights in towns like Tuscaloosa, Lincoln, Norman, Athens, they had big-city media (and the attention that goes with it) right in their backyard. As the season began, it wasn't enough to beat strong opponents – the slate began with preseason No. 5 UNC and featured three ranked teams and Florida State in the first four games. The Panthers had to look the part at all times.

They did not. Fazio, much less of a players' coach than Sherrill, struggled to keep his players on the same page; meanwhile, he was spending quite a bit of time at a nearby hospital, where his wife Norma was fighting (and beating) cancer.

Defense wasn't an issue. Against North Carolina in the season opener, in front of a sellout crowd of 54,449 at the Steelers' Three Rivers Stadium, the Panthers held star running back Kelvin Bryant to 58 yards on 16 carries and limited the Tar Heels to 247 total yards and 12 first downs. That will win you the game just about every time.

Unfortunately, Pitt's offense was completely out of sorts. Marino completed 15 of 27 passes for just 127 yards and four interceptions. He was a perfect 4-for-4 on a scoring drive that finished with a four-yard toss to Thomas. However, that was Pitt's only score in a 7-6 win.

Marino rebounded at Florida State (13-for-22, 133 yards, two touchdowns, one interception), but weather dictated a strategy change. A massive second-half downpour meant the Panthers had to lean on Thomas and fullback Marlon McIntyre, who combined for 40 carries and 156 yards. FSU jumped out to a 10-0 lead, but Pitt took control when the weather went south and turned a 17-17 tie into a 37-17 win.

A Doak Campbell Stadium record crowd of 56,236 watched the Pitt-FSU game; the next week, it was the same story. The Panthers traveled to Champaign to take on No. 19 Illinois, and 71,547 awaited, the second-largest crowd in Memorial Stadium history. The game was billed as a passing showcase – Marino vs. Illinois' star quarterback Tony Eason – but the defenses stole the show. Marino threw four more interceptions in 35 passes, and Eason threw five in 58. Puzzuoli took an interception 95 yards for a score, just as Illinois was about to increase its 3-0 lead. Doleman sacked Eason three times (Eason was brought down nine times in all), but it took Pitt a while to pull away to a 20-3 win. Two of Marino's picks were thrown in the red zone, wiping likely scores off the board.

The first pass of Marino's career was intercepted. The second nearly was, too. The third was a touchdown pass. That was an accurate way of describing what was to come over his four seasons. He had always had a problem with picks. He had thrown 46 of them in his first three seasons, but he had offset that with 62 touchdowns and 6,165 yards. His arm was incredible, and he trusted it too much sometimes, especially on deep balls. But that was all part of the Marino package – wins, big plays, and an occasionally misplaced desire for even more big plays. He would go for the win at all times, and he was unafraid of losing. (He rarely lost.) To both his credit and detriment, interceptions never seemed to dampen his confidence.

Still, nine picks in three games were quite a bit. And he threw two more at Pitt Stadium in October 2's Backyard Brawl. In their third year under Don Nehlen, the West Virginia Mountaineers were quickly picking up steam, and they had Pitt dead to rights when future Buffalo Bill Darryl Talley blocked a punt and recovered it in the end zone for a touchdown. Early in the fourth quarter, WVU suddenly led the preseason No. 1 team, 13-0. Boos rained down

John Short (1970 Dartmouth)

Freddie Solomon (1972 Tampa)

The Big House (1973 Michigan)

Randy Walker coaching his alma mater (1974 Miami-Ohio)

The 1970s Giant Killers (1978 Missouri)

Herschel Walker (1980 Georgia)

Herschel Walker (1980 Georgia)

Florida State vs. Ohio State (1981)

Dan Marino (1982 Pittsburgh)

Doug Flutie (1984 Boston College)

Keith Jackson (1985 Oklahoma)

Errict Rhett (1991 Florida)

Steve Walsh (1988 Miami)

Don James (1991 Washington)

George Welsh (1990 Virginia)

Sam Adams (1993 Texas A&M)

Brent Moss (1993 Wisconsin)

Brook Berringer (1994 Nebraska)

The Blackshirts (1994 Nebraska)

Ahmed Plummer (1998 Ohio State)

Michael Vick (1999 Virginia Tech)

Carson Palmer (2002 USC)

Dennis Dixon (2007 Oregon)

Kellen Moore (2010 Boise State)

Shea McClellin (2010 Boise State)

Tyrann Mathieu (2011 LSU)

Ricardo Louis (2013 Auburn)

The Kick Six (2013 Auburn)

Vince Young (2004 Texas)

on Marino as he walked off the field before the punt. But Talley's score finally lit a fire. Pitt unleashed an 83-yard drive, capped by a three-yard Thomas touchdown, to cut WVU's lead to six, and on the Mountaineers' following possession, a bad exchange between second-string center Billy Legg and quarterback Jeff Hostetler led to a Pitt fumble recovery. The Panthers drove 48 yards and took the lead on a 16-yard pass from Marino to Dawkins.

In the final minute, Hostetler was shoved out of his end zone by Maas for a safety to make it 16-13, but WVU got one last chance by recovering an onside free kick attempt. The Mountaineers advanced to the Pitt 36 with seconds left, but Paul Woodside's 52-yard attempt at the buzzer fell inches short. The Panthers survived.

Marino completed 26 of 36 passes for 344 yards and three touchdowns (and, yes, two more interceptions) in a 38-17 win over Temple – it was tied at 17-17 late in the third quarter until the Panthers pulled away – but fan unrest continued when Pitt traveled to take on a terrible Syracuse team in New York. Dick MacPherson's Orangemen never threatened to score, gaining only 140 yards all day. But the 'Cuse D picked Marino off three times and stuffed two fourth-and-1 attempts. Pitt scored late in the first quarter but couldn't put the 14-0 win away until a one-yard plunge by Joe McCall early in the fourth.

The pressure appeared to be wearing on Fazio's team, but the Panthers still hit November unbeaten after a 63-14 win over Louisville. Marino threw two more touchdown passes – it was his 19th straight game with at least one, breaking an NCAA record – and Pitt led 49-7 at the half. Nevertheless, any good feelings soon subsided.

Gerry Faust's tenure at Notre Dame didn't have too many highlights, but his unranked Fighting Irish came to Pittsburgh and fulfilled what seemed to be a season-long prophecy: a devastating Pitt loss. In front of 60,162, Pitt led 13-10 heading into the fourth quarter, but a 54-yard touchdown pass gave the Irish the lead, and two Allen Pinkett touchdowns (one from 76 yards, one from seven) had the Panthers erupting at each other on the sideline. If you flirt with disaster for long enough, it will strike, and a 31-16 loss to this Irish team definitely qualified as a disaster.

To their credit, the Panthers rebounded when the schedule let up. Marino threw three touchdowns in a 24-6 win at Army, then threw three more in a 52-6 rout of Rutgers in Pitt's home finale. Heading to Happy Valley on Thanksgiving weekend, Pitt's season still had two goals on the table. Ranked fifth, the Panthers could still jump back into the title race with a win over second-ranked Penn State; perhaps as importantly, they could also ruin the Nittany Lions' national title hopes.

The year before, in Pitt's humiliating 48-14 loss to Penn State, all the pressure was on the top-ranked Panthers heading into the game. This time, the shoe was on the other foot. A more relaxed Pitt team took a 7-3 lead into halftime in front of a partisan crowd of 85,522 in windy conditions. But PSU took the lead on a 31-yard Todd Blackledge touchdown pass, and then added two Nick Gancitano field goals. Pitt got back to within 16-10, but one more field goal put the game away. PSU fans tore down the goal posts, and the Nittany Lions agreed to play No. 1 Georgia in the Sugar Bowl for the national title. Pitt was sent to a consolation bowl, the Cotton, to face No. 4 SMU.

Perhaps they should have just passed on a bowl bid altogether. By the end of the season, the divisions between offensive and defensive players had grown, and as tends to be the case when things go south in high-pressure situations, rumors flew. Rumblings about Marino's partying ways, alcohol issues, drug use, etc., had emerged, and while he and his teammates all passed a postseason drug test, it would supposedly go on to hurt his draft stock. (The interceptions didn't help.) Once an assumed top-five pick, Marino fell to Miami at No. 27, behind, among other quarterbacks, Illinois' Eason.

Meanwhile, tragedy struck as the semester was wrapping up: Linebacker Todd Becker, attempting to escape notice from cops storming a dorm party he wasn't supposed to be attending, leaped from a third-floor window and died.

Needless to say, the team didn't play its best game in Dallas. As always, the defense showed up, holding SMU's star running backs Eric Dickerson and Craig James to 178 yards at just 4.3 yards per carry. Marino was a decent 19-for-37 for 181 yards and just one pick. But drops were rampant, Marino's one pick was on a deflection in the SMU end zone, and Pitt could manage only a single field goal. Meanwhile, the Mustangs finally broke through for a touchdown in the fourth quarter. The final pass of Marino's Panther career came on fourth down from the SMU's 37 in the final minutes. A year earlier, he hit Brown for an incredible, defining touchdown. This time around, he threw short to Dwight Collins, who couldn't hold on.

In college football, your trajectory sometimes happens out of order. In this case, any sort of redemption came before the fall.

Pitt would go 8-3-1 in its first year post-Marino, but the disappointment of 1982 still lingered. In 1983, expectations were high again – Pitt was No. 3 in the preseason – and the stumbles were even worse. The Panthers went 3-7-1, and Fazio was gone by the end of 1985. Pitt has not finished in the top 10 since.

1984 BOSTON COLLEGE

You know the Hail Mary. It's been a feature of the American Sports Fan operating system for more than 30 years, installed right between Carl Lewis winning four golds at the 1984 Summer Olympics and the Chicago Bears doing the Super Bowl Shuffle. All someone has to do is say the words "Doug" and "Flutie" and you recall all of it – Flutie in his weird-for-a-QB No. 22 jersey bounding and leaping down the field in celebration, Gerard Phelan at the bottom of the pile, the radio call: "Here we go … here's your ballgame, folks, as Flutie takes the snap. He drops straight back, has some time … now he scrambles away from one hit … looks … uncorks a deep one for the end zone … Phelan is down there … aaaaaand DID HE GET IT? TOUCHDOWN! TOUCHDOWN! TOUCHDOWN! TOUCHDOWN, BOSTON COLLEGE. HE DID IT! HE DID IT! FLUTIE DID IT!"

It was a truly amazing sports moment. And hey, there are worse legacies. If you've got to be a one-hit wonder, this is more "Come On Eileen" than "Rico Suave," more "Baby Got Back" than "Ice Ice

Baby," more "The Message" than "How Do You Talk to an Angel."

But calling Flutie a one-hit wonder would be a massive disservice. Listed at 5'9 and hailing from nearby Natick High School, Flutie had basically one major school offer and went on to win the Heisman. He increased Boston College's admissions. He was a Rhodes Scholar finalist. He threw for over 2,000 yards in the USFL, nearly 15,000 in the NFL, and more than 41,000 in the CFL. He was not only inducted into the College Football Hall of Fame; he was also the first American inducted into Canada's Sports Hall of Fame. He played drums in a band (the Flutie Brothers Band). He had his own cereal (Flutie Flakes). His Wikipedia page is a gold mine, Hail Mary or no.

Meanwhile, distilling Boston College's incredible 1984 season down to a single play ignores countless other moments, wins, and players. This was the culmination of three years of building by Jack Bicknell and was one of two top-five finishes for the school from Chestnut Hill. And it even came with some significant regrets: In a year in which BYU won the national title simply by finishing undefeated, BC came within eight points of doing the same. That Hail Mary was very nearly a title winner.

When Bicknell took over in 1981, returning after once spending eight years as a BC assistant, the Eagles hadn't finished a season ranked in 39 years. They had only spent part of a season ranked three times. Meanwhile, Bicknell was hired despite the fact that, in five years as Maine's head coach, he was just 18-35-1.

Bicknell seemed like a washed up coach. Flutie was an unrecruited quarterback who only got a BC offer late in the recruiting cycle. BC was an afterthought program. And they made magic together.

In Flutie's sophomore year, his first as a full-time starter, the Eagles improved from 5-6 to 8-3-1. They went 9-3 and finished 19th in the AP poll in 1983. And they began 1984 in the same spot. Flutie was joined in the backfield by halfback Troy Stradford, and his receiving corps consisted of not only Phelan, but also future Dallas Cowboy Kelvin Martin and tight end Scott Gieselman. As has remained customary through the years, BC had beef up front – nose tackle Mike Ruth was one of the strongest players in college football.

The season started easily enough. Flutie threw for 330 yards and four touchdowns as BC raced ahead of Western Carolina (34-7 at halftime) and cruised to a 44-24 win. But the season began in earnest the next week, when the Eagles traveled to Birmingham to play No. 9 Alabama at Legion Field. In their third season since Bear Bryant had retired, the Crimson Tide were expecting a breakthrough under Ray Perkins. He had gone 8-4 in each of his first two years. Early on, it seemed Bama would be far too much for BC. Kerry Goode scored two first-half touchdowns – one a 25-yard run, the other an 18-yard reception – and his 99-yard kick return to start the second half gave the Tide a comfortable 31-14 advantage.

Unfortunately for Bama, Goode injured his knee soon after the kick return, and Alabama didn't score again. Flutie scored from five yards out to make it 31-21, and a short field goal made it 31-24.

The script continued to flip: Flutie hit fullback Jim Browne for the game-tying touchdown with six minutes left, and just 2:30 later, Stradford burst for 43 yards up the middle to give BC a stunning lead. A late Tony Thurman interception – his third of the day – sealed the deal.

Goode ended up lost for the season with his knee injury, and Alabama would crater to a 5-6 season, but nobody knew that at the time. And even in the post-Bryant years, going to Legion Field and beating Alabama was a sure way to get national attention. BC shot from 18th to 10th in the AP poll, and in an increasingly unpredictable season – defending champion and No. 1 Miami lost twice in three weeks, No. 2 Clemson lost twice in a row, and Nebraska, just up to No. 1 after Miami's first loss, fell to unranked Syracuse – the

Eagles were poised to move up even further.

BC crushed North Carolina, 52-20, behind 354 passing yards and six touchdowns from Flutie, and by the time Temple came to town on October 13, the Eagles were ranked fourth. They remained there after a tougher-than-expected 24-10 win over the Owls: BC trailed 10-9 until Steve Strachan scored a short touchdown and Dave Pereira put the game away with a 35-yard pick six.

Unfortunately, just as BC was beginning to understand its national title potential, the Eagles had to head to Morgantown. No. 20 WVU had beaten Flutie and the Eagles in each of the three previous years, but it looked like the story would be different this time. BC broke a 6-6 tie with a pair of touchdowns – a 24-yard run by Strachan and a 42-yard pass from Flutie to Martin – to take a 14-point lead. The advantage was 20-9 heading into the fourth quarter, but a couple of touchdowns (and failed conversions) gave the Mountaineers a sudden 21-20 advantage.

Flutie still had time to pull off another comeback. BC got the ball back with just under five minutes left, and Flutie quickly completed three passes to cross midfield. But WVU linebacker Freddie Smalls dragged him down for a sack, and two incompletions later, that was that. WVU ran out the clock and ended BC's unbeaten season. (Flutie's fourth-down pass, by the way, was defended by a backup defensive back named Rich Rodriguez, who would go on to become head coach at WVU, Michigan, and Arizona.)

BC fell out of the top 10 but bounced back against a solid Rutgers team. Up 21-10 at halftime, the Eagles pulled off a 35-23 win behind 318 yards, three touchdown passes, and a touchdown run from Flutie. Back up to ninth, though, BC would trip again, this time in Happy Valley.

In front of 85,690 at Beaver Stadium, BC let a top-10 ranking literally slip through its fingers. The Eagles outgained Joe Paterno's

Penn State squad, 560-429, but Flutie threw two interceptions, and BC fumbled five times, losing three of them. Backup halfback Ken Bell raced 71 yards for the game's first touchdown to give BC a 7-3 lead, but Penn State went on a 21-3 run to take control of the game, and a 39-yard run by PSU's D.J. Dozier put away a 37-30 upset win.

The BC defense was beginning to fade. It became more evident the next week against what would eventually become an eight-win Army squad. BC raced to a 28-14 halftime lead, and Flutie threw for 311 yards, but Army kept scoring in the second half. The Eagles couldn't put the game away until a late, 17-yard score from Flutie to Martin. Final score: BC 45, Army 31. Both teams put up more than 400 yards.

In the New England Patriots' stadium in Foxboro the next week, BC battled both Syracuse and wind. It helped the BC defense, but Flutie completed just 10 of 21 passes for 136 yards. Martin returned a punt 78 yards for a score, however, to put BC up, 24-10. The Eagles eventually won, 24-16, after a Thurman picked off a pass to end a promising, potentially game-tying Syracuse drive.

Now 7-2 and 10th in the country, BC finally made its fateful trip to Miami. The Eagles had played in four games decided by a touchdown or less, and the defense was slipping. Meanwhile, two weeks earlier, Miami had blown a 31-0 halftime lead against Maryland, losing 42-40. It was destiny for this game to get crazy.

It was back and forth from the start on a rainy night at the Orange Bowl. BC went up 14-0, but Miami struck back with two scores. Flutie scored on a nine-yard run, and Miami responded. Flutie hit Phelan for a 10-yard score before halftime, and Miami responded again after half. Miami took a 38-34 lead on a 52-yard run by Melvin Bratton, and a one-yard plunge by Strachan put BC back on top.

With just under four minutes left, Miami got the ball back and pulled off what should have been a perfect, game-clinching drive.

The Hurricanes went 79 yards and ate up all but 28 seconds from the clock. Bratton scored on a one-yard run to give Miami a 45-41 lead.

But Flutie had half a minute and two timeouts. He found Stadford for a 19-yard gain, then hit Gieselman for 13 more. A pass to Peter Caspariello fell incomplete with six seconds left. And then came the play you know. FLUTIE DID IT! and whatnot.

The game was already a classic before the Hail Mary. Flutie finished with 472 passing yards, Miami's Bernie Kosar with 447. Phelan had already caught 10 passes for 178 yards before the last pass, and Martin had added five for 96. Bratton had 134 yards for Miami, and Hurricane receiver Eddie Brown had 10 catches for 220 yards. There were 1,282 total yards and nine lead changes. Nuts from start to finish.

A week later, the regular season ended with a victory lap at Holy Cross. The Eagles led the Crusaders by only a 17-10 margin at half-time, but BC scored four third-quarter touchdowns to put the game away. Flutie found his freshman brother Darren for a 30-yard score, then Darren scored on a 20-yard run. The 45-10 win was icing on the cake: Flutie would win the Heisman voting handily, securing 678 of 807 first-place votes.

Flutie's final game at BC took place in Dallas against a Houston team that eked out a SWC title with a 7-4 record. The Eagles weren't looking to go out on a sour note. BC took a 31-7 lead on touchdown passes from Flutie to Martin (63 yards), Stradford (8), and Phelan (13). But Flutie struggled to maintain a rhythm in freezing temperatures. Houston scored twice, then returned an interception for a touchdown to cut the lead to 31-28.

With the game falling apart, however, BC leaned on the run. It paid off. Strachan and Stradford each scored late touchdowns to put away a 45-28 win and a 10-2 season.

Flutie, Bicknell, and Boston College provided thrills and highs that BC fans hadn't seen in more than four decades. In the process, they proved the lasting legacy football could provide. From an early-February piece by United Press International:

"Nothing like star athletes to boost a college's enrollment. Boston College says the presence and popularity of Heisman Trophy winner Doug Flutie is partially responsible for a 28 percent enrollment increase in the past two years. The influx of students from distant states is especially strong. 'We've experienced a dramatic increase in a declining market,' said BC admissions director Charles Nolan. 'It's not possible nor justifiable to ignore the Flutie phenomenon.'"

It became known as the Flutie Effect, and it gets reinforced every time a school lifts its status in the college football universe. Winning is intoxicating. It boosts morale like few things can. And when you've got a pint-sized, local, running, gunning quarterback leading the way, it boosts it even further.

1985 OKLAHOMA

"Held: The NCAA's television plan violates 1 of the Sherman Act. [...] The NCAA television plan on its face constitutes a restraint upon the operation of a free market, and the District Court's findings establish that the plan has operated to raise price and reduce output, both of which are unresponsive to consumer preference. [...]

"The record does not support the NCAA's proffered justification for its television plan that it constitutes a cooperative "joint venture" which assists in the marketing of broadcast rights and hence is procompetitive. ... Nor, contrary to the NCAA's assertion, does the television plan protect live attendance."

On June 27, 1984, the United States Supreme Court decided *NCAA v. Board of Regents of Univ. of Okla.* For nearly four decades, the NCAA had controlled what and how many college football games could be televised. It limited the number because it held that too many games on television would have a significant, negative impact on game attendance. The Universities of Georgia and Oklahoma challenged the NCAA and won. By a vote of 7-2, the Court held that the NCAA's plan violated the Sherman Antitrust Act, an 1890 law that prohibits anti-competitive practices.

The floodgates opened.

Televised games per year went from double digits to 200-plus the very next season. Schools in the College Football Association (most of Division I sans the Big Ten and Pac-10) negotiated a television deal. The Big Ten and Pac-10 had their own. And the emergence of a new network launched in 1979 – ESPN – created larger availability of potential time slots.

Through the years, *NCAA v. Board of Regents of Univ. of Okla.* changed football almost as significantly as the forward pass. After a few years, Notre Dame would withdraw from the CFA to form its own TV arrangement with NBC. Super-conferences formed, in part, to pull in more television money. College football, like politics, is local … but as television began to play more of a role, it became a little bit more national, too.

Since Oklahoma was the school named in the Supreme Court case, perhaps it made sense that OU would be the first team to take total advantage. The 1985 Sooner team was one of the most high-personality squads in a high-personality era. Brian Bosworth was known as much for his haircuts and antics as his being the best linebacker in college football. Jamelle Holieway flashed a million-dollar smile while running the option as well as any Switzer quarterback ever had. Keith Jackson was one of the fastest tight ends the sport had seen, and took particular pleasure in his touch-down dances. The defense had massive swagger, and the offense had countless halfbacks ready to rip off a 50-yard run.

And, of course, Barry Switzer – the bootlegger's boy, the man who adopted Darrell K Royal's wishbone early on and removed from it any semblance of mercy, the man who could grin and wink at the camera and make you believe you were invited to the party – ran the show.

This team was made for television. And like any good drama, *Oklahoma: 1985* featured one hell of a midseason plot twist.

Holieway, a true freshman from Long Beach, Cal., didn't begin the year as Oklahoma's starter. In fact, until fall camp, it wasn't even assumed he would be the second stringer. Fellow freshman Eric Mitchel came to Norman as or more well touted.

The starter was the local golden boy. Sophomore Troy Aikman, pride of Henryetta, 100 miles east of Norman, was expected to bring more passing prowess to an option offense that had, at times, grown stale in recent years. The blue-chipper started out on the wrong foot at OU; starting for injured Danny Bradley at Kansas in 1984, he completed just two of 14 passes for eight yards and three interceptions. But after a strong performance in spring ball, Switzer and offensive coordinator Jim Donnan felt okay handing him the reins. What he lacked in natural option ability, he made up for in brains and play-action potential.

Quarterback was just about the only question mark for this team. Switzer had begun to get his swagger back.

As Chuck Fairbanks' offensive coordinator in Norman, Switzer went all-in on the wishbone in 1971, and the results were absurd. The Sooners went 22-2 in Fairbanks' last two seasons before he left to take over the New England Patriots. Switzer took over in 1973 and didn't lose until 1975. He went 83-9-2 in his first eight years in charge. The Sooners won two AP national titles and didn't finish lower than seventh in this span. They were constantly dealing with NCAA investigations and were banned from the postseason in both 1973 and 1974, but sanctions did nothing to slow the Sooners down. They were a crimson and cream wrecking machine.

The product fell off dramatically in the early-1980s, however. The Sooners began 1981 ranked second in the polls but finished 7-4-1 and 20th. They started ninth in 1982 and finished 8-4. They started second in 1983 and finished 8-4. They scored 473 points during their 11-0 run in 1974; they barely topped 300 points per year during this iffy span.

In 1984, though, Switzer struck back. And he did so with defense. The offense suffered through injuries and inconsistency, but the Sooners allowed just 12.4 points per game in the regular season. The loss to Kansas was the only one – the Sooners beat 10-win Nebraska and Oklahoma State teams by 10 points each and reached second in the polls heading into the postseason. They probably would have leaped undefeated No. 1 BYU by beating No. 4 Washington in the Orange Bowl; instead, the Huskies won, 28-17, and BYU took the crown.

Oklahoma returned 16 starters and 51 lettermen from the 1984 near-champion. With Bosworth and All-American tackle Tony Casillas anchoring the front seven and players like cornerback Rickey Dixon in the back, the Sooner defense was sure to dominate. Accordingly, OU was ranked No. 1 in the country in the preseason.

The season opener took place on September 28 against a Minnesota team that had already played two games. The Sooners were supposed to begin their season on September 14 against SMU, then have a bye week; only, the SMU game was moved to December 7 for (you guessed it) television, and OU began its campaign three weeks after most of the country.

Under second-year head coach Lou Holtz, Minnesota was able to keep the OU offense under wraps. Two Tim Lashar field goals and a one-yard plunge by Earl Johnson gave the Sooners all the scoring they needed, but Minnesota scored a touchdown in the fourth quarter after a muffed punt, the Golden Gophers got the ball back, down 13-7, with a chance to steal an upset. They could only get to the OU 32, however, and the Sooners survived.

Two early turnovers kept the Sooners from pulling away from an awful Kansas State game the next week, but only for a little while. Leon Perry and Lydell Carr scored touchdowns in the second quarter, and OU pulled away for a 41-6 win. (Once again, KSU's only points were set up by a muffed punt.) Aikman was 10-for-14 for 177 yards, and he had two potential touchdown passes nullified by penalty. It was easily his best game to date.

Next came the annual trip to the Cotton Bowl. No. 17 Texas awaited, and to no one's surprise, another defensive battle ensued. Texas' defense held Oklahoma to 220 rushing yards and limited Aikman to 4-for-9 passing. Unfortunately for the Longhorns, they had no idea how to penetrate Oklahoma's defense. Casillas sprained his ankle in the first quarter, and OU still held the Horns to 70 total yards, didn't allow a single second-half first down, and didn't allow UT past the OU 49-yard line.

Texas scored early when Kip Cooper returned a Lydell Carr fumble for a score, but eventually the Horns wore down. Carr scored in the second quarter, Patrick Collins raced 45 yards for the game-winning points in the third, and OU pulled off one of the most dominant seven-point wins in college football history. After the game, Switzer called it the greatest defensive performance that he'd seen in his time at OU, and he'd been at OU since 1966. Bosworth was dominant, picking up the slack for Casillas and making seemingly every single tackle.

The offense remained a liability, though. It was good enough combined with this otherworldly defense, but it was giving voters pause. The Sooners had sunk to third in the AP poll when Jimmy Johnson's Miami Hurricanes came to town for Oklahoma's October 19 home opener. There was no doubting the defense, but what might happen if some opponent figured out a way to score some points? Would the offense be able to keep up?

A week later, these doubts proved justified. Aikman started the game wonderfully, completing six of seven passes for 131 yards, but Miami's Vinnie Testaverde, with an arm strong enough to win him the Heisman in 1986, burned the Sooner defense. He completed 17 of 28 passes for 270 yards and two huge touchdowns – a 56-yarder to Michael Irvin opened the scoring in the first quarter, and a 35-yarder to Brian Blades in the third; the latter all but put away an incredible upset. Miami only outgained Oklahoma by 13 yards (375-362), but OU suffered two turnovers, and Miami blocked a field goal late in the first quarter. That made the difference in a 27-14 win.

As strange as it sounds, however, Oklahoma's path to the national title began that day. In the second quarter, Aikman was sacked by Miami's Jerome Brown, fracturing his ankle in the process. He was lost for the season, and Holieway took over.

Holieway wasn't enough of a passer to lead a significant comeback – down 27-7 in the fourth quarter, he did engineer a scoring drive, but it took 19 plays and seven minutes. He was only 1-for-6 passing for the day.

Still, his strengths (and limitations) forced Donnan and Switzer to reset the offense. Gone were the I-formation looks and any pro-style tweaks they may have installed for Aikman. Instead, it was back to the full-fledged Wishbone. With Miami in the rearview mirror, it was time to unleash hell. (At the end of the season, Aikman would transfer to UCLA, where he would win 20 games in two years before putting together a hall-of-fame career with the Dallas Cowboys.)

In a way, the loss kept pressure off of Holieway. Aikman had a huge spotlight on him from day one, and he was put in charge of a No. 1 team before he had even won a game. But the loss to Miami dropped OU to 10th in the AP poll, and Holieway could just focus on moving the football.

He did it pretty well. Against Iowa State in his first start, he rushed for 76 yards and completed a 77-yard bomb to flanker Derrick Shepard in a 59-14 win. In a visit from Kansas the next week, he rushed for 162 yards and hit Keith Jackson for a 42-yard score. Final score: OU 48, KU 6. On a trip to Missouri, it was the same story: Holieway rushed for 156 yards and completed eight passes for 168 yards and two scores in a 51-6 win.

On November 16, a solid Colorado team came to Norman. No. 3 Ohio State would suffer a huge upset loss to Wisconsin, and unbeaten No. 4 Air Force would lose to BYU. There was an opportunity to move up in the polls, and No. 7 OU took advantage. In a battle of wishbone attacks, the Sooners converted 24 first downs to the Buffaloes' six. Holieway was held to 80 rushing yards and 2-for-9 passing, but he scored two touchdowns on the ground, and CU couldn't move the ball. OU eased to a 31-0 win.

Then came the game of the year. Tom Osborne's Nebraska Cornhuskers came to town with a 9-1 record. They had fallen to Florida State in the first week of the season but had since beaten ranked Illinois and Oklahoma State teams and had roasted KSU, ISU, and Kansas by a combined 146-9 in the three weeks prior to the trip to Norman. They were more limited than normal throwing the ball, but the run game was more punishing, with Doug DuBose, future San Francisco 49er fullback Tom Rathman, and Paul Miles combining for 2,731 yards.

It was time for OU to unleash its secret weapon. Donnan had kept Jackson under wraps for most of the year, but barely three minutes into the game, he took the ball on a reverse, set up his blocks, then exploded down the right sideline for a jarring 88-yard touchdown. He received great blocking the whole way, and he burned a safety who probably thought he had an angle to make the stop. (He would take two more reverses for another 48 yards, giving him a unique stat line for the day: one catch for 38 yards, three carries for 136 yards. As a tight end.) A few minutes later, on a third-and-7, Holieway kept the ball on an option and weaved his way through ankle tackles for a 43-yard score. He would finish with 110 yards; Nebraska defensive tackle Jim Skow said after the game that trying to tackle him was like getting hold of a field mouse.

Another Holieway score stretched the lead to 27-0 in the fourth quarter, and NU could only score on a late 76-yard fumble return. The Sooners had locked up an Orange Bowl date with top-ranked Penn State with two games left to play.

The Big 8 title was in the bag, but if the Sooners wanted to have a shot at the national title, they first had to survive both a strong Oklahoma State team – the Cowboys had risen to fifth in the polls at one point and sat at 8-2 and 17th heading into the game – and a hellish round of sleet in Stillwater. This weather is not something Oklahomans have to deal with that often, and it's *definitely* not something Holieway was used to dealing with in Long Beach.

The game kicked off at 6:45 p.m. local time because of television. And with the wind chill crossing the wrong side of zero, facing a defense led by All-American end Leslie O'Neal, Holieway and the offense struggled. OU gained only 243 yards on the day, but luckily, OSU was struggling just as much.

This was comedy. The offenses combined for 11 fumbles. Jackson took another tight end around and found wide-open space in front of him, but he couldn't turn his body upfield, basically came to a stop, and got tackled. OSU kicker Brad Dennis attempted a 37-yard field goal and slipped onto his backside instead. (This was great experience for OSU's Thurman Thomas, who rushed for 100 yards – the first player all season to hit triple digits against the Sooners – and got some preparation for his career as an all-pro running back in Buffalo.)

OU's Tim Lasher managed to hit field goals in the second and fourth quarters. A two-yard score by Spencer Tillman late in the first half was the game's only touchdown as OU survived, 13-0.

By the time of the postponed-for-television battle with SMU, the weather had eased up a bit. OU started slowly, trailing 7-0 after one quarter, then cruised. Holieway rushed for another 126 yards and threw a touchdown pass to Lee Morris in a 35-13 win.

That set the table for what might have been a de facto national title game. Oklahoma was still third in the AP poll, but these were the pre-BCS days. No. 1 vs. No. 2 matchups were not common. No. 2 Miami was stuck playing No. 8 Tennessee in the Sugar Bowl, and despite the head-to-head loss to the Hurricanes, an OU win over Penn State would probably give the Sooners the title.

Of course, Miami took any drama out of the potential vote by laying a massive egg against Tennessee, losing 35-7. The Sooners were favored against Penn State because of both their own recent dominance and the Nittany Lions' propensity for eking out mediocre wins (they had beaten just two teams that finished with more than seven wins and won seven games by one possession).

PSU led 7-0 after the first quarter and, with a sturdy front seven led by All-American linebacker Shane Conlan, limited Holieway to just one rushing yard and 3-for-6 passing. But the OU defense was predictably dominant, and one of Holieway's three completions was a perfect, 71-yard play-action bomb to Jackson. OU scored 16 points in the second quarter, and with PSU's defense tired and demoralized, Carr put away a 25-10 win with a 61-yard touchdown run.

In losing his golden boy quarterback, Switzer sent a freshman onto the field, went back to his wishbone roots, and won himself one final national title. He would come close to winning two more; from 1985-87, Oklahoma went 0-3 against Miami and 33-0 against everybody else, but that was enough to come up just short in 1986 and 1987.

1985 represented the final peak. OU would get walloped by the NCAA for recruiting violations in 1988, and Switzer would resign after a series of player arrests in June 1989.

Before his downfall, though, he created one hell of a made-for-TV champion.

1988 MIAMI

It was as if everything had changed overnight.

Miami and Notre Dame had played each other 16 times in 17 years heading into the 1988 season, and they would continue an annual series through 1990. The Fighting Irish owned the first 10 years of this stretch like they were supposed to, winning each game by an average score of 33-10. Only one game was decided by fewer than 13 points.

This was a clear expression of order in college football. Notre Dame was *Notre Dame*, still one of college football's greatest powers. From 1971-80, the Irish won two national titles and finished in the AP top 10 five times.

Miami, meanwhile, was still just a small private school in the planned community of Coral Gables. Football was an afterthought. Through 1980, the Hurricanes had only twice finished in the top 10. In 1956, head coach Andy Gustafson and back Don Bosseler led them to an 8-1-1 record and a No. 6 final ranking. In 1966, Charlie

272

Tate's squad featured a dominant line led by future College Football Hall of Famer Ted Hendricks and went 8-2-1, finishing ninth. That was about it.

When Howard Schnellenberger, former Baltimore Colts head coach and offensive coordinator for Bear Bryant (Alabama) and Don Shula (Miami Dolphins), was hired in 1979, the situation was dire. School officials had weighed dropping the football program altogether.

It feels like an understatement to say that Schnellenberger changed everything. Under Schnellenberger, a pipe-smoking baritone and one of the most unique personalities football has ever produced, this school was no longer seen as some private university – it was the *University of Miami*. He almost exclusively recruited what he called the State of Miami. He reached deep into the inner city and crafted a roster full of speed, passion, and Schnelly-endorsed swagger.

After a 5-6 debut, Schnellenberger won 18 games in 1980-81, rising to eighth in the polls in '81 and thumping Notre Dame, 37-15. The Hurricanes suffered a brief step backwards in 1982, but by 1983, the balance of power had flipped completely. And it remained that way even when Schellenberger left for a (failed) USFL venture in 1984. He was replaced by Jimmie Johnson, maybe the only coach in the country with even more swagger.

1983: Miami 20, Notre Dame 0. Miami finishes 11-1 and wins the national title, Notre Dame finishes 7-5 and unranked.

1984: Miami 31, Notre Dame 13. Miami finishes 8-5 and 18th, Notre Dame finishes 7-5 and unranked.

1985: Miami 58, Notre Dame 7. Miami finishes 10-2 and ninth, Notre Dame finishes 5-6. Not only is head coach Gerry Faust let go; this debacle against Miami is his last game.

1987: Miami 24, Notre Dame 0. Miami finishes 12-0 and wins

the national title, Notre Dame finishes 8-4 and 17th.

Turnaround artist Lou Holtz came to South Bend in 1986 after a nomadic early career that included head coaching stops at William & Mary (1969-71), NC State (1972-75), Arkansas (1977-83), and Minnesota (1984-85). Like Schnellenberger, he began with an up-and-down 5-6 campaign, then took off. In 1987, the Irish finished the season ranked for the first time since Dan Devine's last season (1980). And in 1988, Miami had to come to South Bend. It was the ultimate test of progress for the Fighting Irish.

There was no bigger compliment for how far Miami had come than this: Notre Dame, college football's most famous football program, was using the Hurricanes as the measuring stick for how much it still needed to grow.

That's not to say there was a little brother-big brother relationship going on here. That suggests a level of similarity that just didn't exist. Notre Dame fans still liked to believe that their football team was about More Than Just Football, that there was a higher power involved.

In this way, Holtz was the perfect coach for this program: He carried himself frail and humble, like a friar. But he was more than willing to get down and dirty and do what it took to win. In order to beat Miami in 1988, it was going to take a little bit of attitude.

Miami entered the 1988 season with the 'D' word in mind: dynasty. Indeed, the Canes had won two of the last five national titles and very nearly won the titles in 1985 and 1986 as well. They hadn't lost a regular season game since the first week of 1985. They had made quite a few enemies in recent years, and their No. 1 vs. No. 2 battle with Penn State in the 1987 Fiesta Bowl was all but billed as a battle of good (Joe Paterno's seemingly squeaky clean Nittany Lions) versus evil (Johnson's high-stepping Hurricanes).

When Miami not only created an outlaw image, but also embraced it and doubled down with it, sports fans and writers of a certain age (and, yes, race) were appalled.

But the Canes just kept winning. They had to replace quite a few key contributors from the 1987 title team and were ranked a conservative sixth in the AP poll. In-state rival Florida State, meanwhile, was preseason No. 1. There was reason behind that. The pieces had just about come together for Bobby Bowden; his Noles had surged in 1987, finishing 11-1 with only a one-point loss to Miami marring a title bid. They had ranked second in scoring offense and seventh in scoring defense, and they returned quite a few more known contributors than Miami.

From virtually the opening kickoff, Miami announced that it was not ready to give up its crown. The Hurricanes met FSU in the Orange Bowl and took a 17-0 lead into halftime with touchdowns by running back Cleveland Gary and tight end Pete Chudzinski. They outgained FSU, 450-242, and cruised to a 31-0 statement win. FSU was awesome – the Noles wouldn't lose again for the rest of the season – but Miami was still the king of Florida.

After a bye week evidently spent patting themselves on the back, though, the Canes nearly slipped up in Ann Arbor. Bo Schembechler's 15th-ranked Michigan Wolverines had fallen to Notre Dame, 19-17, the week before and desperately wanted to avoid a 0-2 start. Miami took a 14-6 lead late in the second quarter, but Michigan scored twice in the final minute of the half to take a sudden lead. More shocking: It was 30-14 with six minutes left in the game.

Miami finally put together a rally, though, unleashing a devastating hurry-up offense to strike back. Steve Walsh hit Chudzinski for a seven-yard score with 5:23 left to cap an 11-play, 80-yard drive. The two-point conversion made it 30-22. The Canes quickly forced a three-and-out and drove to midfield, but they faced a fourth-and-1 from the Michigan 48. Walsh threw a short pass to Gary over the middle, and he cut and raced up the right sideline for a touchdown. A second two-point conversion failed, but Miami's Bobby Harden recovered an onside kick.

Walsh found Andre Brown for 14 yards, then Gary pummeled ahead for 17 yards. With 43 seconds left, Carlos Huerta nailed a 29-yard field goal. Miami scored 14 points in the game's first 54:37, then scored 17 points in the next 4:40. And the Canes left Ann Arbor 2-0.

At that point, it was time to start tuning up for the trip to South Bend. Miami never had to take it out of third gear against an awful Wisconsin squad; linebacker Bernard Clark returned a fumble 55 yards for a score, and despite six turnovers, Miami cruised 23-3. The next week, against drastically outmanned Missouri, Walsh threw three touchdown passes in the first 14 minutes (one to Chudzinski, one to Dale Dawkins, one to Randal Hill) in a 55-0 romp.

People still call it maybe the most intense game in the history of Notre Dame Stadium, and it began well before kickoff. After pregame warmups, as Miami players were heading toward the tiny tunnels that both home and visiting teams share, Hurricane players decided to walk through Notre Dame's stretch line instead of around it. Notre Dame players didn't let them through peacefully. In between the end zone and tunnel, one hell of a skirmish broke out.

Holtz's squad was primed and ready. Notre Dame students famously sold "Catholic vs. Convicts" shirts – the Miami players were clearly not the Catholics in reference – but the Fighting Irish weren't going to win this game acting like choir boys.

The fight seemed to focus Notre Dame; it may have also distracted Miami. The Hurricane offense was as explosive as ever, gaining 481 yards and averaging more than 6 yards per play against a defense that would finish third in scoring defense that year. But mistakes destroyed them. Miami committed *seven* turnovers – four fumbles and three interceptions, one of which was returned 60 yards by ND safety Pat Terrell. To say the least, it's hard to keep either a 36-game regular season winning streak or a 20-game road winning streak alive when you give the ball away on half of your possessions. Miami came really, really close, though. Terrell's pick six gave the Irish a 21-7 lead in the second quarter, but every time Notre Dame pulled away, Miami came right back. Two Walsh touchdown passes – a 23-yarder to Leonard Conley and a 15-yarder to Gary – tied the game up before halftime.

It was the same story in the second half. Notre Dame scored 10 points in the third quarter to go up 31-21, but Miami came charging back. Huerta hit a 23-yard field goal to bring Miami within seven, and with just over seven minutes left, Miami faced a fourth-and-7 from the ND 7. There was a tiny space in which Miami could get a first down without scoring. On TV, announcer Brent Musberger called it "fourth down and everything."

With the stadium crowd almost making too much noise to hear the announcers on TV, Walsh took the snap and found his first option covered. He checked down and found Gary in traffic at the 2. Gary caught the ball and spun toward the end zone. He appeared to reach the ball over the goal line for a touchdown, then lose the ball after it hit the ground. Notre Dame recovered the ball as if he fumbled. The only real question was whether his knee hit the ground before the ball crossed the plane of the goal. There was no question that the ball didn't come loose until after it hit the hallowed stadium grass.

At least, there was no question when watching on replay. There was no instant replay for the officials in 1988. They decided Gary had fumbled and gave Notre Dame the ball inside its 1.

Controversy aside, Miami kept attacking. The Hurricanes got the ball back with 3:52 left and got inside the Irish 25 before ND's Frank Stams sacked and stripped Walsh, and the Irish recovered again. But Irish quarterback Tony Rice, so good that season, gave Miami a gift, fumbling the ball back three plays later. Miami got one last chance, and on fourth-and-7 from the ND 11, Walsh lobbed the ball to Brown, who came down with it in the end zone. 31-30, under a minute left.

There's power to staying on brand. Miami was built on confidence and testosterone, and the thought of playing for a tie did not work for Johnson, even though a tie in South Bend would barely ding Miami's national title potential. With the overtime rule still eight years from existence, Miami went for two points and the win. But Terrell was in the right place at the right time again. He broke up one final Walsh pass, and Notre Dame recovered the ensuing onside kick and survived.

There was a little bit of poetry here. Five years earlier, Miami won its first national title over Nebraska by breaking up a two-point conversion attempt on a pass to the right. On October 15, 1988, Miami ever so briefly passed the torch in the same manner.

Notre Dame would go on to finish unbeaten and win the national title. Given the option of playing a rematch against Miami in the Orange Bowl or facing another unbeaten team, West Virginia, in the Fiesta Bowl, the Irish smartly elected to go with the latter and rolled, 34-21.

Miami wouldn't lose again for another calendar year. The Hurricanes angrily plowed through Cincinnati, East Carolina, and Tulsa by a combined 122-13, then headed to Baton Rouge and crushed No. 11 LSU, in Death Valley, 44-3.

Miami almost stumbled on Thanksgiving weekend. The Hurricanes held No. 8 Arkansas to just 186 total yards, but the Razorbacks timed those yards well, gaining 153 of them on two scoring drives to give them a 16-15 lead deep into the fourth quarter. It took a 20-yard Huerta field goal (after a near interception in the end zone) to bail the Hurricanes out. But it was the last close call of the year. Miami stomped BYU 41-17 to finish the regular season 10-1, then dominated Nebraska in the Orange Bowl, allowing only 135 yards and winning, 23-3.

Given a rematch with Notre Dame, Miami would have almost certainly been favored, but there weren't too many rematches in college football in those days. Instead, the Hurricanes had to settle for furthering their brand and remaining the most dominant, scary team in college football. It took seven turnovers (six of them legitimate) for the eventual national champion to beat them at home. Only six giveaways probably wouldn't have done the job.

Miami lost Johnson to the Dallas Cowboys that offseason but hired Dennis Erickson and kept winning. As the NCAA created rules to more significantly punish teams for celebrating and taunting the way Miami tended to, the Hurricanes became a little bit more volatile. Still, they would win the national title again in 1989 and 1991. Eventually the dynasty would crumble for the same reason Oklahoma's did: NCAA sanctions.

1990 VIRGINIA

When you are a fan of a team making a once-in-a-lifetime run, there's almost as much fear as exhilaration. You know that while Alabama or Ohio State (or Notre Dame or USC or …) fans will probably get more than a few chances to watch their team do something incredible, your own team might be flying pretty close to the sun. There might not be another chance. It's called once-in-a-lifetime for a reason.

You can maybe forgive Virginia fans if they still have post-traumatic stress issues when the words "Scott" and "Sisson" are mentioned.

For a couple of months in 1990, it appeared that George Welsh and his Virginia Cavaliers, flying higher than they ever had, would stick the landing. Their timing was impeccable: They had probably the best offense in the country and their best overall team since before World War I, and they were taking the field in a year of upheaval. 1990 would go down as one of the craziest seasons in the history of the sport, with six different teams holding the No. 1 ranking and eight holding No. 2. Two teams split the national title – one began the season unranked and didn't reach the top 10 until November; the other lost a game, tied a game, and benefited from two of the most famous, controversial calls ever.

Welsh had a perfect résumé for turning Virginia into a winner. An All-American quarterback at Navy, he spent 10 seasons as an assistant at Penn State under both Rip Engle and Joe Paterno. He was there when Paterno was turning the Nittany Lion program into a steady winner, and then he spent nine seasons leading his alma mater back into college football's consciousness. In the five years before he took over in 1973, the Midshipmen had gone just 12-41; building and maintaining success at service academies was getting harder and harder, but by his sixth year, he had figured it out. From 1978-81, Navy won 31 games and attended three bowls.

It was time, then, to take on perhaps an even bigger challenge. When Virginia brought him to Charlottesville in 1982, the Cavaliers were desperate. In the last 29 years, they had finished above .500 just twice and had won either zero or one games eight times. In 19 years under Welsh, they would finish *under* .500 just twice.

Welsh was crafty and innovative, and he found a balance between encouraging personal achievement (Virginia's graduation rates were as good as anyone's) and figuring out how to win games with the chess pieces he had compiled. His Cavaliers were sometimes outmanned but rarely beat themselves.

Virginia's talent level peaked in 1989-90. Welsh won quite a few local recruiting battles, securing the services of players like Parade All-American running back Terry Kirby of York County, defensive end Chris Slade of Yorktown, and two great, unrelated Moores: quarterback Shawn of Martinsville and receiver Herman of Danville.

Offensive coordinator Gary Tranquill, who had joined Welsh

in Charlottesville in 1987 after succeeding him at Navy, had the perfect mix of hard-nosed role players and all-world athletes at his disposal, and he found his greatest rhythm in 1990. The Moore-to-Moore connection allowed him to install some principles of the run-and-shoot offense that was beginning to take the sport by storm. Tight end Bruce McGonnigal gave Moore a second big (6'5) option. Virginia's receiving corps had even more size on the outside and Moore (the QB) had more speed than almost any quarterback with his passing ability. There were mismatches all over the field, and UVA did not hesitate to go with a no-huddle attack when they had the matchups they wanted.

Virginia won 10 games for the first time ever in 1989, taking a share of its first ACC title in the process. (The Cavaliers split the title with a resurgent Duke team coached by former Florida quarterback Steve Spurrier.) With so much returning in 1990, even bigger things were expected. For the first time ever, they were ranked in the preseason AP poll. They started at 15th.

The 1990 season was nutty from the very start. Top-ranked Miami, the defending national champion, began the year with a loss at BYU. That set quite a tone. Virginia, meanwhile, simply took care of business. Beginning the season at Kansas, the Cavaliers wasted no time, vaulting to a 31-0 halftime lead and rolling, 59-10. In scorching conditions, the starters got to ice down on the sidelines for most of the second half.

Then came a huge benchmark game. Virginia had played Clemson 29 times; the Cavaliers had lost every time. Former Clemson coach Frank Howard had once called them the "white meat of our schedule," and for good reason. This was a hurdle Welsh just hadn't been able to clear, and he had only come close a couple of times (27-24 in 1985, 10-7 in 1988).

Virginia's Scott Stadium had a listed capacity of 42,000 in 1990; announced attendance for the Clemson game: 46,800. But the incredible environment didn't produce an immediate home field advantage – ninth-ranked Clemson led 7-6 at halftime. After a first-quarter touchdown run by Clemson's DeChane Cameron, the Cavalier defense had begun to take control. Kirby scored from four yards out to give Virginia a 13-7 lead early in the third quarter, and a 12-yard Moore-to-Moore connection made it 20-7 just a few minutes later.

That was all the Wahoo defense needed. In Clemson's next five possessions, the Tigers punted three times and turned the ball over on downs twice. As a last-ditch Clemson incompletion hit the turf and the clock expired, Virginia fans stormed the field with vigor. This win was as cathartic as they come. It was also helpful: Two games into the season, the Cavaliers were already up to 11th.

Now brimming with confidence, Virginia found its own course of white meat. Moore threw four touchdown passes and rushed for a fifth, all in the first half, as the Hoos crushed Navy, 56-14. Then, against a Duke team that had fallen apart with Spurrier now at Florida, Moore threw for three more scores and rushed for another. Final score: UVA 59, Duke 0.

Against William & Mary, the Cavaliers kept the ball mostly on the ground. Kirby and Nikki Fisher combined for 398 yards, and while it took a little while to pull away, three touchdowns in the first five minutes of the second half made it 49-21 Hoos. UVA cruised from there, 63-35.

Then came the most well-timed of byes. While Virginia sat at home, a lot of highly ranked teams stumbled. No. 4 BYU got thumped by unranked Oregon, and No. 3 Auburn and No. 5 Tennessee tied each other as UVA was beating W&M. The next week, top-ranked Notre Dame fell to unranked Stanford while No. 2 Florida State once again lost to Miami. By the time Virginia kicked off against NC State on October 13, Michigan was the No. 1 team in the country, and UVA was No. 2.

Against the Wolfpack, the Hoos' offense picked up right where it left off. Touchdown passes from Moore to Moore and Gary Steele helped them stake out a 24-0 halftime lead. Then, midway through the third quarter, another Moore-to-Moore connection, this one an 83-yard catch and run, gave UVA its final margin of victory: 31-0. Moore (the receiver) had six catches for 162 yards, and Kirby rushed 15 times for 112 yards against what had been the No. 4 defense in the country in total yardage.

Meanwhile, Michigan State, which had nearly knocked off top-ranked Notre Dame in September, got a second chance at a No. 1 team and took advantage. Tico Duckett put the Spartans ahead of Michigan, 28-21; Michigan scored with six seconds left, but a lob to future Heisman winner Desmond Howard was ruled incomplete even though it looked as if Howard had caught the ball. Michigan State won by one, and Virginia was vaulted to No. 1 for the first time ever.

The one-time home of former presidents Thomas Jefferson, James Madison, and James Monroe, Charlottesville is a quaint town of about 43,000, 120 miles southwest of Washington, DC, and 70 miles northwest of Richmond. It has a well-regarded art scene and a pristine, sleepy downtown mall; walking it at any time makes you crave brunch. Celebrities like Muhammad Ali, actresses Sissy Spacek and Jessica Lange, and actor Sam Shepard all owned property near the city at one point, using Charlottesville as a place for maintaining a low profile.

You can eat well in Charlottesville, and you can see a really good show or concert there. (Approximately seven months after UVA beat NC State, a local band called the Dave Matthews Band would play its first public show, eventually taking up residence in a popular club called Trax.) And in the fall of 1990, C'ville was ever so briefly the capital of the sports world.

The team managed to maintain focus, at least for a while. On October 20, in their first ever game as the No. 1 team in the land, the Cavaliers lit up Wake Forest. Virginia kept coming up short of the end zone and settling for field goals early, and Wake managed to take a 14-9 lead early in the second quarter. But after a fourth Jake McInerney field goal made it 14-12, UVA began to finish drives: Moore to Moore for a 49-yard score. Moore to Kirby for a 20-yard score. Gary Steele, 16-yard touchdown run. Fisher, 63-yard touchdown run. Matt Blundin, one-yard plunge. UVA had to break a sweat but cruised, 49-14.

The next week against No. 16 Georgia Tech, Moore scored on a pair of one-yard runs, and two more field goals gave UVA a 21-7 lead in the second quarter. It was 28-14 at halftime, and with the offense as dominant as ever, it looked like UVA would cruise once more.

And then everything fell apart.

A two-week flirtation with the town of Charlottesville hit its peak that Saturday; it was Virginia's first home game as the top-ranked team, and it was against a Georgia Tech team that had already beaten Clemson and No. 25 South Carolina. Bobby Ross' Yellow Jackets had managed only a tie at North Carolina, but they were still 6-0-1. Shawn Jones and a deep stable of running backs powered the offense, and linebackers Marco Coleman and defensive back Ken Swilling led a dominant (to date) defense.

The night before the game, someone sneaked into the stadium and set fire to Scott Stadium's artificial turf, damaging an area near the 50-yard line. Luckily, the grounds crew used turf from the baseball stadium to patch up the spot, and the game was on.

In front of a packed Scott Stadium, and what seemed like an even more crowded press box, Georgia Tech stunned the crowd with a nearly perfect third quarter. Jerry Gilchrist scored on a 12-yard run, then Jones hit Emmett Merchant for a 26-yard score. Another Moore to Moore bomb, this one for 63 yards, gave UVA a 35-28 advantage, but William Bell tied the game with an eight-yard run. It was tied heading into the fourth quarter.

Tech's Scott Sisson gave the Ramblin' Wreck the lead on a 32-yard field goal, but the UVA offense responded. The Cavaliers drove down to the 1-yard line, ready to take the lead, but a team that for so long relied on making fewer mistakes than its opponent committed two illegal procedure penalties and had to settle for a 23-yard field goal with 2:34 left. McInerney nailed it, but Tech's smoking-hot offense had time to make one last drive. The Jackets went 56 yards, and Sisson nailed the game-winning 37-yard field goal.

It was an all-time classic, maybe the best game in the history of either program. And to their credit, the gutted Cavaliers responded. They went to Chapel Hill to take on the team that had tied Tech, and they surged to a 21-3 halftime lead. UNC couldn't score a touchdown until late in a 24-10 win, and UVA was quickly back to No. 8 in the country (Tech, meanwhile: No. 4). The next week, having already accepted a Sugar Bowl bid, the Hoos hosted Maryland and surged to another quick 21-7 lead. But they once again took their foot off the gas. Like Georgia Tech, Maryland scored three third-quarter touchdowns and took a 35-28 lead in the fourth quarter. Moore, meanwhile, dislocated his thumb falling to the stadium turf. Virginia fell, 35-30. Moore would miss the next week's Virginia Tech game, and a demoralized squad got clubbed, 38-13.

Virginia started 7-0 and finished 1-3. The Cavaliers retained their spot in the Sugar Bowl, however, despite how odd it seemed to have what was now an unranked team in a major bowl. And with Moore back in the lineup, the Cavaliers very nearly found redemption against Johnny Majors and the 10th-ranked Tennessee Volunteers. Reenergized, UVA took a 16-0 lead into halftime thanks to TD runs by Steele and Kirby. But Moore's hand was beginning to swell up from taking snaps; his grip on the ball weakened, and his throwing grew erratic. (He finished 9-for-24 with three interceptions.)

Tennessee clawed back into the game. UVA led 19-10 with 7:30 left, but Tennessee scored twice and eked out a 23-22 win. A season that was, at one point, all but guaranteed to become Virginia's greatest ever ended with the Cavaliers sporting an 8-4 record.

To make matters worse, Georgia Tech rolled to 11-0-1. The Yellow Jackets won a share of the national title with Colorado; the Buffaloes had benefited from the famous Fifth Down against Missouri: Down 31-27 in the closing seconds, Colorado received an extra down when the officials didn't change the down marker after quarterback Charles Johnson spiked the ball. (Johnson was credited with a touchdown on said fifth down, but it was unclear whether he actually crossed the plane of the goal line with the ball.) The Buffaloes then beat Notre Dame in the Orange Bowl after a potential game-winning punt return by the Irish's Rocket Ismail was called back because of a controversial clipping penalty.

That Virginia crawled back into the AP poll, finishing 23rd, was the smallest of consolations.

Virginia won between seven and nine games for each of the next nine seasons. Welsh established the Cavaliers as maybe the most consistently decent team in college football. But when you aren't a member of college football's ruling class, you might only get one shot at a national title. And Virginia's ended when Scott Sisson's kick split the uprights on an early-November night in Charlottesville. Moore's dislocated thumb only added insult to injury … or maybe injury to insult.

1991 FLORIDA

Shane Matthews completes 15 of 27 passes for 251 yards, three touchdowns and two interceptions as No. 6 Florida beats No. 16 Alabama, 35-0, in Gainesville. It is the Gators' biggest win ever over the Crimson Tide and the first time Bama has allowed this many points since the 1987 season. Alabama will proceed to win 28 consecutive games, staving off Florida in the 1992 SEC Championship Game. But that will be Bama head coach Gene Stallings' only win over Gators.

"**I** read something once that I think is so true: If you want to be successful, you have to do it the way everybody does it and do it a lot better—or you have to do it differently. I can't outwork anybody, and I can't coach the off-tackle play better than anybody else. So I figured I'd try to coach some different ball plays."

-- Steve Spurrier in a 1995 *Sports Illustrated* profile

There are many self-professed sleeping giants in the college football world, schools that are just the right hire and the right level of commitment away from becoming a force. Ask 50 college football fans, which program is the biggest sleeping giant in the sport, and you'll probably get at least 20 different answers, everyone from UCLA to Maryland to North Carolina. But there's a pretty clear reason for this lack of consensus: In the early-1990s, Florida stopped sleeping.

Against Mississippi State in Orlando, Matthews completes 22 of 35 passes for 322 yards and two touchdowns, and Florida cruises, 29-7. Jackie Sherrill's Bulldogs will get the best of the Gators the next year in 1992, but MSU allows an average of 42 points per game in its next three meetings with UF after that.

Imagine sitting on one of the largest goldmines of football talent in the country, then segregating yourself from it. Imagine failing to take advantage of integration, then finding yourself getting put on NCAA probation just as Miami and Florida State hit their stride. The Florida Gators were college football's biggest underachiever for a significant period of time.

For the first four-plus decades of the AP poll's existence, UF never finished ranked higher than 14th. The Gators had zero SEC titles to their name. They would flash random glimpses of brilliance – quarterback Steve Spurrier won the Heisman Trophy in 1966, and they went 9-1-1 and won the Gator Bowl in 1969 – but no one could consistently harness this potential until Charley Pell came to town. The former Clemson head coach brought the Gators to four straight bowl games. The 1983 team went 9-2-1 and finished sixth in the AP poll, the program's best ever finish. And in 1984, the Gators would finish 9-1-1 and third.

At Death Valley in Baton Rouge, LSU allows 404 total yards to Florida while gaining only 166. Matthews completes 15 of 28 passes for 220 yards, a touchdown, and an interception. Though UF can only manage three field goals in the first half, the Gators pitch their second SEC shutout and coast, 16-0. It is LSU's second straight double-digit loss to Florida, and the Tigers will lose the next five games in the series by an average score of 42-13.

The problem: Pell was fired three games into the 1984 season because the NCAA announced UF had committed over 50 rules violations, ranging from paying players to spying on opponents' practices. Offensive coordinator Galen Hall took over and lost only one of his first 20 games in charge; he led the Gators to back-to-back top-five finishes and the 1984 SEC title (later nullified by the SEC). But Hall couldn't keep up the same level of winning under heavy NCAA punishment – scholarship reduction, bowl ban, live TV ban – and amid rumors of *further* rules violations, Hall was let go in the middle of 1989.

Even as Miami and Florida State were blossoming into dominant forces, Florida had, in the 1980s, proven what it might be capable of under the right guiding hand. Meanwhile, a few hours north of Gainesville, Spurrier, the favorite son, was winning the ACC title at Duke in only his second year. It was a perfect time to bring him home.

Tennessee's defense dominated the Gators in Knoxville in 1990 and begins the 1991 game by sacking Matthews for a safety four minutes into the game. But six minutes later, Matthews hits Terrell Jackson for a one-yard score on fourth-and-goal, then throws a 29-yard score to Tre Everett in the second quarter. Rhett scores twice, and Florida puts away a 35-18 win with a 44-yard pick six by Larry Kennedy. This is Spurrier's first win over Tennessee; he will win seven of the next nine as well. In four years with Peyton Manning as starter in the mid-1990s, the Vols will never beat Florida.

Football in the Southeastern Conference has been, for much of its existence, like parliament. There are proper rules of order you have to follow to win: You establish the run, you put your best athletes on defense, you tilt the field in your favor, and you lean on your opponent until they give out.

Before Steve Spurrier came back to Gainesville, passing was what you did when you either couldn't run or you were behind. LSU led the league in passing yardage in 1989 while going 4-7; Vanderbilt averaged the most passing yards over the 1980s and averaged about three wins per year. Spurrier's tenure as Florida quarterback bucked that trend a bit; he threw for nearly 4,000 yards in 1965-66. And after more than a decade in the coaching profession, he had only become more sold in his preference for the forward pass.

Spurrier didn't want to simply score enough points to beat you; he wanted to score as many as he possibly could. His natural face revealed an easy-going smirk that could turn into a sinister sneer given the right lighting or down-and-distance. He had no interest in coach speak, no interest in dancing around questions asked of him on or off the field. He was a scab-picker, someone who would try a little bit of everything until he figured out your weakness, then exploit it ruthlessly and repeatedly.

Spurrier was scarred by every loss, every setback on his climb up the coaching ladder. And when he reached great heights, he wasn't going to change his approach. In his first spring on the job, he announced that he wasn't sure who would start for him at quarterback but that "whoever it is will lead the SEC in passing next year." Sure enough…

During a 41-10 tune-up win against Northern Illinois, the Florida offensive line struggles to protect Matthews, and he is uncharacteristically inaccurate. At one point in the first half, Spurrier is so frustrated with his line that he briefly subs in the entire second-string line. (His hook will be used more notoriously with quarterbacks during his Florida tenure.) But the line looks just fine at Auburn two weeks later. Matthews throws for 264 yards, Rhett rushes for 106, and the Gators again roll, 31-10.

Florida went 9-2 and averaged nearly 300 passing yards per game in 1990, Spurrier's first season in charge. The Gators were ineligible for a bowl or the conference title because of NCAA punishment, but they proved a point. Spurrier's first ever road win was against Alabama in Tuscaloosa. His Gators beat No. 4 Auburn, 48-7, then whooped Georgia, 38-7. They lost only at Tennessee and Florida State.

That's one hell of a way to send a message. And a year later, against a schedule that featured seven ranked teams, the Gators solidified their gains.

One team has already attempted to adjust to the Spurrier Fun 'n' Gun, not necessarily in trying to stop it, but in trying to keep up with it. Third-year Georgia head coach Ray Goff was so awed by what Spurrier's offense did to him in 1990 that he hired former Florida State offensive coordinator Wayne McDuffie to spruce up his own pass-happy offense. It works to a degree – the Dawgs go 9-3 in 1991 and 10-2 in 1992. But they can't solve the Gators, losing this rivalry game both years. Florida clinches a share of the SEC title by rolling up 512 yards to UGA's 220 in a 45-13 pasting. Matthews completes 22 of 32 passes for 303 yards and four scores, while Rhett outrushes Georgia great Garrison Hearst, 124-37. This is also the beginning of a trend. Florida had lost 14 of 19 to Georgia before Spurrier showed up; the Gators will win 11 of 12 with him in charge.

The 1991 campaign began against defending Big West champion San Jose State. It was a shootout from the opening kickoff, and while the Spartans were able to keep up for a little while – it was 17-14 Florida early in the second quarter – they wilted soon enough. Florida scored four touchdowns in the final eight minutes of the first half, and Matthews was removed with Florida up 52-14. Final score: 59-21. The next week, Spurrier scored his symbolic 35-0 win over Alabama. But while the Gators were redefining football for the SEC, out-of-conference play would only go so well.

Now fifth in the country, Florida flew north to face a Syracuse team that was *ready*. Paul Pasqualoni's Orangemen had tricks up their collective sleeve. Kirby DarDar took a reverse on the opening kickoff and raced 95 yards for a touchdown. Syracuse would go up 14-0 less than five minutes into the game, and with Florida rendered one-dimensional on offense, the Syracuse defense teed off, sacking Matthews seven times. Including sacks, Florida rushed for minus-17 yards for the day, while Syracuse, with a funky option attack, gained 250. The Orangemen cruised to a stunning 38-21 win. Spurrier after the game: "We got a good tail kicking. Royally."

In a year in which Miami and Washington would finish undefeated, this loss eliminated Florida from national title contention
in just the third week of the season. But that was okay; before you
can run (win the national title), you've got to walk (win the SEC).
And Florida responded to this loss with easy wins over Mississippi
State, LSU, Tennessee, NIU, Auburn, and Georgia. Only Kentucky
remained in the quest for an outright SEC title.

*Matthews to Aubrey Hill for an eight-yard score. Matthews to Tre Everett for
a 65-yard bomb the play after Florida recovered a Kentucky fumble. Matthews
to Everett again for 33 yards. Alonzo Sullivan to Matthews for 19 yards
and another touchdown. Florida goes up 28-3 in just 17 minutes. Kentucky
will exploit a blocked punt and a fake punt to score 23 straight points and get
to within 28-26, but with the game in the balance, Rhett gains 41 yards on
seven carries and catches two passes on a 12-play, 71-yard scoring drive to ice a
35-26 win.*

When trying to accomplish something you've never done before,
it's supposed to be hard. But Florida's first SEC title was shockingly
easy. Only one game was decided by fewer than 16 points, and that
one (Kentucky) was mainly a "taking your foot off the gas" situation.
At 9-1, the Gators were back up to fifth in the country, but they still
had the chance to make their biggest statement yet. And it would
require superhuman effort from the UF defense. And one prayer.

Florida and Florida State combined to average nearly 67 points
per game in 1991; in Gainesville on November 30, they combined
for just 23. Florida held FSU's Casey Weldon to 24-for-51 passing,
and FSU held Matthews to 13-for-30 and three picks. In front of
85,461, a record crowd at Ben Hill Griffin Stadium, Florida led just
7-3 at halftime thanks to a short Rhett touchdown.

But midway through the third quarter, FSU's defense suffered
a crippling miscue. With Matthews rolling right, FSU's Terrell
Buckley pursued him, leaving linebacker Reggie Freeman to cover
Harrison Houston deep. Buckley had two interceptions on the day,

but he only got within about one stride of Matthews before the QB heaved a deep jump ball toward Houston. Freeman slipped as he attempted to post up, and Houston made a leaping catch and streaked into the end zone.

The 72-yard strike accounted for more than one-third of Matthews' passing yards. And when a late FSU drive ended with a fourth-down incompletion in the end zone, the bomb made the difference in a 14-9 win. The Gators had lost four in a row to FSU before this win and would lose three of the next four. But this game kick-started a rivalry that would define quite a few national title races throughout the 1990s. The winner of Florida-FSU would either win or play for the national title four times in seven years between 1993-99.

First SEC title. First 10-win season. Spurrier's first wins over Tennessee and Florida State. Then, after the season, a top-five recruiting class. So much of what we came to know about Florida in the 1990s was set in motion in the fall of 1991. Before Spurrier arrived, Florida had only once pulled off a top-10 finish in a year in which they were not banned from the postseason. Despite a 39-28 Sugar Bowl loss to Notre Dame, the Gators pulled off this feat in 1991, and then did it in nine of the next 10 years as well. They played in the first SEC title game (a loss to Alabama), then won four consecutive titles. They won two Sugar Bowls, two Orange Bowls, and the 1996 national title. They forced SEC defenses out of their four-lineman, three-linebacker comfort zone and made them adapt to four- and five-receiver sets. And in 2016, after Spurrier had officially retired following stints with the Washington Redskins and South Carolina Gamecocks, Florida named its field after him.

1991 WASHINGTON

It was better back in the day. You hear that in basically every possible context and every successive decade. The last generation was better, tougher, less coddled. And, according to those of a certain age, your sport of choice was *definitely* better. It was more physical, men could be men, et cetera.

Depending on your preferred style of football offense – and, of course, how tough or coddled you think kids these days are – maybe college football *was* better back in the day. But one thing is certain: The method for determining a national champion was, shall we say, less than optimal.

(Granted, there is a perverse joy in coming to realize that, after the 2015 season, schools had claimed a total of 256 national championships. It allows you to laugh at the thought of teams battling for the title centuries ago. At 5'7, Alexander Hamilton would have made for a heck of an undersized play-maker at nickel back.)

But while teams claiming shares of the mythical national title adds a certain level of socialism to a very oligarchical sport – You get a title! And you get a title! – the bowl system and the given method of determining a champion prevented us from actually getting many No. 1 vs. No. 2 matchups through the years.

For all the issues the BCS era (1998-2013) may have had, it guaranteed a 1-vs-2 game each year, even if we didn't always agree on who should have been No. 1 or No. 2. Before the BCS, college football would sometimes go years without such a battle. For instance, between the 1972 Orange Bowl and the 1979 Sugar Bowl, the top two teams in the AP rankings didn't play even once. That is absurd and counter-productive. And in 1991, bowl obligations prevented us from watching two of the best teams of the 1990s facing off. Miami went undefeated and finished No. 1 in the AP poll and No. 2 in the USA Today/CNN poll. Washington went undefeated and finished No. 1 in the USA Today/CNN poll and No. 2 in the AP. The twain never met.

Both teams got rings; there's nothing particularly wrong with that. But Washington never got a chance to prove itself against the dynasty of its day. This was the best Washington team ever, and in a way, the split title prevented the Huskies from proving they were one of the best *teams* ever.

That Don James was able to put a team this strong together, this late in his career, was a victory in itself. When you lose your cutting edge, it's sometimes hard to get it back, both because it's innately difficult and because, in a low-patience atmosphere, you might not get a chance. In the mid-1980s, James indeed appeared to have lost a step.

A former Miami quarterback and U.S. Army lieutenant, James had served as a defensive coordinator at Florida State, Michigan, and Colorado and spent four years as Kent State's head coach, leading the Golden Flashes to three winning seasons and the 1972 Tangerine Bowl against Tampa. He took over for long-serving

Jim Owens at Washington in 1975, having never coached west of Boulder. He had no built-in recruiting connections, no familiarity with other Pac-10 programs. And it took him all of three seasons to get the Huskies back to the Rose Bowl for the first time in 15 years. They finished 11th or better in the polls four times in six years from 1977-82 and spent time at No. 1 in 1982 before finishing seventh. Two years later, they were back at No. 1 until a 16-7 loss to USC, and their win over No. 2 Oklahoma in the Orange Bowl brought them to within just 20 points of first place in the final AP vote. Undefeated BYU barely held on, and James barely missed a ring.

From 1985-88, however, the Huskies went just 28-17-2. Not terrible, but definitely not great. They went 6-5 in 1988 and missed a bowl for the first time in a decade. You can imagine the rumblings on sports radio. James had lost his touch, he was too loyal to certain assistants, he was past his prime, etc. Almost every successful coach deals with this at one point or another.

According to Gary Pinkel, then James' offensive coordinator, recruiting success had trailed off a bit. "We weren't as good personnel-wise. You never want to say that because that means you recruited poorly. You can't blame it on players. But the truth of the matter was, we had a bit of a lull in recruiting. But we came out of it, then obviously just went crazy."

Fans obsess over recruiting each year because of the truly program-changing effect it can have. Not every star recruit lives up to his billing, and not every team that signs a top-five class is guaranteed a top-five product. But classes like Washington's 1988 signing haul, as uncommon as they may be, happen just frequently enough to make us all hope.

Washington's 1988 class featured the No. 1 pick in the 1992 draft (tackle Steve Emtman), the No. 9 pick in the 1993 draft (offensive lineman Lincoln Kennedy), and six other eventual draftees: receivers Mario Bailey and Orlando McKay, linebacker Jaime Fields and Dave

Hoffman, fullback Darius Turner, and quarterback Mark Brunell.

This was the perfect Washington recruiting class, combining local stars (Bailey), less-recruited local diamonds in the rough (Emtman), and high-caliber imports from California (Brunell, Kennedy). As members of the '88 class began to see the field, Washington's prospects improved drastically. From 6-5, the Huskies improved to 8-4 in 1989, then 10-2 in 1990, with their first Rose Bowl bid in nine years.

By 1991, line coach Keith Gilbertson had replaced Pinkel as offensive coordinator – Pinkel had taken the head coaching job at Toledo; he would spend 10 years there and 15 at Missouri, becoming each school's winningest coach. Gilbertson would face one primary obstacle: In spring practice, Brunell, a second-team all-conference starter in 1990, injured his knee and was relegated to backup status in the fall. Sophomore Billy Joe Hobert would take over.

Washington began the season fourth in the preseason AP poll, but this wasn't the year for much of a rise: Preseason No. 1 Florida State would lose only to preseason No. 3 Miami, and Miami wouldn't lose at all. But that didn't dampen the Huskies' dominance.

In the season opener at Stanford, Hobert threw for 244 yards and two touchdowns, and Washington rolled, 42-7. This turned out to be a pretty good Stanford team, too; Dennis Green's Cardinal would go on to finish 8-4, beating three ranked teams along the way.

After a bye week, the Huskies were off to Lincoln for a major non-conference challenge against No. 9 Nebraska. Tom Osborne's Huskers would go on to finish 9-2-1 and win the Big 8, and they were good enough to lead UW 21-9 in the third quarter. But they were starting to tire, and Washington was only getting warmed up.

Taking advantage of a key fourth-down conversion, the Huskies got to within five points on a 15-yard Beno Bryant score. Touchdowns by McKay and Hobert gave Washington a 29-21 lead, then the Huskies put the game away in style. With six minutes left and the ball at the Washington 19, backup running back Jay Barry lined up behind Hobert in James' patented one-back formation, with a tight end on each side of the line. Barry took the ball on a draw play, cut right to avoid a tackler, hit the right sideline, juked a charging safety just past the 30, and turned on the jets. Only McKay could keep up with him. The 81-yard score punctuated a perfect second-half charge, and Washington went home with a 36-21 win.

A three-game home stand provided minimal challenge. Bill Snyder and Kansas State visited and found themselves trailing 20-0 after one quarter. Hobert completed 13 of 18 passes, and the only drama came when Brunell, who was completing his knee rehabilitation, took the field in garbage time to finish off a 56-3 win. Then, against Dick Tomey's Arizona Wildcats, Brunell saw even more playing time: He filled in for an injured Hobert and completed five of seven passes with two touchdowns to Bailey. Washington's fierce defense sacked UA quarterback George Malauulu six times and forced seven turnovers in a 54-0 destruction of the Wildcats.

October 12 was a homecoming of sorts as Pinkel brought his Toledo Rockets to town. But the pleasantries ended at kickoff. Hobert, back in the lineup, connected with Bailey for three first-half scores; James called off the dogs early, but Washington still won, 48-0.

Washington had only risen to third in the AP poll because FSU and Miami refused to lose; meanwhile, Bruce Snyder's surprising California Golden Bears had begun the season 5-0 and had quickly risen to seventh in the country. To remain unbeaten, Washington would have to pull off its second top-10 road win of the year.

Cal took an early lead on a 59-yard pass from Mike Pawlawski to future Indianapolis Colt and Seattle Seahawk Sean Dawkins; the game was tied at 17-17 at halftime. But, as was the custom, Washington's defense adjusted and wreaked havoc in the second half. One minute into the fourth quarter, it was Bryant's time to apply the dagger. Just as ABC announcer Brent Musberger was saying, "The Huskies are going to dig down and show everybody if they are indeed the best team in the country," Bryant did just that. He took the handoff up the middle, dodged one defender, and raced 65 yards. Washington 24, California 17.

From there, it was destruction after destruction. Hobert threw for 256 yards and Bailey caught seven passes for 108 yards and two scores in a 29-7 win over Oregon. (Oregon *did* become the first team to score a touchdown on Washington in the fourth quarter, the smallest of moral victories.) The only differences the next week against Arizona State: Hobert threw for 228, Bailey's seven receptions went for 139 yards, and ASU was allowed to score *two* garbage-time touchdowns in a 44-16 Washington win.

In the L.A. Coliseum, USC was able to shut Hobert down, but Bryant rushed 26 times for 158 yards and two first-half touchdowns, the only seven-pointers of the game. USC's offense was hopelessly outmanned, and Washington stayed at an arm's length, winning 14-3.

Washington's only defensive weakness was a propensity for occasionally giving up a big pass play. Washington State's Drew Bledsoe was able to take advantage of this a bit in November 23's Apple Cup battle in Seattle. He threw for 295 yards and three touchdowns, including a 33-yarder that briefly gave Wazzu a 7-6 lead. But Washington's Walter Bailey *also* scored off of a Bledsoe pass; his 37-yard pick six was part of a 29-0 UW run that put the Huskies up 35-7. Wazzu got going again, but Washington had already won. Final score: 56-21.

Miami's 17-16 win over Florida State, secured when FSU missed a last-second field goal wide right, meant that the Hurricanes and Huskies would finish 1-2 in the end-of-regular season AP poll. Washington was obligated to play No. 4 Michigan in the Rose Bowl; second-year head coach Gary Moeller, succeeding retired Bo Schembechler, had led the Wolverines to a 10-1 record. Their only loss was to Florida State. Miami, meanwhile, stayed at home to again host No. 11 Nebraska in the Orange Bowl. The Hurricanes did their job, winning 22-0. But in Pasadena, a vengeful Washington squad made a statement.

Michigan was headlined by Heisman-winning receiver and return man Desmond Howard (985 receiving yards, 180 rushing yards, two return touchdowns) and a three-headed running back attack of Ricky Powers, Jesse Johnson, and Tyrone Wheatley (combined: 2,379 yards, 24 touchdowns). The Wolverines came in averaging 36.9 points per game; they barely crossed double digits in Pasadena. Howard caught just one pass while Bailey and little-used Aaron Pierce caught a combined 13 passes for 212 yards to power the Washington attack. Hobert threw two second-half touchdown passes to put Washington up 27-7, and then Brunell and Bailey connected for a 38-yarder. A late 53-yard run by Wheatley accounted for more than a quarter of Michigan's yardage. Yards: UW 404, UM 205. Score: UW 34, UM 14.

Indeed, Washington and Miami would split the national title, with an excellent Hurricanes team stealing some thunder from an all-time Husky squad. Washington would get its revenge in a way: In 2000, the Huskies handed Miami its only loss of the season, a defeat that would narrowly keep the Hurricanes out of the BCS championship game.

Hobert had done such a fantastic job of filling in for the injured Brunell that he kept the starting job even when Brunell had recovered. But during the following season, he was suspended and had his eligibility stripped when it was revealed that he had received $50,000 in loans, with no assets or payment schedule, from the relative of a friend. He became the face of a scandal that resulted in the Pac-10 slapping Washington with sanctions for a lack of institutional control. James would resign in protest of the sanctions after a third straight Rose Bowl campaign. It brought a premature end to James' resurgence, but that did not dampen the achievement of the 1991 squad, one of the best to ever grace the West Coast.

1993 TEXAS A&M

The late-1970s were the heyday for the Southwest Conference. From 1975 to 1986, at least one league team finished sixth or better in the AP's year-end poll, and 28 finished in the top 15. Houston finished in the top 5 twice in the late-1970s, and both Texas (1981) and SMU (1982) nearly won national titles.

This was a huge shift for a conference that was, for a while, dominated by Texas and Arkansas. The addition of Bill Yeoman's Houston Cougars was significant and successful, but Baylor got its act together under Grant Teaff, Texas Tech began to do well under a series of coaches, Texas A&M had its moments under Wishbone champion Emory Bellard, and Ron Meyer was building something spectacular at SMU at the end of the 1970s. By the '80s, the conference only had two real lightweights – TCU and Rice – and TCU even had a great season in 1984.

The reason for this collective upward surge was pretty easy to explain, really: Everybody was cheating. Like their lives depended on it. Even by college football's low standards, programs in the SWC were *brazen* in their rule breaking.

To be fair, Arkansas and Rice were never investigated by the NCAA during this period. That's not the same as being clean and pure, but at the very least, they were not as blatant (or, in Rice's case, successful) in their extralegal maneuverings. But the SWC as a whole was ground zero for NCAA investigations and sanctions.

SMU was always most aggressively courting NCAA investigators. From 1974-85, the Mustangs were put on probation five times, but it seemed boosters were only growing bolder in their efforts to court and retain talented players. In 1986, local media and an NCAA investigation clearly spelled out the details of a comprehensive, well-organized slush fund used to pay players and recruits. And in February 1987, the NCAA's infractions committee handed SMU a death sentence, banning it from playing competitive football in 1987 and allowing only a limited schedule for 1988. (The school would elect to sit out the entire 1988 season as well.)

The Mustangs took the heaviest blow, but they were not alone. In 1986, TCU was slapped with three years of NCAA probation and sanctions, including a scholarship reduction, a one-year postseason ban, and forfeiture of previous television revenue. In March 1987, the month after SMU was handed the death penalty, Texas Tech received one-year probation and a slight scholarship reduction for giving at least one recruit money and a pair of ostrich-skin boots. In June 1987, Texas, the SWC's flagship school, was hit with scholarship reductions.

In 1988, the NCAA had its way with two more schools. Houston wasn't given the death penalty, but it might as well have been – after the discovery of more than 250 violations, the Cougars were given five years' probation, a two-year bowl ban, a one-year television ban, and a massive scholarship reduction. The punishment would have been even worse if Yeoman, the head coach overseeing these violations, hadn't been forced into early retirement. From 1991-2001, UH would win barely three games per year.

Texas A&M, meanwhile, got hit with a two-year probation, scholarship reduction, and a 1988 postseason ban. These sanctions weren't as bad as others', but it still led to Jackie Sherrill's resignation.

Were SWC schools the only ones giving out illegal benefits or paying recruits? Of course not. But sometimes stereotypes are fulfilled; in the era of the TV show *Dallas*, Texas schools came off like *Dallas*' main character, J.R. Ewing: more brazen, more boisterous, and more committed to these deeds than others. (A few hours north on I-35, both Oklahoma and Oklahoma State would also get slapped pretty hard for misdeeds during this period.) This was especially the case at SMU, where booster Sherwood Blount grew so bold as to threaten NCAA investigators.

The effects of these sanctions on overall league quality were predictable; the top-15 finishes became rarer and rarer. Between 1991 and 1994, only one SWC program was able to finish in even the top 20.

When Sherrill resigned in College Station, the job went to his top assistant, defensive coordinator R.C. Slocum. The 43-year old McNeese State graduate had over the previous decade carved out a niche as one of the best defensive minds in college football. He served as Bellard's D.C. in 1979-80, moved on to the same gig at USC, where the Trojans allowed just 14.2 points per game and allowed the fewest yards per game in the country. In 1982, he returned to serve under Sherrill, and despite playing in one of the most offense-friendly conferences in the country, the Aggies didn't allow even 20 points per game between 1983-87.

In Slocum's first year in charge, A&M went 7-5 while banned from the postseason. The growth was slow and steady. In 1989, they went

8-4 and allowed 16 points per game. In 1990, 9-3-1 and 17.8 points per game. And in 1991, the true Wrecking Crew era began. Led by SWC defensive player of the year Quentin Coryatt, A&M went 8-0 in the SWC and 10-2 overall. Over their last five games, which included battles against Arkansas, Texas, and Florida State (a 10-2 loss in the Cotton Bowl), the Aggies allowed a total of just 40 points.

The Aggies began the 1992 season 12-0 before losing 28-3 to Notre Dame in the Cotton Bowl. That dose of reality fed motivation heading into 1993. Led by star defensive tackle Sam Adams and defensive back Aaron Glenn, A&M would allow under 12 points per game that fall. And that average included a dreadful early-season performance.

The Aggies began the season fourth in the country, and they looked the part in their season-opener against visiting LSU. Tiger quarterback Jamie Howard had one of the worst days of his football-playing life, completing just five of 27 passes with three interceptions. LSU gained 206 total yards, and A&M running back Rodney Thomas nearly matched that by himself, rushing for 201 in a 24-0 win. But the next week, things went awry.

Granted, A&M's defense still didn't play too poorly in Norman against Gary Gibbs' No. 17 Oklahoma Sooners; OU averaged just 5.1 yards per play and turned the ball over twice. But OU proved what Notre Dame had in the Cotton Bowl the previous year, and what Florida State had proven the year before that: If you could dominate A&M's offense thoroughly enough, the defense didn't matter. OU intercepted five Aggie passes, three off of A&M starter Corey Pullig, and blocked a punt in rolling to a 44-14 victory, the Sooners' first over a top-five team in six years.

A&M was now in an awkward position. The Aggies had won 19 of their last 20 SWC games but had gotten thumped by each of the last two good non-conference teams they had faced. And with the SWC in relative shambles, they wouldn't get another chance to prove themselves for a while. So instead, they took their frustration out on minnows.

Let's just say that Missouri's trip to College Station came at a pretty bad time. Bob Stull's Tigers ran into an A&M team with a chip on its shoulder and a point to prove. A&M scored 14 points in the first quarter, 24 in the second, and 28 in the third. Thomas and electric redshirt freshman Leeland McElroy combined for 243 rushing yards while Missouri lost five fumbles and gained just 201 yards total. Pullig rebounded from his awful trip to Norman with a 15-for-22 performance, Glenn returned a punt for a touchdown, and A&M rolled up a demonstrative 73-0 win.

A&M was kinder to conference rivals. Texas Tech gained only 169 yards but led 6-3 late in the first half before Pullig and Gene Lowery connected for a 20-yard touchdown, sparking a second-half surge and a 31-6 win. Meanwhile, increasingly depleted Houston gained just 178 yards but trailed just 20-10 in the fourth quarter before a one-yard Thomas score and an 81-yard bolt from McElroy.

Knowing they had a ridiculous defense in their corner, the Aggies could take their time, and offensive coordinator Bob Toledo could remain conservative on offense. At Baylor on October 16, A&M led just 20-17 in the fourth quarter before a four-yard touchdown from Pullig to Clif Groce and a nine-yard McElroy score. At Rice, the offense never even had to shift into second gear – Rice kicked a field goal early in the game, and McElroy returned the ensuing kickoff for a TD; Rice scored again, and McElroy returned *another* kick for a score. Adams recovered a fumble in the end zone, and A&M won 38-10 while gaining only 267 yards.

A valiant effort from SMU in College Station kept A&M from pulling away, but it was the same script as the other games: A&M led 17-6 heading into the fourth quarter, but scored two late touchdowns to pull away, 37-13.

On November 13 came a shot at non-conference redemption as Howard Schnellenberger's 20th-ranked Louisville Cardinals came to town. Schnellenberger had driven an also-ran program to 10-1-1 and a Fiesta Bowl romp over Alabama in 1990; they would eventually finish 9-3 with a Liberty Bowl win over Michigan State in 1993.

After spending the last month in cruise control, A&M was rested and ready. The Aggies took an early 14-0 lead and led 21-7 in the third quarter when Glenn stepped in front of a Jeff Brohm pass and took it 31 yards for a score. The rout was on: Two more late scores made it 42-7; the prolific Brohm was held to 12-for-30 passing with three interceptions.

After a 59-3 destruction of TCU — backup defensive back Dennis Allen recovered a blocked punt in the end zone, Glenn returned another punt 55 yards for a score, and A&M led 35-3 at halftime — it was time for Texas. John Mackovic's Longhorns were just 5-4-1 heading into the contest, but their 5-1 conference record meant that they could still clinch the SWC title with a win.

In front of a Thanksgiving crowd of 74,748 in A&M's Kyle Field (official capacity at that time: 71,100), Texas spent most of the first half controlling the A&M offense. The Longhorns built a 6-0 lead with 8:30 left in the second quarter, but once again the dynamic McElroy struck, taking a kickoff 100 yards for a touchdown. Texas took the lead back, 9-7, but A&M's only touchdown drive of the evening, capped with a 14-yard pass from Pullig to Harrison and a two-point conversion, gave A&M a 15-9 advantage at halftime.

It was still 15-9 when Texas got the ball at its 34 midway through the fourth quarter. The Longhorns proceeded to move all the way to the A&M 2, and on fourth-and-1, UT quarterback Shea Morenz rolled right, looking for tight end Steve Bradley. But Allen, in the game because of a host of injuries in the A&M secondary, stepped in front of the pass and picked it off. Terry Venetoulias kicked a 34-yard field goal to ice both the game and another Cotton Bowl berth.

Rarely do you get a stark opportunity at redemption in the middle of a winning streak. A&M had won 22 straight SWC games and 31 of 32 regular season games, but the Aggies had lost in each of their two previous Cotton Bowl trips.

A year earlier, on New Year's Day 1993, A&M had been humiliated by Notre Dame. Rettig, a one-time Notre Dame commitment, completed just seven of 18 passes, and at one point in the second half, the Irish ran the ball on 34 consecutive plays. Irish backs Jerome Bettis and Reggie Brooks combined for 190 yards, and a proud defense could do little to stop them.

On January 1, 1994, A&M was ready. Against a Notre Dame team ranked second and needing a win to keep national title hopes alive, A&M played daring, composed football. With the score tied at 7-7 in the first half, the Aggies went for it on fourth-and-1 from their own 45; odds greatly favor the offense on fourth-and-1, but most coaches choose to punt regardless. Pullig sneaked ahead for two yards and a first down. Then, on another fourth-and-1 from the Irish 15, Pullig faked another sneak and hit wide open fullback Detron Smith for a 15-yard touchdown.

With the score tied at 21-21 with six minutes left in the game, the Aggies got the ball at their 10 but lost two yards in three plays. Notre Dame's Mike Miller then returned the ensuing punt 38 yards to A&M's 22. The Aggie defense held its ground, but Kevin Pendergast nailed a 31-yard field goal with 2:22 left. One last gasp from the A&M offense came up short. A&M had redeemed itself by playing well against one of the two best teams in the country, but the Aggies still lost their third straight Cotton Bowl.

A&M would have to wait nearly two decades to end the Cotton Bowl losing streak. First, the Aggies again got in trouble with the NCAA. Greg Hill and four other players had received suspensions to start the 1993 season because of money they received for summer work they had not actually completed. Four more ended up involved, as well.

Though Slocum himself was cleared of any wrongdoing, A&M ended up put on five years' probation and banned from both television and the postseason in 1994. (It technically could have been worse – with two major violations in five years, the Aggies were eligible for the death penalty.) They went 10-0-1 that season, getting revenge on Oklahoma, 36-14, beating Texas in Austin by 24 points, and suffering only a surprising tie against SMU.

The Aggies again finished with the best record in the conference at 6-0-1, but since they were ineligible, the SWC title race finished in a five-way tie, with Baylor, Rice, Texas, TCU, and Texas Tech all at 4-3. Tech won the tie-breaker and got stomped by USC in the Cotton, 55-14.

A year later, the SWC was no more. The combination of a lackluster product, sinking television revenue (in part because so many teams were banned from being on TV), and a changing television environment conspired against what was now a one-state league.

Arkansas had left for a new 12-team, two-division SEC in 1992, and teams and conferences were quickly jettisoning the College Football Association to create their own television deals. Texas, Texas A&M, Texas Tech, and Baylor agreed to join Big 8 teams in a super-conference called the Big 12. TCU (narrowly spurned in favor of Baylor), Rice, Houston, and SMU found refuge in mid-major conferences.

Texas A&M would win the Big 12 in its third year, losing to Ohio State in the Sugar Bowl. The Aggies would twice more attend the Cotton Bowl, which was now typically reserved for one of the Big 12's runners up, but lost both times. It wasn't until 2012, their first season in *another* new conference (the 14-team SEC) that they would end a 25-year Cotton Bowl title drought.

1993 WISCONSIN

To find their first Rose Bowl ticket in 31 years, the Wisconsin Badgers had to fly to Tokyo. It's always the last place you look.

When Notre Dame defensive coordinator Barry Alvarez accepted the Badgers' head coaching job at the end of 1989, the UW program was at its nadir. Wisconsin had seen sporadic success in the middle of the century, but things fell apart in the late-1960s. Dave McClain brought some stability to the program in the early-1980s, winning seven games for four straight years between 1981-84. But McClain died of a heart attack at the age of 48 in April 1986. In the four years that followed, UW went just 9-36. The athletic department was running a deficit, and no one was coming to Camp Randall Stadium.

Luckily for Wisconsin, Alvarez saw potential. Alvarez had played for Bob Devaney at Nebraska and spent eight seasons under Hayden Fry at Iowa before coming to South Bend with Lou Holtz. He was confident in his abilities, and he was intensely organized. He had a plan for everything.

As progress isn't linear, it took certain well-placed setbacks to get the Badgers to where they ended up. In his first season, his conditioning program ran off more than 50 players, including walk-ons, and the painfully thin Badgers went just 1-10. The next year, the Badgers started 3-0 and played well in tight losses to Ohio State and a 10-win Iowa team. They lost six games in a row in the middle of the year but rallied to win their final two games and finish 5-6 for the first time in six years.

The 1992 Wisconsin team was, on paper, clearly improved again. A 20-16 win over Ohio State prompted the Camp Randall crowd to tear down the goal posts. But the Badgers lost 23-22 to Iowa, 10-3 to Indiana, and 13-12 to Illinois. Wisconsin was 5-5 with one game remaining; to reach their first bowl in eight years, the Badgers simply had to take down 2-8 Northwestern. Down 27-25 late in the game, they were in position for the game-winning field goal, but running back Jason Burns was hit as he took the ball and fumbled. Northwestern recovered and ran out the clock, but not before a little bit of taunting. According to quite a few players in a Fox Sports oral history piece, Wildcat quarterback Len Williams added some extra notes to his pre-snap cadence in the final plays. "Blue 19, y'all ain't going nowhere." "You ain't going nowhere but home. Set. Hut."

Frustration aside, it was obvious that the Badgers were improving. Heading into the 1993 campaign, Wisconsin boasted two of the Big Ten's best running backs (Brent Moss, Terrell Fletcher), two of its best offensive linemen (Joe Panos, Chuck Belin), a prolific QB-to-WR combination (Darrell Bevell to Lee DeRamus), and the components of a sound, opportunistic defense (lineman Lamark Shackerford, linebacker Gary Casper, defensive back Jeff Messenger).

This was the most physically impressive Wisconsin team in quite some time. Now the Badgers just had to figure out how to close games.

Slowly but surely, the Big Ten was beginning to enter another period of relative socialism. After the "Everybody gets a Rose Bowl bid!" period of the 1960s, either Michigan or Ohio State had snared every bid between 1968 and 1980. The early-1980s brought about some change, as Ohio State began to falter after Woody Hayes' retirement. Someone *other* than the Wolverines or Buckeyes attended four of seven Rose Bowls between 1981 and 1987. Michigan had reasserted its control of late.

Not that it was clear yet, but the Wolverines were about to falter. After 19 top-10 finishes in the 24 years between 1969-92, they would only do the deed twice in the next nine seasons. (Granted, one of those years – 1997 – resulted in a national title.) Ohio State was picking up steam under John Cooper, but the Buckeyes always managed to suffer one surprisingly poor result; they would attend the Rose only once in the 1990s.

That opened the door back up for usurpers. As Wisconsin would come to learn, this was a perfect time to get your act together.

On a perfectly sunny, season-opening Saturday in Madison, Moss and Fletcher combined for 136 yards as the Badgers dominated a decent Nevada team, 35-17. Next came what should have been a pretty easy road test. But Wisconsin was not yet to the point of handling road trips with ease. The Badgers were just 1-12 away from Camp Randall in Alvarez's tenure, and it looked like that record would move to 1-13 when SMU took a 13-0 lead into halftime. But Moss cut SMU's lead to 16-10 with a short score, then Bevell found J.C. Dawkins for a 25-yard touchdown to give UW the lead. Fletcher plunged in and gave the Badgers a 24-16 cushion that held up.

Sometimes disappointing performances can create turning points. Wisconsin dug itself quite a hole in Dallas but responded. That gave the Badgers a confidence they had previously lacked. Now ranked 24th in the country – their first appearance in the AP poll since 1984 – they bolted to a 21-0 halftime lead against Iowa State and cruised, 28-7. They went to Bloomington to face a strong Indiana team (the Hoosiers would finish 8-4) and raced to a 20-2 halftime lead. Indiana responded, but a four-yard Bevell-to-Matt Nyquist connection gave the Badgers a 27-15 win. The next week, they led Northwestern 27-14 at the break (Bevell was 14-for-14 in the first half), and, perhaps still seething from the taunting they received in Evanston a year earlier, scored 26 second-half points to roll, 53-14.

By now, Wisconsin was fully into "firsts" territory. The Badgers were 5-0 for the first time since 1977; the next week in West Lafayette, they raced to a 35-0 lead over Purdue and held off a late Boilermaker charge to win, 42-28. That moved them to 6-0 for the first time since 1912. Alvarez was getting Rose Bowl questions in his press conferences; his response: "Why not Wisconsin?"

The Badgers then proceeded to show why they might not be ready yet. Against an inferior Minnesota team that would finish 4-7, Bevell had one of the worst games of his career. He threw five interceptions, one of which was returned for a touchdown, and despite gaining 605 total yards of offense, the Badgers couldn't erase a 21-0 halftime deficit, falling 28-21.

If there was any fear of Wisconsin's players getting full of themselves, that dissolved in Minneapolis. The very next week, the conference's ruler, Michigan, visited Madison. The Badgers were angry and ready. The first half was near-perfection – Wisconsin gained 226 total yards and held the ball for 20 minutes. Unfortunately, the Badgers had to settle for two field goals; despite dominance, their lead was only 13-3.

Previous Wisconsin teams would have blown this one. This team did not. Michigan opened the second half by driving to the UW 2, but the Badgers recovered a Ricky Powers fumble. Michigan responded with a touchdown to cut the lead to three, and the Wolverines were driving to start the fourth quarter, but Messenger reeled in an interception. In Michigan's last-chance drive, the ball got to the Wisconsin 28, but on fourth-and-6, the Badgers stopped a dump-off pass two yards short of the sticks.

It had been 12 years since Wisconsin had beaten Michigan. The last nine battles had produced an average score of Wolverines 36, Badgers 9. The 13-10 win both provided catharsis and put the Badgers right back into the Rose Bowl conversation.

Unfortunately, the win itself was overshadowed by what happened afterward. As students attempted to rush the field after the win, they were impeded by event staff and a chain link fence. A crush formed, and 73 fans were injured, some severely. Players ended up helping to deliver aid. Alvarez had counselors speak to the team during the week; some players visited victims in the hospital.

Just seven days after the crush, it was game time once again: Ohio State was in town.

The Buckeyes were unbeaten and ranked third in the country. They took a 7-0 lead in the first quarter, but Wisconsin's ball control offense began to find its rhythm. Bevel and DeRamus connected for an eight-yard score late in the second quarter to make it 7-7 at halftime, and Moss scored from three yards out to give Wisconsin a 14-7 lead in the third quarter.

With four minutes left in the game, however, Ohio State was able to do what Michigan could not. Pinned at their one-yard line, the Buckeyes pulled off an improbable touchdown drive. Star receiver Joey Galloway, lined up opposite Wisconsin backup Donny Brady (in the game because of an injury), caught passes of 15 and 47 yards, then reeled in a 26-yard score with 3:48 on a perfect post route.

The Badgers responded, advancing all the way to the OSU 15 with seven seconds left, but the Buckeyes' Marlon Kerner raced in off the left flank and blocked a 32-yard field goal. The game ended at 14-14.

Because of Wisconsin's loss to Minnesota, Ohio State still controlled its Rose Bowl destiny. But that had changed by the next time the Badgers took the field. Early on November 20, Michigan crushed OSU, 28-0; this meant that Wisconsin could tie the Buckeyes for the conference title with wins over Illinois and Michigan State. A tie between the two teams would be broken by who had the longer Rose Bowl absence. To say the least, that tie-breaker favored the Badgers.

Wisconsin came out charging in Champaign. The Badgers led 17-3 at halftime and rolled, 35-10, behind 263 rushing yards from Fletcher and Moss and 17-for-22 passing from Bevell.

Next stop: Japan?

From 1977-93, Tokyo hosted one college football game per year. Sometimes the matchups were reasonably high-caliber – Notre Dame-Miami in 1979, SMU-Houston in 1983, USC-Oregon in 1985, Nebraska-Kansas State in 1992 – but it had never before decided a Rose Bowl bid. During the 1992 offseason, Wisconsin agreed to move its home game against Michigan State there in 1993, in part because athletic director Pat Richter, Alvarez, etc., weren't sure they would make a bowl game and wanted to give their student-athletes a unique, postseason-style experience. Whoops.

Alvarez, of course, had a plan. He created hydration plans and had his players adjust their body clocks by sleeping during the day and waking up in the middle of the night. Whether this was the reason for their success or not, it certainly didn't hurt. In the sold out Tokyo Dome, about 8,000 miles from Camp Randall, Wisconsin spotted Michigan State a 7-3 head start and then hit the jets. Fletcher scored twice in the second quarter, and Moss added a three-yard touchdown to give the Badgers a 24-7 halftime lead on the way to a 41-20 win.

Over the nearly 100 years since the Rose Bowl became an annual event, college football has, in some ways, moved past it. It is no longer the single shining jewel of the college football season – other major bowls moved in on that turf at times, then the BCS Championship gave fans a guaranteed No. 1 vs. No. 2 matchup to finish the season. And then, of course, came the College Football Playoff.

The Rose Bowl has remained steadfast in its desires to pit Big Ten team vs. Pac-10/12 team and kick off on the afternoon of January 1, following the Tournament of Roses Parade. Its hogging of the meat of the January 1 slate can cause logistical issues for the College Football Playoff. It becomes very easy to get frustrated with Rose Bowl officials for holding onto the past. (Hell, the very next season, the Big Ten's adherence to the Rose Bowl meant that the newly-formed Boal Coalition, designed to create stronger major bowl matchups, would have to pair No. 1 Nebraska against No. 3 Miami for the national title while No. 2 Penn State went to Pasadena. It cost the Nittany Lions a shot at the championship.)

But when you actually attend a game at the Rose Bowl, or watch the reaction of a fan base whose team has not been able to make it there in so long – Wisconsin in 1993, Northwestern in 1995, Purdue in 2000, Iowa in 2015 – you start to get it. For the conference's middle class, the wait can be interminable, and an afternoon in a perfect locale, in a perfect climate, can be the ultimate catharsis.

Wisconsin hadn't been to Pasadena for the big game since January 1, 1963. The Badgers lost 42-37 in a spectacular battle against undefeated USC, and they had to wait 31 years to get a shot at victory. Even against UCLA in the Bruins' home stadium, the stands took on a particularly red tint. Wisconsin fans flooded the town north of Los Angeles.

Alvarez's team showed no signs of nerves. They stuck to their ball-control ways, took a 14-3 lead into halftime on two short Moss runs, and ran the lead to 21-10 in the fourth quarter in the most improbable way: Bevell, not the most mobile of QBs, scrambled left to avoid a blitz, found a big opening once out of the pocket, picked up a block at the 5, and somehow completed a 21-yard run in the end zone.

Down 21-10, UCLA would nearly come all the way back. The Bruins cut the lead to 21-16 and forced a punt. But in the closing seconds, the Badgers forced a scramble from quarterback Wayne Cook and tackled him in bounds at the Wisconsin 15. With no timeouts left, the Bruins couldn't get another snap off. Final score: Badgers 21, Bruins 16.

Perhaps the most impressive aspect of Wisconsin's turnaround is that Wisconsin remained turned around. When Gary Barnett took Northwestern to the Rose Bowl in 1995, the Wildcats were back to 3-9 by 1998, and Barnett left for the Colorado job. When Purdue did the deed under Joe Tiller in 2000, the Boilermakers would remain solid for a while but would come up with just one more top-15 finish in Tiller's tenure.

Under Alvarez, Wisconsin remained powerful. The Badgers briefly slid to 4-5-2 in 1995, but they were back in the Rose Bowl in 1998, and again in 1999. A decade later, after Alvarez had retired and handed the baton to Bret Bielema, they attended three in a row from 2010-12. Alvarez built a foundation that was sturdy and sustainable. All it took was a trip to Tokyo.

1994 NEBRASKA

After two decades, infinite close calls, and a battle with blood clots, Nebraska's story is supposed to finally feature a national title. It was in the cards all year, and now the golden boy, quarterback Tommie Frazier, is back in uniform.

But here the Huskers are, once again in the Orange Bowl, once again trailing a Florida team. Since losing to Miami in a stunning upset in the 1984 Orange Bowl, they lost again there to Miami in 1989 and 1992 and to Florida State in 1993 and 1994. And now, a quarter of the way through the 1995 Orange Bowl, third-ranked Miami leads, 10-0.

Hurricane quarterback Frank Costa has been unstoppable. After gouging the NU defense to set up a field goal, he completes a 44-yard bomb, then throws a quick screen to Trent Jones, who gets perfect blocking and takes the pass 35 yards for a score. The indomitable Nebraska defense is getting dominated, and the offense has produced only a punt and interception thus far.

This can't be how the story ends.

In 1975, Nebraska began the season 10-0 and reached second in the country in advance of a trip to Norman. Oklahoma 35, Nebraska 10.

In 1978, the Huskers finally beat Oklahoma to move to No. 2 again and needed only a home win over unranked Missouri to get a shot at the national title. Missouri 35, Nebraska 31.

In 1982, they lost at Penn State, 27-24, thanks to a controversial, patently incorrect call that resulted in a long, late Penn State completion. It was their only loss of the year; Penn State won the national title.

In 1983, they finally got to the end of the regular season undefeated with what many called the best Nebraska team ever. All they had to do was beat underdog Miami in the Orange Bowl to finish No. 1. Miami 31, Nebraska 30.

In 1993, after a decade of mostly two-loss seasons, they finally got another shot. They went 11-0 in the regular season and got a 1-versus-2 battle against Florida State in the Orange Bowl. FSU 18, Nebraska 16.

Since he succeeded resurrection artist Bob Devaney in 1973, Nebraska head coach Tom Osborne had put together a tenure of nearly impossible consistency and constant what-ifs. By the mid-1990s, he had once again put together the pieces of an elite team. Quarterback Tommie Frazier helmed the option beautifully during the 11-1 run in 1993, and the backfield of I-back Lawrence Phillips and fullback Cory Schlesinger was legendary. The line, known as the Pipeline, featured two All-Americans (Zach Wiegert and Brendan Stai).

Meanwhile, with an incredible linebacking corps of All-American Ed Stewart, Donta Jones, and Troy Dumas and safety Barron Miles patrolling in the back, the Huskers would allow the third-fewest points in the country. Nebraska had fallen behind the athleticism curve in the late-1980s, when FSU and Miami were emerging; by

1994, the Huskers had most assuredly caught up.

To start the second quarter, Brook Berringer fills in for Frazier, just as he has for much of the year. The signal caller from Goodland, Kan., has completed more than 60 percent of his passes and guided the Huskers through a couple of late-season landmines.

At first, Miami treats Berringer just like it did Frazier. With future NFL great Ray Lewis roaming the middle of the field, another future all-pro, tackle Warren Sapp, sacks Berringer for a huge loss, and NU punts. At this point, Miami has outgained NU, 143-57. But NU's vaunted Blackshirts are finding their rhythm; the Huskers will allow only 134 yards over the final three quarters.

After a nice punt return sets Nebraska up in Miami territory, Berringer, with his no-frills release, flicks a beautiful 19-yard pass to tight end Mark Gilman for a touchdown. It's 10-7 at halftime. Game on.

The season began with a statement. Nebraska, ranked fourth in the preseason poll, went to New Jersey to take on No. 24 West Virginia in college football's Kickoff Classic. Nebraska led 3-0 after one quarter, but scored three touchdowns in the second on the way to a 31-0 win. The Pipeline more than did its job – Frazier rushed 12 times for 130 yards and three long touchdowns, while Phillips rushed 24 times for 126 yards.

After a bye week came a tricky trip to Lubbock to face Texas Tech. The Huskers took a 14-0 lead in the second quarter on two Frazier scores, but Tech clawed back to within 14-9 in the third quarter. No worries – Phillips scored twice (the second a 56-yarder), and NU pulled away, 42-16.

NU bolted to a 28-7 halftime lead over UCLA in the home opener and rolled 49-21. Phillips rushed for 178 yards, then posted 138 on just nine carries the next week against overwhelmed Pacific. NU led 28-0 after one quarter, and Osborne emptied the bench in a 70-21 rout.

Heading into October, Nebraska was rolling. But then Wyoming came to town.

Led by future Purdue head coach Joe Tiller, the Cowboys were putting together a dominant offense. By 1996, they would rack up more than 40 points per game with Tiller's version of what would become known as the spread. They weren't quite at that level in 1994, but they gave Nebraska fits. Quarterback Jeremy Dombek threw two early touchdown passes, and Wyoming had Memorial Stadium stunned and quiet, taking a 14-0 lead into the second quarter. Call it revenge for NU stealing Bob Devaney from UW three decades earlier.

One other thing had Nebraska fans uneasy: Frazier wasn't in the lineup. He had played only two series against Pacific because of what was deemed a sore leg; by the middle of the week, it was determined he had a blood clot behind his right knee. After an incredible start to the year, Frazier would miss the rest of the regular season. Backup Brook Berringer was a better passer than Frazier but wasn't nearly the runner, and the NU offense sputtered out of the gates against UW.

The Huskers rallied, though. Berringer scored on runs of five, 24, and 10 yards as NU took a 35-24 lead into the fourth quarter. Wyoming cut it to 35-32 before a late Phillips score sealed the deal with a score. Berringer was 15-for-22 passing but got hit hard and finished the game with a partially collapsed lung.

Again, the Nebraska secondary shows a crack. Miami's Jonathan Harris catches a short pass from the NU 44, then cuts against the grain, from left sideline to right, to score a spectacular touchdown and give Miami a 17-7 lead. An excessive celebration penalty means Miami is backed up on the kickoff, which gets returned to midfield.

Nebraska goes three-and-out but, thanks to the good field position, pins Miami at its 3 with a punt and two Miami penalties. Nebraska rushes just four defenders but swarms Costa regardless; Dwayne Harris takes him down for a safety before he can throw the ball away, and it's 17-9.

After the teams trade punts, Berringer completes four passes, two to Abdul Muhammad, to get Nebraska into Miami territory. But on the final play of the third quarter, a muffed exchange between Berringer and his running back puts the ball on the ground at the Miami 40. After originally saying Nebraska had recovered it, officials reverse ground and give the ball to Miami. Nebraska enters the final stanza down eight.

Berringer played in the first half against Oklahoma State the week after Wyoming, but by the second half had ceded the ball to third-string walk-on Matt Turman. No matter – Nebraska had Lawrence Phillips, and OSU did not. The Cowboys took an early 3-0 lead, but Phillips scored three times and rushed 33 times for 221 yards. Turman was just 1-for-4 passing, but it didn't matter; NU still cruised, 32-3.

A rising Kansas State squad welcomed Nebraska to Manhattan on October 15. With Berringer clearly struggling and Turman doing no better, NU leaned on Phillips and the defense. The formula eventually worked. The score was 7-6 after three quarters, but backup fullback Jeff Mackovicka went 15 yards up the gut of the KSU defense for a score, and Darin Erstad (future Major Leaguer and Nebraska head baseball coach) tacked on a 24-yard field goal. NU would fall from second to third in the polls due to ongoing concerns with the offense, but the Huskers still won, 17-6.

After a 42-7 breather the next week at Missouri came the game of the year. Colorado, the 1990 national co-champion, was undefeated and up to No. 2 in the country. Due to NU's issues, the Buffaloes were favored by a point.

Unfortunately for the Buffs, they couldn't move the ball on the Blackshirts, and Berringer was healthy and ready. He completed 12 of 17 passes for 142 to punish CU for ganging up to stop Phillips.

Schlesinger scored on a 14-yard as NU built a 17-0 halftime lead, then Berringer put a 24-7 win away with a 30-yard scoring strike to Alford. The Buffalo offense, led by quarterback Kordell Stewart and eventual Heisman running back Rashaan Salaam, came to town averaging over 500 yards per game. They managed just 89 in the first half and 314 for the game. To celebrate the Huskers' first win over a higher-ranked opponent in eight years, students rushed the field and tore down both goal posts.

Another setback: After Miami bombs a snap over the punter's head, NU takes the ball at the Hurricanes' 4-yard line early in the fourth quarter. But Berringer makes an ill-advised pass to the corner of the end zone, and Miami's Earl Little picks it off. After a Miami punt, Frazier takes over again at quarterback. NBC's Cris Collinsworth says, "This is turning into a movie." He has no idea.

The teams trade punts, and with eight minutes to go, Frazier pitches right to Phillips for a huge gain to the Miami 15. From there, it's the most Nebraska call of all: Again running the option to the right, Frazier sticks the ball into the gut of fullback Cory Schlesinger, who sets up his blocks and bursts into the end zone. Frazier's two-point conversion pass to Alford is complete. 17-17, 7:38 to go.

The post-Colorado momentum carried over to the next Saturday. Kansas came to town and found itself down 24-3 after one quarter thanks to interceptions on two of the Jayhawks' first three plays from scrimmage. Berringer threw for 267 yards, the most for a Nebraska passer since 1978, and the Huskers romped, 45-17.

Osborne had feared a letdown against KU, but he got one a week later. Against a winless but pumped up Iowa State team playing its final game for head coach Jim Walden (who would be replaced by Wisconsin assistant Dan McCarney), Nebraska outgained the Cyclones by a 478-213 margin but led only 14-12 heading into the fourth quarter. Both teams missed huge late opportunities – ISU had a long touchdown pass called back because of a holding penalty, and Phillips fumbled into the end zone at the end of a 61-yard run. Eventually, though, NU pulled away, 28-12, thanks to touchdown runs by Damon Benning and Phillips. But that was far tougher than it should have been.

So was the season-ending trip to Norman. With Frazier available if needed but remaining on the bench, NU's offense sputtered, gaining just 302 yards. But the Blackshirts held OU to 47 yards in the second half, and a late Berringer plunge put away a 13-3 win without Frazier seeing the field. The last two games were unimpressive, but the win over Colorado had all but clinched NU's position in the national title race. The Huskers would play Miami in the Orange Bowl.

Miami gets the ball back and gains just one yard in two plays. On third-and-9 with 6:46 left, Costa finds little-used receiver Taj Johnson wide open down the left sideline, with no defender within 15 yards of him. But the pass rush forces Costa to throw it before his feet are set, and he overshoots Johnson by about a yard. Costa stays on the ground for a while after the play, both because he is hit pretty hard and because he probably knows what's coming next.

Against a Miami defense starting to wear down and lose discipline, Frazier keeps the ball on the option and bounces for 25 yards to the Miami 27. Phillips spins for another six yards, and Frazier again cuts upfield on an option keeper to the 14. The Hurricanes are toast. As the clock creeps under three minutes to go, Frazier goes back to Schlesinger. The junior from Columbus, Neb., bolts up the middle, past flailing Miami arms, for a 14-yard score.

On Miami's ensuing drive, Terry Connealy sacks Costa on second down, and three defenders meet at Costa to swallow him up on third. A desperation pass on fourth down finds the arms of NU's Kareem Moss. Ballgame. Torched in the first quarter, Nebraska didn't allow a single first down in the fourth. Nebraska 24, Miami 17.

This was how the story was supposed to end. As the clock hits 30 seconds, Osborne remains uptight, chomping away on his gum. But he accepts a hand-shake from a member of the chain gang, and as Frazier downs the ball for the final time and points at the sky, Osborne calmly removes his headset, takes the most stoic Gatorade bath you'll ever see, and strolls to the middle of the field. In his postgame interview with NBC, he finally permits himself a smile.

The story never actually ends, though. The Huskers romped to the 1995 national title as well, outscoring opponents 638-174 and humiliating Florida in the 1996 Fiesta Bowl; snubbed of the Heisman, Frazier pulled off one of the most famous runs in the sport's history in the third quarter. He gained about 10 yards before he was hemmed in by a gang of Florida tackles, but none of the Gators actually wrapped him up, and Frazier squirted out of the other side of the pile and raced for a touchdown.

Meanwhile, Berringer, the most important backup quarterback in Nebraska history, finished his career with a one-yard QB sneak for Nebraska's final score in the 62-24 win.

Off the field, the story took on a tragic tone. In April 1996, Berringer died when a plane he was flying crashed into a field near Raymond, Neb. Phillips, meanwhile, made headlines for the wrong reasons, too.

A character risk from the start, Phillips was charged with assault during the 1994 season, then was arrested again the next fall. Osborne stuck by him and continued to play him, which put a bit of a stain on his record. Phillips would go on to play in the NFL and CFL but was eventually jailed for good in 2008. He hanged himself in a prison cell in January 2016.

1998 OHIO STATE

The moral of Tom Osborne's story at Nebraska is that if you keep fielding really good teams for a long period of time, eventually you'll break through. The most powerful quality is consistency.

John Cooper might beg to differ.

The Iowa State graduate worked for Tommy Prothro at Oregon State and UCLA and spent time as an assistant at Kansas and Kentucky, and wherever he went, his teams had unprecedented success. UCLA won the Rose Bowl in Prothro's first season in 1965; Kansas won the Big 8 in 1968 and went to the Orange Bowl with him as defensive coordinator; and in 1976, with Fran Curci leading the way, Kentucky won eight games for the first time in 25 years.

When Cooper took over as head coach at Tulsa in 1977, the Golden Hurricane had only won eight or more games once in 11 years. Under Cooper, they did so four times in a six-year span. He moved on to Arizona State in 1985 and had the Sun Devils into their first Rose Bowl by 1986.

Cooper brought heretofore unseen success in every stop of his career, so when Ohio State was looking to rejuvenate itself following a stagnant run in the 1980s, Cooper was almost a no-brainer. He was selected over West Virginia's Don Nehlen and introduced on December 31, 1987.

Earle Bruce certainly hadn't done a terrible job in succeeding Woody Hayes in Columbus. He took the Buckeyes to two Rose Bowls and three top-10 finishes, and he never won fewer than nine games in a season. The problem was that, after his first year in charge, he never lost fewer than three. Ohio State went either 9-3 or 10-3 for seven consecutive years between 1980-86. That led to obvious frustration for a fan base with such high expectations, and Bruce was fired the first time he lost more than three games (the Buckeyes went 6-4-1 in 1987).

Cooper proceeded to lose *four* games per year over his first five seasons in Columbus, but the pieces were coming together. In 1993, the Buckeyes began the year 9-0-1 with only a tie to Wisconsin marring a perfect record. But a 28-0 loss at Michigan wrecked Rose Bowl plans. In 1995, they began 11-0 but again lost at Michigan, 31-23. In 1996, it was the same story: 10-0 start, followed by a 13-9 upset loss to Michigan at home. In 1997, they went 10-0 against teams outside of the top five but lost to No. 1 Michigan, No. 2 Penn State, and No. 4 Florida State. They had a chance to turn the tables when playing an undefeated Michigan team that year; they lost, 20-14.

The constant ability to fall one win short created an interesting dynamic in Columbus in 1998. On one hand, Buckeye fans were prepared for another excellent season but were braced for the worst, especially with a brutal schedule that would feature five ranked opponents, three in the first four weeks. On the other hand ... goodness, was this team talented.

Even by Ohio State standards, the 1998 Buckeyes were loaded. Quarterback Joe Germaine was ready for a star turn after splitting time as starter the previous two years. Michael Wiley and Joe Montgomery would combine for 2,001 rushing yards and 17 touchdowns. David Boston was the best receiver in college football; he would catch 85 balls for 1,435 yards and 13 scores, completely overshadowing an awesome season from No. 2 target Dee Miller (59 catches, 915 yards). Meanwhile, the defense was led by the best defender in the nation, defending Butkus Award winner Andy Katzenmoyer, and an untouchable pair of cornerbacks, Antoine Winfield and Ahmed Plummer.

This team had everything, and it was taking the field on the 30th anniversary of Ohio State's last national championship. The stars had aligned. The Buckeyes began the season No. 1.

Like Nebraska had in 1994, Ohio State began the season by hitting the road to face West Virginia. Nehlen's Mountaineers were ranked 11th in the country and boasted a dynamic offensive attack, but while the Mountaineers would eventually get untracked offensively, it was too late – the Buckeyes scored on four of their first five possessions on their way to a 20-7 lead and a 34-17 win. Boston and Miller caught 13 passes for 239 yards, and Wiley rushed for 140.

After a 49-0 romp over Gary Pinkel's Toledo Rockets, the Buckeyes welcomed No. 21 Missouri to town. In front of 93,269, Ohio State would suffer some early adversity; late in the first half, Germaine was stripped by Barry Odom (who would succeed Pinkel as Missouri's head coach 18 years later); Carlos Posey picked up the loose ball and took it 65 yards for a score. Missouri would lead 14-13 midway through the third quarter, but the Buckeye defense had locked down the Tiger offense, and the Buckeye attack eventually got going. Ohio State scored three times in the final 21 minutes to cruise to an easy 35-14 win.

The Buckeyes were talented and deep enough to create a feeling of inevitability. Even if you found early success, you probably weren't going to be able to sustain it. No. 7 Penn State visited

Columbus on October 3 and ran into the same issue as Missouri; up 3-0 late in the first half, Penn State then allowed three touchdowns in seven minutes and fell, 28-9. The Nittany Lion defense slowed Ohio State down (Boston had only two catches), but the Buckeyes shut PSU out for the final 25 minutes of the game.

Nobody else on the October docket could keep up. In the first half at Illinois, the Buckeyes outgained the Fighting Illini, 326-69, eventually rolling to a 41-0 win. Boston scored twice the next week against Minnesota as Ohio State put up 586 yards and cruised, 45-15. Gary Barnett's final Northwestern team (he would leave for Colorado the next year) kept up for a little while in Evanston – Ohio State led by only seven, 17-10, late in the first half – before the dam broke in a 36-10 win. And a 70-yard punt return by Boston set an early pace in a 38-7 win at Indiana.

As the calendar flipped to November, it seemed obvious where this was headed. Only 4-4 Michigan State and 3-6 Iowa remained before the big game against Michigan, and Cooper's Buckeyes hadn't lost a game to an unranked team for more than four years. They had a reputation for slipping up at bad times, but it was almost always to really good teams.

Michigan State was led by a young, talented head coach (and former Ohio State assistant) by the name of Nick Saban. The Spartans had been volatile in 1998, as many athletic, inexperienced teams are. They had beaten No. 10 Notre Dame by 22 and lost at Minnesota. The week after the trip to Ohio State, they would lose to Purdue at home on their way to just a 6-6 finish. Still, this was a different, more mature Ohio State team. No reason to fear a slipup, right?

The 1998 season was a significant one. College football leaders had formed the Bowl Championship Series (BCS) to assure college football of a No. 1 vs. No. 2 battle to finish the season. Over the previous 25 years, there had been only 16 such matchups, seven in bowls. In so many seasons, the No. 2 team had to win its bowl and hope that No. 1 lost to take the title. It was possible that wouldn't even be enough: If No. 3 beat No. 1, No. 2 could get hopped. It was convoluted and messy – so very, very college football.

The original iteration of the BCS formula combined poll averages (the AP poll and the *USA Today* coaches poll) with the averages of well-regarded computer rankings, a strength of schedule adjuster, and a penalty for losses. Beginning in late-October, the BCS standings would be unveiled weekly, and everyone would know where they stood. The national championship game, then, would pit the top two teams in the standings, rotating between four bowls: the Fiesta, Sugar, Orange, and Rose Bowls. The Fiesta was up first.

Through the years, the BCS would frustrate fans and analysts, mostly for its inability to fit three teams onto the same football field (there was often minimal difference in the résumés of the No. 2 and No. 3 teams). And it was beginning to look like, in its very first year in existence, it might be used to choose between more than two unbeaten, power-conference teams.

Heading into the Michigan State game, Ohio State was 8-0 and No. 1 in the BCS, but No. 2 Tennessee, No. 3 UCLA, No. 4 Kansas State, No. 8 Wisconsin, No. 11 Arkansas, and No. 16 Tulane (of non-BCS Conference USA) were also undefeated, and there was minimal overlap – aside from Tennessee and Arkansas, none of these teams would play each other.

Heading into the final weekend of the season, four of these teams would remain undefeated. Somehow, Ohio State wasn't one of them.

The Michigan State game started out like many others that season. An early MSU field goal made it 3-3, but but Ohio State scored twice in the latter stages of the first quarter—once on a 41-yard pass from Germaine to tight end John Lumpkin and once on a one-yard Wiley score—to take a 17-3 lead. Two MSU field goals cut it to 17-9, and the Spartans were driving early in the third quarter, but Damon Moore picked off a Bill Burke pass and returned it 73 yards for a score. Ohio State led 24-9, then quickly forced a punt; here's where the flood gates were supposed to open.

Fate had other ideas. Craig Jarrett's low punt hit an Ohio State blocker, and MSU recovered near midfield. Four plays later, Burke completed a 23-yard pass to Lavaile Richardson to cut the lead to 24-15. Then Germaine fumbled, and a 49-yard field goal got the Spartans to within 24-18 heading into the fourth quarter.

Then, the unthinkable: Suddenly confident, Michigan State drove 93 yards in eight plays and took the lead when Burke and Plaxico Burress connected for a 37-yard score. Ohio State fumbled *again*, and Michigan State's fourth field goal of the day made it 28-24 Spartans.

The Buckeyes got their feet back underneath them, however, and started moving. They drove inside MSU's 30, but big Joe Montgomery was stuffed on fourth-and-1 with 3:33 remaining.

MSU couldn't run out the clock. The Spartans punted with 1:51 left, and Boston returned it 26 yards to midfield. Germaine quickly completed passes to Boston and Lumpkin, and OSU was at the Sparty 15. However, two passes to Boston fell incomplete, and Renaldo Hill broke up a pass to Miller on third down.

On fourth-and-everything, Hill one-upped himself: He picked off a ball intended for Miller. It was Ohio State's fifth turnover of the day, and it capped a momentous upset. Ohio State was a 28-point favorite and fell, 28-24.

To their utmost credit, the Buckeyes responded. They pasted Iowa, 45-14, gaining 627 yards in the process, and they ended a three-game losing streak to Michigan with a 31-16 win on a beautiful November day in Columbus. In Boston's final game at Ohio Stadium, he caught 10 balls for 217 yards.

Meanwhile, chaos was unfolding in college football. On December 5, BCS No. 2 UCLA fell to Miami, 49-45, in a game that had been postponed from early in the year due to Hurricane Georges. That same day, BCS No. 3 Kansas State got upset in overtime by Texas A&M in the Big 12 title game. That gave a lot of teams national title hope, but with 12-0 Tennessee an easy No. 1, the BCS formula spit out 11-1 Florida State's name as the No. 2 team instead of KSU, UCLA, or Ohio State. The Seminoles were playing without injured starting quarterback Chris Weinke and would fold against Tennessee, 23-16.

With Wisconsin in the Rose Bowl, the Buckeyes would settle for the Sugar Bowl against Texas A&M. And again, they moved past their disappointment. A&M scored first in New Orleans, but OSU responded with three first-quarter scores of its own – a touchdown pass from Germaine to Reggie Germany, a 10-yard Montgomery run, and a 16-yard blocked punt return – and tacked on a second-quarter field goal. That was that. The Buckeyes won, 24-14, and finished with just one loss. For the third time in six years.

This was supposed to be the year Ohio State broke through and avoided that single, crippling loss. But the Buckeyes would have to wait a little while longer. Cooper went just 14-10 in 1999-2000 and was sent packing; he finished with 111 wins in 13 years of coaching the scarlet and gray, but only two of them came against Michigan. And one of his three losses to Michigan State was particularly devastating.

Cooper's replacement, Jim Tressel, went 14-0 in 2002.

1999 VIRGINIA TECH

October 16, 1999.

The thing is, Syracuse was a pretty good team in 1999. Paul Pasqualoni's Orange were coming off of back-to-back major bowl appearances – Fiesta Bowl in 1997, Orange Bowl in 1998 – and had established themselves as one of the Big East's steady powers. They were 5-1 and ranked 16th in the country when they came to Blacksburg. They had won at Pitt the week before, and their only loss was a gripping, 18-13 stumble against No. 6 Michigan.

They weren't the only ones in western Virginia that Saturday. ESPN's *College GameDay*, quickly becoming a staple of every fan's Saturday, had come to Tech's city, with a record crowd of 10,000. Virginia Tech had started the season strong and had moved up to fourth in the AP poll thanks to an exciting quarterback, a dynamic defense, and Frank Beamer, the head coach who had built it all.

Now came the ultimate test, a chance to prove to doubters that the Hokies were to be taken seriously. (And for a new riser, there are always plenty of doubters.)

The Hokies had malice in their hearts. They dominated in every way Beamer teams dominated. The scoring began when Tech's Anthony Midget stripped a Syracuse receiver; Cory Bird caught the ball in the air and took it 26 yards for a score. Tech's Shyrone Stith scored twice, Ricky Hall caught a short touchdown pass, and Tech led 31-0 at half. The Hokies scored another 31 in the second half.

Total yards: No. 4 Virginia Tech 411, No. 16 Syracuse 120.

Turnovers: Syracuse 5, Virginia Tech 0.

Touchdowns: Virginia Tech offense 5, Virginia Tech defense 3, Syracuse 0.

Syracuse – a good team! – had three first downs and 58 yards after three quarters. The 62-point margin was their worst since the Taft administration and the worst-ever loss for a ranked team.

There are statements, and then there are statements.

We remember the teams that transcend our imaginations. The 1999 Hokies did everything a little differently, a little faster, a little nastier. They scored with defense and special teams, and their quarterback was lightning in a bottle.

Late January, 1998.

Southeastern Virginia – the Newport News/Hampton area, specifically – has always been a hotbed of athletic talent. But in the class of 1998, the area that had produced basketball great Allen Iverson a few years earlier figured out how to top itself. Basically every key recruiter came to the area because of two stunning talents: Hampton High School's Ronald Curry and Newport News Warwick's Michael Vick.

Curry was the bigger name. An all-around athlete and high school All-American in both basketball and football, he would end up winning the McDonald's All-American slam dunk contest, throwing 28 touchdown passes for North Carolina and catching 193 passes in six seasons with the Oakland Raiders.

Vick had his list narrowed down to Syracuse and Virginia Tech. At Syracuse, he could succeed the great Donovan McNabb and play for a school that, decades earlier, had been one of the first to embrace African-American players. At Virginia Tech, he could not only play closer to his family; he could create a path for himself.

In late-January 1998, he chose the latter.

December 23, 1986.

Compared to expectations, Bill Dooley had been pretty successful. He spent nine years as VT's head coach, attended three bowls, and finished with a winning record (albeit as an independent with a sometimes shaky schedule) seven times. He was the winningest coach in school history at the time. However, he also served as the school's athletic director, and his team committed NCAA infractions. He was fired as A.D. and resigned as head coach.

Two days before Christmas 1986, the school announced it was replacing Dooley with Murray State head coach Beamer, a former Tech cornerback.

Beamer inherited NCAA sanctions and had a pretty long rope. He used up most of it. His Hokies went 22-32-1 in his first five seasons, then 2-8-1 in 1992, his sixth. It took a leap of faith for the school to retain him.

Over the next six years, however, the Hokies won 53 games and finished ranked four times. They were built around an aggressive, modern defense – eight men in the box with nasty, aggressive defensive backs on the perimeter – and dynamic special teams. With pro-caliber talent like quarterback Jim Druckenmiller (a first-round pick in 1997) and receiver Antonio Freeman (third-rounder in 1995), the offense was catching up.

Tech had joined the newly-formed Big East in 1991, along with fellow independents Boston College, Miami, Pitt, Rutgers, Syracuse, Temple, and West Virginia. They had one of the least proven football programs of the bunch, but they changed that script quickly.

And Beamer was beginning to utilize the school's improving cachet to his advantage in local recruiting battles.

September 4, 1999.

It took two plays for Vick, a redshirt freshman, to become a fan favorite throughout the country.

About 10 minutes into the season opener against James Madison, he took a shotgun snap from his 46-yard line and ran a designed QB draw against a blitz. He shook off a shoulder tackle in the backfield and started to his right, then made one cut and raced toward the left hash mark. About three different JMU defenders looked like they had an angle on him. None came close before he crossed the goal line.

About 12 minutes later, he became a legend.

On third-and-goal from the JMU 7, with Tech leading 17-0, he found his first passing option covered, then took off. With two tacklers converging on him, he leaped from the 4, got flipped by tackler No. 1, springboarded off of tackler No. 2, and landed on his feet in the end zone.

It was his last play of the game. Tech didn't need any more help in what was eventually a 47-0 win, but when Vick landed from his spectacular dive, he injured his ankle. His Superman leap had a Clark Kent landing. The ankle would still be hampering him when Syracuse came to town and beyond.

Vick was a quarterback for the video game era. It seemed he could do everything a quarterback had ever been able to do, only better. With a flick of the wrist, his left arm could fire a ball as far as any receiver could run. He seemed to go from zero to "faster than any linebacker" in half a step. In the open field, he was a blur.

Vick threw for 2,065 yards and rushed for 682 in 1999. On one ankle.

January 4, 2000.

Tech had become a respectable program without many star recruits, and in 1999, the blue-collar roots of Beamer's recruiting efforts showed.

Corey Moore was an undersized fullback and linebacker in high school who, after a detour in junior college, became one of the celebrated defensive ends of all-time, racking up 35 sacks in three seasons in Blacksburg. Thousand-yard receiver Andre Davis, who appeared on the cover of Sports Illustrated in December behind a "They Belong!" header, was a track star and soccer player in New York until late in his high school career. Stith barely played during his senior year in high school. Ike Charlton was a high school quarterback in Orlando who was passed on by Florida State and ended up a second-round draft pick at cornerback.

Adding just a little bit of star power took Tech to the top of college football. Briefly.

The Sugar Bowl, which was to host the top two teams in the Bowl Championship Series standings in the BCS' second year, pitted Tech against No. 1 Florida State.

Everything that could go wrong for the Hokies early, did. The nation's best passing combination – FSU's Chris Weinke to Peter Warrick – struck for a 64-yard score late in the first quarter, and within the next eight minutes, the Seminoles would score on both a blocked punt and a Warrick punt return to take a 28-7 lead. This Cinderella run looked like it was coming to a rude conclusion, but Tech surged back. Vick scored late in the first half to make it 28-14 at the break, then a field goal and two Andre Kendrick TD runs gave the Hokies a stirring 29-28 lead heading into the fourth quarter.

Unfortunately, things took a turn in the final stanza. Two Weinke touchdown passes (one to Ron Dugans, the final to Warrick) and a field goal gave FSU 18 points in a five-minute span, and the Seminoles burst ahead for a 46-29 win.

The Hokies were definitively the second-best team. And they were only sparsely tested on their way to the title game.

With Vick sitting out the second game of the year, backup Dave Meyer threw three interceptions against UAB, but the Tech defense held the Blazers to 63 yards in 53 plays in a 31-10 win. In a dogfight against Tommy Bowden's Clemson Tigers on a Thursday night in late-September, the Hokies found themselves leading only 14-11 with 11 minutes left before the Tech defense once again struck. A 47-yard Shayne Graham field goal extended the lead, then the Hokies scored on a 34-yard Charlton interception return and a 32-yard Moore fumble return to win, 31-11.

Vick struggled against Clemson, completing just seven of 17 passes with three picks, but in October, he found his stride. He was 7-for-9 for 222 and a touchdown in a 31-7 win over Virginia, then threw four touchdown passes (two to Davis, two to Ricky Hall) as the Hokies used a 35-0 second quarter to ease to a 58-20 win over lowly Rutgers.

After the destruction of Syracuse, Tech briefly showed some cracks. Now third in the country, the Hokies raced to a 27-7 lead over Pitt and held on, 30-17, but allowed 427 passing yards.

And the next week at WVU, they had to survive in a classic. With No. 2 Penn State losing at home to two-touchdown underdog Minnesota, Tech had a chance to advance in the rankings, but

WVU backup Brad Lewis completed two fourth-quarter touchdown passes to suddenly put the Mountaineers up, 20-19.

Vick had completed only 11 of 27 passes against WVU to that point, but with the game on the line, he thrived. He found Terrell Parham for 14 yards, then hit Hall for nine. But Hall was tackled in bounds, and the clock ticked under 35 seconds by the time Tech was able to get off another snap.

The Hokies still had to gain probably 30 yards to get within field goal range for Graham. Vick looked to his left but found no open receiver; he narrowly avoided a WVU lineman in the pocket but escaped to his right and crossed the line of scrimmage. He looked like he was going to run out of bounds, but darted for a 31-yard gain, hurdling out of bounds at the WVU 36 with 21 seconds left. After another short pass to Hall, Vick spiked the ball with five seconds left. Graham nailed a 44-yarder from the right hashmark. Tech 22, West Virginia 20. The Miracle in Morgantown.

The next week, at home against No. 19 Miami, the hungover Hokies quickly fell behind, 10-0. But they proceeded to score the next 43 in pure Tech fashion: two touchdown runs by Stith, a 64-yard punt return, a 51-yard fumble return, and a fumble recovery in the end zone.

The next week at Temple, they allowed an early touchdown, then scored 62 straight.

On the day after Thanksgiving, against No. 22 Boston College, they clinched a date in New Orleans by jumping to a 24-0 halftime lead and cruising, 38-14, behind Vick's 290 passing yards and 76 rushing yards. Fans tore down the goalposts at Lane Stadium. Tech's first perfect regular season in 81 years was complete.

April 21, 2001.

A loss like that Sugar Bowl against FSU hurts doubly, because you never know when you might get another shot. Tech went 11-1 again in 2000, with Vick struggling even further with injury, and in April 2001, Vick became the school's second No. 1 draft pick (the first: end Bruce Smith in 1985).

Vick was a four-time Pro Bowler and became a redemption story of sorts. He served nearly two years in prison for his role in an interstate dog-fighting ring. After his release, he lobbied for stronger animal protection laws and became the NFL's 2010 Comeback Player of the Year.

Tech continued to cruise at a high altitude. The Hokies won at least 10 games every year from 2004-11 and pulled off another four top-10 finishes in Vick's absence. The quarterback for one of those seasons: Marcus Vick, Michael's brother.

Beamer retired following the 2015 season, his 29th in charge of a program that, for all intents and purposes, he built. His Hokies spent parts of nine seasons ranked in the AP top 5, but they never again reached the title game.

2002 USC

In early-December 2000, a resurgent Oklahoma locked up a BCS title game bid with a Big 12 Championship win over Kansas State. It was only Bob Stoops' second season as Sooner head coach, and the turnaround had been dramatic. Barry Switzer had left in 1989, leaving successor Gary Gibbs with NCAA sanctions to deal with, and while Gibbs managed to tread water for a while, he was dismissed following a 6-6 campaign in 1994. Howard Schnellenberger strutted into town and strutted right back out after a 5-5-1 season.

The school took a reach on 34-year old Dallas Cowboys assistant John Blake and won just 12 games in three seasons. And then, *poof* – Stoops walked in the door, went 7-5 in his first year, then won the national title in his second. Order restored.

As Oklahoma was eking out a tough 27-24 win over Kansas State in Kansas City, however, USC athletic director Mike Garrett was driving up and down the West Coast looking for someone to lead his team. The former Trojan star running back had led the USC program since 1993 and hadn't scored many points with his handling of the firing of John Robinson in 1997. He openly searched for a new coach before firing Robinson, and the replacement he hired, Paul Hackett, went just 19-18 with one bowl appearance in three seasons.

USC is like an old muscle car: In the wrong hands, it stalls out and stumbles; in the right hands, it purrs and roars, faster and louder than anyone else. It is perhaps harder to find a good driver than you think it's going to be. For a while, Garrett couldn't find someone willing to give it a shot – not Oregon State's Dennis Erickson (a former national champion at Miami), not Oregon's Mike Bellotti (engineer of three nine-win seasons for the burgeoning power in Eugene), not the San Diego Chargers' Mike Riley (Robinson's offensive coordinator in the mid-1990s).

Colorado State's Sonny Lubick … recently fired Washington Redskins head coach Norv Turner (another former Robinson assistant) … Wisconsin's Barry Alvarez … Utah's Ron McBride … a lot of names floated around in the rumor mill as Garrett's search stretched on for nearly three weeks. And in the end, the name Garrett chose – former New England Patriots and New York Jets coach Pete Carroll – inspired few.

Once regarded as a coaching wunderkind, the University of the Pacific grad hadn't coached at the college level since serving as his alma mater's defensive coordinator in 1983. He went 6-10 in one disastrous season leading the Jets, and while he won 27 games in three years with the Patriots, he was succeeding legendary Bill Parcells in Foxborough and couldn't meet that standard.

Local media railed against the hire and mocked Garrett for overvaluing NFL experience and replacing one Hackett with another Hackett. But Carroll was something different. He had head coaching experience, obviously, and he paired a fantastic defensive mind with bounding charisma – he was able to recruit well enough to stockpile absurd offensive talent.

In a few brief weeks of work, Carroll landed blue-chippers like quarterback Matt Leinart and defensive lineman Shaun Cody in his February 2001 signing haul; after a 6-6 debut campaign, he inked future stars in players like offensive lineman Fred Matua, Winston Justice, and Kyle Williams, receiver Mike Williams, tight end Dominique Byrd, and safety Darnell Bing. His recruiting classes from 2003-07 were works of art, top-ranked classes all (or really close to it).

At the turn of the century, the Pac-10 was in flux. Over the seven seasons before Carroll was hired, the conference had sent seven different programs to the Rose Bowl: Oregon in 1994, USC in 1995, Arizona State in 1996, Washington State in 1997, UCLA in 1998, Stanford in 1999, and Washington in 2000. The conference produced plenty of strong teams, but consistent standouts were rare.

And then, *poof*.

Carroll's tenure started with five losses in seven games. USC was competitive against ranked Kansas State, Oregon, and Washington teams — they lost by a combined nine points to these three — but had to rally to finish 6-5. A 27-0 pasting of No. 20 UCLA in the season finale both earned a bowl bid and sent a message. And despite a meek Las Vegas Bowl loss to Utah, USC's clear potential (and, yes, historical reputation) got the Trojans ranked 20th in the 2002 preseason.

USC's young talent was beginning to show, but the Trojans headed into 2002 led by veterans. Senior and former blue-chip quarterback Carson Palmer had one last chance to fulfill his promise, while the defense's identity was formed around hard-hitting safety Troy Polamalu. An incredible schedule tamped down expectations — the Trojans would end up playing *nine* ranked teams, plus an Auburn team that would finish ranked — but Carroll's guys were ready for a breakthrough.

USC had to get resourceful against Auburn in the season opener. Unable to run the ball against a stout Auburn front, the Trojans

had to lean on the pass, and Palmer found success throwing to …
a running back. Sixth-year senior Malaefou MacKenzie caught six
balls for 117 yards, and one-yard sneak by Palmer early in the fourth
quarter gave USC a 24-17 win.

The next week, it was time to send a message. On the road against
Gary Barnett's No. 18 Colorado Buffaloes, a team that would go on
to reach the Big 12 title game, the Trojans raced to a 20-0 halftime
lead with two touchdowns by MacKenzie and a 62-yard run by
Sultan McCullough. And in the fourth quarter, they scored three
more times to win, 40-3. Total yards: USC 425, Colorado 61.

The Trojans' ceiling was becoming clear, but they still had a couple
of setbacks to work through. The week after Colorado, they had to
travel back to the Midwest to face Kansas State in Manhattan, and
Bill Snyder's Wildcat defense frustrated Palmer. USC gained only 86
yards in the first half, and K-State led 27-6 early in the fourth quarter.
Two touchdowns, however, brought the Trojans back: Palmer and
Keary Colbert connected on a five-yard score, then McCullough
raced 25 yards to make the score 27-20 with 6:31 left. After a Wildcat
fumble, USC had a chance to send the game to overtime but turned
the ball over on downs in KSU territory.

After a 22-0 win over Erickson's No. 23 Oregon State squad came
setback no. 2. In Pullman against No. 17 Washington State, Polamalu
suffered a high ankle sprain and missed most of the game. Wazzu's
Jason Gesser threw for 315 yards, and though USC quickly erased a
24-14 fourth-quarter deficit with two touchdowns (the second a 55-yard
strike from Palmer to emerging freshman Mike Williams), Ryan Killeen
missed the PAT, and Wazzu sent the game to overtime at 27-27 with
a late field goal. Killeen then missed a 52-yard field goal, and Wazzu's
Drew Dunning made a 35-yarder for a 30-27 Cougar win.

The very next week against Jeff Tedford's rising Cal Bears, USC
nearly slipped again; the Trojans fell behind 21-3 early in the second
quarter before rallying to win, 30-28.

The successful rally was evidently the last piece of the puzzle. Over the following four games – home wins over No. 22 Washington and Arizona State, road wins over No. 14 Oregon and Stanford – Palmer hit a remarkable stride. He completed a combined 94 of 142 passes for 1,327 yards, 15 touchdowns, and only two interceptions. Williams caught 31 passes for 497 yards in this span, Colbert 23 for 387. Palmer threw three first-half touchdown passes as USC bolted to a 28-7 halftime lead over UCLA (final: 52-21), and a week later he painted his masterpiece.

The Notre Dame-USC game featured two top-10 teams for the first time since 1989, when the No. 1 Irish took down the No. 9 Trojans, 28-24. Tyrone Willingham's first Notre Dame squad – he came from Stanford, where he had led the Cardinal to a surprise Rose Bowl bid – was 10-1 and seventh in the AP poll after wins over Michigan and Florida State. USC, meanwhile, was sixth with a bullet after its run of six dominant wins.

The Trojans played one of their greatest games ever. Total yards: USC 610, Notre Dame 109. First downs: USC 31, Notre Dame 4. Mike Williams caught 10 passes for 169, and leading Irish receiver Arnaz Battle caught two for six. Justin Fargas rushed 20 times for 120 yards, Notre Dame's Ryan Grant 10 times for 16.

Palmer was magnificent. He completed 32 of 46 passes for 425 yards, four touchdowns, and two picks. That this performance was against a good Irish team probably carried extra weight; Palmer passed Iowa's Brad Banks to win the 2002 Heisman Trophy voting by 233 points.

Palmer then finished his career by destroying Banks, too.

The BCS featured some awkward pairings in 2002. With Big Ten champion Ohio State facing Miami for the national title in the Fiesta Bowl, the Rose Bowl ended up choosing Oklahoma instead of Big Ten co-champion Iowa. Meanwhile, Washington State's overtime win over USC gave the Cougars the tiebreaker edge in the Pac-12 race and Wazzu headed back to the Rose Bowl. As a result, college football got a classic Big Ten-Pac-10 matchup … in Miami. USC and Iowa faced off in the Orange Bowl for what was a de facto national third-place game.

Iowa put its best foot forward. C.J. Jones returned the opening kickoff 100 yards for a touchdown, and the Hawkeyes led 10-7 late in the first half. But the Hawkeye defense was laboring to keep USC out of the end zone.

Killeen kicked a 35-yard field goal to tie the game at halftime, and USC laid the hammer down in the second half. Palmer and Williams connected for an 18-yard touchdown, Fargas ripped off a 50-yard run, McCullough scored from five yards, and reserve Sunny Byrd capped a 31-0 run. Iowa scored again late, but Palmer completed 21 of 31 passes to Banks' 15-for-36 performance, and USC romped, 38-17.

The 2002 season was a statement of intent for USC. After finishing outside of the AP top 5 every year from 1980 to 2001, the Trojans would rip off seven consecutive finishes of fourth or better. Matt Leinart succeeded Palmer at quarterback in 2003 and went 37-2 over the next three years, winning two national titles. Only a dramatic finish against Texas in 2005's BCS title game prevented a third straight championship.

Then again, the third one wouldn't have counted anyway. Carroll courted celebrities and star recruits, but like so many other immensely successful coaches, he eventually courted trouble, too. An NCAA investigation centering on Reggie Bush, the jewel of Carroll's incredible 2003 recruiting class and the 2005 Heisman winner (Leinart won in 2004), turned up evidence of improper benefits. Carroll's open-access policies with media and fans were resented to some degree in the NCAA offices – Garrett's general crankiness toward the NCAA probably didn't help – and the NCAA attempted to send a message by severely sanctioning the program with scholarship restrictions, a bowl ban, and the vacating of previous wins, including the last two games of the 2004 season and all of its 2005 wins. Bush was forced to vacate his Heisman, too.

Following the 2009 season, USC's first with more than two losses since 2001, Carroll left to go back to the NFL, where he would win a Super Bowl with the Seattle Seahawks.

Vacated wins don't vacate memories, however. After 20 years of up-and-down play, it took Carroll only one year and a couple of recruiting classes to restock USC's depth chart and make the Trojans look like the Trojans again. They were brash and exciting, and they gave the Pac-10 a national power around which other programs would orbit.

For 90 years, USC has been one of college football's most confusing powers. The proximity to star recruits and the Hollywood sign create a high-attention, high-pressure atmosphere. When things aren't going according to plan, the echo chamber and attention can become toxic. And when things are going well, no team in the country looks more awesome. That Carroll wasn't Garrett's first (or second, or third…) choice, and that the national reaction to his hire was mostly mockery, tells us all we need to know about how unpredictable hires can be.

That won't stop us from overreacting every December, though.

2004 TEXAS

"**Fourth**-and-5, the national championship on the line here. He's going for the corner ... he's got it!"

The last great call of announcer Keith Jackson's career was also the last snap of Vince Young's in a Texas uniform. In front of a packed Rose Bowl crowd, in the closing seconds of the greatest national title game of the BCS era and one of the best games of all-time, Young took the shotgun snap on fourth down from the USC nine-yard line and looked to his left. With his receiver covered and USC's blitzing (and gassed) pass rushers all accounted for, he tucked the ball and made a long, loping run toward the front right corner of the goal line.

As was the case throughout the 2005 season, he made it. He hopped through a throng of media surrounding the field, glanced up at jubilant Longhorn fans in the stands, then continued on, clutching the ball to his chest as he walked back toward the Texas sideline, taking a hug from the Texas mascot along the way.

Nineteen seconds later, Texas was the national champion. The Longhorns had taken down the two-time defending champ, 41-38, capping Young's career and defining head coach Mack Brown's.

Young threw for 3,036 yards and 26 touchdowns and rushed for 1,050 and 12 as the Longhorns plowed through the 2005 season unscathed. He became one of the most celebrated college football players of the 2000s, an all-world recruit who lived up to his billing and delivered to Texas its first national title in a generation.

Barely 14 months earlier, Young was sitting in a locker room in the bowels of Austin's Darrell K Royal Stadium as both Texas' 2004 season and his own career were threatening to unravel. The Longhorns trailed Oklahoma State, 35-14, done in by both defensive breakdowns and two Young turnovers. Within the previous month, they had been shut out by Oklahoma, and Young had been benched for costly mistakes in a near-loss to Missouri. Young was built like a truck with long-striding speed and all the arm strength you need, but with expectations increasing, his mistakes were holding him back.

The successes of players like Michael Vick spoil expectations for everyone else. Sometimes it takes you a little while to grow into your role. That was certainly the case for Young, a 6'5 product of Houston Madison High School whom Rivals.com named the No. 1 recruit in the country in the 2002 class.

With senior starter Chris Simms still in uniform for Texas, and with Young in need of bulking up, Brown elected to redshirt his new star in 2002, and he alternated between spellbinding and maddening during a 10-3 campaign in 2003. He was 6-for-14 for just 15 yards as the Longhorns lost the 2003 Holiday Bowl to Washington State, but Texas still began 2004 ranked seventh in the country.

As important as 2004 would be for Young's development, it was just as important for Brown. By any definition, he had been a rousing success in Austin. Through most of the 1980s and 1990s, the Longhorns had been defined by brief bouts of success followed by massive underachievement. Fred Akers went 11-1 in 1983, then won just 20 games in his final three seasons. David McWilliams went 10-2 in 1990 and 21-24 in his other four years. John Mackovic won a surprising 1996 Big 12 title with an upset of mighty Nebraska, then went 4-7 the next year and got fired.

Hired away from North Carolina in 1998 following back-to-back top-10 finishes, Brown was the quintessential CEO coach. He signed great recruits, hired good assistants, and got out of the way. He was a politician in a school polo, and he was really good at what he did.

But Brown's 'Horns were developing a reputation as an offseason national champion, so to speak. Elite recruiting classes were producing only very good results – Texas had finished lower than it started in the AP poll in three of the last four years – and potential breakthroughs were constantly done in by losses to Oklahoma and random upsets. The 'Horns could have made the BCS title game in 2001, but lost the Big 12 title game to Colorado. They blew a shot at the 2002 Big 12 title with a late-season upset loss to Texas Tech. And while Young showed promise in 2003, Texas got its doors blown off, 65-13, by Oklahoma. It seemed that if Brown was ever going to break through, it was going to be with Young, the bluest of blue-chippers, leading the way.

2004 began well enough. Running back Cedric Benson, who gave up a baseball side gig before the season to focus on football, rushed for a 38-yard touchdown just two minutes into the season as Texas strolled to a 65-0 win over lowly North Texas. The next week, the Horns headed to Fayetteville to face Arkansas, an old SWC rival. In front of 76,671, Young avoided turnovers while throwing for 150 yards and rushing for 56. Texas trailed 17-16 at halftime, but with a defender hanging off of him, Young completed a short pass to Benson, who took it 13 yards for the go-ahead score.

Thanks to an opportunistic defense that forced two turnovers in the last three minutes, Texas held on for a 22-20 win. They tuned up with easy wins over Rice (35-13) and Baylor (44-14) – Young completed a combined 26 of 38 passes for 350 yards, five touchdowns, and two picks, and rushed for 119 yards – and then hit the road to Dallas for the annual loss to Oklahoma.

Texas beat Oklahoma in 1998 and 1999 – John Blake's final year at OU and Stoops' first – but the Sooners had won four straight since. The 2000 and 2003 losses were utter domination; the 2004 loss would almost be more humiliating. The Texas defense fought as hard as it could, bending and bending but allowing just two short field goals and a single touchdown. OU's flashy new toy, freshman running back Adrian Peterson, rushed for 225 yards, but the Sooners scored just 12 points.

That was 12 more points than Texas could manage. Young completed just eight of 23 passes, and Texas punted seven times, lost three fumbles, turned the ball over on downs late, and went home with a meek shutout loss.

Back home against Missouri, Texas powered to a 14-0 first-quarter lead, thanks to a short pick six by Brian Robison and two impressive Young plays – a 48-yard reception on a trick-play pass from Ramonce Taylor and a 23-yard rush over left end. But the Tigers scored midway through the second quarter, and Young threw a bad interception to set up another Mizzou score. Young threw *another* interception, and then took a seat on the bench.

Chance Mock, part-time starter in 2003, subbed in, and while he completed only four passes, he stopped throwing the ball to the other team. Benson's 150 yards and two scores powered a 28-20 win.

Young's bounce back came in fits and starts. He rushed for 158 yards and threw for 142 in a 51-21 romp at Texas Tech, but he threw an early pick six and went just 8-for-15 against Colorado.

Luckily, Texas still had a defense. Linebacker Derrick Johnson (who would go on to win the Butkus and Nagurski Awards) and safety Michael Griffin combined for 16 tackles, two sacks, and two forced fumbles, and combined with 225 rushing yards from Benson and Taylor, Texas still cruised, 31-7.

Next came Oklahoma State.

You never really see turning points until after the fact. About 29 minutes into the game, Young was 3-for-5 passing with two picks and a sack, and the Longhorns trailed by 28. But not long after Young's second interception, everything changed, both in the Oklahoma State game and in Young's career trajectory.

Over the last 31 minutes or so, Young completed 15 of 16 passes for 222 yards and rushed seven times for 86 yards. Texas scored on its final seven possessions, and Young put away a 56-35 win with a 42-yard touchdown run over right end. It was the biggest comeback in school history, and it seemed to instill a new level of calm and confidence. Suddenly, this was a New Vince and a New Texas.

The calm would pay off the very next week. Texas gained 581 yards at Kansas but consistently shot itself in the foot; Young threw two interceptions inside the Kansas 30, and UT settled for three field goals, missing one. They found themselves down 23-13 with less than eight minutes left, but New Vince rushed for an 18-yard score with four minutes left, then converted a fourth-and-18 with an incredible 22-yard scramble. He connected with Tony Jeffery for a 21-yard score with 11 seconds left, and while KU coach Mark Mangino stole headlines by claiming an officiating conspiracy, Young had once again pulled himself and his team out of the fire. After a bye week, Texas handled Texas A&M, 26-13, to finish the season 10-1.

The official record states that Texas scored a bid in the Rose Bowl and wrote the prologue for its incredible 2005 with a late comeback win over Michigan. Young threw for 180 yards and rushed for 192 in his best all-around performance to date. It was an amazing game and an amazing performance.

The detail that gets lost: Texas barely earned a trip to Pasadena at all. Having a politician leading the program paid off.

The top four teams in the BCS standings were guaranteed a spot in a BCS bowl, but Texas stood at fifth heading into championship weekend. The top three teams – undefeated USC, Oklahoma, and Auburn squads – were obvious, but Brown began to politick, talking up his team on television and lobbying like crazy.

When No. 4 Cal, led by eventual Super Bowl champion quarterback Aaron Rodgers, finished the season with a fine but unimpressive win over Southern Miss (in a game rescheduled because of Hurricane Ivan), the Golden Bears dropped on quite a few poll ballots while No. 6 Texas, on bye, suspiciously moved up in quite a few. The shift in polling average, combined with computer rankings, allowed the Longhorns to cke ahead of Cal by 0.0129 points per the BCS formulas.

Instead of Cal making its first trip to the Rose Bowl since the 1958 season, Texas would make its first trip ever. The controversy ensuing from both this and the exclusion of Auburn from the BCS championship game (in a nutshell: three teams finished undefeated, the BCS could only select two; since USC crushed Oklahoma, hindsight established that Auburn should have gone instead), resulted in the AP withdrawing itself from the BCS formula.

A letdown Cal team ended up in the Holiday Bowl, where it laid an egg and lost 45-31 to a fired-up Texas Tech team. The Longhorns, meanwhile, made magic.

Michigan was a worthy foe; Lloyd Carr's Wolverines had beaten two top-15 teams but fell at Notre Dame early in the year and got upset at Ohio State late. Their defense wasn't quite up to the Michigan standard, but a prolific offense featured quarterback Chad Henne, running back Michael Hart, and receiver Braylon Edwards.

The teams traded punts early, but once Young opened the scoring with a 20-yard run late in the first quarter, it was off to the races. Henne and Edwards connected from 39 yards to tie the game, then Young found tight end David Thomas for an 11-yard score. A Taylor fumble set up an eight-yard score by Edwards, and the game was tied at halftime.

Those late to their seats to start the second half missed some hay-makers. Texas took the second-half kickoff, and on the Longhorns' sixth play, Young bolted 60 yards for a touchdown. Michigan needed only three plays to respond: Henne found Steve Breaston for a 50-yard score. Henne and Edwards connected once more for a nine-yard touchdown, and Young threw an interception; with 2:35 left in the third quarter, Michigan's Garrett Rivas hit a 44-yard field goal to put the Wolverines up 10.

New Vince, of course, wasn't done. Early in the fourth quarter, he scored on third-and-goal to bring Texas to within 31-28, and Michigan had to settle for a field goal on its next drive. Texas got the ball with six minutes left and drove 69 yards in three plays (Young scored on a 23-yarder), but Breaston returned the ensuing kickoff 53 yards to set up another Rivas field goal with three minutes remaining. Michigan was back up, 37-35.

Rather than continue to trade scores, Texas instead decided to eat clock. Young found Bo Scaife for a first down into Michigan territory, and then rushed for 14 yards to the Michigan 30. Three Young carries generated another 11 yards, and the Horns positioned themselves for a field goal. With two seconds left, Dusty Mangum booted a 37-yarder for a thrilling 38-37 win.

The shutout loss to Oklahoma was Young's last in burnt orange. Texas limped through the next month with some close calls, but the Longhorns would win the final 20 games of Young's career. When the switch got flipped, the light stayed on.

2007 OREGON

Football innovation spreads like a virus. Random coaching camps or hires create conversation, networking opportunities, and bursts of creativity. Two coaches interact, then go back to their schools and infect those staffs.

In 1989, new Iowa Wesleyan coach Hal Mumme hired an offensive coordinator named Mike Leach. That partnership would stretch to Valdosta State and Kentucky; Leach took the Oklahoma coordinator job, then spent 10 years coaching Texas Tech. Former assistants and players at Kentucky, Oklahoma, and Tech tweaked their own versions of the Mumme-Leach air raid. A few became major-college head coaches.

Twenty-five years after two coaches met in Mount Pleasant, Iowa and traded ideas on a campus of about 500 students, their vision of a pass-heavy, spread-out offense had proliferated throughout football.

Another chance interaction took place in 1988 in Durham, New

Hampshire. At a clinic held by the University of New Hampshire staff, 34 of 35 high school coaches in attendance went to listen to defensive line coach Jack Bicknell Jr., son of Boston College's celebrated 1980s coach. That left two men in another session: 31-year-old UNH offensive coordinator Gary Crowton and a 24-year-old UNH alum and high school coach by the name of Charles "Chip" Kelly.

The two discussed the fundamentals of Crowton's pass-heavy attack. He would parlay its success into eventual head coaching opportunities (Louisiana Tech, BYU) and a brief stint as the Chicago Bears' offensive coordinator. When Oregon head coach Mike Bellotti wanted a version of the spread at Oregon in 2005, he brought in Crowton to work out the details.

Two years into the experiment, results were mixed. Oregon averaged nearly 35 points per game while surging to 10-2 and a No. 12 finish in 2005, but the Ducks faded miserably in 2006, losing four games in a row to finish 7-6. They scored just 14 points per game during the losing streak.

Crowton was dealing with a quarterback controversy, with Dennis Dixon and Brady Leaf alternating and struggling. Leaf's passes weren't going anywhere, and Dixon was throwing too many balls to the other team.

Dixon's dual-threat skill set wasn't being utilized in the 2006 version of the offense. He was a decent passer and a fantastic runner, but quarterbacks weren't asked to run much in Crowton's system.

Earlier in 2006, Crowton had consulted with an old friend about further spread ideas to implement in Eugene. And in 2007, that old friend replaced Crowton.

After a few years of bouncing around as a college assistant, Kelly became Johns Hopkins' defensive coordinator in 1993, then landed a gig at his alma mater.

He coached running backs at UNH until 1996, moved to offensive line for two years, and then took over Crowton's old position, UNH offensive coordinator, in 1999.

The results were scattershot for a while (30 points per game in 2001, 18 in 2002), but by 2003, the Wildcats weren't looking back. They scored 34 points per game in 2004 and 42 in 2005. They won games in the I-AA playoffs for three straight seasons, going 30-9 from 2004-06 and pummeling FBS' Rutgers in 2004 and Northwestern in 2006. Kelly moved across the country, hesitantly agreeing to become Bellotti's new coordinator.

You can't buy your way into college football's ruling class, no matter how much Nike money resides nearby. Oregon was on an unprecedented, sustained run; the Ducks had pulled off their first Rose Bowl bid in nearly 40 years in 1994, and when head coach Rich Brooks left to take over the NFL's St. Louis Rams, Bellotti, his offensive coordinator, took the reins. They had been to 10 bowls in 12 years and went 11-1 with a No. 2 finish in 2001.

Growth had stalled out, however. Since 2002, the Ducks were averaging only about 7.5 wins, and with Nike CEO Phil Knight plugging more money into the program (and helping to usher in an era of constantly changing uniforms), that wasn't good enough. Bellotti was under pressure to win and innovate, to produce a quality product unique to UO. Two years with Crowton were mixed. It was time to go further.

Kelly's offense was the spread id seen to completion.

It took the idea of a no-huddle attack to a new level. It utilized many of the read option concepts that were coming back into vogue (a quarterback reads a defender and decides whether to keep the ball or pitch it), only it read all sorts of defenders and incorporated run-pass options. It chose speed over size. It spread from sideline to sideline so the defense couldn't hide its intentions, then ran over teams with old-school run-it-down-your-throat concepts. When Kelly found a play that worked, his team would line up as quickly as possible and run it again.

No single element was unique. The wishbone utilized speed and options over girth, and coaches like Woody Hayes had grumbled about tempo moving toward 100 plays per game since the 1960s.

But this blur of an offense was relentless and anti-social, like Kelly himself. A Barry Switzer-esque bundle of charisma, he was not. But he would change the balance of power on the West Coast.

Dixon not only saw bench time in 2006; he frustrated his head coach by electing to pursue professional baseball in the summer of 2007.

Kelly spun this into a positive, citing the mental toughness that you develop in a sport like baseball, when failure is frequent. Whatever the circumstances, Dixon took to Kelly's system like a duck to water. (Sorry.) And he would put an end to any criticism by going almost failure-free in the first two months of the football season.

The Ducks opened the season against Houston, a team thriving behind its own version of the spread. Head coach Art Briles (who had spent three years as a Mike Leach assistant) would take the Baylor job after winning 18 games in 2006-07, and his Cougars would keep up for a while in Eugene. They tied the game at 20-20 early in the third quarter, but the Ducks took charge. Dixon threw two third-quarter touchdown passes, then ripped off an 80-yard touchdown run. A three-yard score by Jeremiah Johnson put away a 48-27 win.

Next came a trip to Ann Arbor and a chance to show off the new offense to the world. Michigan had just lost a classic upset to

Appalachian State, falling from fifth to unranked in a single week, but the Wolverines were still a name program, and the game was still on national television.

The final score was 39-7. It felt a lot worse. Oregon gained 624 yards. Dixon completed 16 of 25 passes for 292 yards and rushed for 76 more. Jonathan Stewart and Johnson combined for 200 rushing yards. Oregon trailed 7-3 when Dixon connected with Brian Paysinger for an 85-yard touchdown. Michigan was a step behind the rest of the way. After a successful Statue of Liberty play (the quarterback fakes a pass and hands it to the running back behind his back), Kelly called a fake Statue of Liberty; in what became one of the most memorable moments of the Kelly era, Dixon faked a handoff and, as defenders all moved toward the running back, walked untouched into the end zone for a nine-yard score.

With three minutes left in the first half, Dixon completed a 61-yard touchdown pass to Derrick Jones. It was 32-7 at halftime, and the home fans booed their Wolverines into the locker room. Oregon showed mercy in the second half, but the statement was resounding.

Now ranked, the Ducks returned home and rolled to a 52-21 win over Fresno State. A week later, on the road against Jim Harbaugh's first Stanford team, Dixon threw four touchdown passes and rushed for another score. Stanford surged to a 31-21 lead late in the second quarter, but Oregon finished the game on a 34-0 run. Stanford would eventually rise to power as an anti-Oregon, getting mileage out of a plodding tempo and tightly packed, tight end-heavy sets. But the Cardinal weren't ready just yet.

The nation was paying attention. Oregon was up to 11th per the AP, and when No. 6 California came to Eugene on September 29, ESPN's *College GameDay* was waiting. The popular Saturday morning preview show was in Eugene for the first time in seven years.

In a surprisingly low-scoring affair (for a while), a 42-yard pass from Dixon to Cameron Colvin gave the Ducks a 17-10 lead heading into the fourth quarter. Cal scored twice to take the lead, but Dixon scored with seven minutes left to tie the game at 24-all. Cal went ahead on a one-yard Justin Forsett run with three minutes left, but Oregon charged back. Dixon drove the Ducks to the Cal 5 with 30 seconds left. He completed a short pass to Colvin near the left sideline, but instead of stepping out of bounds to stop the clock, Colvin went for the score. He was hit at the 1 and fumbled into the end zone for a Cal touchback. The Golden Bears held on, 31-24.

Luckily, this was a good year to slip up. Everybody else was doing the same. Because of the Ducks' impressive display, and because of other losses, they had actually risen to ninth in the rankings by the time they hosted Washington State on October 13. Dixon completed 21 of 28 passes for 287 yards in a 53-7 rout, then stepped aside as Stewart and Andre Crenshaw rushed for 364 yards in a 55-34 romp at Washington.

Now fifth in the country, Oregon again welcomed *GameDay* for a huge battle against No. 9 USC.

Though the Trojans had fallen off a bit from their 2003-05 heights, this was still an awesome USC team. The offense was struggling through injury issues at quarterback, but the Trojans would allow just 16 points per game, second-fewest in the country. The key to the game would be remaining patient and staying ahead of the chains, and Oregon succeeded. The Ducks gained only 339 yards, but Dixon completed 64 percent of his passes, and the defense picked off USC freshman Mark Sanchez twice. Stewart and Dixon grinded out 179 yards on the ground, and Stewart's two second-half touchdowns gave Oregon a 24-10 lead. Sanchez threw a touchdown pass with five minutes left, but a late interception by Matthew Harper sealed a huge win.

Oregon entered November fourth in the country, the program's highest poll standing in six years. The Ducks would rise to second the next weekend, and Dixon would enter the season's home stretch as a Heisman favorite. Oregon was turning the football world on its ear.

And then came a Thursday night trip to Tucson.

The entire 2007 season turned football on its ear, actually. Some seasons are blips, years in which everything we thought we knew is brought into question. The 1984 and 1990 seasons were particularly wild, with top team after top team falling from atop the ladder. But 2007 was one of the zaniest in memory.

It began on the season's first Saturday. The Big Ten Network had launched on August 30 – it would soon be one of the driving forces of a crazy round of conference realignment – and on its third day of existence, it televised Appalachian State's spectacular upset of Michigan. The Mountaineers roasted Michigan with their version of a run-heavy spread, then blocked a potential game-winning field goal in the final seconds.

That was the first of many astounding results. On October 6, No. 2 USC fell to 41-point underdog Stanford. The next week, new No. 2 Cal lost to Oregon State. Five days later, new No. 2 USF lost to Rutgers. Two weeks after that, No. 2 Boston College lost to Florida State.

By the end of the season, everyone from Kentucky to Rutgers to Hawaii had spent time in the top 10, seven different No. 2s had lost over a nine-week span, and upstart Missouri had beaten upstart Kansas to move to No. 1 in the BCS standings. The Tigers and West Virginia each came within a half of playing the other for the national title.

Seemingly, the only non-chaotic outcome was the finale. So many teams fell from the top that LSU, the preseason No. 2 team, circled back to No. 2, then beat Ohio State in the BCS title game.

2007 reflected a sea change for college football.

In the ACC, Florida State was limping along in Bobby Bowden's final years, and Miami was a national afterthought as leadership shifted from Larry Coker to Randy Shannon. There was such a power void that Jim Grobe's Wake Forest Demon Deacons were able to surge to a conference title in 2006.

In the Big 12, Nebraska had grown unstable. In 1997, the Huskers replaced Tom Osborne with right-hand man Frank Solich; he did well, but apparently not well enough. He was replaced by the NFL's Bill Callahan, who would finish under .500 in both his first (2004) and last seasons in charge (2007). The Cornhuskers were outscored, 117-45, in losses at Missouri and Kansas, against whom they had gone 48-0 from 1979-2002. And with Kansas State struggling after Bill Snyder's temporary retirement and Colorado falling directionless, Mizzou stepped into the Big 12 North void, taking the division in 2007 and 2008 and going 22-6.

In the SEC, Alabama had gone 26-24 in four years under Mike Shula and was starting over under high-priced Nick Saban, who had won a national title at LSU in 2003 before heading to the NFL. Tennessee was beginning to labor under Phillip Fulmer; after losing 14 games in seven seasons between 1995-2001, the Vols lost 25 in six from 2002-07.

Out West, USC was losing its stranglehold on the Pac-10. The excellent Trojans were growing increasingly prone to upsets. They fell at Oregon State in both 2006 and 2008 and, of course, lost to Stanford in between.

The spread had something to do with this. With most elite recruiting teams still catering to old notions of the pro-style offense and 4-3 defenses, the spread was proving capable of creating mismatches for teams with two- and three-star talent.

It wasn't a total coincidence that spread teams like West Virginia,

Missouri, Kansas, and Oregon rose to power at the same time. But a lot of older powers had grown stagnant as well. This year presented once-in-a-lifetime opportunities for so many programs.

Of course, chaos might not have reigned for quite so long in 2007 if not for Dixon's knee.

"Dennis is going to be fine. He would have gone back in if we felt he was needed."

That's what Bellotti told the press after Oregon's 35-23 win over No. 6 Arizona State.

A crowd of 59,379, the largest to ever attend a game in the state of Oregon, saw its party mellowed with a late scare. Dennis Erickson's Sun Devils entered 8-0, having just taken down California at home, but the Ducks put together their most complete performance of the year. They went up 21-3 early in the second quarter on a 27-yard touchdown pass from Dixon to Jaison Williams, already Dixon's third scoring strike of the game. His fourth made the score 35-16 heading into the fourth quarter.

Two minutes into the fourth, Dixon took a shot to his left knee and limped off the field. It dampened the mood for a team that was about to move to second in the country.

A well-timed bye week allowed Dixon to rest his leg, and then the Ducks traveled to Tucson to face 4-6 Arizona on a Thursday night ESPN game. In pregame warmups, Dixon told coaches he was feeling great, and barely two minutes in, he ripped off a 39-yard touchdown. Oregon went up 8-0 after a surprise two-point conversion (another Kelly staple). With six minutes left in the first quarter and Oregon driving, Dixon planted his left leg to attempt a shovel pass and crumpled to the ground.

The three scariest words in football: "non-contact injury." Dixon had a torn ACL, and it turned out he had actually suffered it against Arizona State. Having just watched its leader taken out of the game, a stunned Duck squad gave up a 24-0 run before rallying. They were down just 31-24 late in the game, but an Arizona field goal put away a 34-24 upset.

It's one thing to watch your national title hopes go down the drain. It's another to watch your Heisman-favorite quarterback leave with an awful injury. It is yet another to do both on the same night.

Dixon's injury came after a run of issues. Paysinger, Johnson, and others had also gone down in recent weeks. Oregon fell into a definitive funk. The Ducks gained just 148 yards in a 16-0 loss to UCLA; three Oregon quarterbacks combined to go 11 for 39 with three interceptions, and Stewart gained 33 yards in 13 carries. (UCLA proceeded to nearly steal Oregon's coach; Bellotti interviewed for the vacant Bruin gig in December before electing to remain.) They rallied at home against Oregon State on December 1, turning a 21-7 deficit into a 28-21 lead, but the Beavers prevailed in overtime, 38-31.

The final chapter was bittersweet. With time to recover, Oregon went to El Paso and stomped South Florida, another former No. 2 team from earlier in the season, in the Sun Bowl. The Ducks led 18-14 at halftime but exploded for four third-quarter touchdowns and rolled to a 56-21 win. It was a reminder of what Oregon was capable of ... and a reminder of what could have been.

This wasn't the end of Oregon's run. The Ducks went 10-3 in 2008, and Bellotti retired to become UO athletic director. Kelly was the no-brainer replacement and won 46 games in four seasons, reaching the 2010 BCS title game and losing in the last second to Auburn. He would depart for the NFL's Philadelphia Eagles, leaving the program to deal with a few NCAA violations, but his replacement, Mark Helfrich, got Oregon right back to the title game in 2014. (They lost to Ohio State.) Oregon finished in the AP top 5 four times in a five-year span from 2010-14.

The 2007 run was just the beginning.

Still, the regret was palpable, the what-ifs immense. In 2007, Oregon helped to reinvent football – over the next decade, even Saban's Alabama would adopt aspects of offensive tempo and change his defense to account for the spread-'em-out attacks that had become so lethal – but was deprived of a defining moment because of a left knee ligament.

2010 BOISE STATE

In 1958, Oklahoma was logging its seventh consecutive top-five finish and its fifth straight season with at least 10 wins. A school named Boise Junior College, meanwhile, was winning the national junior college championship, beating Tyler (Texas) 22-0 in the finals.

In 1980, Georgia rode an all-time great running back (Herschel Walker) to an unlikely, unbeaten season and thrilling national title. Boise State, now a four-year school, beat Grambling and Eastern Kentucky on its way to the 1-AA national title.

In 1994, Oregon won the Pac-10 and attended its first Rose Bowl in 37 years. Boise State, meanwhile, beat future FBS schools Nevada, North Texas, Appalachian State, and Marshall on the way back to the 1-AA national finals.

In 1999, Virginia Tech rode an all-time great quarterback (Michael Vick) to an unlikely, unbeaten regular season and national runner-up finish. Boise State made history of its own, winning its first bowl game, a Humanitarian Bowl victory over Louisville, in its fourth season at the FBS level (formerly known as Division 1-A).

In 2006, the Broncos beat Oklahoma in the Fiesta Bowl. In 2008-09, they swept a home-and-home against 10-win Oregon teams. In 2010, they beat an eventual 11-win Virginia Tech team. In 2011, they beat 10-win Georgia.

The "small western school makes good" stories mostly died out in the 1930s with schools like St. Mary's. But from 2006-12, barely a decade after moving up to college football's top subdivision, Boise State went 84-8, finishing in the AP top 10 four times and in the top five twice. The Broncos went 9-2 against major-conference opposition in this span.

How, exactly?

Boise State's rise was a testament to the power of commitment, good hires, and talent identification. It is very difficult to make two straight good-to-great head coach hires, but BSU made five: Pokey Allen, Houston Nutt, Dirk Koetter, Dan Hawkins, and Chris Petersen. The Broncos returned to 1-AA power under Allen, rebounded under Nutt after Allen died of cancer, won 26 games in three years under Koetter, won 53 in five under Hawkins, then went stratospheric under Petersen. The school got local buy-in, built its facilities up to carry itself like a major program, kept the blue artificial-turf branding its home field, and, for half a decade, played elite football.

In Petersen's first season on the job, Boise State made history. The Broncos plowed through the regular season, going 12-0 and outscoring teams, 473-187. With help from a glorious hook-and-lateral play late in regulation, then a successful Statue of Liberty play on the game-winning two-point conversion, they beat Oklahoma in overtime, 43-42, in the Fiesta Bowl. After a retooling job in 2007, they went 12-1 in 2008, then beat No. 3 TCU in the Fiesta Bowl to finish 14-0 in 2009. They finished fourth in the AP poll. With almost everybody back, they would begin the next season third.

The 2010 roster was an unholy mix of overachieving local prospects, overlooked players from talent-rich areas, and diamonds in the rough from what you might call 'exotic' locales. There were All-Americans and/or draft picks in nearly every unit, and they were coached by a staff of future head coaches and coordinators.

Crafting an elite roster required looking near and far. Quarterback Kellen Moore, a human computer and Heisman finalist, was from Prosser, Wash., a town of about 5,700 in southern Washington. All-American offensive lineman Nate Potter and tight end Kyle Efaw were from Boise, and defensive lineman Shea McClellin was from Caldwell, a Boise suburb. Linebacker Byron Hout was from Coeur d'Alene, Idaho's largest northern city.

While local recruiting wins provided beef, Petersen looked to California for speed. Running backs Doug Martin (Stockton) and Jeremy Avery (Bellflower), receivers Titus Young (Los Angeles) and Austin Pettis (Anaheim), and defensive backs Jeron Johnson (Compton) and Brandyn Thompson (Elk Grove) were all from the Golden State. Safety George Iloka, an eventual starter for the Cincinnati Bengals, was from Houston, Texas, another talent-heavy area. All-American defensive tackle Billy Winn was from Las Vegas.

Then there were the exotic additions. Defensive end Tyrone Crawford and defensive tackle Michael Atkinson were from Windsor, Ontario. Defensive back Cedric Febis, defensive tackle Ricky Tjong-A-Tjoe, and receiver Geraldo Boldewijn hailed originally from Holland.

Easy formula, right? Make a ton of great hires and do spectacular legwork in compiling your roster, and you, too, can field an elite football team! Boise State's success was not a mistake, a blip in the space-time continuum; it was simply a product of the surest, most thorough coaching job of the late-2000s.

The Broncos had already proven themselves on a national stage, going 49-4 to date under Petersen, 4-2 against ranked teams; in 2010, it was time to take one more step forward. The season began with a primetime, nationally televised Monday night battle.

Frank Beamer's Virginia Tech Hokies would go 11-3 in 2010, eventually taking down Florida State to win the ACC. Their offense was guided by dual-threat dynamo Tyrod Taylor, their defense by All-American cornerback Jayron Hosley. BSU and Tech met in front of 86,587 at FedEx Field in Landover, Md., to wrap up Week 1 of the season.

BSU wasted no time attempting to make a statement. Kyle Brotzman nailed field goals of 44 and 47 yards, and Moore threw touchdown passes to Pettis and Tommy Gallarda to stake the Broncos to a 20-7 second-quarter lead. However, Virginia Tech unleashed a 23-6 run to take a 30-26 lead midway through the fourth quarter. The Hokies' fantastic secondary had slowed down the Bronco passing attack, forcing mostly shorter passes and tackling well. However, after the teams traded punts, BSU got one last chance to claim a huge win. Moore strolled onto the field with 1:47 left and proceeded to complete passes to Gabe Linehan for 11 yards, Mitch Burroughs for five, Pettis for 14, and Pettis again for a 13-yard touchdown with 1:09 left.

Pettis finished with six catches for 73 yards and bookend touch-downs. BSU quickly forced a four-and-out to seal the 33-30 win.

Having proven themselves and solidified their No. 3 ranking, the Broncos returned west. Tjong-A-Tjoe and Atkinson powered a dominant defensive effort at Wyoming; the Cowboys gained just 135 yards while Moore threw for 370 as BSU cruised to a 51-6 win. Then, in the long-awaited home opener, the Broncos held an explosive Oregon State offense in check. The Beavers got touchdowns via punt return and fumble recovery but averaged only 4 yards per play, and a 17-3 second-quarter run paced a 37-24 win over the Pac-10's

Beavers. Former walk-on Ryan Winterswyk basically lived in star running back Jacquizz Rodgers' back pocket; the exciting scatback gained just 46 yards on 18 carries.

After an almost unfair 59-0 romp at New Mexico State (Moore was asked to throw only 18 passes before ceding to the second string), BSU returned home to face what should have been a tricky Toledo team. After struggling through four straight losing years, the Rockets were rising again under head coach Tim Beckman. They would go 8-5 in 2010, their first of six consecutive winning seasons.

However, Toledo was overwhelmed from the get-go against the class of the mid-major universe. Avery and Efaw scored early, Winn recorded two sacks, and McClellin, a future first-round pick well into a huge season (he would record 13.5 tackles for loss, four of which had come against Virginia Tech), opened the second half with a 43-yard interception return for touchdown. BSU led 57-7 after three quarters and won, 57-14.

Once conference play began for BSU, it became difficult to judge the Broncos. No matter who they managed to schedule early, they would disappear to the west to play mostly weak Western Athletic Conference opponents, overshadowed by marquee national battles elsewhere. They had fallen to fourth in the polls when they played Toledo, bumped down in favor of a hot Oregon squad.

But over the course of two weeks, No. 1 Alabama got upset by Steve Spurrier's South Carolina Gamecocks, then new No. 1 Ohio State was thumped at Wisconsin. With a 48-0 win over lowly San Jose State, in which the Spartans gained just 80 total yards, BSU moved to No. 2 in the polls. The Broncos were officially in the national title mix, and other contenders were falling by the wayside: The next week, as BSU was cruising over Louisiana Tech – Moore completed 20 of 28 passes for 298 yards, and Shoemaker caught six for 124 in a 49-20 victory – No. 3 Oklahoma (the top team in the first BCS rankings) lost to Missouri and No. 6 LSU lost to Auburn and its star quarterback, Cam Newton.

Auburn's rise was complicating matters, however. If both Auburn and Oregon were to finish the regular season undefeated, Boise State would probably fall to third in the BCS standings because of strength-of-schedule differences. Nevertheless, even in that scenario, this former Episcopalian junior college could still score a Rose Bowl bid. There is no surer signifier of one's arrival than that.

It was quickly becoming a one-game schedule. The November slate began with Hawaii, Idaho, and Fresno State, and while all of those programs had provided resistance (or superiority) in the past, that was not going to be the case in 2010. It was all about the November 26 trip to Nevada.

Under head coach Chris Ault, Nevada had embarked on a lengthy run of success. The Wolf Pack had been to five consecutive bowl games and revolutionized college football offense with their Pistol formation, a short shotgun in which the running back lined up directly behind the quarterback. The formation allowed the running back to hit the line more quickly, and with star quarterback Colin Kaepernick running the read option, the results were devastating. He would throw for 3,000 yards and rush for 1,200 in 2010 (barely a decade after Clemson's Woody Dantzler became the first 2,000/1,000 guy); go-to running back Vai Taua would rush for 1,610 yards.

The Wolf Pack suffered a blip of a loss at Hawaii in mid-October, falling 27-21 to the Rainbow Warriors. But they had destroyed BYU and California early on, and they were manhandling other WAC foes almost as easily as BSU.

Boise State beat Hawaii, Idaho, and Fresno State by a combined score of 145-21. Moore completed a combined 76 of 101 passes for 1,056 yards, 10 touchdowns, and three interceptions. The defense allowed just 3.4 yards per play and 212 yards per game. The Broncos headed to Reno in fifth gear.

The entire game was spectacular. Boise State raced to a 24-7 halftime lead thanks to two Martin touchdowns, but Nevada clawed back. A Wolf Pack defense that was overwhelmed in the first half settled down to force four consecutive punts, and Kaepernick eventually guided three scoring drives to tie the game with five minutes left. Then things got *really* crazy.

On BSU's first play after Nevada tied the game, Moore dumped a screen to Martin, who ran past three well-blocked defenders, juked a fourth, ran through the tackle of a fifth, and outran a sixth and seventh to score a thrilling 79-yard touchdown. But that had a negative effect: An already gassed BSU defense had to go back on the field. Kaepernick and Taua alternated body blows, Nevada engineered a 14-play drive, and a seven-yard pass from Kaepernick to Rishard Matthews tied the game at 31-31 with 13 seconds left.

The drama was only beginning. Not content with playing it safe for overtime, BSU went deep. Moore stepped up into the pocket and heaved a perfect bomb to Titus Young, who made a diving catch at the Nevada 9 with two seconds left. The Broncos' last two snaps had gained 132 yards, and it looked like they would survive Reno. All they needed was a 26-yard field goal from Brotzman, an All-American candidate who had made 13 of 16 field goals on the year.

He missed, wide right.

In overtime, he missed a 29-yarder wide left.

Nevada freshman Anthony Martinez nailed a 34-yarder, and the Wolf Pack won, 34-31.

The WAC produced countless incredible shootouts before dying a realignment-related death in the early-2010s. This may have been the greatest game in conference history, and it could not have been more of a gut punch for what had become the WAC's bell-cow program. There would be no tour to the national title game, no consolation trip to Pasadena.

At its cruelest, college football forces you to believe in something amazing, then not only takes it away, but does so in unimaginable fashion.

To their everlasting credit, the Broncos rebounded. In their final home game, against Utah State, Derrell Acrey picked off a pass and returned it for a touchdown just 14 seconds into the game, and BSU rolled from there, 50-14.

Despite inevitable disappointment about being relegated to the Maaco Las Vegas Bowl instead of the Fiesta (Auburn vs. Oregon) or Rose (Wisconsin vs. Boise replacement TCU), Boise State handled its business against an excellent Utah team. The No. 20 Utes had lost only to undefeated TCU and Notre Dame, but they gained only 200 yards with eight first downs. Moore threw for 339, Martin rushed for 147, and Pettis caught 12 passes for 147. The Broncos started slowly, but Martin's 84-yard scoring run midway through the second quarter ignited an eventual 26-3 win.

The best teams lose sometimes. On paper, the 2010 Boise State team mark the peak of Petersen's incredible run at the university. The Broncos would again go 12-1 in 2011, Moore's senior season, moving as high as fourth in the AP poll until a 36-35 home loss to TCU.

They were in position to pull that one off, too, but they missed a 39-yard field goal at the buzzer. Sometimes fate is as repetitive as it is unkind.

2011 LSU

After a 53-yard punt by thunder-legged Aussie Brad Wing, LSU nickel back Tyrann Mathieu tracks Oregon's Kenjon Barner down, strips the ball from him, then recovers the ball and walks three yards into the end zone. Safety Eric Reid lays a Mississippi State receiver out on a short pass with a perfect shoulder-to-shoulder shiver. Mathieu violently bats a West Virginia pass into the air, then reels it in and returns it to the Mountaineers' 1.

Mathieu overshoots on a blitz against Kentucky but karate chops the ball out of the quarterback's hand on his way by, then tracks the ball down and takes it for a touchdown. Cornerback Morris Claiborne makes a leaping interception of a Tennessee bomb attempt, maintains his balance, then returns the ball 89 yards in the other direction. Cornerback Ron Brooks lunges to reel in a short Auburn pass and takes it 28 yards for a touchdown.

Safety Brandon Taylor darts into the backfield to bring down Alabama running back Trent Richardson like a roped calf. Deep into the second half of the biggest game of the year, Reid wrestles a potential go-ahead touchdown away from an Alabama receiver, saving the game.

Brooks catches scrambling Ole Miss quarterback Zack Stoudt and separates him from the ball, then recovers the fumble. Brooks falls for an Arkansas pump fake, leaps into the air to block a pass that isn't thrown ... and then sacks the quarterback anyway after he lands. On a rare Arkansas completion, Mathieu pops the ball away from the tight end, catches it in the air, and returns it for 19 yards.

Cornerback Tharold Simon tracks down a bomb in the SEC championship game and outjumps the intended Georgia receiver for the ball. Claiborne jumps an iffy Georgia pass and races in the other direction, juking out offending quarterback Aaron Murray on his way to the end zone.

The college football universe was very offense-friendly in 2011. Eighteen teams averaged at least 35 points per game, and only three allowed fewer than 15. Defenses were still trying to adjust to the matchup advantages the spread offense was able to create.

LSU, however, came up with a pretty ingenious solution: Field one of the most dangerous, aggressive, and downright entertaining defensive backfields in the history of the game. Voila! Mathieu, Reid, Taylor, Claiborne, Simon, and Brooks combined for 16 interceptions, 39 pass breakups, 27 tackles for loss, six sacks, 11 forced fumbles, and 10 fumble recoveries. LSU allowed seven touchdown passes all season; including special teams returns, these six players combined for eight touchdowns of their own.

John Chavis had already spent more than 15 years as a successful defensive coordinator in the SEC, first at Tennessee and then at LSU. This was his masterpiece. Combined with an offense that was both efficient and drastically overshadowed, head coach Les Miles' Bayou Bengals took down an incredible eight ranked teams (three in the top five) on their way to the BCS Championship game. But they failed the final test.

This was Miles' seventh season in Baton Rouge. The former Michigan offensive lineman had recruiting prowess and a strange, ballsy charisma. His teams would run trick plays in huge moments.

They would go for bombs on fourth down. Even despite generally conservative offensive schemes, they would play unafraid to lose. Despite dealing with the dramatic fallout of Hurricane Katrina, his first LSU squad went 11-2 in 2005; the Tigers went 11-2 in 2006, then 12-2 with a national title in 2007. They fell to just 8-5 and 9-4 post-title, but rebounded in 2010 to 11-2 with their fourth top-10 finish in six years.

LSU was the perfect team to lead college football through the on- and off-field chaos of 2011. Change was inescapable throughout the landscape. Not only did the product *look* different because of the increasing prevalence of the spread; the conferences housing this product were also building strange, huge new rosters for themselves.

Near the end of 2009, the Big Ten began serving notice that, due in part to the success of the Big Ten Network and the desire to expand its reach, it would be increasing its current roster of 11 teams to at least 12, maybe eventually more. The Big 12, forever unstable due to the power plays and the perceived unequal treatment of its more powerful members, began to look like it would fall apart. Nebraska and Missouri were vying for the spot in the Big Ten (it eventually went to Nebraska), while new Pac-10 commissioner Larry Scott swung for the fences. With a TV network in mind as well, he aimed to decapitate the Big 12 altogether, inviting Texas, Oklahoma, Oklahoma State, and a fourth school, be it Texas A&M, Colorado, or Texas Tech.

A Pac-16 would have murdered a power conference in broad daylight, but it didn't come to pass. Still, the Big 12 would lose three other members as Texas started its *own* national network, the Longhorn Network, through ESPN.

By the time the dust had settled in the mid-2010s from a chaotic round of realignment, Missouri and Texas A&M were in the SEC, Rutgers and Maryland had joined Nebraska as junior members in the Big Ten, Utah and Colorado had gone to what was now the Pac-12, the Big 12 had narrowly survived by adding West Virginia and TCU, and the ACC had added Louisville, Pittsburgh, Syracuse, and, in a strange half-membership, Notre Dame. (The Irish would not "join" the conference for football but joined in other sports and agreed to play a certain number of ACC opponents per year.) Within this new landscape sprouted an SEC Network (also through ESPN) and a Pac-12 Network; eventually, the ACC would announce it was joining the network frenzy as well.

2011 was a year for change. It was also a year for the honey badger. In January, a silly YouTube video called "The Crazy Nastyass Honey Badger" went viral for a bit, eventually scoring nearly 80 million views. And at some point before the 2011 college football season began, LSU fans noticed that Mathieu, their emerging star nickel back, with his bleached, cropped hair, bore a slight resemblance to the animal. The Honey Badger nickname took hold. Google searches for "honey badger" were 100 times higher in January 2012 than in January 2011.

Despite starting only one game as a freshman in 2010, Mathieu finished the season as LSU's fourth-leading tackler, and despite his diminutive, 5'9, 175-pound stature, he lived behind the line of scrimmage, recording 8.5 tackles for loss and forcing five fumbles to go with his aggressive pass defense.

In 2011, he would one-up himself in every way, so much so that he would finish fifth in the Heisman voting, despite no offensive presence. (The Heisman should go to the supposed 'most outstanding player' in college football, but it has been an almost completely offense-based award since offense-defense platoons were introduced for good in the 1960s.) And he might not have even been the best defensive back on his own team – Claiborne won the Jim Thorpe Award for nation's most outstanding DB. Reid, meanwhile, had to settle for being *merely* an eventual All-American and first-round draft pick.

Of course, the run defense was pretty good, too. Against an Oregon team that would lose only twice in 2011, LSU limited the

Ducks' LaMichael James to 54 yards on 18 carries, and the big-play Ducks averaged only 4.1 yards per play. The Tigers went up 33-13 early in the fourth quarter and won, 40-27.

After a tune-up against Northwestern State (the Tigers outgained the Demons by a 400-95 margin and won, 49-3), LSU visited Starkville to take on a Mississippi State team coming off of a top-15 finish. The offense kept having to settle for field goals (four in all), but MSU gained just 193 yards in a 19-6 Tiger win.

Against a West Virginia team that would score 70 points on Clemson in the Orange Bowl three months later, LSU built a 27-7 lead in the first half. Lee hit both Randle and Odell Beckham Jr. for long scores, and though WVU would cut the lead to 27-21, Claiborne returned a kickoff 99 yards for a touchdown. LSU added two more scores to cruise, 47-21.

Now No. 1 in the AP poll, the Tigers played like they had no intention of letting go of that mantel. Lee and Beckham combined for a 51-yard touchdown in a 35-7 win over Kentucky, then Randle scored on a 46-yarder three minutes into the next week's game against No. 17 Florida. LSU rolled, 41-11.

Derek Dooley's floundering Tennessee squad stayed close for a while, trailing only 14-7 late in the first half. But touchdown drives of 7:01, 8:44, and 6:08 gave the Tigers a 38-7 win. And despite suspensions to Mathieu, Simon, and running back Spencer Ware, LSU faced minimal challenge from 19th-ranked defending national champion Auburn. Randle scored on passes of 42 and 46 yards in the second quarter, and Brooks' pick six headlined a 45-10 win.

Fans of offense were indeed spoiled in 2011. Baylor, led by eventual Heisman winner Robert Griffin III, began the season with a 50-48 shootout win over TCU (maybe the best game of the season) and closed it with a 67-56 win over Washington in the Alamo Bowl. Those are basketball scores. It was like watching a completely different sport than what LSU and Alabama put on display in Tuscaloosa on November 5.

Neither team gained 300 yards or averaged even five yards per play. (Baylor averaged 7.6 per play in 2011, while Baylor *opponents* averaged 6.4.) The teams' two defenses combined to field 28 future draft picks, 10 first-rounders. It was a sumo match to Baylor's lucha libre, but it was absurdly tense.

Alabama moved the ball well but kept settling for field goals, missing the first three. Lee had a miserable time, completing just three passes to his receivers and two to Alabama defenders, but Jordan Jefferson, who had been playing a secondary role in the offense all year, offered enough of a change of pace to keep things even in the field position battle.

Alabama took a 6-3 lead into the fourth quarter, but Claiborne intercepted Bama quarterback AJ McCarron and returned the ball to the Bama 15. Drew Alleman's 30-yard field goal tied the game and, thanks to Reid's interception of a trick-play pass at the LSU 1, the Tigers forced overtime.

On Alabama's overtime possession, Sam Montgomery came up with a huge sack of McCarron to force a 52-yard field goal, which Cade Foster missed short. Alleman's 25-yard shot gave LSU a 9-6 win.

With the biggest hurdle cleared, LSU broke into a sprint: The Tigers beat Western Kentucky, 42-9, then went to Oxford and delivered a 52-3 knockout to Ole Miss.

The Tigers did face some adversity back home against Bobby Petrino's best Arkansas team; the third-ranked Razorbacks raced to a 14-0 lead, but Kenny Hilliard scored a six-yard touchdown, and then Mathieu struck: He returned a punt 92 yards for a touchdown, forced a fumble that Brooks recovered, then forced another one late. Jefferson, now LSU's primary QB, threw for 208 yards and rushed for 53 as LSU raced to a 41-17 comeback win.

It was the same dynamic the next week in Atlanta. Facing 10-2 Georgia in the SEC Championship game, the Tigers spotted the Dawgs the first 10 points, then Mathieu locked up his spot as a Heisman finalist by returning a punt 62 yards for a score, recovered a fumble, and returned another punt 47 yards. Three Hilliard touchdowns in the third quarter gave LSU a cushion, then Claiborne's pick six punctuated a 42-10 win.

Teams from the SEC had won the last five national titles (Florida in 2006 and 2008, LSU in 2007, Alabama in 2009, Auburn in 2010) and in a normal year, the streak would be up for grabs in January. Instead, the streak was extended in early December. On a late-November Friday night in Ames, Iowa State beat unbeaten Oklahoma State in overtime, in part because OSU missed a field goal by, at most, inches late in regulation. Because of this classic, Alabama was able to claw back up to No. 2 in the BCS standings, holding off OSU by decimal points. It would be a Bama-LSU rematch for the national title.

In a season of change, the rematch may have prompted a little bit more of it. Though Alabama and LSU probably *were* the two best teams in the country, the game had the third-lowest TV rating of the BCS era, and in retrospect, the unenthusiastic reaction likely played a role in college football's decision makers finally taking the plunge on a long-discussed playoff. By the following summer, they had finalized a plan for a four-team College Football Playoff, beginning in 2014. Sentiment had been growing for quite a while; Alabama-LSU II pushed it over the top.

In theory, LSU would have had to survive a rematch anyway, even with a CFP in place. Regardless, the Tigers and Tide did indeed play a second time. And only one team gained more than 100 yards.

In 11 possessions, LSU went three-and-out six times and turned the ball over twice. The Tigers didn't cross the 50 until midway through the fourth quarter, and when they did, they lost 18 yards and fumbled back at midfield. The defense did all it could, again holding Alabama to field goal after field goal, and the Tide only led 15-0 well into the fourth quarter. They teased the Tigers by keeping it close enough for a comeback while offering not a single ounce of hope that LSU would ever score. Trent Richardson finally put away a 21-0 win with a late 34-yard touchdown, but it had grown hopeless long before that. Les Miles took heat for not subbing in Lee for Jefferson like he did Jefferson for Lee in Tuscaloosa. But that was like complaining about not putting a Band Aid on a bullet wound.

A bad ending can completely wreck a great movie. It's the hardest part of the script to nail. But LSU's 13-game run through a rugged regular-season slate was one for the ages, powered by a revolutionary defense and an offense that was mostly dominant against every defense not named Alabama. The Honey Badger-style nickel backs, cover men who can fly into the backfield, would come into vogue as a tactic for slowing down spread offenses, even if few could come close to the standard that Mathieu set.

LSU's defense would take a step back in the following seasons. It was never bad, but it was without Claiborne (first-round pick in 2012), Taylor (third-rounder), Brooks (fourth-rounder), tackle Michael Brockers (also a first-rounder), and, surprisingly, Mathieu (dismissed from the team the following August, allegedly due to failed drug tests). That will make you mortal awfully quickly. But for a few months in the fall of 2011, the Tigers were transcendent.

2013 AUBURN

Everything has fallen apart. Auburn led by 20 with 10 minutes left, but Georgia has scored 21 points to take a 38-37 lead. Auburn got the ball back with 1:45 left, but quarterback Nick Marshall took a costly sack, and the Tigers now face a fourth-and-18 from their 27 with 36 seconds remaining. Marshall steps into the pocket and heaves the ball into double coverage ... and Auburn wins.

Alabama has created nearly twice as many scoring opportunities as Auburn, but missed field goals have again cost the Crimson Tide. A 39-yard touchdown pass from Marshall to Sammie Coates tied the game at 28-28 with 32 seconds left. Still, Alabama was able to advance the ball to the Auburn 38 with one tick remaining. Adam Griffith lines up to attempt a 57-yard field goal ... and Auburn wins. In regulation.

Tre Mason's 37-yard run gave the Tigers a 31-27 advantage over Florida State with 1:19 left in the BCS title game in Pasadena. Heisman winner Jameis Winston, however, responded by finding Kelvin Benjamin for the go-ahead score with just 13 seconds remaining. Auburn has to gain 83 yards on its final play to salvage its second national title in four years.

Marshall completes a short pass to C.J. Uzomah, who laterals to Quan Bray near the right sideline at the Auburn 18. Bray flips back to Marshall at the 10, and he wings the ball across the field to Mason at the 6. Mason has blockers ahead of him and acres of space ...

If you saw it, you didn't believe it *could* happen, you almost thought it *would*. For a few seconds, it looked as if Auburn might actually complete the craziest, most unlikely finish ever to a national title game, a play that could almost never be topped.

It was almost a little surprising when the play didn't work. Mason advanced the ball past the 30, but his gassed linemen couldn't hold their blocks well enough. Instead of racing down the sideline, he had to cut inside and was brought down at the 36. In 2013, we were conditioned to believe the unbelievable, but the bag of magic tricks was finally empty.

Life is rarely boring on the Plains. Since winning the 2010 national title behind workhorse quarterback Cam Newton, Auburn had completely collapsed. Head coach Gene Chizik's Tigers lost Newton, lost five games in 2011, and then lost offensive coordinator Gus Malzahn as well. With a new, shall we say *un*coordinated offense in place, Auburn went 3-9 in 2012, and Chizik was fired not even two years after lifting the BCS' crystal ball trophy.

In desperate need of an offensive identity again, Auburn turned back to Malzahn. The 47-year old Henderson State grad trod a unique path to coaching stardom; he cut his teeth as a high school coach in tiny Hughes, Ark., then rose through the state's ranks to Springdale's Shiloh Christian School, then Springdale High. He mastered the art of a hurried-up, wide-open offense, won two state titles with Shiloh Christian, then won a third at Springdale. He joined Houston Nutt's Arkansas staff in 2006, bringing most of his Springdale stars with him. But his philosophy didn't mesh well with Nutt's, and after a soap-opera season, he took the Tulsa offensive coordinator job in 2007.

Even as offensive totals were skyrocketing throughout the country, Tulsa's stood out. The Golden Hurricane were first in the country with 544 yards per game in 2007, then improved to 570 in 2008. They were devastating via both ground and air. When Chizik took the Auburn job after the 2008 season, he brought Malzahn aboard. The results were immediate, and a year after Malzahn took the Arkansas State head coaching job, Auburn brought him back to town to replace Chizik.

It stood to reason that it might take him a while to get things figured out, even though he knew most of the personnel. Auburn had, after all, averaged just 18.7 points per game in 2012 (114th in the country), 11.1 against power conference opponents. They had lost 10 SEC games in a row.

It took him about six weeks.

The Tigers had to grind out a few early wins. They were out-gained by Mike Leach's Washington State Cougars in the season opener but rode a 100-yard Mason kick return and a 75-yard Corey Grant touchdown run to a 31-24 victory.

After an easier 38-9 win over Malzahn's former employer, Arkansas State, came a second dramatic finish. Mississippi State led Auburn by a 20-17 margin late on the evening of September 14 at Jordan-Hare Stadium, but Marshall, a converted defensive back who began his career at Georgia, completed four passes to Marcus Davis on Auburn's last-gasp drive, then converted a third-and-10 with an 11-yard scamper. With just 10 seconds left in the game, he found tight end C.J. Uzomah for an 11-yard touchdown and a 24-20 win.

In most seasons, a win like that would be a team's most memorable. But the Tigers were just getting started. They fell on the road, 35-21, to No. 6 LSU on September 21, but they proved resilient, battling back a bit from a 28-7 deficit. After a bye week, they hosted Hugh Freeze's Ole Miss Rebels, who were making waves with their own version of the spread and a precocious, exciting defense. Ole Miss outgained the Tigers by 89 yards and limited the Auburn attack to only 65 snaps, but the Rebels kept falling short of the end zone, and Auburn did not. The Tigers got an early 78-yard pick six from Robenson Therezie and held on to win, 30-22. Following a 62-3 win over Western Carolina, the 5-1 Tigers made their first appearance in the polls since dropping out late in 2011.

On October 19, it was time to serve notice.

The Tigers traveled to College Station to take on defending Heisman-winning quarterback Johnny Manziel and No. 7 Texas A&M. The Aggies were 5-1, their only loss a shootout defeat against mighty Alabama. A&M led 24-17 at halftime, thanks to three long Manziel-to-Mike Evans touchdown passes, then took a 34-24 lead early in the fourth quarter. But Auburn scored on touchdown drives of 75, 69, and 75 yards, and Mason's five-yard score gave the Tigers a 45-41 lead with 1:19 left.

A&M responded immediately. Manziel hit Evans for gains of 19 and 22 yards to bring the Aggies to the Auburn 18. But Dee Ford sacked Manziel for a loss of eight with 28 seconds left, and on fourth-and-13 from the Auburn 21, with all of Kyle Field and a national TV audience assuming that Manziel was still going to figure out a way to escape with a win, Ford sacked him again. Ballgame.

The Tigers followed up this upset with wins of 45-10 over Florida Atlantic, 35-17 at Arkansas, and 55-23 at Tennessee. In a single month, they had gone from unranked to seventh in the country. But it looked like the run was coming to an end when Georgia's Aaron Murray scored late on November 16. On fourth-and-goal from the Auburn 5, Murray fought his way toward the goal line and, by the skin of his teeth, was credited with a touchdown. This completed a spectacular fourth-quarter collapse by Auburn. Murray led three straight touchdown drives while Auburn twice went three-and-out, turning a 37-17 AU lead into a 38-37 deficit. And when Jordan

Jenkins sacked Marshall, Auburn faced a fourth-and-ballgame with 36 seconds remaining.

Take it away, Auburn radio announcer Rob Bramblett: "Alright, here we go, fourth-and-18 for the Tigers. Here's your ballgame. Nick Marshall ... stands in ... steps up ... gonna throw downfield, just a home run ball, and it is tipped up and LOUIS CAUGHT IT ON THE DEFLECTION. LOUIS IS GONNA SCORE. LOUIS IS GONNA SCORE. LOUIS IS GONNA SCORE. TOUCHDOWN, AUBURN. TOUCHDOWN, AUBURN. A MIRACLE AT JORDAN-HARE. A MIRACLE AT JORDAN-HARE. SEVENTY-THREE YARDS. AND THE TIGERS, WITH 25 SECONDS TO GO, LEAD 43-38."

With no better options, Marshall had to simply heave the ball downfield in the general direction of receiver Ricardo Louis. Young Georgia defensive backs Josh Harvey-Clemons and Tray Matthews were much closer to the ball than Louis, but both went for the interception instead of batting it to the ground. They collided with each other, and the ball popped perfectly into the air. Louis, still running full-speed, managed to catch a glimpse of it, and it fell into his hands at the Georgia 12. He trotted into the end zone in front of an apoplectic home crowd.

Murray heroically completed two passes for 50 yards to give the Dawgs a shot at instant redemption. But his final pass couldn't find intended receiver Michael Bennett, and Auburn held on, 43-38.

This was the second-most amazing finish of the month in Jordan-Hare Stadium.

The team that was eking out wins against decent teams early in the year was now one upset away from the SEC title game. Top-ranked, undefeated Alabama was a clear favorite in the 2013 Iron Bowl and was, for most of the way, the clearly superior team. But as with their 2011 loss to LSU, the Crimson Tide were doomed by place-kicking. Cade Foster missed a 44-yarder in the first quarter, then missed a 33-yarder early in the fourth. As a result, when Bama's AJ McCarron connected with star receiver Amari Cooper for a 99-yard bomb with 10:28 left, it gave the Tide only a 28-21 lead. After back-to-back fourth-and-1 stuffs – Marshall was stopped at the Auburn 35, then Carl Lawson stopped Bama's T.J. Yeldon on the AU 13 – Alabama's Christian Jones returned an Auburn punt to the Tiger 25. Three plays later, with 2:32 left, Foster had a chance to redeem himself and put the game away. Instead, his 44-yard field goal attempt was blocked by Ryan Smith.

Auburn had one last chance to tie and took advantage. Six straight Mason runs gained 26 yards to the Alabama 39, and with barely half a minute left on the clock, Marshall pulled off the perfect run-pass option. The newest en-vogue tactic gave the quarterback not only an opportunity to hand the ball off or keep it, like most option runs for the last 70 years; it also gave him an opportunity to throw the ball if a defensive back committed to stopping the run. Marshall faked to Mason and ran wide to his left. Right before he crossed the line of scrimmage, he caught a glimpse of Sammie Coates uncovered by the left sideline. He threw to Coates, who ran untouched into the end zone to tie the game.

There would be no overtime. With seven seconds left, from the Bama 38, McCarron handed to Yeldon, who gained 24 yards and managed to step out of bounds right before the final tick of the clock. With a last-gasp chance to save the game, head coach Nick Saban turned to big-legged redshirt freshman Adam Griffith to attempt a 57-yard field goal.

Take it away again, Rob Bramblett: "Chris Davis is gonna drop back into the end zone, a single safety. I guess if this thing comes up short, he can field it and run it out. Alright, here we go … 56-yarder … it's got … no … does not have the leg. And Chris Davis takes it in the back of the end zone. He'll run it out to the 10 … 15 … 20 … 25, 30 … 35, 40 … 45, 50 … 45 THERE GOES DAVIS." Color commentator Stan White: "OH MY GOSH." Bramblett: "DAVIS IS GONNA RUN IT ALL THE WAY BACK. AUBURN'S GONNA WIN THE FOOTBALL GAME. AUBURN'S GONNA WIN THE FOOTBALL GAME. HE RAN THE MISSED FIELD GOAL BACK. HE RAN IT BACK A HUNDRED AND NINE YARDS. THEY'RE NOT GONNA KEEP 'EM OFF THE FIELD TONIGHT. HOLY COW. OH MY GOD. AUBURN WINS."

The Iron Bowl has been one of the most intense rivalries in college football's long history, so intense that the schools wouldn't even play each other for most of the first half of the 20th century. The rancor grew when the teams each won national titles in back-to-back years in 2009 and 2010. Following Auburn's '10 title, an outraged Alabama fan poisoned the two trees standing at Toomer's Corner. The corner had long been Auburn fans' place of celebration; they would throw rolls of toilet paper into the trees.

The trees were gone in 2013, removed the previous April. Following Davis' return, to be known in lore as the Kick Six, Tiger fans rushed the field, then eventually congregated across from Toomer's Drugs and rolled the power lines instead. Auburn was going to the SEC title game.

By any other standard, the conference championship in Atlanta was crazy in its own right. In a back and forth affair against Gary Pinkel's 11-1 Missouri Tigers, Auburn trailed 34-31 with under four minutes to go in the third quarter, but Mason made sure Malzahn's troops would not be denied. He rushed for 304 yards, securing his place as a Heisman finalist, and his two fourth-quarter touchdowns put away a 59-42 win. This team of destiny needed one final break to reach the national championship against Florida State, and of course, it got it: Michigan State upset undefeated Ohio State in the Big Ten title game in Indianapolis. Auburn slid into the No. 2 spot.

Alas, though Auburn's dramatic flair was the story of the season, the Tigers had to settle for being the second-best team. The Tigers raced to a 21-3 lead over undefeated FSU, but as they did to Michael Vick and Virginia Tech in 1999, the Seminoles put an end to the 'team of destiny' talk. FSU scored 24 second-half points, and when Mason was finally tackled on the game's final play, Jimbo Fisher's 'Noles had secured their first national title in 14 years.

In the absence of titles, though, we collect moments. Auburn gave its fan base two of its greatest ever moments, against its two chief rivals, in a three-week span in November 2013. Sure, Alabama would win another national title two years later, its fourth in seven years under Saban. Sure, Saban would establish a Bryant-esque dynasty in Tuscaloosa. But Auburn fans would always be able to lord the Kick Six over their neighbors to the west-northwest.

That fall, the Tigers also reminded college football fans exactly why they are college football fans: If you keep watching, just in case, you might see something you've never seen before. Believe the unbelievable in this silly, ridiculous sport.

AFTERWORD

In the first week of the 2016 season, Alabama and USC took each other on in front of 81,359 bystanders in Dallas Cowboys owner Jerry Jones' monstrosity, AT&T Stadium, in Arlington, Texas. The equipment was different, and the athletes were bigger, but these were the same programs that fielded Sam Cunningham against Johnny Musso in their revolutionary (evolutionary?) Birmingham battle in 1970, the same programs that went through similar "We love this sport, and we want to be really good at it" epiphanies in the 1920s.

Two weeks later, Georgia Tech and Vanderbilt met in a non-conference battle, just as they did in 1917. Paul Johnson's Yellow Jackets got the best of Derek Mason's Commodores but didn't quite have the same advantage that John Heisman's crew did over Dan McGugin's squad 99 years earlier: a 38-7 win in 2016 paled in comparison to the 83-0 destruction led by Joe Guyon and company.

A little more than a month after that, on October 22, Illinois and Michigan took each other on in cavernous Michigan Stadium; it was completed three years after Red Grange famously ripped a hole in the proud Wolverine defense and four years after Grange led the Illini to a national title.

That same day, Ole Miss and LSU kicked off in Tiger Stadium, almost exactly 57 years after Billy Cannon's glorious punt return.

Because of its longevity and pure quantity – hundreds and hundreds of schools have football teams – college football has a deeper, richer history than any sport this side of English soccer. That allows us to explore its history right alongside that of the country it lives in.

College football has survived huge rules changes and tiny ones. It has survived enormous cultural shifts, often begrudgingly. It has seen its balance of power move from one area of the country to another, and back again.

As the country itself continues to (begrudgingly) evolve, this sport will try to do the same. Its decision-makers will continue to make frustrating, often hypocritical decisions. Its coaches will continue to look for tiny tweaks that can shift tectonic plates. Its rules makers will attempt to address the need for further player safety. And no matter who is covering it, or how, no matter which direction strategies, tactics, safety, salaries, and television take this sport, we will probably continue to watch it. If we could stop, we would have a long time ago.

PHOTO INDEX

Team	Credit	Page#
1906 Chicago	Special Collections Research Center, University of Chicago Library	*i*
1917 Georgia Tech	Georgia Tech athletics	*ii*
1923 Illinois	Illinois athletics	*i, ii*
1924 Notre Dame	Notre Dame athletics	*iii*
1925 Alabama	University of Alabama Athletic Photography/Crimson Tide Photos	*iii*
1930 Utah	Utah athletics	*iv*
1931 USC	Getty Images	*iv*
1938 TCU	TCU athletics	*v*
1938 Tennessee	University of Tennessee/1938-39 Volunteer	*v*
1940 Minnesota	Minnesota athletics	*vi*
1941 Northwestern	University archives, Northwestern University Libraries	*vi*
1943 Iowa Pre-Flight	Center for Media Production Photographs Collection, University Archives, The University of Iowa Libraries	*vii*
1945 Army	Army athletics	*viii*
1947 Notre Dame	Notre Dame athletics	*viii*
1951 Michigan State	Michigan State athletics	*ix*
1955 Oklahoma	Western History Collections, University of Oklahoma Libraries	*ix*
1957 Auburn	Auburn athletics	*x*
1959 Ole Miss	Ole Miss athletics	*xi*
1959 Syracuse	USA Today Sports Images	*xii*
1960 Iowa	Center for Media Production Photographs Collection, University Archives, The University of Iowa Libraries	*xii*
1962 Nebraska	Nebraska athletics	*xiii*
1965 UCLA	UCLA athletics	*xiii, xiv*
1968 Purdue	Purdue athletics	*xiv, xv*
1968 Texas	Texas athletics	*xv*
1970 Alabama	University of Alabama Athletic Photography/Crimson Tide Photos	*xvi*

Team	Credit	Page#
1970 Dartmouth	Dartmouth athletics	*xvii*
1972 Tampa	Tampa athletics	*xvii*
1973 Michigan	Michigan athletics	*xviii*
1974 Miami-OH	Miami (Ohio) athletics	*xviii*
1978 Missouri	University of Missouri/1979 Savitar/©Keith Graham	*xix*
1980 Georgia	Georgia athletics	*xix, xx*
1981 Florida State	Florida State athletics	*xx*
1982 Pittsburgh	Pitt athletics	*xxi*
1984 Boston College	Boston College/1985 Sub Turri	*xxi*
1985 Oklahoma	Western History Collections, University of Oklahoma Libraries	*xxii*
1988 Miami	Miami athletics	*xxiii*
1990 Virginia	USA Today Sports Images	*xxiv*
1991 Florida	Florida athletics	*xxii*
1991 Washington	USA Today Sports Images	*xxiii*
1993 Texas A&M	Texas A&M athletics	*xxiv*
1993 Wisconsin	Wisconsin athletics	*xxv*
1994 Nebraska	Nebraska athletics	*xxvi, xxvii*
1998 Ohio State	USA Today Sports Images	*xxvii*
1999 Virginia Tech	USA Today Sports Images	*xxviii*
2002 USC	USA Today Sports Images	*xxviii*
2004 Texas	Texas athletics	*xxxii*
2007 Oregon	USA Today Sports Images	*xxix*
2010 Boise State	Boise State athletics	*xxix, xxx*
2011 LSU	USA Today Sports Images	*xxx*
2013 Auburn	Auburn athletics	*xxxi*

ACKNOWLEDGMENTS

You can find a living bibliography for this project at http://www.footballstudyhall.com/pages/50-best. Because there were quite a few interesting links and videos among the sources, I wanted to do them justice, and since I have a web page available to me already, I thought I would use it.

I did want to acknowledge a few sources that were particularly valuable for this project. First, I cannot recommend Newspapers.com highly enough. The subscription fee is more than worth it, and the ability to sift through historical AP, UPI, etc., recaps and box scores is invaluable. It would have taken me months at the library to do what I ended up being able to do in seconds or hours through that site.

Another useful site: TipTop25.com, run by a man named James Vautravers. He wrote in depth about basically every good team in the 20th century in the "Fixed AP Polls" section of his website, and I ended up drawn back to it for basically every team in the book pre-World War II.

I want to thank university athletic and archive departments for assisting me with photos. Many athletic departments sent some to me free of charge, and employees of a few different university archive departments helped me to procure others. Most were incredibly responsive.

You can find references to useful books and websites throughout the text here.

This book began as a Kickstarter project. I was intrigued by Kickstarter from the first time I heard about it, and I wanted to test it out if I ever had a good idea for it. Then I found one.

I asked for $22,000 to help fund paying for an assistant, acquiring photographs, etc., and I ended up getting $25,140 from 610 backers. That was humbling. One of the potential rewards was

"Spend $X, and you can get your name (or whatever you want) in the Acknowledgements section," and quite a few backers hit that donation level.

So without further ado, I would like to thank and acknowledge Jason Amyett, Joey Bentschneider, Randy Bernhoft, David Bonnewell, Dan Bray, Hooter Brown, BST, Hamilton Cook, Ross Cunningham, Austin and Jana Deardorff, Bill DiFilippo, Rob Dreier, Nate Edwards, Electrolightsllc, Griffin D. Francis, Ph.D., Kimberly L. W. and Mark D. Griffis, Chris "Bear Down" Halligan, Ben Herrmann, Ryan Hoes, Paul Horn, Johnny Hutchinson, John Iezzi, Bill Kenney, Chris Mastenbrook, Von Miller, Nick Polak, Poseur (And the Valley Shook), Jon Preble, Nathan Saper, Jefferson M. Shelton, Ricky Sirois, Jay Sparks, Sarah Sprague, Karl Strength, Stroot Land Services, LLC, Wes Sutton, the tailgate queen, Walt Terry, THEKEYPLAY.COM, Sam Thomas, THIS SPACE INTENTIONALLY LEFT BLANK, Brandon Tolle, Cam, Shana, Abbie, Carter and Griffin Williams, www.scenehound.com, Takao Yamada, and George Young & The Closers. Without your support, this book wouldn't have come to fruition.

That's obviously not the entire list of thank yous, however. Jamie and Erin are awesome companions in this odd little universe we've created for ourselves. My parents, Mike and Betty Connelly, were supportive of the sports-and-writing addiction from the start (even when they didn't really understand the dice games I had created to entertain myself in the back seat during car trips). Jamie's parents (Jim and Suzan Tuley) have been beyond supportive, even when I was the proverbial blogger in the in-laws' basement. Seth and Katie Rosner didn't think they'd get mentioned in this book. Joke's on them. And Eric Ratterree and Jon Walsh are terrific trip mates.

To everyone else who has helped me through the years, as this strange career has taken shape, I cannot thank you enough. Hopefully this book was as enjoyable to read as it was to write.

Love you guys.

Bill Connelly is the author of *Study Hall: College Football, Its Stats and Its Stories.* He is a college sports editor and analytics director for SB Nation, co-host of Podcast Ain't Played Nobody with Steven Godfrey, co-founder of D1 Labs with Colin Davy, and editor of Football Study Hall and Rock M Nation. His work has also been featured at Football Outsiders, ESPN Insider, the Wall Street Journal, and in the Football Outsiders Almanac and annual Athlon previews. You can follow him on Twitter at @SBN_BillC.